ERICH FROMM:
THE COURAGE TO BE HUMAN

ERICH FROMM: THE COURAGE TO BE HUMAN

Rainer Funk

With a Postscript by
ERICH FROMM

CONTINUUM · NEW YORK

Translated by Michael Shaw

1982

The Continuum Publishing Company
575 Lexington Avenue, New York, NY 10022

Printed in the United States of America

Library of Congress Cataloging in Publication Data

Funk, Rainer.
Erich Fromm: the courage to be human.

Translation of: Mut zum Menschen.
Bibliography of Fromm's writings: p. 374
Bibliography: p. 384
Includes index.
1. Fromm, Erich, 1900– 2. Humanism—History—20th century I. Title.
B945.F754F8613 191 81-22186
ISBN 0-8264-0061-2 AACR2

CONTENTS

1. Quotations in this study omit all italicization that may be found in the original text.
2. Numbers in parentheses (1955c) indicate the date the work was first published. In the bibliography of Fromm's writings, they precede the title.
3. The notes give only author and title of the works listed in the bibliographies.

Preface

A preface to a study of Erich Fromm should be programmatic and typical of both the subject and the author. It should be "dis-illusionment." In Andersen's fairy tale "The Emperor's New Clothes," the child discovers that the emperor's splendid garments are mere figments of the imagination, that he is, in fact, naked. To take away those garments, to "dis-illusion" his subjects, to make both emperor and subjects into human beings and to give them the courage to be human—this is the scientific and ethical interest that pervades Erich Fromm's life and work. If one is to do his work justice, one must allow it to impose its direction on one's research.

The first interest of this study is, therefore, the most comprehensive understanding possible of Fromm's insights and views. After providing some biographical and bibliographical information, this study sets forth Fromm's sociopsychological approach (Chapter I) and characterology (Chapter II), which, being empirical insights, are fundamental to all further reflections and views. The philosophical-anthropological and historical-philosophical reflections on the nature and history of man follow (Chapter III). Part Two deals with Fromm's humanism. It contains a critical discussion of the humanistic critique of religion and of humanistic religion (Chapter IV), and presents the humanistic ethic (Chapter V). The relevance of the humanistic ethic to a theological ethic is then examined (Chapter V). In the final section of Chapter V, the second object of interest is articulated, namely, the significance of Fromm's insights and humanistic ideas for a theological ethic.

Dealing with Fromm's empirical discoveries and humanistic concerns prompts a third interest, which is to understand his intellectual antecedents. Part Three attempts this in two sections. In the first, four sources of his thought—Moses Maimonides, Hermann Cohen, Shneur Zalman, and Karl Marx—are introduced (Chapter VI). In the second (Chapter VII), the attempt is made to develop the usefulness of the insights that were derived from the critical discussion of Fromm's humanistic religion in Chapter IV, and of what was discovered about the sources of his thought. It is shown that Fromm is indebted to a particular pattern of thought, that is, a particular kind of dialectics. Such an endeavor may appear questionable because it involves the risk of labeling, and labeling runs counter to Fromm's living thought. But Fromm himself confirmed that this demonstration of his dialectical thinking does not put him into a straitjacket but accurately interprets his thought and makes a deeper comprehension of it possible.

The cognitive value of a search for patterns of thought becomes apparent in Part Four, which sets forth the having/being alternative. This last part of the book summarizes all that precedes it, because the question "to have or to be?" is the common denominator of Fromm's scientific and religious-ethical humanism. The presentation of the characterological and religious concept of the having/being alternative (Chapter VIII) is followed by a critical appreciation of Fromm's humanism, which takes the form of reflections concerning a possible dialogue between him and Christian theologians (Chapter IX). The emphasis here is on arriving at the most consistent and persuasive understanding of the distinctiveness of Fromm's humanism possible. The purpose is to provide an impulse for the discussion of Fromm's humanism—and that is the fourth interest of this study. The final pages attempt to provide an impetus to theological and theological-ethical discussion by proposing some questions about the self-understanding of theology and mysticism, and the relation between the two.

There is an objective reason for the intensive discussion of the concept of religion, the religious ethos, and mysticism in these pages. A deeper understanding of Fromm's insights and ideas is possible only against the background of his humanism, and this humanism is religio-critical for religious and ethical reasons. In fact, that is what makes Fromm's humanism distinctive. If justice is to be done to its distinctiveness, therefore, religious-philosophical and theological-ethical questions must be discussed.

The difficulties that attend such an enterprise are considerable, for dealing with Fromm's work means participating in the difficulties that proceed from these problems. To evaluate Fromm fairly, to arrive at a final judgment, one would need to be competent in all the various disciplines and sciences, for to Fromm's credit, he risked a global view of man and his history at a time when the sciences were becoming ever more specialized. His scientific work, its understanding and critique, propose a task one can never discharge in a wholly satisfactory manner. That is why this study reports discoveries from the most diverse disciplines and advances interpretations even though the author lacks expertise in most of these areas. Examples are the human and social sciences that are touched on in connection with Fromm's social psychology and characterology, philosophical questions, Marxism, Eastern and Western mysticism, and the general humanism discussion.

The author must beg the reader's indulgence for failing to treat extensively two men who influenced Fromm's thought, Meister Eckhart and Spinoza, an omission ascribable in part to a lack of competence, in part to a lack of space. For the same reasons, it proved impossible to compare Fromm's discoveries and views with the opinions currently held in the various relevant disciplines, even though it would certainly be illuminating to compare Fromm's work with Max Scheler's, Arnold Gehlen's, and Helmut Plessner's anthropologies, for example.

The literature about Fromm presents a special problem. The scientific reception of Fromm's work in the German-speaking countries is still in its initial stages, so it seemed both necessary and justifiable to offer this study as the first comprehensive presentation of his discoveries and ideas. The considerable resonance his thought has found in the English-speaking countries is more remarkable for its volume than for its quality. To the extent that the secondary literature was available and warranted it, it was given consideration. The bibliography lists monographs, essays, and reviews, and identifies them accordingly.

One reason for the generally limited discussion of Fromm's thought in the German-speaking countries is the contemporary scientific establishment's prejudice that a persuasive and appealing style necessarily indicates scientific inadequacy. Another reason has greater justification: although the present study will show that Fromm's thought can be stringently developed from his fundamental humanistic convictions as an experiential value, and that it can be understood in all its detail as the result of that approach, his own presentation frequently suffers from an imprecise and inconsistent use of concepts and too limited a systematic interest—both deficiencies in a scientific discussion.

The last-named difficulties provide the motive for extensive quotations from the sources, not just the sources of Fromm's thought but his thought itself. The attempt was also made to refer the reader to the greatest possible number of passages in Fromm's work that bear on a particular problem. The bibliography includes the most comprehensive listing of Fromm's works presently available.

It was the author's personal contact with Fromm that most decisively contributed to bringing this study to a successful completion. Fromm began taking an interest in this book in 1972. Intensive discussions and a half-year stay at his home corrected many a misinterpretation of his written statements, directed attention to those questions and dimensions of experience that deepened understanding, and clarified those problems and approaches that furthered scientific discussion.

It is therefore to Fromm himself that the author owes the largest debt of gratitude: gratitude for his willingness to engage in dialogue; for the trouble he took to ensure the completion of this study; for the tolerance of much, sometimes unqualified, questioning; and for his hospitality, which the author availed himself of time and again. I also wish to thank Alfons Auer for his scholarly help and advice in the preparation of the manuscript. His untiring concern about structure and direction, clarity of language and style, but principally his sincere and cordial manner, contributed significantly to its completion. For helpful suggestions and conversations on the New Testament and New Testament problems and exegesis, I thank Herbert Leroy. And I owe special thanks to my wife, Renate Oetker-Funk, for assistance in correcting the manuscript.

Tübingen, November 1977

Preface to the American Edition

To add one more study to the many English and American dissertations and monographs on the work of Erich Fromm was not a sufficient reason for translating this book. I believe that the special value of this study lies in the fact that it is the first to consider Fromm's entire opus, especially the earliest writings, some of which have never been translated. It should also be said that it is a scientific discussion of Fromm's work that has been significantly shaped by personal acquaintance with Erich Fromm. And finally, it represents an attempt to understand Fromm's thought against the background of the Jewish and German intellectual history from which he derives. Except for a few minor corrections in the Introduction, this version corresponds to the German text. Even the comments on guiding cognitive interests, such as the significance of Fromm's humanism for questions of theological ethics (Chapter V: 4) and for Christianity generally (Chapter IX), were retained in order to give the reader some insight into the relevant discussion in German-speaking countries.

The bibliography of Fromm's writings was reworked: it contains all presently known titles with the internationally used logograms and indications of first publication, but omits versions, prepublications, reprints, and translations. Readers who are interested in such bibliographical data are referred to the complete bibliography of Fromm's writings in Volume X of the *Collected Works* (*Erich Fromm Gesamtausgabe in 10 Bänden*, edited by Rainer Funk, Stuttgart: Deutsche Verlags-Anstalt, 1981). The general bibliography in this study was enlarged by a few titles from the secondary literature.

I thank the translator for his trouble, Inter Nationes for the financial support that made this translation possible, and Märitt Schütt (Deutsche Verlags-Anstalt, Stuttgart) as well as Werner Mark Linz and Ulla Schnell (Continuum Publishing Co.) for making this book accessible to the English-speaking public.

Tübingen 1981

Introduction:

ERICH FROMM'S LIFE AND WORK

Fromm has been called "one of the most influential and popular psychoanalysts in America."[1] "Of all the psychoanalytic theorists who have tried to formulate a system better suited than Freud's to problems of contemporary life, none has been more productive or influential than Erich Fromm."[2] Even one of his sharpest critics, John Homer Schaar, had to admit that Fromm's writings "make his name a prominent one in any serious discussion of modern social problems."[3]

The increasing number of dissertations on Fromm is testimony to the ongoing scientific discussion of his thought and discoveries. Their authors come from the most varied scientific disciplines and are interested in determining the relevance of Fromm's insights to their field of specialization.[4] The breadth of this interest in Fromm reflects the breadth of his writings and his thought.

A short sketch of his life and intellectual antecedents is in order before we undertake a summary of his literary work.[5] Erich Fromm was born on March 23, 1900, in Frankfurt am Main, the only child of Orthodox Jewish parents. He characterizes his parents as "highly neurotic" and himself as "a probably rather unbearable, neurotic child."[6] The Jewish faith practiced by his parents (his father came from an old rabbinical family), and Fromm himself up to his twenty-sixth birthday, had a profound influence on him. Fromm studied the Old Testament intensively and was especially fascinated by the prophets Isaiah, Amos, and Hosea because they had promised universal peace. As a young man, he studied the Talmud with Rabbi J. Horowitz, and later, as a university student, he took instruction from Salman Rabinkov in Heidelberg and Nehemia Nobel and Ludwig Krause in Frankfurt. The influence of these teachers was considerable: Rabinkov's socialist and Nobel's mystic orientation are thematically present in Fromm's writings and fields of interest.

The suicide by which a twenty-year-old female friend of the family thought to assure her burial alongside her recently deceased and excessively loved father is mentioned by Fromm as the childhood experience that was responsible for his later interest in Sigmund Freud and psychoanalysis.[7] There is probably also a connection between that suicide, which occurred when he was twelve, and Fromm's reinterpretation of the Oedipus complex, his profound skepticism concerning all irrational and symbiotic relations of dependence, and his thesis that there are two possible life projects, the biophilous and the necrophilous.

Fromm's sympathy for the prophets and their messianic visions of the harmonious coexistence of all nations was profoundly shaken by the First World War, which made him increasingly distrustful of all official doctrines and vainglorious prophecies of national victory. "When the war ended in 1918, I was a deeply troubled young man who was obsessed by the question of how war was possible, by the wish to understand the irrationality of human mass behavior, by a passionate desire for peace and international understanding. More, I had become deeply suspicious of all official ideologies and declarations, and filled with the conviction 'of all one must doubt.' "[8]

His political interests deepened when he became acquainted with the work of Karl Marx, for in it he saw "the key to the understanding of history and the manifestation, in secular terms, of the radical humanism which was expressed in the messianic vision of the Old Testament prophets."[9]

Considering the problems that preoccupied him, it was only natural that Fromm's scientific career should have begun with the study of psychology, philosophy, and sociology. After two semesters spent at the University of Frankfurt, he went to Heidelberg in 1919 to study under Alfred Weber, Karl Jaspers, and Heinrich Rickert. As early as 1922, he obtained his doctorate in philosophy with a dissertation on the sociopsychological structure of three

Jewish Diaspora communities: the Karaites, the Hasidim, and the Reformed Jews.[10] After further studies in psychiatry and psychology in Munich, he married Frieda Reichmann in 1926, but this marriage was brief. From 1928 through 1929, he received psychoanalytic training from Dr. Landauer and Dr. Wittenberg in Munich, and also in 1929, he became a student of Hans Sachs and Theodor Reik at the psychoanalytic institute in Berlin. In 1930, Fromm and others founded the South German Institute for Psychoanalysis in Frankfurt am Main. In that same year, he became a member and *Dozent* at the Institut für Sozialforschung (Institute for Social Research) at Frankfurt University, where he taught psychoanalysis.[11] It is from this institute that the "Frankfurt School" emerged.

Around 1926, Fromm had become acquainted with Buddhism, an important event in his intellectual development that was followed, decades later, by the intensive study of Daisetz T. Suzuki's works on Zen Buddhism. Fromm's estimate of religion, his critique of all appeals to irrational revelation and authority, and his preference for combining rational insight and mysticism were significantly molded by this experience.

Another important event in Fromm's intellectual life before 1930 was his reading of Johann Jakob Bachofen's (1815–1887) *Mother Right.* Bachofen's insights into the link between matriarchal or patriarchal social structures and cultural and psychic phenomena influenced Fromm's ideas on the reciprocal influence of social and psychic structure, which went beyond Freud's.

From 1930 on, Fromm's research was directed toward a synthesis of these various insights and sciences. "I wanted to understand the laws that govern the life of the individual man, and the laws of society—that is, of men in their social existence. I tried to see the lasting truth in Freud's concepts as against those assumptions which were in need of revision. I tried to do the same with Marx's theory, and finally I tried to arrive at a synthesis which followed from the understanding and the criticism of both thinkers."[12]

For this project, Fromm developed his own sociopsychological method, which—in contrast to Wilhelm Reich's and Herbert Marcuse's—did not rely on Freud's sexual theories. When one surveys

Fromm's large literary output, one notices that all his later works are explications and—albeit far-reaching—modifications of these spiritual and intellectual antecedents and methodological discoveries.

National Socialism forced the Frankfurt Institute for Social Research to emigrate, first to Geneva, and then in 1934, to Columbia University. After a rather long illness during which he stayed at Davos, Fromm accepted an invitation by the Chicago Psychoanalytic Institute to give a series of lectures in 1934. When the Institute for Social Research found its new home in New York, he moved there and resumed work at the institute while continuing his psychoanalytic practice. In New York, he made the acquaintance of Karen Horney, Clara Thompson, Harry Stack Sullivan, and William Silverberg.[13] From 1935 to 1939, he was visiting professor at Columbia. His connection with the Institute for Social Research continued into the late thirties, when Max Horkheimer and Herbert Marcuse came out against his elaboration of the Freudian theory of drives, the latter denouncing him as a "neo-Freudian or neo-Freudian revisionist."[14] Fromm continued to develop his thought, which, though bearing some kinship with that of the so-called Neo-Freudians, Karen Horney, Harry Stack Sullivan, and Abram Kardiner,[15] in its emphasis on "culture," did not prevent him from clearly distancing himself from these thinkers.[16]

During the war years, Fromm tried to enlighten the American public concerning the real intentions of the National Socialist system. In 1945, he and others founded the William Alanson White Institute of Psychiatry, Psychoanalysis, and Psychology, and from 1946 to 1950, he was chairman of the faculty and chairman of the institute's training committee. All through the forties, he taught extensively. From 1945 to 1947, he was professor of psychology at the University of Michigan, and in 1948–49, he was a visiting professor at Yale. From 1941 to 1949, he also was a member of the faculty of Bennington College, and in 1948, he became adjunct professor for psychoanalysis at New York University.

Fromm had married a second time in 1944 and that same year he became an American citizen. On the advice of a physician that his ailing wife would benefit from a more favorable climate, he moved from Bennington to Mexico in 1949 and became professor at the

National Autonomous University in Mexico City, where he established the psychoanalytic section at the medical school. He taught there until 1965, when he became professor emeritus. In addition to his teaching duties in Mexico, Fromm attended to his responsibilities at the William Alanson White Institute, held a position as professor of psychology at Michigan State University from 1957 to 1961, and was adjunct professor of psychology at the graduate division of Arts and Sciences at New York University after 1962. Despite his extensive teaching activities, he kept up his psychoanalytic practice (for more than forty-five years), remained active as a supervisor and teacher of analysis,[17] and participated in sociopsychological fieldwork in Mexico over the years.

Since childhood, Fromm had been passionately interested in politics, and in the middle fifties, he joined the American Socialist party and attempted (fruitlessly, as it turned out) to provide it with a new program.[18] Although he recognized that he was temperamentally unsuited to practical politics, he did considerable work to enlighten the American people about the current possibilities and intentions of the Soviet Union.[19] Fromm taught a socialist humanism that rejects both Western capitalism and Soviet Communist socialism and sympathizes with the interpretation of socialism of the Yugoslav "praxis" group.[20]

His strongest political interest was the international peace movement. In this, he was motivated by the insight that the present historical situation will decide whether humanity will take rational hold of its destiny or fall victim to destruction through nuclear war.[21] He was a co-founder of SANE, "the most important American peace movement, which not only fought against the atomic arms race but also against the war in Vietnam."[22] His last important political activity was his work on behalf of Senator Eugene McCarthy during the 1968 campaign for the Democratic presidential nomination.[23]

After 1965, Fromm concentrated more and more on his writing. Beginning in 1968, he spent the summer months in the exceptionally benign climate of the Tessin, to which he moved permanently in 1974. He and his wife Annis took up residence in Muralto, far from the hectic pace of modern life, and it was in Muralto that he died on March 18, 1980. But solitude and retirement on the Lago

Maggiore did not lessen Fromm's interest in contemporary problems, a fact that is clearly evidenced by his literary productivity during the last years of his life.

As one surveys Fromm's literary output, one is struck by the variety and breadth of his interests and research. The sociologically-oriented dissertation he wrote as a twenty-two-year-old doctoral candidate examines the "correlation between social structure and the (religious) idea entrusted to its charge"[24] among the Jews of the Diaspora. A number of shorter essays written between 1926 and 1930 reveal Fromm as an orthodox Freudian.[25] The treatise "Die Entwicklung des Christusdogmas. Eine psychoanalytische Studie zur sozialpsychologischen Funktion der Religion" (The development of the Dogma of Christ. A psychoanalytical study on the sociopsychological function of religion), written in 1930, demonstrates his interest in the relevance of religion and the religious idea for social and cultural reality. This essay represents the first instance of Fromm's particular type of sociopsychological analysis of these phenomena. It is a method that differs from both the vulgar Marxist base-superstructure theory and the psychologizing cultural analysis *à la* Freud.

In his next essays, Fromm explicated the method of "analytic social psychology."[26] An understanding of the importance of Bachofen's and Robert Briffault's theories of the matriarchy plays a particular role here, and the investigation on authority and family that utilized this sociopsychological method represents a kind of testing of it.[27]

After a few years during which he wrote nothing, Fromm published his first important sociopsychological monograph, *Escape from Freedom,* in 1941. Based on an analysis of the relation between Protestantism and the development of early capitalism, the work demonstrates modern man's incapacity to value his "freedom from" as a "freedom to." Instead, Fromm wrote, modern man attempts to escape from freedom by placing himself in authoritarian relations of dependency, and in the process becomes destructive and conformist. The book's insights into the contemporary situation in Nazi Germany made a considerable impression on the American public, although Fromm's sociological interpretation of the Reformation provoked sharp criticism from some.[28]

There followed years of intensive effort to shed light on the connections between socioeconomic structures on the one hand, and human needs as psychic necessities in the process of orientation of assimilation and socialization on the other. In this effort, Fromm developed a characterology that widens the perspective of Freudian libido theory and its narrow human image, while simultaneously indicating the ethical relevance of the various character orientations. The results of this research found expression in what may well be Fromm's central work, *Man for Himself: An Inquiry into the Psychology of Ethics.*

The Sane Society, published in 1955, develops the themes found in *Escape from Freedom* and *Man for Himself.* Written from the viewpoint of a humanistic ethic, the book points to the socioeconomic reasons that today prevent the realization of the human project. An analysis of the modern capitalist and bureaucratic social structure lays bare the universal phenomenon of alienation that can be overcome only if economic, political, and cultural conditions are fundamentally changed in the direction of a democratic and humanist socialism.

In addition to these three works with their abundant observations and discoveries, Fromm wrote a number of monographs during the fifties and sixties in which the horizons of his thought emerge more clearly. In 1950, he published a shorter work, *Psychoanalysis and Religion,* in which he discusses his understanding of a humanistic religion as influenced by psychoanalysis and Buddhism in greater detail. *The Forgotten Language,* a discourse on fairy tales, myths, and dreams[29] as universal and revelatory phenomena of human existence, appeared the following year. Fromm's best seller was the short *The Art of Loving,* first published in 1956, which was translated into twenty-eight languages and had sold more than one and a half million English-language copies by 1970. Using the concept of "productive love," Fromm here shows the consequences of a humanistic ethics for the understanding of self-love, love of one's neighbor, and love of one's fellow man.

In three further books,[30] Fromm paid tribute to Freud and Marx, while at the same time attempting to define his position in relation to these seminal modern thinkers. His *Marx's Concept of Man* is of special significance because it drew the attention of the American public to Marx's early writings.

The importance of religion for a successful human existence and the future of man is clarified in two works: the essay "Psychoanalysis and Zen-Buddhism," which reflects Fromm's study of the latter; and *You Shall Be as Gods,* a "radical interpretation of the Old Testament and its tradition"[31] that pleads the cause of a nontheistic religion. Fromm develops a historical-philosophical perspective that views the Old Testament account of God and man as a process in the course of which man comes increasingly into his own. Thus God as idea becomes identical with man's complete "being at home with himself," and belief in a revealed god is understood as a stage on the path toward a "humanistic religion" that develops in and through itself.[32]

Subsequently, Fromm focused principally on two problems, one of which is the historically decisive question whether man will once again become the master of his creations or whether he will perish in an overtechnicized industrial world. Fromm's writings on politics, especially on nuclear armaments and the peace movement,[33] and his *Revolution of Hope: Toward a Humanized Technology* (New York, 1968), which can be considered a continuation of *The Sane Society,* address this question. The second problem relates to the syndrome of decay of the individual and of mankind as a species. Using the types of nonproductive life that Fromm had previously explicated (principally in *Man for Himself*), *The Heart of Man: Its Genius for Good and Evil* presents a systematic treatment of the polarity of possible orientations on the basis of character. The related questions concerning the antithesis of instinct and character, the inherent human destructive instinct postulated by behavioral research, and the skepticism concerning man's potential goodness that this view entails (and the doubt this skepticism casts on humanism) were the interests that guided Fromm's research for some five years. The results of his work over this period are summarized in *The Anatomy of Human Destructiveness.*

His last major publication, *To Have or to Be?,* is an attempt to synthesize sociopsychological insights and humanist religion and ethics. Here, Fromm identifies two fundamentally antithetical orientations of human existence—having and being—and links his abundant insights into the individual and society's psyche to the tradition of humanistic religion and of significant historical figures.

Again and again, Fromm has been reproached for being excessively "speculative," for not providing enough scientific data.[34] This criticism derives, in part, from his occasional predilection for not quoting sources in detail and failing to reflect adequately on what the pertinent intellectual traditions have had to say about the specific problems he is discussing. Then, too, his language is clear and uncomplicated, although with no loss of depth in either the formulation of problems or the presentation of insights, and this makes him suspect in some quarters. There is every reason to believe Fromm when he says, "There is not a single theoretical conclusion about man's psyche, either in this or in my other writings, which is not based on a critical observation of human behavior carried out in the course of this psychoanalytic work."[35] The same applies to the insights into character structures that his sociopsychological method helped him formulate: a study on *Social Character in a Mexican Village*[36] that is based on five years of fieldwork is persuasive because of the extensive coincidence of findings and theory. So it is not the lack of rigorous research that inspires the charge of unscientific speculation. Rather, such attacks are the result of Fromm's disputes with positivistic tendencies that have no use for anything but precisely demonstrable, objective insights confined to a single discipline. Fromm believed that responsible scientific work cannot ignore the ends of its activity or refuse to synthesize insights from a variety of disciplines. Neither can it be neutral toward the ethical relevance of its findings. Science therefore requires a frame of orientation that is ultimately not deducible from the insights of any single humane discipline.

Part One

THE SOCIO-PSYCHOLOGICAL INSIGHTS AND PHILOSOPHICAL-ANTHROPOLOGICAL IDEAS OF ERICH FROMM

1

SOCIAL PSYCHOLOGY

THE QUESTIONING OF FREUD's CONCEPT OF MAN

The Molding of Man by Socioeconomic Conditions: The Sociopsychological Method

Erich Fromm has no doubts on this matter: Sigmund Freud "is the founder of a truly scientific psychology, and his discovery of unconscious processes and of the dynamic nature of character traits is a unique contribution to the science of man which has altered the picture of man for all time to come."[1] Yet Freud's psychoanalysis is just a "contribution" to the science of man, and Fromm's critique of Freud relates precisely to Freud's claim that he can define man scientifically, which here means psychoanalytically.

For "as the motor of human behavior, [psychoanalysis] has shown drives and needs which are fed by physiologically anchored 'drives' which are themselves not directly observable."[2] Initially, Freud had postulated two groups of drives: self-preservation and sexual drives.[3] The latter are fed by the energy inherent in them, the libido, which is of a relatively constant quality. "This libido causes painful tension, which is reduced only by the act of physical release; to this liberation from painful tension Freud gave the name of 'pleasure.' . . . This dynamism which leads from tension to release of tension to renewed tension, from pain to pleasure to pain, Freud called the 'pleasure principle.' "[4] This principle is so central to man that it essentially defines him, which means that man fundamentally tends toward the maximal pleasurable release of tensions. According to Freud, man develops his social nature, his culture, his religion and science, only secondarily and modificatorily—that is, by way of reaction formation or sublimation. This occurs in partnership with the "reality principle," which opposes the individual's pleasure principle and embodies the demands of reality and society, insisting on the renunciation or postponement of pleasure so that greater displeasure may be avoided or greater future pleasure gained.[5] If these two principles cannot be brought into a tolerable equilibrium, neurotic or psychotic phenomena result. "The active and passive adaptation of biological facts, the drives, to social facts is the core concept of psychoanalysis."[6]

In a number of ways, Freud failed to develop this insight. While it is true that in his late works[7] he deals more intensively with the social conditions that generate the psychic structure and development, he continues to view man as a self-sufficient individual who is governed by the pleasure principle and limited and modified by the reality principle.

Erich Fromm's first objection to this understanding of man is addressed to Freud's nonchalant acceptance of society's structure and demands as givens.[8] Fromm proposes to follow Karl Marx in examining social structure as determined by economic factors. If such a determination of social structure is discoverable, it must be asked whether psychic structure is not also shaped by socioeconomic conditions through the family as the "psychological agency of society."[9] If so, socioeconomic conditions rather than libidinous energy have the primary shaping influence. In that case, it would not be the structure of drives that determines man's nature and behavior; instead, "in the interplay of interacting psychic drives and economic conditions, the latter have primacy."[10] In connection with the elaboration of his sociopsychological method, Fromm posits this dominance of the "socioeconomic" structure over the libidinous structure of drives. Viewed superficially, this method represents a fusion of Marxist social theory and Freudian psychoanalysis; concretely, it involves the application of psychoanalytic insights to social phenomena. In contrast to Sigmund Freud, Theodore Reik, and others who view social entities as structured by psychic mechanisms and laws that resemble those at work in the individual, and who analyze the psychic structure of social entities in analogy to the structural regularities of the individual psyche, Fromm maintains that the psychic structure of social entities must be understood through their social structure—that is, through their "socioeconomic" situation.[11] The difference thus does not lie in the psychoanalytic method itself but in the absence of a sociological starting point, a lack that subsequently becomes methodologically relevant. It is in his reinterpretation of the Oedipus complex that Fromm's different understanding of the psychic structure of social entities becomes apparent.[12]

In Freud's psychology, the phase of the Oedipus complex is of central importance to a successful maturation process. The male child develops sexual desires for his mother, which simultaneously occasion hatred of the father as rival and avenger. This phase must be passed through if further psychological maturation—the rise of the superego, the development of guilt feelings and of conscience, the capacity for genuine love, and so on—is to occur. Neurotic symptoms in later life are essentially traceable to an unsuccessfully negotiated oedipal phase.

Fromm raises the following objection to this Freudian view: "The absolutizing of the Oedipus complex led Freud to base the whole development of mankind on the mechanism of father hatred and the resultant reactions,[13] without any regard for the material living conditions of the group under study."[14] Such regard for "material living conditions" was made possible by Johann Jakob Bachofen's investigations of matriarchy.[15] Viewing Greek mythology and religion as the expression of a shift from a matriarchically to a patriarchically organized and defined social structure and religion, Fromm[16] interprets the Oedipus myth as an element of the entire trilogy (*Oedipus Rex, Oedipus at Colonus,* and *Antigone*), "as a symbol not of the incestuous love between mother and son but as the rebellion of the son against the authority of the father in the patriarchal family."[17] Comparative research in cultural anthropology[18] confirms Fromm's interpretation in the sense that it shows that the Oedipus complex in psychic development is an important element only in clearly patriarchal social structures, where it is primarily the expression of an authority conflict and only secondarily a sexual, incestuous fixation.

Fromm's reinterpretation of the Oedipus complex suggests not only that Freud interpreted his phylogenetic knowledge incorrectly, but also that he was mistaken in his ontogenetic interpretation of the Oedipal phase in the child. While the sexual, incestuous fixation of the child often plays a significant role, the element that produces the Oedipus complex is actually the conflict between the father's demand that he be obeyed and the contrary interests of the son, a conflict that is provoked by the patriarchal social structure.[19] More importantly, here, Fromm's insights make clear that both the psychic structure of the individual and that of social entities is properly grasped only when seen against the background of social structure (which here means the effect of influences that prevail in a matriarchal or a patriarchal society).[20]

For the analysis of social phenomena, this leads to the following sociopsychological method: "the phenomena of social psychology can be understood as processes involving the active and passive adaptation of the instinctual apparatus to the socio-economic situation. In certain fundamental respects, the instinctual apparatus itself is a biological given; but it is highly modifiable. The role of primary formative factor goes to the economic conditions. The family is the essential medium through which the economic situation exerts its formative influence on the individual's psyche. The task of social psychology is to explain the shared, socially relevant, psychic attitudes and ideologies—and their unconscious roots in particular—in terms of the influence of economic conditions on libido strivings."[21]

If economic conditions are the primary shaping factors, a view of psychic facts that differs from Freud's must result. Fromm shows "that a psychological agency like the super ego and the ego, a mechanism such as repression or sado-masochistic impulses which condition man's feelings, thinking and acting decisively are not 'natural' things but are ultimately conditioned in part by man's existence, the mode of production and the social structure resulting from it."[22]

The Shaping of Man by His Relation to the World: The Formation of Character

Fromm elaborated his thesis that psychic agencies, mechanisms, and structures are shaped by socioeconomic conditions in the doctrine of the genesis of character. According to Fromm, character is not formed by the phases of libidinal development but is a psychic entity that is created by the various ways in which man relates to the world. From a formal point of view, what is involved here is the opposition between Freud's biologically and Fromm's sociologically oriented characterology. Both believe "that character traits underlie behavior and must be inferred from it."[23] Both also agree "that the fundamental entity in character is not the single character trait but the total organization from which a number of single character traits follow."[24]

But in their understanding of the genesis of character Freud and Fromm decisively differ. Freud's theory of character is based on two observations.[25] He notes that character traits are relatively constant passionate strivings that cannot simply be abandoned as learned forms of behavior may be. He also became convinced that all innate passions except the drive for self-preservation have their roots in sexual and libidinous desires.[26] Freud's libido theory combines these two observations and "explained various character traits as sublimation of (or reaction formation against) the various kinds of pre-genital libido.[27] The libido was assumed to develop from primitive pre-genital forms to the mature genital orientation and the various character orientations were explained as outcomes of those different phases of libido development."[28]

Freud makes the most extensive use of this theory in his analysis of the anal character, which he describes as "pedantic, parsimonious and stubborn." It appears when the anal phase of libidinal development is beset by special difficulties in what is referred to as toilet training.[29] Traits such as parsimony, punctuality, orderliness, and stubbornness are not chance qualities but are anchored in the specific instinctual structure of the individual as it developed during the anal phase.[30] In corresponding fashion, traits that typically relate to other phases of libidinal development can also be determined.

Fromm elaborates a wholly different perspective. For him, the development of character is not tied primarily to libidinal development, its sublimations, and reaction formations. Nor does he subscribe to the causal relation between erogenous zones (mouth, anus, genitals) and a given character structure that the Freudian theory postulates.[31] Character is not formed by the various phases of libido development but rather by the various ways man relates to his world: "(1) by acquiring and assimilating things, and (2) by relating himself to people (and himself)."[32] The first, Fromm calls the process of assimilation; the second, the process of socialization.[33]

Fromm's comments on the sociopsychological method show that

he developed this important new approach because he ascribed primary influence to socioeconomic conditions rather than to libidinous strivings.[34] The critique of Freud's image of man that this fundamental decision entails makes Fromm's new approach to the understanding of the genesis of character appear as no more than a logical consequence: "Freud's essential principle is to look upon man as an entity, a closed system endowed by nature with certain physiologically conditioned drives, and to interpret the development of his character as a reaction to satisfactions and frustrations of these drives; whereas, in our opinion, the fundamental approach to human personality is the understanding of man's relation to the world, to others, to nature, and to himself. We believe that man is *primarily* a social being and not, as Freud assumes, primarily self-sufficient and only secondarily in need of others in order to satisfy his instinctual needs. In this sense, we believe that individual psychology is fundamentally social psychology or, in Sullivan's terms, the psychology of interpersonal relationships; the key problem of psychology is that of the particular kind of relatedness of the individual toward the world, not that of satisfaction or frustration of single instinctual desires. The problem of what happens to man's instinctual desires has to be understood as one part of the total problem of his relationship toward the world and not as *the* problem of human personality. Therefore, in our approach, the needs and desires that center about the individual's relations to others, such as love, hatred, tenderness, symbiosis, are the fundamental psychological phenomena, while with Freud they are only secondary results from frustrations or satisfactions of instinctive needs."[35]

For this reason, Fromm defines character as "the (relatively permanent) form in which human energy[36] is canalized in the process of assimilation and socialization."[37]

THE "SOCIAL CHARACTER" AS MEDIATION BETWEEN THE SOCIOECONOMIC STRUCTURE AND THE IDEAS AND IDEALS THAT PREVAIL IN A SOCIETY

If it is true that man's character is formed by socioeconomic conditions, it must be asked in what "medium" the mediation between socioeconomic conditions and psychic and intellectual phenomena takes place.

Fromm received the initial impetus toward the solution of this question from Marx's distinction between the "constant drives" (the sexual drive and hunger fall into this category) whose form and direction, though nothing else, social conditions can change, and the "relative drives" or "desires" that owe their origin to a particular type of social organization.[38] "Here Marx already linked the relative appetites with social structure and conditions of production, and communication, and thus laid the foundation for a dynamic psychology which understands most human appetites—and that means a large part of human motivation—as being determined by the process of production."[39]

Only the sociopsychological method, which gains an insight into the instinctual structure of a group because it has a precise knowledge of the fate of this group, can discover such a shaping influence and make it accessible to scientific formulation.[40] "The value of social-psychological investigation, therefore, cannot lie in the fact that we acquire from it a full insight into the psychic peculiarities of the individual members, but only in the fact that we can establish those common psychic tendencies that play a decisive role in their social development."[41]

As long as Fromm subscribed to Freud's libido theory, he usually referred to these tendencies or "certain psychic attitudes common to members of a group"[42] as "libidinal structure": "The libidinal structure of a society is the medium through which the economy exerts its influence on man's intellectual and mental manifestations."[43] After he had rejected Freud's libido theory and developed his own view of the genesis of character, Fromm stopped using the term "libidinal structure" and spoke of "social character" instead.[44]

To explain the psychic attitudes shared by a society, one must assume a formation process of psychic energy. "This process of transforming general psychic energy into specific psychosocial energy is mediated by the social character."[45] By "social character," Fromm means "the core of the character common to most members of a culture, in contradistinction to the individual character, in which people belonging to the same culture differ from each other."[46] What is of interest, therefore, is not individual pecularities, which make the individual unique and which are the result of chance factors of birth (such constitutional factors as temperament) and particular life experiences.[47] Rather, research into the social character tells us "how human energy is channelled and operates as a productive force in a given social order."[48] If the energy of most members of a social group takes the same direction, it follows that their motivations are the same and that they are receptive to the same ideas and ideals.[49] From a formal point of view, social character is something like the "transmission belt between the economic structure of society and the prevailing ideas."[50] "It is not only the 'economic basis' which creates a certain social character which in turn creates certain ideas. The ideas, once created, also influence the social character and, indirectly, the social economic structure."[51] The social character thus mediates in both directions,[52] and the concept of social character can be clarified in the following way:[53]

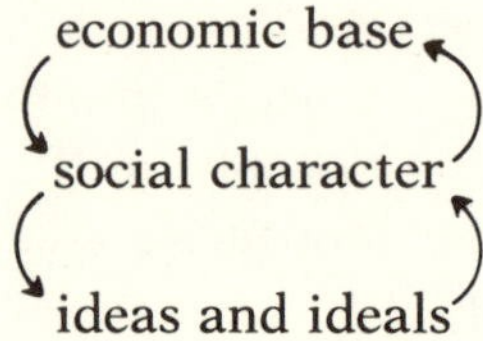

The real meaning of the social character lies in the fact that this concept makes possible a new understanding of social processes. Fromm defines its function as follows: "Every society is structuralized and operates in certain ways which are necessitated by a number of objective conditions; such conditions are the methods of production and distribution which in turn depend on raw material, industrial techniques, climate, etc.; furthermore political and geographical factors and cultural traditions and influences to which society is exposed. There is no "society" in general but only specific social structures which operate in different and ascertainable ways. Although these social structures do change in the course of historical development, they are relatively fixed at any given historical period and society can exist only by operating within the framework of its particular structure. The members of the society and/or the various classes or status groups within it have to behave in such a way as to be able to function in the sense required by society. It is the function of the social character to shape the energies of the members of society in such a way that their behavior is not left to conscious decisions whether or not to follow the social pattern but that *people want to act as they have to act* and at the same time find gratification in acting according to the requirements of the culture. In other words, the social character has the function of molding human energy for the purpose of the functioning of a given society."[54]

The individual who, being a member of a given society, has been shaped by the character of that society is spared all confrontation with the society's demands because he wishes to think, feel, and act as he must (and is happy in so doing because he is behaving in what is, for him, a psychologically satisfactory manner).[55] The social character is the essential stabilizing (system-maintaining) factor for the survival of the society and its underlying economic base because "the energies of people are molded in ways that make them into productive forces that are indispensable for the functioning of that society."[56] The social character of an individual or a society is molded largely by the socioeconomic conditions of a given society.[57] But where man's natural, fundamental needs are concerned, this formative influence encounters limits.

When one considers the factors that shape the social character, one observes the interplay of the following elements:[58]

1. Social and economic factors, which have a certain preponderance because it is difficult to change them.

2. Religious, political, and philosophical views ("ideas and ideals"), which, though rooted in the social character, also define and stabilize it.

3. Fundamental human needs such as those for relatedness, rootedness, and transcendence, which all must be satisfied and are indispensable to successful human life, play an active role in this interplay.[59]

As long as the interaction between these elements remains harmonious and stable, the social character has a predominantly stabilizing function. But if conditions change so that a discrepancy develops between the factors that determine social character and the already existing social character, the social character becomes an element of disintegration, "dynamite instead of a social mortar, as it were."[60]

The concept of a social character thus explains "how psychic energy in general is transformed into the specific form of psychic energy which every society needs to employ for its functioning."[61] Social character includes "the functional aspect of character—the part of character structure which has developed to make culture or society proceed and operate."[62] A misunderstanding of this significance of the social character is the cause of a good many false interpretations of Fromm's social psychology.[63]

All of Fromm's sociopsychological research aims at discovering various kinds of social character within the context of the factors that determine it; he then wishes to confront this social character with the teleological ideas entailed in a humanistic concept of man and history. These ideas themselves are largely determined by the results of his sociopsychological analyses.

SUMMARY: THE CRITIQUE OF FREUD'S CONCEPT OF MAN

Freud's concept of man can be described as a physiological and mechanical one: "Freud's man is the physiologically driven and motivated '*homme machine*.' "[64] The mechanistic element in this concept found its most conspicuous expression in Freud's theory of instincts, according to which man is a primarily self-enclosed unit driven by two forces: the instinct for self-preservation (ego drives) and sexuality (sexual drives—in Freud, comprising everything that relates to the senses).[65] These two basic drives are anchored in chemical and physiological processes and obey their own laws; they demand optimal satisfaction.

Viewed as a being controlled by the dynamics of his libido development, man is fundamentally unrelated: his relation to those who make up his environment, to society, culture, and history, is not primary. His "social being" is seen as the product of his striving for optimal satisfaction and as only a secondary phenomenon. Man must use others (mother, father, and other persons) as objects; that is, he "is forced by his drives into relationships with others"[66] in order to satisfy his libidinal interests. Only the limits imposed on his libidinal interests by the individuals used to satisfy them produces, by sublimation and reaction formation, social attitudes that make possible a productive life with others, culture, and history. Thus both phylogenetically and ontogenetically, sociality, character qualities, society, and cultural manifestations such as art, religion, technique, and science are the products of physiologically determined instinctual action—"nothing but" frustrations of the primarily libidinal striving for satisfaction.

The primary striving for satisfaction that the pleasure principle postulates is based on the need to eliminate displeasure; that is, it is based on a want, a lack.[67] This means, on the one hand, that pleasure is not something that comes from plenitude and leads to the intensification and enhancement of human experience but is the necessity of a physiologically determined process. On the other hand, love and tenderness are surplus phenomena that can play no role in Freud's system. Although the term "pleasure principle" conjures up fulfillment, joy, happiness, these goals cannot be realized in Freud's system because his pleasure principle, which determines man, is a principle of want.

Closely connected is Freud's rejection of the view that man is a morally good being.[68] "Man develops exclusively under the influence of his self interest which demands the optimal satisfaction of his libidinal impulses, always on the condition that they do not endanger his interest in self-preservation (reality principle)."[69] Man's driving force is his egoism. Conscience is not a constructive impetus toward altruism but merely the internalization of the reality principle that curtails egoistic libidinal strivings for satisfaction.

The picture of history that this concept of man implies is characterized by both an optimism concerning the possibilities of progress and a tragic aspect.[70] Man's capacity to suppress his drives makes possible spiritual and intellectual development and greater cultural achievements. Freud differs from Herbert Marcuse in opting for the partial suppression of drives that makes culture possible, and he harbors an optimism that implies the necessity of renunciation (this is the tragic element). For Freud, there can be no free society, but only a civilized one that is purchased by the suppression of instincts.

Freud's introduction of the death instinct into his system caused a fundamental change in his concept of history and of man. The death drive is posited as the root of human destructiveness in both its directions—that is, by man against himself and by man against the outside world.[71] Presumably because of the impression the catastrophe of World War I made on him, Freud discarded the ego drives and libidinal drives and proceeded to postulate an opposition between the life instinct (Eros), which comprised both ego and sex drives, and the death instinct (Thanatos). He became convinced[72] there was a drive in man that had the same importance as the drive serving the preservation of life, so that both drives are constantly active as tendencies, combat each other, and merge, "until finally the death instinct proves to be the stronger force and has its ultimate triumph in the death of the individual."[73] An essential point in Freud's new theory that must be examined critically is the assumption that the destructive tendency that is posited with the death instinct is grounded in man's nature, and is thus a biologically rooted element inherent in all life.[74]

Freud developed the implications of this theory for the concept of man only partially and hesitantly, for he was uncertain how to verify his hypothesis.[75] He was also unable to establish a connection with his earlier theory of drives in which the libido theory had been the decisive component. The following aspects of his changed image of man can nonetheless be observed:

The self-sufficient and asocial quality of man as defined by the libido theory now becomes his aggressive and destructive nature: "*homo homini lupus*."[76] The manifest realities of profound hatred, an irrational destructive urge, and destructive aggressivity in human beings find an apparent solution. But the actual import is that man must resign from the task of determining his own fate. "On the basis of his instinctive orientation and also of a profound conviction of the wickedness of human nature, Freud is prone to interpret all 'ideal' motives in man as the result of something 'mean.' "[77] As a result, all man's striving for constructive values—for love, truth, freedom, right—is ultimately an illusion, love's labor lost, for "Man is only a battlefield on which the life and death instincts fight against each other. He can never liberate himself decisively from the tragic alternative of destroying others or himself."[78] Human history and society and culture also take on a tragic quality. Freud himself acknowledges, "As a result of this primary hostility of man for man, society is constantly threatened by disintegration."[79] According to Fromm, "the skeptical enlightenment philosopher, overwhelmed by the collapse of his world, became the total skeptic who looked at the fate of man in history as unmitigated tragedy."[80]

Some of Fromm's most important arguments against Freud's view of man and history are summarized in the following paragraphs.

Concerning the knowledge of man's nature and of social processes, Fromm's sociopsychological starting point, shaped by Marxism and sociology, is fundamental. In contrast to Freud, Fromm begins with the "sociobiological" question: "What kind of ties to the world, persons and things must—and can—man develop in order to survive, given his specific equipment and the nature of the world around him?"[81] This question presupposes that man is primarily a social being, molded phylogenetically and ontogenetically by the social conditions in which he lives. "The ideological, religious, economic and political forces that operate in the social process have a dynamism of their own. A product of man, they also create man."[82]

The fundamental difference between Freud and Fromm is found in their opposing views of psychic energy and its function in the shaping of man. For Freud, the libido is a psychic energy that develops as an instinct according to its own, physiologically determined law, so that the development of man's character remains tied to the phase-by-phase development and psychic energy of the libido, and social processes depend on the latter. Fromm, on the other hand, believes that what makes man specifically human is his relative independence from the instincts. Against the libido theory, he sets the vision of an individual and social character that makes possible a new understanding of social processes and therefore of the things that shape man.

A further important insight of Fromm's, which has been hardly touched upon so far, leads to an even more fundamental critique of Freud: the analysis of the social character of certain socioeconomic structures with their corresponding ideas and ideologies yielded a set of criteria for evaluating the concept of man, of history, and of the world that had a determining influence on Freud's psychoanalytic insights.[83]

In Freud's concept of man as a primarily isolated, egoistic being who is forced into relatedness because he seeks optimal satisfaction, Fromm recognized a parallel to the *homo economicus* of nineteenth-century bourgeois market economy, a being who can satisfy his economic needs only through exchange in the marketplace. "In both variants, the persons essentially remain strangers to the other, being related only by the common aim of drive satisfaction."[84] Fromm subjects Freud's theory of a duality of life instinct and death instinct to a sustained critique.[85] In part, he objects to Freud's lumping together of hostility, aggression, destruction, and sadism under the death instinct, because reactive aggressiveness, for example, stands wholly in the service of the preservation of life. Much more important is Fromm's critique of the instinctual nature of Thanatos. For Fromm, the death instinct is no biological necessity. While Eros must be viewed as the biologically normal goal of development, the death instinct should be seen as the expression of the failure of normal development and "in this sense as a pathological though deeply rooted striving."[86] The affinity for death is therefore a secondary pathological phenomenon[87] that occurs when the conditions of life make a biophilous unfolding impossible:[88] "The only basic biological drive Fromm recognizes in man is the drive to live and to grow."[89]

This view formulates Fromm's critique of the concept of instinct in a general way, a critique that will be set forth more explicitly when we examine Fromm's view of character as a substitute for animal instinct and discuss the debate concerning an aggressive drive that was provoked by behavioral research.[90]

2

THE CHARACTER THEORY

THE DYNAMIC CONCEPT OF CHARACTER

Fromm sees character as that constitutive part of the personality that is acquired and shaped and that is the opposite of the inherent, innate psychic qualities. "The difference between inherited and acquired qualities is on the whole synonymous with the difference between temperament, gifts and all constitutionally given psychic qualities on the one hand and character on the other."[1] Here the concept "character" is used exclusively to designate those psychic qualities that were acquired as reactions to experienced events. It thus differs from both everyday usage and the understanding of the term in other branches of science.[2]

An important distinction is the *difference between character and temperament*: "temperament refers to the mode of reaction and is constitutional and not changeable; character is essentially formed by a person's experiences, especially those in early life, and changeable, to some extent, by insights and new kinds of experience."[3] In contrast to temperament, which reveals whether a person will react cholerically or in a melancholy, phlegmatic, or sanguine manner, character and situation clarify what the reaction refers to.[4] Character, in other words, gives information about the nature of the individual's relatedness to the world, to others, and to himself, and, in turn, is formed by this relatedness. Fromm calls this kind of relatedness "orientation." When a choleric individual feels attracted by cruelty, for example, the fact that he reacts quickly and severely is to be ascribed to his temperament, while the fact that he feels attracted to cruelty is to be attributed to his sadistic character orientation.

A further fundamental *difference* is that *between character and behavior*. From a behaviorist perspective, behavior is "the ultimately attainable and at the same time scientifically satisfactory datum in the study of man. From this standpoint, behavior traits and character traits are identical and from a positivistic standpoint, even the concept 'character' may not be legitimate in scientific parlance."[5]

In opposition to this view of a "superficial" equation of character trait and behavior, psychoanalysis has the merit of having recognized different—conscious, and especially unconscious—motivational nexuses. "The same behavior can spring from different motives, while of course the same motives can give rise to the most variegated behavior."[6] It is in its criticism of every kind of behaviorism that the decisively different approach of psychoanalysis becomes apparent. Behaviorism does "not recognize that 'behavior' itself, separated from the behaving person, cannot be adequately described."[7]

The difference between a form of conduct and a character trait is this: While there are forms of conduct that must be seen as essentially momentary or practiced adaptations to the demands of circumstance, there are typical, pervasive forms of behavior—and these are really what so-called behaviorism is concerned with—that can be properly understood and interpreted only when viewed as character traits that persist under changed circumstances, even when they disadvantageously affect the person who conducts himself typically in this fashion. For this reason, Fromm makes a strict terminological distinction between forms of behavior and character traits. The term "forms of behavior" is reserved for "adaptive responses to a given social situation and [is] essentially a result of learning."[8] "Character trait," in Fromm's definition, is something that typically remains the same in the most widely differing social situations.[9] This "dynamic" quality of the character trait suggests that the trait is only one part of an entire character syndrome and that it is charged with psychic energy—or, as Fromm usually puts it, it is part of a character system or structure.[10]

Freud perceived the *dynamic quality of character* and recognized in the character structure of an individual the specific form through which psychic energy is channeled in the development of life. He derived the psychic energy of individual character traits from the sexual drive, which is to say he combined his characterology and his libido theory and "interpreted the dynamic nature of character traits as the expression of their libidinous source."[11] The tie-in with the libido theory meant that the individual character trait had to be understood as an element in the organization of the character as a whole.

In contrast to Freud, Fromm ascribes to man a primary relatedness to the world, to others, and to himself. It follows that the genesis of character must be understood through this antecedent relatedness. Accordingly, character traits are not the sublimations or reaction formations of various forms of the sexual drive but rather a syndrome "which results from a particular organization or . . . orientation of character."[12]

In the process of assimilation and socialization, every human being must somehow "relate" ("orient" himself). The specific form of relatedness is expressed in the individual's character and is at the same time an expression of that character. "These orientations, by which the individual relates himself to the world, constitute the core of his character" so that "character can be defined as the (relatively permanent) form in which human energy is canalized in the process of assimilation and socialization."[13]

Unlike forms of behavior, which are adaptive and learned responses to a given social situation, *character traits* are parts of a dynamic system, the character structure,[14] and change only as the character structure does. The character structure as a whole is formed by the entire social configuration—that is, "it is the result of a dynamic interrelation between system-man (with the needs, possibilities and limitations deriving from man's nature) and the system-society in which he lives."

What character means for man is properly understood only when *character is seen as a substitute for animal instinct* and its functions. Since character is the relatively permanent form in which human energy is channeled, this channeling has an extremely important biological function. For the character structure can then be viewed as the "human substitute for the instinctive apparatus of the animal."[15] It is precisely the comparison with the animal kingdom that clarifies the distinctiveness of man.

Equipped with an innate instinctive apparatus, an animal either adapts autoplastically to changed conditions and is in harmony with nature, or it becomes extinct. Man, in contrast, came into existence at that very point in evolution when an enlarged brain mass made possible an alloplastic behavior vis-à-vis the environment. Human instinctual adaptation to the environment therefore decreased to a minimum and character took over the functions of instinct, thus becoming "man's second nature."[16]

Though initially this thesis may appear vague and even insignificant, it is fraught with consequences. To begin with, it means a consistent rejection of the Freudian theory according to which man is shaped instinctually, by the development of the sexual drive. It also repudiates behaviorist thinking, which proposes to understand human behavior as conditioned reflex. And it is most opposed to the kind of research that takes its cue from the analysis of animal behavior to explain, for example, that aggressive behavior is inherent in man, a legacy of his animal ancestors, and the implication of this view for the image of man.[17]

When character is defined as a substitute for animal instinct, the function of human character is clarified.[18] For character is then seen as determining the decisions everyone makes constantly—and occasionally very suddenly—and this to such an extent that conscious acts of judgment are not required time and again. It stabilizes human reactions and ensures the internal consistency of human thinking, feeling, and acting (which is why we use such turns of speech as "having character," being "faithful" to one's character, and being "characterless").

Character also has a selective function as regards an individual's ideas and values. And finally, it is the basis for adaptation to society. It is shaped by the family as the "psychic agency of society." As "social character," it is functional for social processes and the survival of the individual in any given society.[19]

If character is defined as "relatively" permanent form, there is a further sense in which it differs from instinct. For Fromm as well as for Freud, the first years of life are decisive for the shaping of the character structure.[20] But the importance of the early years does not preclude later changes in character structure and character traits. On the contrary, Fromm's different understanding of the genesis of character and its independence from instinctive behavior patterns leads him to say that character structure continues to be modifiable up to an advanced age.[21] A change in the conditions that shaped an individual's character in a particular way and inhibited the rise of different character orientations can bring about a change in his character structure by allowing a hitherto latent orientation to become dominant.[22]

CHARACTER ORIENTATIONS

The character traits of a person and a social group correspond to a specific orientation of the character structure. In what follows, various such character orientations will be set forth. The term "orientation" reveals that the statement that some person or group has a certain character orientation, does not mean that this orientation is the sole determinant of their character. Rather, "the character of a given individual is usually a blend of all or some of these orientations in which one, however, is dominant."[23] The dominant orientation must therefore be understood as an "ideal type" in Max Weber's sense of the word.

Because he is not simply describing the character of a given individual,[24] Fromm speaks not only of orientations of the character structure or of character orientations but also of character types.

In keeping with Fromm's distinction between assimilation (as a relationship to things) and socialization (as an interpersonal relation), we will first consider orientations in the process of assimilation.

Orientations in the Process of Assimilation[25]

In both the assimilation and socialization process, Fromm differentiates between productive and nonproductive orientations, and this distinction is fundamental to a clear definition of orientations. In actual individuals and societies, of course, we are always dealing with a mixture of these two forms of orientation, but since one or the other dominates, an ideal-typical classification is possible.

The following presentation follows Fromm in the sense that it is the negative aspects of these orientations that are first set forth.[26]

The Nonproductive Orientations

Fromm distinguishes five orientations in the process of assimilation that are characterized as nonproductive: the receptive, the exploitative, the hoarding, the marketing, and the necrophilic-destructive.

"In the *receptive orientation*, a person feels 'the source of all good' to be outside, and he believes that the only way to get what he needs—be it something material, be it affection, love, knowledge, pleasure—is to receive it from that outside source."[27] In the religious sphere, such individuals expect everything from God; in the interpersonal sphere, they depend on what others give them so that, when on their own, they cannot live contentedly and find it difficult to make decisions. They are loyal and affectionate, however. Eating and drinking are very important to them.

The receptive orientation plays a dominant role in twentieth-century civilization: it is the orientation of our present-day social character. "*Homo consumens*"[28] is the eternal suckling, and it is a matter of indifference to him whether the consumption goods are cigarettes, alcohol, and sex, or books, lectures, art galleries, and TV. He relates to all things receptively. "I expect others to feed me if I'm nice to them"[29] is his motto.

Like those dominated by the receptive orientation, those marked by the *exploitative orientation* expect everything good to come from outside. The difference is "that the exploitative type does not expect to receive things from others as gifts, but to take them away from others by force or cunning."[30] Believers in the adage "stolen fruits are the sweetest," such individuals always try to appropriate something that isn't theirs: they break up marriages, become kleptomaniacs, or when they work as scientists, tend to plagiarism. Mistrust, cynicism, envy, and jealousy are other characteristics of individuals with this orientation. Their entire lives are based on the conviction that they are incapable of producing anything whatever.

In primitive cultures, this orientation would be called cannibalism. In our century, the exploitative orientation is less often dominant than the receptive orientation, although the current capitalist system is essentially designed to be exploitative.

The *hoarding orientation* "makes people have little faith in anything new they might get from the outside world; their security is based on hoarding and saving. . . . "[31] These people view everything from the perspective of possessing and owning. To them, love equals taking possession of but never giving. Out of avarice and stubbornness, but also orderliness and punctuality, they reject and resist all questioning by others. Order and punctuality are their highest values: "No experiments" and "There is nothing new under the sun" are their mottos.

As a social character, the hoarding orientation was probably most at home among the middle and upper classes of the eighteenth and nineteenth centuries, that is, during the ear of private capitalism when lust for possessions and an eagerness to save were necessary to economic progress. Today these qualities tend to prevail only among the petite bourgeoisie.[32]

Although exchange is one of the oldest economic mechanisms, the *marketing orientation* that is shaped by exchange did not become a dominant influence in relations to the world until our own century. Today it is not characterized by use value but rather by the mechanism of supply and demand, and extends beyond the commodity market to the market for persons. The individual whose dominant orientation is marketing relates to the world by perpetually asking how he can best sell himself—that is, he needs constantly to determine whether and how he can best make himself acceptable to others, and he must do, think, and feel what the market prescribes. In contrast to the receptive hoarding orientations, which are intent on preserving, taking, and receiving, the marketing-oriented individual's process of assimilation is characterized by exchange.

The marketing orientation is the social character of present-day Western industrial civilization generally. It expresses itself in the person's increasing alienation from himself, his work, and his environment, and derives from the conviction that he is no longer his own master, or the master of his products and capacities. Instead, it is the products and capacities that, as objects of supply and demand, control man.[33] Modern man experiences himself both as commodity and as the seller of that commodity.

Compared to the three nonproductive orientations just discussed, the distinctive feature of the marketing orientation is "that no specific and permanent kind of relatedness is developed, but that the very changeability of attitudes is the only permanent quality of such orientation."[34]

Only much later did Fromm elaborate an additional orientation. Because of its destructive character, he called it the necrophilous-destructive orientation, a term that does not refer to a sexual perversion, but to an attraction for everything dead and destructive.[35] In the assimilation process, the necrophilous and destructive individual is oriented toward the inorganic and objectlike. "The person with the necrophilous orientation is one who is attracted to and fascinated by all that is not alive, all that is dead: corpses, decay, feces, dirt."[36] He lives in the past, cultivates feelings he had yesterday, and is devoted to "law and order." Because he loves what is dead, he loves violence, for violence aims at limiting and destroying life. "All living processes, feelings, and thoughts are transformed into things. Memory, rather than experience; having rather than being, is what counts."[37] He enjoys talking about illnesses, difficulties, accidents, and deaths.

For Fromm, necrophilous destructiveness as a social character is especially apparent in the buildup of nuclear armaments. The sheer madness already apparent in calculating how many millions of deaths a nuclear war may cause is understandable only in a social character where *"people are not afraid of total destruction because they do not love life."*[38] Aside from the question of the life and death of mankind, the individual in our bureaucratized, industrial culture[39] is a *homo mechanicus* who believes he can make his relations to the world purely mechanical and thus avoid all direct, spontaneous, and productive contact. He turns all relations into something mechanical in an attempt to control them and to suppress the spontaneous and creative elements of all relationships: "Necrophilia constitutes a fundamental orientation: it is the one answer to life which is in complete opposition to life."[40]

The Productive Orientations

From a formal point of view, Sigmund Freud's concept of the genital character parallels the productive orientation in Fromm's theory of character.[41] Fromm, however, attempts a very precise definition of productivity. In so doing, he not only fills a gap in Freud's account of the "mature" character but also establishes an important link between psychoanalytic and sociopsychological insights on the one hand, and an anthropology on the other. For this reason, his *concept of productivity* will be examined first.[42]

The concepts "spontaneity" and "spontaneous activity" represent the first step in Fromm's attempt to define productivity. "Spontaneous activity is free activity of the self and implies, psychologically, what the Latin root of the word 'sponte' means literally: of one's free will."[43] The historical and conceptual background of the phrase "spontaneous activity" is somewhat different. For Hegel, man is only himself when "actively related to the world."[44] Karl Marx, whose image of man is rooted in Hegel's thought and whose concept of "self-activity" quite clearly lies behind Fromm's concept of productivity, sees man at home only when he relates actively to other human beings and to nature.[45]

In contrast to animals, which are completely at one with their activity, man "makes his activity itself the object of his willing and his consciousness. He has conscious life activity."[46] And whenever this life-activity or self-activity is not directed toward making him productive, whenever man remains receptive or passive, he is alienated from himself,[47] at home with neither himself nor nature nor other people. "Auto-activity is, then, nothing less than freedom, freedom in the sense of the voluntary and unconstrained activity, stimulated by one's own profound internal needs."[48]

Against the background of this understanding of activity, Fromm developed his concepts "spontaneity" or "spontaneous activity,"[49] which he later expanded to mean "productivity" and "productive orientation" in *Man for Himself.* In this book, he first defines these concepts negatively.[50] Productivity is not the same as artistic creativity, since the latter presupposes a specific gift, while every individual who is not an intellectual or psychological cripple is capable of productivity.[51] More important, productivity does not mean activity in the modern sense of simply being active—a hypnotized person is "active" though it is not he himself who acts but rather the hypnotist who acts through him. Similarly unproductive are activities that are reactions to fear, submission, dependence, or irrational passions such as avarice, masochism, envy, jealousy, and other forms of greed. In all these, man is active but he is not productive, for Fromm's concept of productivity is the opposite of what is commonly meant by that word. It is not an activity that *necessarily* leads to practical results but an "attitude, a mode of reaction and orientation toward the world and oneself in the process of life.[52] It is identical with biophilia.[53]

For this reason, productivity is the realization of man's own faculties, the use of his capacities and his power, though what is involved here is the very opposite of "power over." Rather, it is "power to" (bring something about): "The ability of man to make productive use of his powers is his potency."[54]

With this concept of productivity as a basis, *the productive orientation* in the process of assimilation can be defined. "The world outside oneself can be experienced in two ways: reproductively by perceiving actuality in the same fashion as a film makes a literal record of things photographed (although even mere reproductive perception requires the active participation of the mind); and generatively by conceiving it, by enlivening and re-creating this new material through the spontaneous activity of one's own mental and emotional powers."[55] When the generative experience of the world is atrophied, the result is a relatedness to the world that is proudly called "realism," but that is actually nothing but a superficial kind of perception. The individual is then incapable of enlivening and newly creating the perception from the inside, with all the fibers of his capacity for experience. When reproductive perception is totally lacking, man has only his imagination. Such an individual is psychotic and cannot function in society.

In the productive orientation, the reproductive and the generative faculties represent two poles that in their interaction are the dynamic source of productivity.[56]

Compared with a "realistic" orientation, the productive orientation is characterized by the fact that man "is capable of relating himself to the world simultaneously by perceiving it as it is and by conceiving it enlivened and enriched by his own powers."[57] What the productive orientation produces are not primarily material things, works of art, or systems of thought. "By far the most important object of productiveness is man himself,"[58] for everything that takes place between the conception and the death of an individual is a process of birth of that individual's possibilities and capacities. In contrast to the process of physical maturation, which occurs spontaneously when conditions are favorable, the development of the individual's psychic and intellectual capacities requires productive activity. Therefore it is only through the productive orientation in the process of assimilation and socialization that an individual can realize the possibilities and capacities that lie dormant within. Productive relatedness to the world (as activity) simultaneously implies and evokes the individual's relatedness to himself and to others and is an essential factor in the process of individuation.[59]

The Orientations in the Process of Socialization

A person's character structure is molded not only by the process of assimilation but also by that of socialization. As in the case of the assimilation process, in the following discussion of the possible forms of interpersonal relatedness we will first distinguish between nonproductive and productive orientations.

The Nonproductive Orientations

Describing the orientations in the process of socialization is made more difficult by the fact that after his book *Escape from Freedom* was published in 1941, Fromm repeatedly defined the various orientations more precisely and also elaborated them.[60] But one fundamental differentiation persists throughout his work: nonproductive interpersonal relatedness can be either symbiotic and unfree—be it masochistically or sadistically—or fail to develop at all because the individual lives indifferently-conformistically, destructively or narcissistically. The first type is characterized by symbiosis and includes masochism and sadism in authoritarian relations of dependency. The orientations characterized by distance include indifference, necrophilic destructiveness, and narcissism.

When Fromm uses the term *symbiotic relatedness,* he means by symbiosis "the union of one individual self with another self (or any other power outside of the own self) in such a way as to make each lose the integrity of its own self and to make them completely dependent on each other."[61] This kind of nonproductive orientation is embodied in two apparently diametrically opposed forms of relatedness: masochistic and sadistic interpersonal relatedness.[62]

Masochism is the passive form of symbiotic relatedness. In it, the individual makes himself part of another person who guides, directs, and protects him and without whom he can no longer live.

"The power of the one to whom one submits is inflated, may he be a person or a god; he is everything, I am nothing, except inasmuch as I am part of him. As a part, I am part of greatness, of power, of certainty."[63]

Submissiveness expresses itself in a variety of forms. Most frequently it manifests itself in feelings of inferiority, impotence, and personal insignificance. What is special here is that people with this orientation are unconsciously driven to make themselves small and weak. Sometimes this inclination expresses itself in persistent avowals of weakness and of the difficulty of life. Usually the tendency of the weak to submit to a strong individual is rationalized "as love or loyalty, inferiority feelings [are rationalized] as an adequate expression of actual shortcomings, and one's suffering as being entirely due to unchangeable circumstances."[64] In extreme cases, the tendency to submit to external forces like a small child becomes a crazed desire to hurt oneself and to make oneself suffer so as to guarantee the protection and care of a powerful being. Such submission may no longer be conscious. The forms of masochistic self-inflicted harm extend from self-accusations and the tendency to become psychically ill, to the creation of accidents and being blocked during examinations, and even to provocative criminal acts and various addictions that could be called suicide by installments.[65]

The common denominator of all forms of masochism is the incapacity to be one's own person, to stand on one's own feet, to use "freedom to."[66] Instead, the masochistic individual attaches himself to an authority in order to make his personal self disappear to the point where he no longer feels in conflict between his desire for independence and his sense of insignificance. He can then surrender his self and be "overwhelmed by pain and agony." The person with a masochistic orientation deals with the fear of being alone that is involved in "freedom from" by humiliating himself, by suffering and hiding.[67] "But pain and suffering are not what he wants; pain and suffering are the price he pays for an aim which he compulsively tries to attain.[68]

From the perspective of the person who seeks a symbiotic tie, submission to an authority means becoming a part of a larger, more powerful whole (another individual, an institution, god, the people, or, in internalized form, his own conscience or obsession), to share in its power and superiority, and thus to become equally powerful and superior, even though all this may be unconscious.[69] As social character, masochism (as well as sadism) is the ideal precondition for fascist and totalitarian systems[70] because this orientation toward authority satisfies "both the need for a lessening of anxiety and that for greatness and power."[71]

Sadism is the active form of symbiotic relatedness. It differs from the masochistic orientation in that "the sadistic person commands, exploits, hurts, humiliates, [while] the masochistic person is commanded, exploited, hurt, humiliated."[72] Both forms have in common the desire for a union without independence and integrity, the sadist being as dependent on the masochist as the masochist is on him. Indeed, every sadist is also a masochist, and vice versa, albeit in different respects.[73]

The inner affinity between sadism and masochism does not mean that their manifestations are similar. In fact, it is precisely by its destructive and other damaging tendencies that the sadistic orientation differs significantly from the masochistic one.

Fromm distinguishes three forms of sadistic orientation. The first is "to make others dependent on oneself and to have absolute and unrestricted power over them so as to make of them nothing but instruments, 'clay in the potter's hand.' Another consists of the impulse not only to rule over others in this absolute fashion, but to exploit them, to use them, to steal from them, to disembowel them and, so to speak, to incorporate anything eatable in them. . . . The third kind of sadistic tendency is the wish to make others suffer or to see them suffer. This suffering can be physical but more often it is mental suffering. Its aim is to hurt actively, to humiliate, embarrass others, or to see them in embarrassing and humiliating situations."[74]

Because such sadistic tendencies are not nearly so socially innocuous as the corresponding masochistic ones, they are usually more conscious and frequently veiled by a misleading justification. Examples of such rationalizations are: "I rule over you because I know what is best for you" (a pedagogic maxim parents may use toward their teenagers in order to prolong their symbiotic fixation on their children); "I have done so much for you, and now I am entitled to take from you what I want" (to validate exploitative claims on inferiors in the world of work); "I have been hurt by others and my wish to hurt them is nothing but retaliation."[75]

All forms of sadistic orientation have in common the passion "to have absolute and unrestricted control over a living being, whether an animal, a child, a man, or a woman."[76] Humiliation and enslavement are often means to that end, though the goal of ruling over others is best attained when suffering is inflicted on the other, "since there is no greater power over another person than that of inflicting pain on him to force him to undergo suffering without his being able to defend himself."[77] The need of the sadistically oriented individual to rule over others has its deepest root in an incapacity to live his freedom (the same is true of the masochist). Instead he attaches himself to others and can survive only if he can exercise power over them. The nonproductive element of both the sadistic and the masochistic orientation lies in the symbiotic relatedness of these individuals to each other where the one lives, and is dependent on, the other.

An examination of the relations between the orientations in the processes of assimilation and socialization yields the following conclusion: The receptive orientation in the process of assimilation corresponds to the masochistic one in the process of socialization; the exploitative orientation corresponds to the oral-sadistic; while the hoarding orientation parallels the anal-sadistic orientation.[78]

If the characteristic of symbiotic relatedness is a close dependence of one person on another, the following nonproductive orientations in the process of socialization are characterized by *withdrawal*—that is, a relatedness that is *marked by a distance* whenever the other is experienced as a threat.[79] We are dealing here with the indifferent, the necrophilous-destructive, and the narcissist orientations.

In the indifferent orientation, modern society has produced a new type of interpersonal relatedness that is of considerable importance because it is widespread, yet it has hardly been recognized for what it is because it is veiled by illusions. As in all nonproductive orientations, the individual self stops being itself. Instead the individual "adopts entirely the kind of personality offered to him by cultural patterns, and he therefore becomes exactly as all others are and as they expect him to be."[80] The individual self withdraws by conforming with others, becomes an automaton, and gives up the "freedom to," a freedom that is experienced as loneliness and isolation. He withdraws into an indifference that is "often accompanied by a compensatory feeling of self-inflation."[81]

The levels at which the indifferent orientation becomes manifest are as numerous as the individual points of contact with society and its culture; they extend from the latest fashion to theories about equality as uniformity in the women's movement.[82] The compulsive quality of the anonymous "one" of this orientation points up another aspect of conformist relatedness. While in earlier times adaptation to visible authorities such as state, church, parents, school, and moral codes demanded an equally visible conformism, authority in the middle of the twentieth century has become anonymous and invisible and all the more compelling because its invisibility renders it invulnerable. The only authority is the "one," and that may be "profit, economic necessity, the market, common sense, public opinion, what 'one' does, thinks, feels."[83]

The submission to *anonymous* authorities that indifference implies explains why this orientation, although a submission and surrender of the individual self, has the power to give people security and even an inflated sense of what they are. As in the masochistic orientation, the individual who conformistically submits to the dictates of anonymous authorities participates in the power of these authorities, a power that increases precisely because it is anonymous. In a manner of speaking, he himself is the power of the anonymous "one."[84] The anonymity of the authorities that enforce conformism also explains why the majority of people in our society have this orientation, yet firmly believe that they are individualists who think, act, and feel freely. First, "one" surrenders to the illusion that it is the (relative) freedom from external authorities that made individuality and responsibility possible to begin with, and the reason is that external authorities can no longer enforce conformism. Second, being determined by anonymous authorities is rationalized as interest, social attitudes, "having both feet on the ground," individuality, "leading a productive life," and the like (such rationalizations are suggested by the anonymous authorities themselves). In reality, of course, these rationalizations only disguise the loss of individual self and veil the conformist orientation that, like its counterpart in the process of assimilation, the marketing orientation, is nonproductive because on a deeper emotional level it means detachment from others.[85]

If indifference is the passive form of the relatedness characterized by distance, *the necrophilous-destructive* orientation is its active form. But before we discuss this active form we must explain what Fromm means by destructiveness.[86]

We must distinguish between three different forms of destructiveness, each differently motivated: there is reactive or defensive aggression, sadistic-cruel destructiveness, and necrophilous destructiveness.[87] Reactive or defensive aggression stands in the service of life and appears when an individual's vital interests are being threatened.[88] Sadistic-cruel destructiveness, which is unique to man, is something altogether different. It uses violence to control and incorporate others. In this process, the object of the destructive act must not perish because it is needed for symbiosis. Sadistic-cruel destructiveness is thus merely a means to an end. Necrophilous destructiveness is also unique to man. The person who acts necrophilously aims to destroy the object because he is attracted by everything that is dead: by decay, illness, nonlife, and nongrowth. This is the kind of destructiveness that is meant when the necrophilous-destructive orientation in the process of socialization is mentioned. In contrast to reactive aggression, it is profoundly irrational—that is, if no objects for its passion to destroy can be found, it turns upon itself so that serious illnesses or even suicide may result.

Of all the orientations, the necrophilous-destructive is the most damaging both socially and individually. It is hardly conscious and usually recognizable only by its rationalizations. Sacrificial love, strict fulfillment of duty, the call of conscience, patriotism, personal honor, racial consciousness, and the desire to defend and protect are some of the rationalizations used to hide a necrophilous-destructive orientation from oneself and others. The purpose of such rationalizations is always the same: it is to disguise the destructive impulse as reactive aggression, as effort with a high moral purpose.[89]

Though negative and totally nonproductive, the necrophilous-destructive orientation is an attempt to relate to oneself and to others. The need to relate derives from man's loneliness and the powerlessness it entails. The individual with a necrophilous-destructive orientation believes he can escape from this situation by seeking to destroy possible objects of relatedness. His attempted "solution" is determined in part by two factors that also have their roots in man's isolation and powerlessness, and these are the fear and the thwarting of life.[90]

All isolation is experienced as a threat to vital interests and produces anxiety. Resistance to such anxiety normally provokes an aggressive attitude toward the threatening objects, and if this attitude is not overcome (as, for example, when such objects turn toward the individual with love), the individual develops an inclination toward destructiveness that becomes constant and governs all his relations to life. The thwarting of life results from an inner blocking: sensual, emotional, and intellectual capacities go unrealized, and this is intensified by cultural, religious, and moral taboos on enjoyment and pleasure. The result is an interpersonal orientation that is necrophilous and destructive because it could not and cannot develop love for life. "Destructiveness is the outcome of unlived life."[91] The necrophilous-destructive orientation in the process of socialization has its parallel in the process of assimilation.

The final nonproductive orientation in the process of socialization is the narcissistic orientation.[92] It is characterized by a greater degree of withdrawal than the nonsymbiotic orientations. In contrast to the indifferent and the necrophilous-destructive, the individual with a narcissistic orientation acknowledges only his own inner world as real and is incapable of seeing and experiencing the world and others "objectively," as they are.

It was only at a relatively late date in his career, and then as a result of his reinterpretation of Freud's view of narcissism, that Fromm recognized the fundamental importance of this orientation.[93] Freud distinguishes between "primary" and "secondary narcissism."[94] By "primary narcissism," he means the phenomenon whereby the libido of the small child is wholly self-directed and does not yet extend to objects in the outside world. Freud believed that during the maturation process the libido turns outward, but that in pathological conditions it detaches itself from objects and is reflected back on one's own person ("secondary narcissism").[95] Because of its connection with Freud's libido theory, secondary narcissism was seen as limited to pathological, usually psychotic, manifestations, but Fromm recognized that it was, in fact, typical of many "normal" individuals in their interpersonal relatedness.

"Narcissism can . . . be described as a state of experience in which only the person himself, his body, his needs, his feelings, his thoughts, his property, everything and everybody pertaining to him are experienced as fully real, while everybody and everything that does not form part of the person or is not an object of his needs is not interesting, is not fully real, is perceived only by intellectual recognition, while *affectively* without weight and color."[96] Such individuals only truly know a single reality, that of their own thoughts, feelings, needs. "The world outside is not experienced and perceived objectively, i.e. as existing in its own terms, conditions and needs."[97] For that reason, the narcissistically oriented individual can never make a value judgment that truly measures what is to be evaluated, for example, because he knows only himself, what he thinks and feels. For the same reason, he is hypersensitive to any criticism of his person, however fair it may be.[98] He compensates for his nonrelatedness to the world outside him by excessive estimate of his own worth, and this compensation makes it possible for him to live only for himself, his body, his possessions, his illnesses, his guilt, his beauty, his virtues, and so on. "If I am 'great' because of some quality I *have,* and not because of something I *achieve,* I do not need to be related to anybody or anything."[99] The only thing such a person represents is an inflated ego that can only cultivate itself.[100]

The narcissistic orientation is found not only in individuals but, as "social narcissism," in groups, classes, races, and nations. In conjunction with destructive tendencies, it constitutes a source of violence, genocide, and war.[101] The analysis of group narcissism yields results that are quite similar to those found in the analysis of individual cases. What is common is primarily the incapacity to see reality objectively. There is also the unflagging concern to underline the superiority of one's group, race, or religion by recourse to all manner of ideologies.[102] The narcissistic orientation is probably the most pronounced nonproductive orientation in the socialization process because it supplants relatedness to others with a pure self-relatedness, and therefore totally misses man's task, which is to relate to others and the world.

The Productive Orientations[103]

The nonproductive orientations mentioned so far have illuminated the paradox of human existence: "that man must simultaneously seek for closeness and independence; for oneness with others and at the same time for the preservation of his uniqueness and particularity."[104] Only a productive orientation to the world (i.e., to nature, to others, and to oneself) can ensure such a twofold effort. Productivity here means that man realizes his capacities for active and creative relatedness.[105] "In the realm of thought, this productive orientation is expressed in the proper grasp of the world by reason. In the realm of action, the productive orientation is expressed in productive work. . . . In the realm of feeling, the productive orientation is expressed in love which is the experience of union with another person, with all men, and with nature, under the condition of retaining one's sense of integrity and independence."[106]

We have already discussed productive orientation in the realm of action.[107] Now we will deal with the productive orientation of love and reason, which are but two different forms of the same productive relatedness, though they must be treated as the expression of two different powers in man: feeling and thinking.

Today the word "love" is illegitimately used for all manner of inclinations, sympathies, dependencies and obsessions. Yet such misuse should not be taken to mean that every human being does not have the fundamental capacity for productive love, even though "its realization . . . is one of the most difficult achievements."[108] The mere attempt to list the characteristics of such love is beset by difficulties. The essential criteria for productive love are neither its object nor its intensity and quality. Rather, the fundamental elements that are typical of every form of productive love are care, responsibility, respect, and knowledge. They define productive love whether it be the mother's love for her child, the love for humanity, the erotic love between two individuals, the love of one's neighbor or of oneself.[109] "Care and responsibility denote that love is an activity (in the sense of "productive activity") and not a passion by which one is overcome, nor an 'affect' which one is affected by."[110] It is the criterion of "responsibility" that makes it clear that love cannot refer to a duty imposed from without but is rather a response to the expressed and implicit needs of another person, and that it comes from inside.[111]

Care and responsibility then, are indispensable elements of productive love. But love can degenerate into the desire to dominate and the greed to possess unless respect and knowledge of the other person are also present. Respect is possible only when the loving person is free to see the other as he is in his individuality and uniqueness and neither uses nor exploits him. Respect thus presupposes knowledge of the other. "Knowledge" here means putting oneself into another's place in order to understand his needs, fears, limits, and capacities.[112]

All four characteristics of productive love are interdependent and determine one another. "They are a syndrome of attitudes which are to be found in the mature person."[113]

The capacity for productive thought that is called reason "enables man to penetrate through the surface and to grasp the essence of his object by getting into active relation with it."[114] This definition is based on the distinction between reason and intelligence.[115] Whereas intelligence sees things merely as appearance and in terms of their use value, "reason involves a third dimension, that of depth, which reaches to the essence of things and processes."[116] Penetration of the object means two things: From the point of view of the cognizing subject, it means an interest (in the etymological sense), an existential engagement, and a relating of oneself. It also means, however, that one allows oneself to be determined by the object and its nature so that one may understand its essence, its hidden ramifications, and its deeper meaning. The object is thus not "experienced as something dead and divorced from oneself and one's life. . . . On the contrary, the subject is intensely interested in his object and the more intimate this relation is, the more fruitful is his thinking."[117]

Productive thinking (reason) makes objectivity possible because it combines both the subject's interest in the object and the respect of the thinker for his object. Respect for the object as it is implies that the observer always takes seriously the object in the totality of its appearances and does not isolate individual aspects without seeing the whole (which is what intelligence does). Finally, objectivity, as respect for the object as it is, also means that the cognizing subject becomes aware of the special constellations within which it is interested in the object.[118] "Objectivity does not mean detachment, it means respect."[119]

It is only under these conditions that productive thinking—reason—can occur. In its specific quality, it corresponds to productive love and productive action. Productive reason and love as expressions and characteristics of productive activity are central concepts in Fromm's characterology, anthropology, religion, and ethics.

The Affinity and the Blends of the Various Orientations[120]

Our discussion of the various possibilities of orientation in the processes of assimilation and socialization has repeatedly brought out *the affinity of the orientations.* In what follows, these affinities will be set forth schematically.

Figure 1 is based on the preceding explanations and differs in some points from Fromm's in *Man for Himself.*[121] To view the various orientations merely as the dimensions of a person's character would be to misunderstand Fromm's characterology. The various orientations are the ultimate fundamental tendencies of

FIG. 1
Relationship of the Orientations in the Process of Assimilation and Socialization

Orientations	**In Assimilation Process**	**In Socialization Process**	
nonproductive	receptive	masochism	*symbiosis* (authoritarian)
	exploitative	oral — sadism	
	hoarding	anal — sadism	
	marketing	indifference	*withdrawal*
	necrophilic-destructive	necrophilic-destructiveness	
		(narcissism)	
productive	working	loving, reasoning	

human relatedness in the sense that an individual's character traits and forms of conduct are largely determined by his underlying orientation. The various orientations are of significance primarily in the investigation of the social character and the factors that determine it.

The listed orientations are to be understood as ideal types in Max Weber's sense. No single orientation ever determines what a person is; in every individual we find a blend of all orientations. The important thing is the relative strength of these orientations and their dominance in an individual or a social group.

We must begin by making a distinction between combinations of nonproductive orientations and those of nonproductive and productive orientations.[122] The former are almost always blends of receptive and exploitative orientations. The conformist (as the passive element) and the necrophilous-destructive orientation (as the active element) also tend to combine. Finally, there is a relatively frequent mixture of hoarding and necrophilous, or narcissistic and necrophilous-destructive, orientations.

Before we explore the combination of nonproductive and productive orientations, we should note that "there is no person whose orientation is entirely productive, and no one who is completely lacking in productiveness."[123] What is decisive in a given individual is the relative weight of the productive and the nonproductive orientations in his character structure. The weight of the former determines the quality of the latter. In someone who has so little productiveness that his nonproductive orientation predominates, the single most salient nonproductive orientation, with its negative aspects, will become dominant. For example, a person will then think, feel, and act predominantly necrophilously and destructively. But the greater the "weight" of the productive orientation, the less negative will be the role played by the nonproductive orientation, for every nonproductive orientation has not only the negative aspects we have described but also positive ones that emerge when the productive orientation is dominant. The aggressive component in the exploitative and sadistic orientation, for example,[124] emerges as the positive capacity to seize the initiative. Similarly, the arrogant individual becomes self-confident, the indifferent tolerant, the one-sided intellectual intelligent. Thus are the character traits of an individual determined by the degree of his productive orientation. In addition, a given orientation can be of varying strength, depending on whether one considers the realms of action, feeling, or thinking. "If we add to the picture of personality the different temperaments and gifts, we can easily recognize that the configuration of these basic elements makes for an endless number of variations in personality."[125]

THE SYNDROME OF GROWTH AND THE SYNDROME OF DECAY[126]

The description of the various character orientations and their affinities and mixtures has demonstrated that though the number of combinatory possibilities is considerable, there are two fundamental tendencies of character orientation: one is directed toward the greatest possible realization of love for life, the other aims at inhibiting life and is destructive in nature. This observation caused Fromm to investigate more closely the presuppositions and conditions for the development of these opposing tendencies, to elucidate the factors that determined their intensity, and to set forth more precisely how these tendencies were correlated. The result of his investigations was the discovery of a syndrome of growth and a syndrome of decay. The latter develops only as a consequence of the failure of the former, which means that the syndrome of growth is prior. Viewed formally, these investigations involve a more precise account of the orientations in the process of socialization and their systematization in two fundamental orientations, the syndrome of growth and the syndrome of decay.

Biophilia and Necrophilia and Their Relation to Freud's Eros and Thanatos

Starting from the observation that everything that lives is governed by the biological principle of growth, Fromm agrees with "the assumption made by many biologists and philosophers that it is an inherent quality of all living substance to live, to preserve its existence,"[127] that is, to fight death. This struggle for existence brings with it reactive aggression when a living being must defend itself in order to survive. But the preservation of existence also means that all living substance has the tendency to integrate and unite. "The cycle of life is that of union, birth, and growth."[128] Fromm calls this tendency, which also holds for man, biophilia, love for life and the living. "The full unfolding of biophilia is to be found in the productive orientation."[129] This love for life opposes necrophilia, whose nature and manifestations we have already discussed,[130] and whose essence is the love for everything that is dead and does not grow, everything inorganic, thinglike, mechanical.[131]

Though Fromm's biophilia and necrophilia resemble Freud's Eros and Thanatos, the two theories differ fundamentally.[132] While agreeing with Freud that the affinity for what is alive and the affinity for what is dead constitute a basic contradiction in man, Fromm does not see this duality as the expression of two equally basic, biologically anchored drives that are relatively constant and fight each other until Thanatos overwhelms Eros. Rather, he posits a duality "between the primary and most fundamental tendency of life—to persevere in life—and its contradiction, which comes into being when man fails in this goal. In this view, the "death instinct" is a *malignant* phenomenon that grows and takes over to the extent to which Eros does not unfold."[133] The phenomena that Freud ascribes to the death instinct are thus not part of a primary biological given to which everyone necessarily succumbs but a secondary possibility of psychopathological development that either does not set in at all or never becomes a competing entity if the primary possibility of a love for life develops under the appropriate circumstances.

The essential difference between Freud's and Fromm's understanding is this: In Freud's theory, the strength of Thanatos is constant, and environmental influences can do nothing but direct the death instinct more toward one's own person or toward others. According to Fromm, however, both the development of necrophilia and its intensity depend on nonbiological factors. "The most important condition for the development of the love for life in the child is for him to be with people who love life."[134] The shaping influence such people have on the child does not so much depend on their express affirmations of a love for life as on their nonverbal and unreflected forms of communication such as gestures and intonation. In other words, they must themselves be biophilous in their character structure if they are to influence the child in this direction. This fundamental condition implies specific pedagogic postulates such as warmth, heartfelt contact, freedom, protection from threats, and a stimulating life style.[135]

Social conditions also play a decisive role in the growth of biophilia. "Love for life will develop most in a society where there is: *security* in the sense that the basic material conditions for a dignified life are not threatened; *justice* in the sense that nobody can be an end for the purposes of another; and *freedom* in the sense that each man has the possibility to be an active and responsible member of society."[136]

It is these individual and social conditions and not two biological drives inherent in man's nature and strictly determining his development, as Freud thought, that decide whether a person is biophilously or necrophilously oriented.[137]

Narcissism and Incestuous Symbiosis

We have already discussed narcissism and incestuous symbiosis as orientations in the process of socialization, the latter under the concept of symbiotic relatedness, as masochistic and sadistic orientation.[138] They are decisively important for the progressive or regressive development of the life of an individual or of groups, and for this reason, Fromm made them components of the decay syndrome.

An adult is narcissistic because his development from the so-called primary narcissism of the small child to that object relatedness that first makes possible man's productive relatedness to nature, others, and himself did not proceed as it should have.[139] The extreme forms of narcissism are rare. Instead, it appears in many shadings, from markedly malignant, solipsistic forms to less malignant ones in which it is coupled with productive activity, even including the capacity for love of one's neighbor, of strangers, or of humanity in general.[140] Ontogenetically and phylogenetically, the intensity of individual or social narcissism is the measure of regression to earlier developmental levels. Love of one's neighbor or of humanity, on the other hand, is the expression of progression and of the overcoming of individual and social narcissism. In its malignant forms, narcissism thus works against life and growth and for destruction and death, and is therefore an essential component of the syndrome of decay.

Similar considerations apply to the final orientation, incestuous symbiosis,[141] which derives from an incestuous fixation. But Fromm's interpretation goes beyond the one Freud advanced in connection with the Oedipus complex. While every child experiences incestuous wishes, they are not primarily the result of sexual desires nor are they tied to a specific—the oedipal—phase of libido development; instead, they "constitute one of the most fundamental tendencies in man: the wish to remain tied to an all-protective figure, the fear of being free, and the fear of being destroyed by mother, the very figure with whom he has made himself helpless."[142] "Mother" here must be understood literally, for genetically, the mother is the first personification of the power that protects and guarantees safety. In the course of psychic development, "mother" is supplemented and supplanted by motherly elements such as family, clan, blood, nation, church, political party, or—archaically—nature, earth, the sea. Every individual has the tendency to remain tied to a motherlike person or an equivalent, and this tendency conflicts with his more fundamental tendency to be born, to develop, to grow. If this tendency to develop fails, the regressive tendency of symbiotic relatedness will prevail and become the source of hatred, destructiveness, and irrationality, as well as the basis for both the sadistic and the masochistic orientations.[143] For the incestuous tie to the mother implies not only love and security but usually also anxiety, which results from dependence and lack of freedom, especially when the "mother" herself is necrophilously oriented.

To what extent ties to the mother are benign or malignant depends on the degree of regression. Malignant ties that prevent the individual from fulfilling his task of becoming independent are called incestuous symbiosis by Fromm.[144] In the most extreme regressive form, the unconscious longs for a return to the womb in order to recover total harmony with nature, even though this means the surrender of individuality and the desire to live.

The Convergence Within the Syndromes of Growth and Decay and the Correlation of the Syndromes[145]

The more malignant the components of the syndrome of decay—necrophilia, narcissism, and incestuous symbiosis—the more readily they merge, while in less malignant forms they can be distin-

FIG. 2

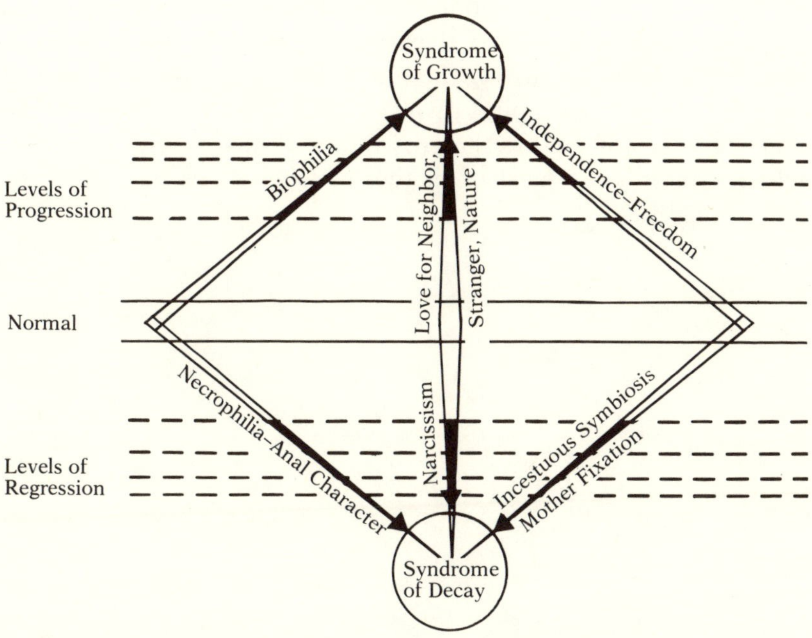

guished from one another, and, in fact, often occur in isolation in a given individual. Still, the more archaic the form of any one such orientation in the syndrome of decay, and the greater the regression, the more all three orientations will fuse in a syndrome of decay that will determine the individual so completely as to shape his entire personality.[146] Conversely, if an individual advances to biophilia, to love of neighbor and stranger, these orientations converge in a syndrome of growth that represents the greatest plenitude and productivity of human life.

The more markedly the orientations converge in a syndrome, the more they exclude one another. An individual with a growth syndrome will therefore be incapable of relating necrophilously, narcissistically, or symbiotically to others. The person with a decay syndrome will be incapable of exhibiting aspects of the growth syndrome in his relationships. But although one syndrome excludes the other, it is nonetheless true that the decay syndrome is the result of a growth syndrome that primordially characterizes man but failed to develop. As early as 1941, Fromm recognized that "the amount of destructiveness to be found in individuals is proportionate to the amount to which expansiveness of life is curtailed" and that destructiveness is "the outcome of unlived life."[147] The thesis regarding the correlation of destructiveness and the unfolding of life he put forward at that time also applies to the other orientations and to the growth and decay syndromes themselves. Fromm's summary of his thesis is shown in schematic form in figure 2.[148]

3

CONCEPTS OF THE NATURE AND HISTORY OF MAN

MAN'S NATURE

In the preceding comments on Fromm's theory of character, it was constantly necessary to recur to assumptions that could only be postulated and that did not result directly from clinical observation. While it is true that analyses of human relatedness point to the necessity of such relatedness, clinical observation alone allows one neither to infer such a necessity nor to establish a classification of positive or negative kinds of relatedness. The correctness of clinical observation is proved only when the assumptions are corrected by analysis. Only in the constant interplay between the philosophical and anthropological model and the continuous modification of this model by analytic work according to the methods of the discipline in question does it become possible to arrive at scientific insights in the human and social sciences that, as statements about man and his nature, are relevant to ethical questions. For this reason, we will now set forth the *conditio humana* as Fromm sees it. For every psychology "must be based on an anthropologico-philosophical concept of human existence."[1]

The "Essence" or "Nature" of Man[2]

The question whether there is such a thing as a human "essence" or "nature" increasingly preoccupied Fromm. As he systematically justifies his humanistic view of man and man's destiny, this question becomes ever more urgent.[3]

Fromm did not overlook the difficulties that lie in postulating a definable human "nature": apart from the fact that the concept of a "human essence" or "nature" has been misused to bolster certain claims to domination and certain types of society,[4] the modern sciences have questioned the possibility of a universally persisting human nature. Historical research, discoveries in cultural anthropology, and evolutionary theory all suggest a relativist perspective[5] according to which the real problem would be "to infer the *core* common to the whole human race from the innumerable manifestations of human nature . . . to recognize the laws inherent in human nature and the inherent goals of its development and unfolding."[6] Such attempts have been made repeatedly in the course of history by a distinguishing between the essence itself and certain qualities or attributes that all human beings share. Examples of such shared attributes are reason (*animal rationale*), the capacity for production (*homo faber*), the capacity for social organization (*zoon politikon*), and the capacity for language (creation of symbols).[7] But the mere multiplicity of possible attributes shows that they do not "constitute the totality of human nature."[8]

Fromm proposes a model that transcends both the perspective of an immutable human nature and the position that, some essential attributes notwithstanding, disputes that there is something all human beings share. It is the mathematical idea of constants and variables: "One could say that in man, since he began to be man, there is something that remains constantly the same, a nature, but within man, there are also a great number of variable factors that make him capable of novelty, creativity, productivity and progress."[9]

Behind this model lies Marx's differentiation between human nature in general and the human nature that is historically modifiable in each and every epoch. The concept of human nature here is no abstraction; rather, "It is the *essence* of man—in contrast to the various forms of his historical *existence*."[10] While Marx defines the species character as "free, conscious activity"[11] and sees man as a being that produces "with foresight and imagination,"[12] Fromm does not feel that such definitions tell us anything about man's nature but only about human traits.[13]

What is constant in man, man's "essence," can only be established in a comparison between man and animal. "We have to arrive at an understanding of man's nature on the basis of the blend of the two fundamental biological conditions that mark the emergence of man. One was the ever decreasing determination of behavior by *instincts* . . . the other . . . is the *growth of the brain, and particularly the neocortex.*"[14] Seen from this biological perspective, man "emerged at the point of evolution where instinctive determination had reached a minimum and the development of the brain a maximum."[15] The growth of the brain enabled man to increase his "instrumental intelligence."[16] But beyond that, his thinking "acquired an entirely new quality, that of self-awareness."[17] Along with this self-awareness, there also came "his ability to remember the past, to visualize the future, and to denote objects and acts by symbols; his reason to conceive and understand the world; and his imagination through which he reaches far beyond the range of his senses."[18]

From the perspective of the animal kingdom, man is the most helpless animal. But this biological weakness also makes possible his specific human qualities—self-awareness, reason, and imagination. These distinctive human qualities preclude interpreting man wholly according to instinctual, animalistic, or biological categories. Man understands himself adequately only when, as he defines who and what he is, he makes his specific human qualities his point of departure and asks what their relevance for his self-understanding is.

But it is these new qualities that have destroyed the harmony between man and nature. Man is "a 'freak of nature,' being in nature and at the same time transcending it."[19] When the definition of man's nature or essence is involved, therefore, "the answer, in my opinion, is to be found in the fact that man's essence lies in the very contradiction between his being in nature, thrown into the word without his will, and taken away against his will, at an accidental place and time, and at the same time of transcending nature by his lack of instinctual equipment and by the fact of his awareness—of himself, of others, of the past and the present."[20] Man is separated from nature, yet part of it. He is homeless, yet chained to the home he shares with all creatures. "Man is the only animal who does not feel at home in nature . . . for whom his own existence is a problem that he has to solve and from which he cannot escape."[21]

Fromm's briefest definition of man's nature is this: "the questions, not the answers, are man's 'essence.' "[22] The questions as man's essence are the contradictions and the resultant disturbances of his inner equilibrium. "The answers, trying to solve the dichotomies, lead to various manifestations of human nature"[23] but are not themselves man's nature or essence, for "the various kinds of solutions of these contradictions depend on socio-economic, cultural and psychic factors."[24]

By defining man's nature or essence as a contradiction containing the potential for its own resolution, Fromm steers a sure course between the dogma of natural law on the one hand and total relativism on the other. The specific qualities of self-awareness, reason, and imagination give rise to this contradiction and are at the same time the conditions for its resolution. Whether the specific human qualities are actually employed to bring about an optimal and positive solution—Fromm refers to them briefly as "human qualities of reason and love"[25] as they realize themselves in the productive character orientations—depends on a variety of factors, not least among them an appropriate ethical goal. But because there is more to this than the fact of contradiction and the specifically human qualities that give rise to it, neither the specifically human qualities nor human capacities as essential attributes suffice to constitute the essence or nature of man.[26]

Man's Dichotomies[27]

If animal life is defined by its fundamental unity with surrounding nature, human existence is defined by the fact that man "is a part of nature, subject to her physical laws and unable to change them, yet he transcends the rest of nature."[28] The human situation is determined by this fundamental contradiction which manifests itself in a number of ways that man perceives existentially. It is the distinctive quality of these contradictions that they are rooted in man's existence and therefore called "existential dichotomies"[29] to distinguish them from contradictions that are historically determined. And while there exists a solution to these contradictions, they cannot be abolished. They are "contradictions which man cannot annul but to which he can react in various ways, relative to his character and his culture."[30]

The most important existential dichotomy comes from the

awareness of death as unavoidable. The dichotomy of life and death cannot be abolished. Rather, the fact of death must be taken seriously and not denied (by postulating an immortal soul, for example). Love for life and the living is therefore the only human reaction to this dichotomy, for our specifically human qualities entail a need to resolve the dichotomy defined by the fact of death.[31]

The inevitable death of the person is the source of a further existential dichotomy between the unfolding of all a person's potential and the shortness of human life, which even under favorable conditions hardly permits a full unfolding. Here again, ideologies attempt to persuade man that these dichotomies are not tragic. They suggest that life is fulfilled only after death, that the present historical period represents the goal of human development, or that the individual's happiness must take second place to society's. Faced with such attempts to deny these existential dichotomies, man must accept the tragic brevity of his life and react by the optimal unfolding of his potential.

The existential dichotomies are explications of the situation and of the special conditions of human existence. All of them show that man is subject to nature, yet "transcends all other life because he is, for the first time, *life aware of itself.*"[32] This conflict is man's essence and it enables and obliges him to find an answer to his dichotomies. According to Fromm, this answer can only come from the specific human qualities of self-awareness, reason, and imagination that give rise to those dichotomies in the first place: "There is no meaning to life except the meaning man gives his life by the unfolding of his powers, by living productively."[33]

In contrast to the existential dichotomies that constitute man's essence because they are inextricably part of his existence, there are contradictions in individual and social life that are produced by man himself. They can therefore be resolved where they appear, even if at a later time in human history. Fromm calls these contradictions "historical dichotomies." They emerge wherever a technical, economic, social, cultural, emotional, or physical development begins to contradict the dispositive and creative powers man potentially has to deal with such developments. The present contradiction between the abundance of technical resources for the satisfaction of human needs and the incapacity to use these resources exclusively for peaceful aims and for the well-being of mankind, for example, is not an existential dichotomy but a historical one that can be solved by man.[34]

The difference between the existential and the historical dichotomy is extremely important. It shows which contradictions in the individual's life and in the life of mankind can be resolved because men produced them and can therefore deal with them, and which constitute man's essence and can only be reacted to as his specifically human qualities dictate. The observation that only a historical dichotomy is involved in a certain contradiction unmasks the motto of all ideologies and individual rationalizations, that what cannot be must not be, and thus makes man conscious of himself and able to create a productive relatedness to the world.[35]

The Needs of Man as Human Needs[36]

Man's essence lies in the contradiction that he is subject to nature, yet can transcend it by self-awareness, reason, and imagination, and this existential conflict produces certain psychic needs that are common to all men. Man "is forced to overcome the horror of separateness, of powerlessness and of lostness, and find new forms of relating himself to the world to enable him to feel at home."[37] Fromm calls these psychic needs "existential needs" because they are rooted in the very conditions of human existence.

Like physiological needs, existential needs are common to all men and must be satisfied if the person is to remain healthy. Unlike physiological needs, however, existential ones can be satisfied in a variety of ways, depending on social conditions, and these various responses express themselves in varying character traits and character orientations. In his later publications, Fromm also refers to them as "rooted in the character" or simply as "human passions." Depending upon whether they are productive or nonproductive, human passions are "rational" (love, tenderness, striving for justice, for example) or "irrational" (hatred, sadism, destructiveness).[38] Individuals differ because the dominant passion in each varies and therefore the responses to common needs (existential needs) must also vary.

The view of man as a contradictory being who has existential-human needs because of his contradictions calls for a new estimate of those needs that man, remaining subject to nature, shares with animal life, such as hunger, thirst, and sexuality, the so-called *physiological needs*. Like other animals, man must satisfy these needs, but while in animals their satisfaction is synonymous with being in harmony with nature, in man they only attain a similar value when they are satisfied within the framework of the specifically human needs as determined by the existential dichotomies.[39]

Finally, what is referred to as existential or human needs must be distinguished from the "inhuman needs" that are suggested to man. Artificially produced, these needs are meant to draw his attention away from his true human needs. The historical background for this distinction is Karl Marx's concept of needs that are created to force man to make new sacrifices and to place him in new dependencies.[40] Alienated man and a society characterized by alienation create artificial needs that enslave the individual even more and thus alienate him increasingly from his own needs because they make him the means for the satisfaction of others' needs.

For Fromm, this distinction between human and inhuman needs is central. Psychology can only make a contribution to the knowledge of human nature if it stops taking alienated man as its point of departure—someone who feels the need for wealth to be his primordial human need, for example—and addresses itself to man in his nonalienated existence, which is determined only by existential dichotomies. Authentic human needs can be discovered only if one puts oneself in the psychological position of the person who has lost unity with nature as a result of his specific human qualities, and seeks to recover that unity.

Fromm identified the human needs, though without being wholly consistent as to their number or names.[41] The most comprehensive explication is found in *The Sane Society*,[42] where he identifies five of them: the need for relatedness, for transcendence, for rootedness, for a sense of identity, and for a frame of orientation and an object of devotion.

In *The Anatomy of Human Destructiveness*,[43] the "need for a frame of orientation and an object of devotion" (and, as part of this, "the need for transcendence") and "the need for rootedness" recur. The older formulation of "need for identity" becomes a "need for a sense of unity." There is an aspect that is influenced by the neurophysiological studies on the question of aggression and that is renamed the "need for effectiveness," while the "need for relatedness" is not expressly mentioned because it manifests itself in the other needs.[44] The following presentation adds the need for effectiveness to the five needs listed above.

A first *need* is *for relatedness*. "Man is torn away from the primary union with nature, which characterizes animal existence. Having at the same time reason and imagination, he is aware of his aloneness and separateness, of his powerlessness and ignorance."[45] It is precisely the severance of primary ties—that is, of the instinctual unity with nature—that makes it necessary for man to create human forms of relatedness to nature, to others, and to himself, and this with the aid of specifically human qualities. Where this need for relatedness is not realized, human life is impossible. Just as the physiological need, hunger, causes death if not satisfied, so intellectually and spiritually healthy human life is possible only where the specifically human need for relatedness is responded to. Without this response, man becomes psychotic, "spiritually" ill. But the necessity to respond to the human need for relatedness does not suffice to ensure that the kind of relatedness achieved will be appropriate to the specifically human situation. As our discussion of the various character orientations showed, only productive relatedness does full justice to this need and the human situation that creates it.

The *need for transcendence* is another aspect of the human situation that is closely connected to the need for relatedness. It "concerns man's situation as a *creature,* and his need to transcend this very state of the passive creature."[46] Through the acquisition of his specifically human qualities, man is obliged to overcome the role of being merely created. Here also, two fundamentally different kinds of reaction are possible. In the case of the productive reaction, the person himself takes on the role of creator by creating life and culture. In the case of the other transcendent reaction, the nonproductive, man destroys life and creation, for "to destroy life is as transcendent as to create it."[47] Fromm's concept of "transcendence" is to be understood humanistically; it has nothing to do with God as a transcendent entity. It means instead "a need to transcend one's self-centered, narcissistic, isolated position to one of being related to others, to openness to the world, escaping the hell of self-centeredness and hence self-imprisonment."[48]

The *need for rootedness* directly results from the fact of birth. Once born, man loses that safety and security that up to this moment had been guaranteed by his rootedness in nature. He can renounce his rootedness in nature and become truly human only if he finds new roots that are appropriate to him; only then can he (once again) feel at home in this world. Ontogenetically, this rootedness in nature is realized in an elemental sense in the child's tie to his mother. The child's development to maturity is a continuous birth, the ever-renewed cutting of the umbilical cord that symbolizes rootedness in nature. Ontogenetically and phylogenetically, man's birth is the same as the acquisition of genuine independence and freedom,[49] which are realized when man reacts to the need for rootedness by planting new roots for his existence.

Man has two possibilities of reacting to his need for rootedness: "either to persist in his craving to regress, and to pay for it by symbolic dependence on mother (and on symbolic substitutes, such as soil, nature, god, the nation, a bureaucracy), or to progress and to find new roots in the world by his own efforts, by experiencing the brotherhood of man, and by freeing himself from the power of the past."[50] Here again we find different kinds of reaction, negative (all forms of incestuous fixation) and productive, the latter ultimately a rootedness in the experience of a universal brotherhood that transforms man's world into a truly human one.

The *need for an experience of identity or unity* is closely akin to that for rootedness. "Man, being torn away from nature, being endowed with reason and imagination, needs to form a concept of himself, needs to say and feel: 'I am I.' Because he is not lived, but *lives*, because he has lost the original unity with nature, has to make decisions, is aware of himself . . . he must be able to sense himself as the subject of his actions."[51] But the problem of the experience of identity is not only a philosophical one that concerns our intellect and thinking. It takes in the entire person and expresses itself as the search for the experience of unity with oneself and the natural and human environment. The ways of realizing the need for the experience of identity or unity are even more intimately dependent upon the degree of mankind's and the individual's development than is the case with the need for rootedness. The more closely the possibility of the experience of identity is tied to the consciousness of class or clan, or some kind of conformism through which the self experiences itself only if it is as others wish it to be, the less developed and productive this experience of identity will be. Conversely, it may be said that the need for an experience of unity or identity is realized most strongly when man experiences his individual identity as productive activity, because then it is in line with specific human qualities. While the negative type of response to this need is always a forgetting and a self-forgetfulness in the sense that the individual's reason is being narcotized, "there is only one approach to unity that can be successful without crippling man. Such an attempt was made in the first millennium B.C. . . . by fully developing human reason and love."[52]

The specific human qualities that cause man to become aware of his break with nature are the conditions for man's developing a *need for a frame of orientation and an object of devotion*. Man, being endowed with reason, must also orient himself intellectually in his world if he is to understand himself and the meaning of his life. In this process, it does not matter initially whether the interpretation he gives himself, his life, and his world is correct or false. At first, there is simply the necessity to find any frame of orientation for his existence so that he may react to the dichotomies inherent in that existence. Such frames of orientation or systems are all sorts of religion (animism, totemism, theistic and nontheistic religions), philosophies, and world views including the idolatrous striving for money, prestige, success, and so on.[53] It is only at a second level that the question concerning the content and the truth of such frames of orientation arises. The answer depends on the capacity for seeing the world, nature, others, and oneself objectively, as they truly are. This means that reality must be grasped by reason and not veiled by illusions and rationalizations. The more reason and the less irrational elements determine the content of the frame of orientation, the more adequate the answer to this need will be, and the more fully will man realize his own distinctive qualities. The instinctual animal need not worry about a frame of orientation, nor does it ask itself toward what end its life and action are to be directed. "But man, lacking instinctive determination and having a brain that permits him to think of many directions in which he could go, needs an object of 'ultimate concern,' to use Tillich's expression; he needs an object of devotion to be the focal point of all his strivings and the basis for all his effective—and not only proclaimed—values."[54]

The need for an object of devotion is an essential part of man and *must* be satisfied. The kinds of reaction to this need differ considerably. Man can devote himself to the most various goals and idols: "He can be devoted to the growth of life or to its destruction. He can be devoted to the goal of amassing a fortune, of acquiring power, of destruction, or to that of loving and of being productive and courageous."[55]

A final interpretation of the contradictory being that is man, of his characteristic of having specified and specifiable needs to which he must always respond and to which he does in fact respond, is the *need for effectiveness*. Time and again, it has become clear that the various needs can be understood as aspects of a single fundamental human need, and this is why the descriptions of the individual needs are very similar. This observation also applies to the description of the need for effectiveness, although this need identifies an aspect that is not covered by the other needs. The loss of harmony with nature when man is born results from the loss of instinctive adaptation to nature. The break with nature means not only man's superiority over nature but also nature's superiority over that "defective being" that is man. And this superiority is experienced as life threatening. The human need for effectiveness is the expression of this dichotomy between nature and man. Man needs to experience himself as "able to do something, to move somebody, to 'make a dent' or, to use the most adequate English word, to be 'effective.' . . . To effect is the equivalent of 'to bring to pass, to accomplish, to realize, to carry out, to fulfill'; an effective person is one who has the capacity to do, to effect, to accomplish something."[56] There are many ways of responding to this need. If the need for effectiveness is frustrated by prohibitions, for example, it can express itself in a variety of flawed forms in which what is forbidden or even impossible has a special attractiveness. Basically, two opposite reactions can be observed here as well: "In the relationship to others, the fundamental alternative is to feel either the potency to effect love or to effect fear and suffering. In the relationship to things, the alternative is between constructing and destroying."[57] When the response to the need for effectiveness is productive, productivity results, though the need for effectiveness does not necessarily entail the concept of productivity and activity;[58] rather, this concept is only the expression of a reaction to that need. It follows that the need for effectiveness cannot be understood as a need for productive activity: the needs themselves are neutral, but the designations for the reactions to the needs are value terms that acquire their positive or negative quality from psychoanalytic ideas about what constitutes a sick and what a healthy psyche.

THE HISTORY OF MAN

Man is a creature of needs and can only be understood when he is seen as a historical and history-making being. To the extent that man originates and makes his history and frees himself from his ties to nature by developing his own powers, he is a historical being in whose hands the responsibility for history lies. Man, then, is accountable for history and therefore needs an idea about its meaning and direction. The point of departure for such a historical view is man's break with the original unity with nature and his striving for a new unity in reason and love. "This new harmony, the new oneness with man and nature, is called in the prophetic and rabbinic literature 'the end of the days,' or 'the messianic time.' It is not a state predetermined by God or the stars; it will not happen except through man's own effort. This messianic time is the historical answer to the existence of man. He can destroy himself or advance toward the realization of the new harmony. Messianism is not accidental to man's existence but the inherent logical answer to it—the alternative to man's self-destruction."[59]

The History of the Messianic Idea as a Historical-Philosophical Theory[60]

"While for the Greeks, history had no aim, purpose or end, the Judaeo-Christian concept of history was characterized by the idea that its inherent meaning was the salvation of man."[61] In the Judaeo-Christian tradition, history unfolds in three stages: history before man's existence, the history of man as a contradictory being, and the history of saved man. Thus history has a direction. When this direction is defined as the new unity of man with himself, with mankind, and with nature, history is understood as the realization of the messianic idea.

A survey of the history of the messianic idea, of the history of Jewish belief and of the Jewish people, reveals an inner dynamic in the development of the messianic idea that allows one to recognize the goal of history in its contours. At the same time, the history of the messianic idea shows that man can, and has the responsibility to, work out his own salvation.[62] "Man . . . has to give birth to himself, and at the end of the days, the new harmony, the new peace will be established, the curse pronounced against Adam and Eve will be repealed, as it were, by man's own unfolding in the historical process."[63] For Fromm, this religio-critical aspect of man's self-salvation is part of the messianic idea: "The Messiah is a symbol of man's achievement."[64] From the perspective of the messianic idea as understood in these terms, we first get an interpretation of biblical prehistory. Before the fall, man finds himself in a state of undifferentiated harmony with nature. It is only the development of his reason that opens his eyes. His first act is both the first act of disobedience and of freedom, the expression of the genesis of his consciousness of himself. When the Bible states that the curse is enmity and struggle between man and beast, between man and the soil, between man and woman, between woman and her natural functions, this means that while man has lost the original unity because of his specifically human qualities, it is through these same qualities that he "creates himself in the process of history which began with the first act of freedom, with 'sin.' "[65] Fromm sees the biblical *Urgeschichte* as the mythological portrayal of the beginning of the history of man's self-liberation: "his sinning is justified in the process of history."[66]

Both the beginning of human history in the Bible and the history of the Hebrews are characterized by the renunciation of a paradisiacal home. With his renunciation of a home, Abraham symbolizes the exodus that becomes the essence of the messianic idea and of Israel's theology of history.[67] A second realization of this *"leitmotif"*[68] of the exodus is Moses' exodus from Egypt,[69] a third the journey through the desert and the revelation of the laws to

Moses.[70] With Moses' death and the return of the people to slavery and idolatry, this "first revolution"—as Fromm calls the attempts to realize the messianic idea—fails and ends.[71] "After the failure of the first prophet, Moses, new prophets continued his work, deepened and clarified his ideas, and developed a concept of history which . . . was to flower only in the prophetic literature, in the concept of the messianic time, which was to have the deepest influence on the development not only of the history of the Jews but of the whole world."[72] The new prophets have a fourfold task whose first and most important part is the passing on of the message "that man's goal is to become fully human; and that means to become like God."[73] Beyond that, they indicate the alternatives between which man can choose. They protest when man takes the wrong path and, opposing all individualistic concern for salvation, call for a society that is ruled by love, justice, and truth.[74]

The self-understanding of the prophets also stamps the prophetic theory of messianic time.[75] Messianic time is the "time when man will have been fully born,"[76] a time within history, in other words (and not, as in Christianity, a metahistorical and merely spiritual entity[77]). It is not given to man in an act of grace but is the result of his own effort to resolve his dichotomies through reason and love and thus to arrive at a new unity. The paradisiacal, original unity of man with nature at the beginning of history corresponds to the messianic time as a new, historical unity of man with himself, with others, and with nature. Paradise and messianic time, however, are different "inasmuch as the first state of harmony existed only by virtue of man's *not yet* having been born, while the new state of harmony exists as a result of man's having been fully born."[78]

The elaboration of the idea of messianic time and of the circumstances of its realization by the biblical prophets is varied. The principal characteristics of messianic time are peace and universalism. While the prophets of the Hebrew Bible do not know the word "messiah" in the sense of a hoped-for redeemer, this sense of the term does emerge during the time of Herod the Great. But "it is only after the Jews had lost their kingdom and their king that the personification of the messianic time in the figure of the anointed king becomes popular."[79]

The postbiblical development of the messianic idea is fundamentally different. With the Book of Daniel, messianic time becomes metahistorical and personified so that it stops signifying the perfection of man's history through man. Apocalyptically, messianic time now becomes the "supernatural being who descends from the heavenly heights to end history."[80] The only element the secular-historical and the transcendent-metahistorical ideas of salvation have in common is that salvation is not individual but collective.[81] After the destruction of the Temple, rabbinical Judaism renounces sacrifice and priests and develops its own idea of messianic time, which, though differing widely in its forms, everywhere holds the conviction that messianic time occurs within history.[82] According to the Talmud, two versions concerning the preconditions for messianic time persist throughout the history of the messianic idea: "One is that the messiah will come only when suffering and evil have reached such a degree that men will repent and thus be ready. There are numerous descriptions of this catastrophic situation . . . the other concept is that the messiah will come, not after catastrophes, but as the result of man's own continuous improvement."[83]

Clinging to the historical realization of messianism during this era made it easier to give a direct historical interpretation of a person as the messiah, so that the history of Jewish messianism is at the same time one of the "false messiah figures," from Bar Kochba (C.E. second century) to Moses the Cretan (fifth century), Abraham Abulafia and Nissim ben Abraham (both thirteenth-century figures), to the "greatest" false messiah, Sabbatai Zvi (seventeenth century), and his imitators Michael Cardozo and Jacob Frank (seventeenth and eighteenth centuries, respectively).[84] The messianic idea flowered again in eighteenth-century Hasidism, which incorporated much of the original prophetic hope for messianic time through man's self-improvement.[85]

Fromm believes that the prophetic idea of man's new unity with himself and his human and natural world in a universal society found its ultimate valid realization in Karl Marx's conception of history, which strives for socialism as the goal of man as he attains new unity in history.[86] Marx's concept is a valid realization of prophetic messianism because it takes wholly seriously the view of man as creating and making his history, and Marx thus represents a humanism that renounces any power that transcends man.[87] Fromm believes that "Marxist and other forms of socialism are the heirs of prophetic messianism. . . ."[88] In spite of many a false turn—especially in its final realization in Marx's writings—the history of the messianic idea reveals the contours of the goal of all history: the realm of freedom in humanistic socialism on the basis of a socialist humanism.[89]

Fromm's View of History as a Continuation of Karl Marx's Theory of History

Fromm sees in the history of the messianic idea the dynamic unfolding of a theory of history whose climax is prophetic messianism. This prophetic messianism has its final and valid—because humanist—realization in Karl Marx's view of history. For this reason, Marx's views form the starting point for Fromm's own reflections on the theory of history. His historical-philosophical theses are therefore a reception of the Marxist view of history and can only be presented as such.[90]

To avoid the misunderstandings associated with such terms as "materialist" and "economic," Fromm writes that "Marx's interpretation of history could be called an anthropological interpretation of history . . . it is the understanding of history based on the fact that men are 'the authors *and* actors of their history.' "[91] An anthropological interpretation of history as formulated here has a variety of consequences: "The first premise of all human history is the existence of living human individuals. . . . They themselves begin to *produce* their means of subsistence, a step which is conditioned by their physical organization. By producing their means of subsistence men are indirectly producing their actual material life."[92] This occasions a fundamental change in man's relationship to nature: "Man, at the beginning of his history, is blindly bound or chained to nature. In the process of evolution, he transforms his relationship to nature, and hence himself."[93] The factor that mediates between man and nature, that changes man's relationship to nature and therefore man himself, is labor.[94]

"Initially, work is a process between man and nature, a process where man mediates, regulates and controls his metabolism with nature through his own act. He confronts the natural substance as a natural force. He puts into motion the natural powers that are part of his physical nature, arms and legs, head and hand, to appropriate the natural substance in a form that his own life can use. By acting on nature outside of him in this fashion and by changing it, he simultaneously changes his own nature."[95] Labor, accordingly, is not a necessary evil, not a means toward the end of producing, but rather "the meaningful expression of human energy; hence work is enjoyable."[96]

Man's self-production through work makes him free and independent and allows him to make his own history.[97] This implies that the manner of working—the mode of production of material life—determines the social, political, and intellectual life process. "It is not the consciousness of men that determines their social being, but, on the contrary, their social being that determines their consciousness."[98] The course of history is shaped by conflicts between the productive forces (which include not only raw materials, energy, capital, and labor, but also, and increasingly, the sciences and all of man's capacities[99]) and the mode of production in a given social organization. "When a mode of production or social organization hampers, rather than furthers, the given productive forces, a society, if it is not to collapse, will choose such forms of production as fit the new set of productive forces and develop them."[100]

"Together with the conflict between productive forces and sociopolitical structures goes the conflict between social classes."[101] Man is involved in the dynamics of this process; indeed, he is its propulsive force and progressively frees himself through these conflicts in the productive process from what ties him to nature. Along with the work process, his intellectual and psychological powers become more independent and attain full development. Since man in an everchanging unity with nature is both origin and goal of history, what counts in all modes of production and social relations is that man and the unfolding of the powers with which he can dominate nature always remain the center of all efforts.

Once man has extended his control as governed by his reason over all of nature, he will be completely independent and free. Society will then lose its antagonistic class character and the true history of man will begin, "in which free men plan and organize their exchange with nature, and in which the aim and end of all social life is not work and production, but the unfolding of man's powers as an end in itself. That is, for Marx, the realm of freedom in which man will be fully united with his fellow men and with nature."[102]

The realm of freedom is the goal of socialism. For both Marx and Fromm, socialism means independence and freedom.[103] It is identical with man's self-realization "in the process of productive relatedness and oneness with man and nature. The aim of socialism was the development of the individual personality."[104] Thus both Fromm and Marx refuse to identify the aim of all of history with socialism.[105] Socialism is the "condition of human freedom and creativity, not . . . in itself . . . the goal of man's life."[106] It is only when man creates a socialist, that is, rational,[107] form of society that the goal of life becomes achievable: "the development of human power which is its own end, the true realm of freedom. . . ."[108] Then man will have fully given birth to himself in the historical process. Being free and independent, he will be at one with nature and his fellow man, in reason and love.[109]

"Since, however, for socialist man, the whole of what is called world history is nothing but the creation of man by human labor, and the emergence of nature for man, he therefore has the evident and irrefutable proof of his self-creation, of his own origins."[110] Once man is truly born, his "prehistory" will have ended and true human history will begin.[111] With this view, Marx, and Fromm along with him, clearly stand in the tradition of prophetic messianism. Yet there is another essential aspect to their theory of history that proposes to do justice to actual historical development. Fromm called this aspect idolatry—that is, man's alienation in the historical process.

MAN'S ALIENATION IN HISTORY

In Fromm's work, the concept of alienation is closely linked to the historical-philosophical interpretation of man and his nature. The literature on the concept of alienation in the intellectual history of the last one hundred and fifty years, a literature that has grown enormously in recent times, cannot be considered here. Only sources that influenced Fromm and the way he developed his own concept of alienation against this intellectual background will be discussed.[112]

The Roots of Fromm's Concept of Alienation in Intellectual History

"The thinker who coined the concept of alienation was Hegel. To him, the history of man was at the same time the history of man's alienation."[113] Objectification, alienation, and reunification are part of the life process, and in this movement, Hegel sees man's innermost nature. Through the creation of an objective world, the absolute spirit becomes alienated from itself so that it may return to itself. "Hegel, taking God as the subject of history, had seen God in man, in a state of self-alienation, and in the process of history God's return to himself."[114] For man, this means that his existence is alienated from his essence, that he, in other words, *"is not what he ought to be, and that he ought to be that which he could be."*[115]

Karl Marx's adoption of Hegel's concept of alienation was influenced by Feuerbach's inversion of Hegel's "theology" into an anthropology. Ludwig Feuerbach sees in God a projection of man's being, which means that alienation becomes a movement within man's consciousness. "In the thought of Feuerbach, God's self-externalization in nature becomes, through inversion, man's projection of his own essence into an imagined objectivity."[116] In contrast to Feuerbach, however, Marx sees alienation primarily as man's losing himself in the things he makes, and religious alienation as only a reflection in consciousness of the alienation of "real life." This "real life" is shaped by labor, which is man's active relationship to nature, the creation of a new world, and of man himself.[117] "For Marx, [alienation means] that man does not experience himself as the acting agent in his grasp of the world, but that the world (nature, others, and he himself) remain alien to him. They stand above and against him as objects, even though they may be objects of his own creation. Alienation is essentially experiencing the world and oneself passively, receptively, as the subject separated from the object."[118]

This process began with the rise of private property and the division of labor, with the result that labor ceased to be the expression of human powers. "The object produced by labor, its product, now stands opposed to it as an alien being, as a power independent of the producer. The product of labor is labor which has been embodied in an object and turned into a physical thing; this product is an *objectification* of labor."[119] Along with man's alienation from his own product, which, having become independent, now controls him, there is the alienation of productive activity itself. Man is no longer active; instead, all activity appears merely as alienated man's livelihood. "A direct consequence of the alienation of man from the product of his labor, from his life activity and from his species life is that man is alienated from other men. When man confronts himself, he also confronts other men."[120]

Marx believes that alienation can be overcome where the liberation of the human being aims at the restoration of the nonalienated and therefore free activity of all men, at a society whose end is man, not the production of objects.[121] This view of alienation and the overcoming of it, which Fromm documents principally by quotations from Marx's early writings, is of importance because it means that, contrary to certain Marxist doctrines, efforts to deal with alienation must go beyond mere socioeconomic manipulations. Rather, the point of departure must be an encompassing image of man and history, and the goal of all effort must be to overcome man's estrangement from life, from himself, and from his fellow man.[122]

Alienation as Idolatry

The intellectual background outlined above is essential to Fromm's view of alienation. But by an analysis of the prophetic struggle against idolatry, he also attempted to make his understanding of it more precise. "I use 'alienation' as it was used by Hegel and later by Marx: instead of experiencing his own human powers, for example love or wisdom, thought or reason, acting justly, a person transfers these powers to some idol, to force or forces outside himself. In order then to get in touch with his own power, he must submit completely to this idol. . . . What I'm saying is that the biblical concept of idolatry is essentially the same as the Hegelian and Marxian concept of alienation."[123]

The essence of idolatry is not the worship of this or that idol but that idol worship itself represents a certain human attitude.[124] It is equally unimportant whether many gods are worshipped or a single one. The core notion of the prophetic struggle against idolatry is that idols are the work of human hands, so that man "transfers to the things of his creation the attributes of his own life, and instead of experiencing himself as the creating person, he is in touch with himself only by the worship of the idols."[125] The idol thus represents man's own powers in alienated form to which he must submit and by which he allows himself to be dominated.

Idols and the objects of idolatry vary from culture to culture and from period to period. "Once, idols were animals, trees, stars, figures of men and women. . . . Today they are called honor, flag, state, mother, family, fame, production, consumption, and many other names."[126] It is the function of such idols to serve crippled and self-alienated man as crutches that, though expressions of his loss of himself, enable him to preserve a minimal self and a minimal experience of identity.

It is not only in relation to other objects and persons that Fromm speaks of idolatry or alienation. When someone is controlled by his irrational passions, he worships his own partial striving as an idol and is "obsessed" by it: "In this sense, the neurotic person is an alienated person. His actions are not his own; while he is under the illusion of doing what *he* wants, he is driven by forces which are separated from his self."[127] The psychotic represents the extreme case. He is a person who is alienated from himself, who has totally lost his self as the center of his experiences.[128]

What is common to all these phenomena of idolatry is that "man does not experience himself as the active bearer of his own powers and richness, but as an impoverished 'thing,' dependent on powers outside of himself, unto whom he has projected his living substance."[129] This is especially true of contemporary industrial civilization, in which alienation is nearly total and pervades the individual's relations to his work, to the objects he uses, to his fellow man, and to himself. Modern man has become "the object of blind economic forces which rule his life."[130] In contrast to Marx's view, Fromm observes that the entire work force, management even more than the traditional working class, is exposed to the alienating dictate of economic forces.[131]

A typical feature of our industrial society that is independent of the social system is the hypertrophy of the administrative apparatus in all spheres, in the industrial-technical bureaucracy, in unions, and in political, military, church, and social institutions. "They function rather like electronic computers, into which all the data have been fed and which—according to certain principles—make the 'decisions.' When man is transformed into a thing and managed like a thing, his managers themselves become things; and things have no will, no vision, no plan."[132] It is on the basis of such insights that Fromm refers to our contemporary society as an "insane society" in which men have become incapable of experiencing themselves as active but have instead idolatrously surrendered to enslavement by their own achievements and powers.

The Possibility of Overcoming Alienation

Does Fromm believe that the phenomena of alienation are purely the result of modern capitalism? The question must be answered negatively in two respects. First, he notes that typical alienation phenomena are also observable in socialist economic systems.[133] Second, by showing the structural affinity between the biblical concept of idolatry and the alienation concept in Marx, Fromm suggests that alienation is not a distinctive characteristic of capitalist or state-capitalist systems or some corresponding social structure. Conversely, it demonstrates suicidal blindness to ask in the atomic age "to what extent the bad features of alienation [are] simply the price we have to pay for the good features of modern economic and political freedom and progress."[134] Fromm believes that the need to overcome alienation today is a matter of life and death, and he is persuaded that the attempt can be successful. Following Marx, he recognizes "that contemporary idolatry is rooted in the contemporary mode of production and can be changed only by the complete change of the economic-social constellation together with the spiritual liberation of man."[135] This insight also contains a criticism of Marx's position that brings out Fromm's point of view more sharply. For change to be possible, Fromm believes, there must also be spiritual liberation. It is his view that Marx "had not sufficiently recognized that human nature has itself needs and laws which are in constant interaction with the economic conditions which shape historical development."[136] The socialization of the means of production is, then, a necessary but not a sufficient condition for overcoming alienation.[137] So long as the needs that are a consequence of man's self-consciousness—and this includes their deformations by socioeconomic conditions—are not recognized, and recognized as essential needs that have a share in fundamentally determining and stabilizing socioeconomic conditions, and so long as man's unfolding does not become a driving element in development, one cannot expect alienation to be overcome.[138]

From this insight into human needs and their pseudo-solutions in nonproductive orientations, Fromm proceeds to establish guidelines for changes in economic factors and social structures. His insights are provided by a dynamic psychology: "A concept like alienation, to be meaningful beyond a relatively speculative level of description, must be studied empirically by dynamic psychology. . . . If alienation isn't thus investigated, it remains in itself an alienated term."[139] This does not mean that Fromm concedes that the power of human consciousness to bring change is greater than that of economic or social forces.[140] He is not concerned with establishing the primacy of consciousness but with respecting the specifically human qualities that imply specific, inalienable human needs whose reality and effectiveness no effort to overcome human alienation can ignore. And because alienation is possible only in the human sphere, every insight into alienation and every attempt to overcome it depend on the specific human quality of consciousness and illuminate the conscious and unconscious forces that determine man in his unique situation. This is why psychology "must empirically study key concepts of religion, philosophy and sociology,"[141] why psychology is given priority in the process of cognition.[142] And it is also this circumstance that makes the "spiritual liberation of man" the necessary condition if alienation is to be overcome.

Fromm lived up to this insight in his writings. In *The Sane Society,* his principal work on this problem, he starts out by setting forth the human situation and the human needs resulting from it, and ends with practical reflections on ways to overcome alienation.[143] For alienation must be overcome if individuals are to be spiritually healthy and there is to be a society in which productive persons can exist. Nonalienated man "relates himself to the world lovingly, and . . . uses his reason to grasp reality objectively . . . experiences himself as a unique individual entity, and at the same time feels one with his fellow man . . . is not subject to irrational authority, and accepts willingly the rational authority of conscience and reason . . . is in the process of being born as long as he is alive, and considers the gift of life the most precious chance he has."[144]

Progress toward spiritual liberation begins when the conflict between human needs and the existing social structure is pointed out. The next step is to raise consciousness about this conflict and what has been lost through it. Then practical changes in the economic, political, and social, as well as the cultural, sphere must be initiated.[145] These practical changes aim at a "sane society in which no man is a means toward another's ends but always and without exception an end in himself; where nobody is used, nor uses himself, for purposes which are not those of the unfolding of his own human powers; where man is the center, and where all economic and political activities are subordinated to the goal of his growth . . . where the individual is concerned with social matters so that they become personal ones, where his relation to his fellow man is not separated from his relationships in the private sphere. . . ."[146]

To a considerable extent, these postulates were realized in the so-called work communities (*communautés de travail*) that came into existence during the Second World War and, especially, in the period following it in France, Switzerland, Belgium, and Holland.[147] These agricultural and industrial communities, which consisted of as many as one thousand working individuals, were characterized by a fundamentally new kind of life with others,[148] ranging from the abolition of the distinction between employer and employee and institution of the common ownership of capital, to democratic codetermination in such matters as production, management of the enterprise, and personnel policies, the dynamic acting out of conflict management, leisure-time management, the formation of neighborhood groups, and the establishment of a specific catalogue of norms. The communities were successful in considerably raising production levels, even though this was not one of their goals, but were more remarkable for instilling a new experience of human value whereby man "knows what he is doing, has an influence on what is being done, and feels united with, rather than separated from, his fellow man."[149]

While such experiments cannot be transferred en bloc to larger social structures, they proved to Fromm that alienation is not fated. In contrast to all previous attempts at a one-sided manipulation of socioeconomic elements without concurrent consideration of inalienable human needs—attempts such as the Communist states and England have undertaken—the work communities demonstrate the possibility and rightness of a "humanistic communitary socialism."[150]

On the Ambiguity of the Concept of Alienation

The historical-philosophical context of Fromm's concept of alienation is indispensable to an adequate understanding of it, but it is also essential to grasp the differing use of the term he makes in his writings. The history of man (both individual and mankind) originates in the break with nature that is due to the emergence of specifically human qualities and must therefore be seen as the process of man's birth. "History is seen as an extension of nature, moving through stages of growth toward the full realization of human potentialities."[151] This goal of history means a new unity between man and nature, his fellow human beings, and himself, on a higher, a conscious level.

The stretch of history that extends from the origin of man to the full realization of human potentialities is necessarily marked by alienation. The new unity can only be attained "after man has experienced his separateness, after he has gone through the stage of alienation from himself and from the world, and has been fully born. This new unity has as a premise the full development of man's reason, leading to a stage in which reason no longer separates man from his immediate, intuitive grasp of reality."[152] Until he has overcome it by the total unfolding of his productive capacities of reason and love, alienation is thus an essential characteristic of man's condition.[153] It has a positive aspect in that it is both a necessary step and a constructive stimulus toward the full unfolding of human potentialities—but only if man's reaction to his alienated situation is productive.

This use of the term "alienation" is supplemented by another that, although related to the first, must be distinguished from it, even if Fromm himself did not always do so. Where man does not react productively but nonproductively to his alienated situation, Fromm also speaks of alienation. His use of the concept of alienation, which he took from Hegel and Marx to define idolatry as a nonproductive response to the human situation, shows that the second alienation concept is problematical. Idolatry is not alienation pure and simple but a nonproductive and regressive result of man's alienated situation (regressive because it strives to restore man's original unity).[154] A distinction must be made here between alienation as a positive necessity if the specifically human qualities are to unfold toward a new unity of man in a nonalienated society, and unnecessary negative alienation as regression that manifests itself in the decay syndrome as a nonproductive and therefore pathological reaction to man's alienated situation.

This distinction also becomes relevant to an understanding of the difference between the existential and the historical dichotomies.[155] Something can be done about the historical dichotomies because they are flawed developments caused by man, and therefore can be overcome by him during this historical period. Existential dichotomies, on the other hand, are contradictions that are inherent in human nature and can therefore never be resolved. Man's only productive reaction to them is to counteract their potential for fettering his developmental possibilities—that is, to refuse to succumb to regression. Historical dichotomies arise when man reacts to his alienated situation in a manner that is not adequate to specific human qualities, meaning in a manner that is nonproductive. To the extent that man deals with these dichotomies consciously, using his productive powers, they can be overcome.

This raises a question concerning the correlation between alienation as a positive necessity and the pathological regression that is the negative result of alienation. It also raises a more fundamental question concerning the legitimacy of distinguishing between existential and historical dichotomies, and between man's alienated situation and the regression reaction that may or may not be a necessary consequence of it.

Fromm's insufficient clarity and his confusion about these distinctions is probably due to the fact that his thinking proceeds from two points in intellectual history. On the one hand, he follows Marx in seeing a form of alienation that is essentially the product of alienated socioeconomic conditions; this alienation of man from himself, from nature, and his fellow man can be resolved by changing socioeconomic conditions. On the other hand, in the psychological analysis of the human situation he discovers contradictions within man that cannot be resolved by a change in socioeconomic conditions. Via Hegel's theory of history he links these contradictions with the theory of alienation. Thus the contradiction between nature and reason as it expresses itself in inalienable human needs itself appears as alienation, alienation that only the unfolding of the productive forces of reason and love can overcome.

Fromm was dissatisfied with the truncated concept of alienation that takes the historical development of economic factors for the sole cause of man's alienation from the world and himself, and that therefore can understand consciousness only as the reflection of socioeconomic conditions and consequently maintains that it can overcome all alienation merely by changing socioeconomic conditions. Opposing this view, Fromm proceeds from an image of man that characterizes him as marked by existential dichotomies that are not caused by socioeconomic conditions and, for that very reason, cannot be overcome by changing these conditions. What is required instead is an autonomous response. Because these dichotomies are part and parcel of man's endowment with reason, it is reason that permits man to become conscious of the need for an autonomous response and also makes it possible for such a response to occur. Fromm thus assigns to the modifying power of reason a place that is independent of socioeconomic forces. This view implies that a reason that is tied to nature while also transcending it can be overcome by those capacities that are given along with reason.

This final consequence represents the logical limit of Fromm's idea of man's liberation from himself through himself. Because he feels that the break between nature and reason constitutes man's alienation (i.e., because he does not make economic and social forces the only cause of, nor their change the panacea, for alienation), yet does not postulate a metahistorical entity beyond nature and human reason but sees the productive forces that have to overcome this break as deriving from the break itself, he must bank on man's undivided belief in himself and those positive powers within him that press toward unfolding.[156]

In the course of history, therefore, everything depends on the unfolding of man's productive forces. An indispensable condition of this unfolding is the alteration of alienating socioeconomic conditions because these conditions prevent the full unfolding of the productive powers and produce inhuman needs. The criterion for all change, however, is that it make possible a productive reaction to human needs as determined by the existential dichotomies.

In the end, Fromm's view of man and his history remains subject to the dilemma of all immanent beliefs in perfection. On the one hand, man is capable of much greater things than he has so far achieved. On the other, the risk of failure remains an integral part of his condition and historical situation. Because of this risk, it is necessary to postulate that the project that is man will succeed. But it is possible that the actual consequence of this constitutive risk of man's failure will be that he is seen to be capable of less than he needs to prevail.

Part Two

THE HUMANISM OF ERICH FROMM AND ITS CRITIQUE

The reflections on philosophical anthropology and the theory of history presented up to this point have made it clear that Fromm interprets man in view of a specific idea that breaks through the frame of purely scientific observation—that is, his concrete statements on man and history are influenced by such an idea. This idea is part of the humanistic tradition and unfolds in Fromm's understanding of humanistic religion and humanistic ethics. The necessity and legitimacy of both explications result from the human situation itself, namely from reflection about the existential need for a frame of orientation and an object of devotion.

Before giving a more precise religious and ethical definition of Fromm's concept of humanism, that concept must be defined systematically and historically and placed within a specific context: "Humanism, both in its Christian religious and in its secular, nontheistic manifestations is characterized by faith in man, in his possibility to develop to ever higher stages, in the unity of the human race, in tolerance and peace, and in reason and love as the forces which enable man to realize himself, to become what he can be."[1] In this sense, there has been a humanistic tradition for the last two thousand five hundred years. In antiquity, its representatives were Buddha, the prophets of Israel, Socrates, and Jesus Christ.[2]

The most important idea of humanism is that *humanitas* (in the sense of both mankind and humanness) is not an abstraction but a reality, which means that all of humanity is contained within every single individual and that all people are the same in their fundamental human qualities.[3] The concept of such an equality of all people is rooted in the Judaeo-Christian tradition of the Old and New Testaments. Since early modern times, its representatives have been thinkers like Nicolas Cusanus, Leibniz, Spinoza, Hume, Herder Lessing, Goethe and Albert Schweitzer.[4]

Sigmund Freud's discovery of the unconscious and of the dream as man's universal language[5] provided scientific support for the belief in the equality of men:[6] "Making the unconscious conscious transforms the mere idea of the universality of man into the living experience of this universality; it is the experiential realization of humanity."[7]

This version of the belief in the reality of *humanitas* makes a "normative humanism" possible. If man's nature or essence is not understood as "a fixed substance which exists in man and which does not change in the historical process but [as referring to] the potentialities and possibilities existing in all men,"[8] then man's nature is the same as the *humanitas* common to all men. As man's nature, it persists through all the variations of human diversity, is normative for all action and creation, and therefore the condition for the possibility of a "normative humanism."[9]

Closely linked to the belief in the quality of all men on the basis of a *humanitas* they all share are other elements of the humanism concept:[10] the concept of man's dignity, and the belief in man's potential goodness and capacity for freedom. They represent the basis for Fromm's understanding of humanism as "radical humanism." "By radical humanism I refer to a global philosophy which emphasizes the oneness of the human race, the capacity of man to develop his own powers and to arrive at inner harmony and at the establishment of a peaceful world. Radical humanism considers the goal of man to be that of complete independence, and this implies penetrating through fictions and illusions to a full awareness of reality."[11] "Radical" is thus to be understood in its etymological meaning: both the root and the goal of this humanism is man, and nothing but man.[12]

Methodologically, "radical" means a radical questioning of all postulates and institutions "which have become idols under the name of common sense, logic and what is supposed to be 'natural.' "[13] Such radical questioning as attitude and method follows the motto *"de omnibus dubitandum."* "It is the dawning of the awareness that the emperor is naked, and that his splendid garments are nothing but the product of one's own phantasy."[14] Since Fromm believes that this concept of humanism coincides with Marxist theory, he also uses the term "socialist humanism."[15]

The discussion in Part Two will first take up Fromm's humanistic religion. We will not shy away from critical comment where Fromm, in setting forth his understanding of humanistic religion, avails himself of a religio-critical humanism that is justified only when it is understood as the counterconcept to a theistic concept of religion. There will be no detailed examination of his religio-critical humanism until Karl Marx is discussed as the source of Fromm's thought. The discussion of humanistic religion will be followed by a discussion of humanistic ethics, whose relevance for a theological ethics will be taken up at the end of this part.

4

HUMANISTIC RELIGION

Fromm's interest in religion resulted from the possibility of contrasting the position of humanism with the traditional idea. His interest is confined to an essential criterion that cuts across nontheistic and theistic religions like a dividing line. It is the distinction "between authoritarian and humanistic religions."[1] The understanding of humanistic religion presupposes a detailed comprehension of rational and irrational authority.

AUTHORITY AND RELIGION

Rational and Irrational Authority

Though the concept "authoritarian religion" already plays a central role in Fromm's 1930 study, "Die Entwicklung des Christusdogmas,"[2] it is only in the sociopsychological part of the "Theoretische Entwürfe über Autorität und Familie" (Theoretical sketches on authority and family)[3] that the concept of authority is closely examined. Though the multiplicity of its manifestations makes it impossible to give an ultimate definition of authority in the psychological sense, it can be stated with certainty that an authoritarian relationship is not just enforced behavior and that "the emotional tie of a subordinate to a superordinate person or authority is an element in every authoritarian relationship."[4] What is decisive is the way authority manifests itself and how the authoritarian relationship takes shape.

An authoritarian relationship is relatively uncomplicated when authority confronts the individual as a person or an institution and demands obedience. Since the beginning of the modern period, such "external authority" has been increasingly supplanted by an "internal authority" that is called duty, conscience, or superego, and whose rule can be even more rigorous than that of an external authority because the individual perceives its commands as his own.[5]

In the twentieth century, a still more invisible form of authority has come into existence. It may be called "anonymous authority." To distinguish it from all overt authority, "it is disguised as common sense, science, psychic health, normalcy, public opinion. It does not demand anything except the self-evident."[6] The distinctive efficacy of anonymous authority lies in the fact that it presents itself as nonauthoritarian, which means that not only the one giving orders but the order itself remains invisible.[7] Modern man is ruled by anonymous authorities whose goal is the total conformism of adapted man.[8] Psychologically, this has the same effect as total dependence on an external or overt authority: man is no longer his own master; he is alienated from his being and his productive forces of reason and love. The individual who is ruled by anonymous authority is himself only to the extent that he is part of an anonymous "one" that determines what he does.

Although the modern authority problem is decisively shaped by the problematics of anonymous authority, central to Fromm's thought is a distinction relating to overt authority:[9] the distinction between rational and inhibiting or irrational authority.[10] Because authority is not a quality of a person but an expression of the interpersonal relationship of superiority or inferiority,[11] everything depends on whether the authority involved is rational or irrational.

"Rational authority has its source in competence. The person whose authority is respected functions competently in the task with which he is entrusted by those who conferred it upon him. . . . The source of irrational authority, on the other hand, is always power over people. This power can be physical or mental, it can be realistic or only relative in terms of the anxiety and helplessness of the person submitting to this authority."[12] As an example of a relationship characterized by rational authority, Fromm points to that between teacher and student; as an example of an irrational authority, he cites that between slaveowner and slave.[13]

Both authority relationships differ in these essential respects:

1. If the superiority is rational, it wishes to help; where it is irrational, it is intent on exploitation.

2. The goal of a rational authority relationship is its own dissolution; the irrational authority relationship is intent on widening the gulf and thus the dependence.

3. The psychological condition is dissimilar in the two cases: in the rational authority relationship, the authority is a model and the elements of love, admiration, and gratitude dominate. In the irrational authority relationship, on the other hand, resentment and hostility—or their opposites, blind admiration and the worship of authority—are dominant.

Defining authority as rational or irrational authority and relation of dependence requires a better understanding of the concepts "rational" and "irrational." When these terms are used adverbially, they usually have the ordinary meaning of "reasonable" and "unreasonable."[14] But where the concepts are epithets, they qualify the object in a consistent, clear manner. Thus Fromm speaks of rational and irrational faith, and advances this definition: "By irrational faith I understand the belief in a person, idea, or symbol which does not result from one's own experience of thought or feeling, but which is based on one's emotional submission to irrational authority. . . . Rational faith, in contrast, is a firm conviction based on productive intellectual and emotional activity."[15]

By his very choice of concepts to define rational belief Fromm makes clear the specific sense in which he uses the terms "rational" and "irrational." In all those cases in which an attitude or quality springs from man's powers of reason and love—and thus has the quality of productive activity and therefore presses toward its unfolding and growth—he uses the term "rational." It therefore seems indicated to "call rational any thought, feeling or act that promotes the adequate functioning and growth of the whole of which it is a part, and irrational that which tends to weaken or destroy the whole."[16] The word "irrational" thus defines a nonproductive or alienated activity: "In alienated activity, I do not experience myself as the active subject of my activity; instead, I experience the outcome of my activity as something 'over there,' separated from me and standing above and against me."[17]

If the irrational means that man does not experience himself as the subject of his activity, then "irrational" applies fundamentally to all nonproductive reactions to the need for relatedness. But Fromm employs the term "irrational" especially to characterize orientations that are marked by a symbiotic dependence on an authority. In his thought, "authority" is an expression for the interpersonal relationship of superiority and inferiority.[18] Rational authority therefore means that an authority-related interpersonal relationship must aim at furthering the powers of reason and love in the weaker individual. The external mark of rational authority is its competence. Although competence implies a position of superiority, its aim is not to enslave the dependent person and to increase his dependence, but rather to lessen the distance between superior and subordinate and promote in the dependent person those powers that will ultimately make a relationship of dependence unnecessary and rational authority superfluous.[19] Irrational authority, on the other hand, strives to increase the power of the superior at the expense of the weaker. Its goal is total dependence and greater distance, which are to be brought about by suppressing and exploiting the subordinate person's powers of reason and love, to make that person's life wholly dependent on the glory of the superior.

Apropos authoritarian religion, it should be remembered that the distinctive quality of irrational authority is not who is superior but whether the implied intent of the dependence is to strengthen or weaken the subordinate—differently expressed, whether the stronger is competent or exploitative. Therefore authority can be distinguished as rational or irrational independently of the question concerning a divine being. The declaration that God is the superior does not in itself tell us whether the resultant relation of dependence furthers or enslaves man—that is, whether God is a rational or an irrational authority.

The Authoritarian and the Revolutionary Character and Their Dialectic

To understand the authoritarian character, one must first understand the *genesis of irrational authority*.[20] Irrational authority characterizes an interpersonal relation of dependence, the origin of which lies in the conditions of human existence: Man is not only dependent on nature. His reason makes him aware how much he depends not only on his natural environment and its laws but also on certain needs that only emerge along with his capacity for reason and his transcendence of nature.[21]

Man's answer can take two directions: he may either acknowledge his dependencies as limitations of his possibilities and confine himself to the optimal unfolding of his powers of love and reason, or he may give in to those dependencies and begin to worship the powers on which he depends.[22] If man chooses the second alternative, he enters into a relation of dependency that is characterized by an irrational authority: he becomes alienated from his primordial powers, subjects himself to the ideologies of an irrational authority, and is forced into idolatry.[23] The consequence is that man "wants to be ruled."[24]

Phylogenetically, there is a connection between man's surrender of himself and the genesis of the division of labor and the rise of classes. Ontogenetically, there is a dependence on the prevailing social structure and its character, though such dependence is not, strictly speaking, a determinant. Man can always attempt to mobilize his inner faculties, and to the extent that a human being does unfold them, irrational authority loses its power over him.[25]

If a person responds to his need for relatedness by subjecting himself to an irrational authority, his character structure should be called "authoritarian." The *concept of the authoritarian character* has its own history.[26] During the early thirties, the Frankfurt Institute for Social Research undertook an investigation of the authoritarian character of the German worker and employee in order to gauge Hitler's chances of being elected and "authoritarian character" is a concept that was formulated in this connection.[27] The various elements of the authoritarian character correspond to those orientations of sadism and masochism that were described by the collective term "symbiosis."[28] In the authoritarian character, feelings of strength and the experience of identity are based on "a symbiotic subordination to authorities, and at the same time a symbiotic domination of those submitted to his authority."[29] Two specific traits of the authoritarian character deserve special mention. They can be conceptualized as the paired opposites "power-impotence" and "obedience-disobedience."

Power is a distinctive mark of the irrational relation of dependence. Correspondingly, the attitude toward power is the most important trait of the authoritarian character. "For the authoritarian character, there exists, so to speak, two sexes: the powerful ones and the powerless ones."[30] Since he experiences himself as lacking all power of his own,[31] he can acquire strength to act only if he submits to a higher power and attains power through his identification with it. When the authoritarian character acts, his activity means "to act in the name of something higher than one's own self."[32] He is persuaded "that life is determined by forces outside his own self, his interest, his wishes. The only possible happiness lies in the subjection to these forces."[33] Psychologically, the need for power is the expression of impotence: "It is the desperate attempt to gain secondary strength where genuine strength is lacking."[34] This explains why an authoritarian character who has come to power by symbiotic submission to an irrational authority must demonstrate his lust for power vis-à-vis those weaker than himself.[35] Irrational authority has such strong meaning for the authoritarian character that he perceives any weakening of the power of the irrational authority as life-threatening. Therefore the greater the distance from irrational authority, and the more unattainable and superior it is, the better the protection it affords and the more stable both the authoritarian character as social character and the power relations in a social system will remain.[36]

This function of authority makes the excessive stress the authoritative character places on obedience understandable,[37] for in obedience, the act of submission to irrational authority becomes conscious. The authoritarian character "is happy when he can obey orders, provided merely that they come from an authority that he can fear for its power and the assurance of its bearing, that he can worship and love. The desire to receive orders and the wish to be able to execute them, to subordinate himself to something higher, indeed to lose himself in it, can go so far that he will even enjoy being chastised and mistreated by the stronger."[38]

Yet even in the authoritarian character, there exists a kind of defiant and oppositional disobedience that rebels against irrational authority. It manifests itself when various irrational authorities compete and the security that irrational authority ordinarily gives the person who submits to it is no longer fully guaranteed. Rebellious disobedience toward the "beloved" authority is to be understood as a provocative act, intended to force the irrational authority to uphold and strengthen its control. It can also lead to a turning away from one irrational authority in order to submit to another, more powerful one. In either case, the mechanism of submission to an irrational authority at the expense of one's own productive independence is unchanged, as is the dominance of the authoritarian orientation in the character structure of the rebel.[39] Only when that person's own power of love and reason is mobilized so that he no longer needs to subject himself to a powerful authority because he experiences his own powers as potencies that enable him to productively and actively turn to the world and others without anyone's help does the character structure also change: the nonproductive authoritarian character then becomes the productive revolutionary character.

The "revolutionary character"[40] is the opposite of the "authoritarian character."[41] "The most fundamental characteristic of the 'revolutionary character' is that he is independent, that he is free."[42] Freedom and independence only exist when it is man that thinks, feels, and decides. "He can do so authentically only when he has reached a productive relatedness to the world outside himself which permits him to respond authentically."[43] The revolutionary character has a critical attitude toward everything that may become an external determinant of human beings. His independence is complete: "The revolutionary . . . is the man who has emancipated himself from the ties of blood and soil, from his mother and his father, from special loyalties to State, class, race, party or religion."[44] The only thing to which he gives his allegiance is a universal humanism: within himself, he wants to experience all of humanity so that nothing human is alien to him.[45]

Although the preceding quotation suggests that the character type who has achieved all these forms of liberation actually exists, it must be said that the revolutionary character remains but a goal. A glance at Fromm's own research in the field proves this. In the report on an extensive investigation into the character orientation of the inhabitants of a Mexican village, only a single individual is claimed to have a revolutionary character—and even this claim is not certain.[46] The report gives great attention to the special nature of this ideal. The revolutionary character is not simply the free and independent one but one who "expresses a particular quality of independence and the wish to liberate life from conditions that block its free growth."[47] While this description suggests that the revolutionary character is the fully developed, wholly productive individual who lives in complete independence and wholly through himself, Fromm makes it clear that the revolutionary character is but a step toward the ultimate human being. "Once all are awake, there need no longer be any prophets and revolutionary characters—there will be only fully developed human beings."[48]

It is the revolutionary character's life to criticize all irrational authorities. He thereby becomes the countertype of the authoritarian character, and, as such, has his right to exist. Fromm never really clarifies whether the revolutionary character is able to relate to rational authority or is merely an antiauthoritarian construct that does not believe that rational authority might exist anywhere outside himself. We will examine this question by taking a detailed look at the attitude of the revolutionary character toward obedience and disobedience.

"The revolutionary character is capable of saying 'no.' Or, to put it differently: the revolutionary character is a person capable of disobedience."[49] But by "disobedience" Fromm does not mean the disobedience of the "rebel without cause . . . who disobeys because he has no commitment to life except the one to say 'no.' "[50] The definition of the revolutionary character as an individual who is capable of saying "no" points up the contrast with the authoritarian and conformist who can only obey irrational and anonymous authorities and are therefore incapable of saying "no." Then there is this alternative: who is to be obeyed? "I am speaking of the man who can disobey precisely because he can obey his conscience and the principles which he has chosen."[51]

In spite of this definition of "obey," Fromm consistently uses the concepts in such a fashion that "disobedience" is always the positive, and ethically positive, concept, while "obedience" is used only negatively. Thus he repeatedly judges Eve's disobedience as man's first act of self-liberation, while labeling the danger of mankind's nuclear self-destruction an act of obedience: "Human history began with an act of disobedience, and it is not unlikely that it will be terminated by an act of obedience."[52] Analogously, historical development is always a history of disobedience where it is a story of man's self-liberation.

This clear-cut use of the concepts "obedience" and "disobedience" has its background in Fromm's understanding of autonomy and heteronomy. "Obedience to a person, institution or power (heteronomous obedience) is submission; it implies the abdication of my autonomy and the acceptance of a foreign will or judgment in place of my own. Obedience to my own reason or conviction (autonomous obedience) is not an act of submission but one of affirmation. My conviction and my judgment, if authentically mine, are part of me. If I follow them rather than the judgment of others, I am being myself; hence the word "obey" can be applied only in a metaphorical sense and with a meaning that is fundamentally different from the one in the case of heteronomous obedience."[53]

This last statement is especially significant, for "obey" here means primarily attending to an external authority that is almost necessarily hostile to one's own authentic self, so that it is only in a metaphorical sense that heeding one's own authentic judgment can be called "obeying." It is insinuated that everything that exists outside the authentic self is heteronomous and hostile to it and demands a heteronomous obedience that means submission to an alien power. Without further elucidating "autonomy" and "heteronomy," Fromm attempts to forestall the misunderstanding that "obedience to another person is ipso facto submission."[54] He does this by calling attention to the difference between rational and irrational authority, and again explains this difference by the examples of teacher-student and slaveowner-slave. He also gives reasons why rational authority does not imply submission: " 'Rational authority' is rational because the authority, whether it is held by a teacher or a captain of a ship giving orders in an emergency, acts in the name of reason which—being universal—I can accept without submitting."[55]

Contrary to his usual practice, Fromm here uses the epithet "rational" not in the sense of "conducive to productive unfolding" but in the ordinary sense of "reasonable." It must also be noted that he speaks of rational authority only as that of a person and does not raise the question whether an institution may not also embody rational authority. This "concession" to the possibility of obedience to a rational authority does not affect his understanding of the revolutionary character.

In one of his last books, Fromm discusses the connection between sin and disobedience.[56] Here, in the context of the opposition between the authoritarian and the revolutionary character, the ambivalence of his understanding of obedience once again finds expression. While every act of disobedience by the authoritarian character is a sin, the disobedience of the revolutionary character as represented by Prometheus is viewed as a heroic act of liberation: "Prometheus does not submit, nor does he feel guilty. He knew that taking the fire away from the gods and giving it to human beings was an act of compassion; he had been disobedient, but he had not sinned. He had, like many other loving heroes (martyrs) of the human race, broken through the equation of disobedience and sin."[57]

Fromm's general description of the revolutionary character already led to the conclusion that it represents the negation of the authoritarian character and must therefore be seen primarily as its antiauthoritarian function. His definition of obedience as disobedience toward (almost) all authorities and his refusal to call the heeding of a rational authority "obedience" make it clear that Fromm saw a *dialectical nexus between the revolutionary and the authoritarian character.* In view of the omnipresence of irrational authority and the authoritarian character, there remains only the principle of disobedience, of negative criticism, of naysaying, of the revolutionary principle, if man's self-liberation is to seem possible.

The analysis of the authoritarian character as the alienation of man from his productive powers of reason and love suggests the authoritarian character will be negated with the help of the revolutionary character, provided history is understood as a dialectical process. In this dialectic, the authoritarian character represents the negation of productive man—that is, it represents nonproductive and alienated man. The revolutionary character, on the other hand, is the negation of the negation. The goal of the dialectical process is sublation in the wholly productive and fully developed human being. The revolutionary character is antiauthoritarian and disobedient, and must have these qualities. His determination as the negation of the negation also explains why he is not definitive even though he embodies productive and developed man. It is only in the sublation of the antagonism between authoritarian and revolutionary that the fully developed individual of messianic time comes into existence. And only if the principle of disobedience determines the future will obedience to irrational powers have no chance and will it be possible to avoid man's premature end by nuclear self-destruction.

Fromm himself only hints at the identification of authoritarian and revolutionary character as negation and negation of the negation, respectively; he does not elaborate it.[58] This identification shows Fromm's divergent and willful positions, especially as regards questions of obedience to authority. But it also reawakens interest in the question *whether rational authority is possible at all.* Using the concepts of irrational authority and revolutionary character as starting points, we will examine this matter once again.

What first strikes one is that the idea of irrational authority as a relation of dependence that deprives man of his inherent productive forces is pervasively present throughout Fromm's work in a great many variations. The discussion of rational authority, on the other hand, is not nearly so extensive. A comparison with the significance of irrational authority in Fromm's work indicates that while rational authoritarian relations, and especially obedience to rational authority, are postulates of everyday life (where they play a large role), he fails to assign them any place in the reality he understands as a dialectical process. Consequently he does not set over against the authoritarian character a productive character orientation as determined by rational authority; rather, the function of stripping the irrational authorities of their power to subject and exploit man is taken on by the revolutionary character, whose primary aim is the negation of irrational authorities and who demonstrates no positive interest in the necessity of rational authorities. This explains why Fromm does not attach very much importance to presenting a psychological description of the individual who is caught up in a variety of rational dependencies, who must obey the dictums of reason and competence, and who must consciously compromise with the constraints of irrational relations of dependence. Despite Fromm's view of authority as primarily irrational, he provides another, parallel perspective that allows for the reality and efficacy of rational authority, although he consigns it to a specific phase in the historical process.

"Freedom and independence are the goals of human development, and the aim of human action is the constant process of liberating oneself from the shackles that bind man to the past, to nature, to the clan, to idols."[59] In biblical terms, this process begins with Adam and Eve's awakening from their original tie to blood and soil. "With this first step of severing the ties between man and nature, history—and alienation—begins."[60] The movement toward independence requires first that the tie to father and mother be cut, and then that one free oneself from social ties that make one the slave of a master and the worshipper of an idol.[61]

In discussing ties of dependence, it is necessary to distinguish between two wholly different kinds of bond.[62] The first is the usually unconscious, emotional tie to the mother, to blood and soil, and its equivalent, which is called "incestuous fixation."[63] The second is the act of submission to an authority, a form of conduct that normally becomes conscious when obedience is demanded. Historically, obedience is usually obedience to the father and his representatives—that is, reason, conscience, law, moral and spiritual principles, and, most importantly, God.[64] "Incestuous fixation is by its very nature a bond with the past and a hindrance to full development."[65] "In the process of the development of the human race, there was perhaps no other way to help man liberate himself from the incestuous ties to nature and clan than by requiring him to be obedient to God and his laws."[66] Of course, the patriarchal principle has this function only where the authority demands an obedience that promotes the independence and full development of man. Obedience to a rational authority is therefore assigned a relatively high and positive place value as man comes into his own. "Obedience to rational authority is the path that facilitates the breaking up of incestuous fixation to pre-individual archaic forces."[67] In this phase of man's development toward what he ought to be—a phase that is characterized by a belief in God as a rational authority—belief and obedience have an even more essential function. When man acts obediently toward a god who represents a rational authority, his obedience implies the rejection of all other gods, idols, rulers, and systems of powers that are enslaving and irrational authorities: *"obedience to god is also the negation of submission of man."*[68]

But the process of man's self-liberation does not end with obedience to an authority. The next step is to enable "him to acquire convictions and principles, and thus to be eventually 'true to himself,' rather than to be obedient to an authority."[69] The goal of the entire process is independence. But the dissolution of incestuous ties and emancipation from obedience to authorities are not tantamount to the attainment of independence. "Independence is possible only if, and according to the degree to which, man actively grasps the world, is related to it, and thus becomes one with it. There is no independence and no freedom unless man arrives at the stage of complete inner activity and productivity."[70] The greatest plenitude of being human can be experienced only when one is free of all determinations. Man is able to relate to all of mankind in a universal manner only when he has renounced all relations of authority, which always imply the distinction of superior and inferior (i.e., differences), and has become altogether independent. It is only in complete independence that man experiences "all of humanity in himself so that nothing human is alien to him."[71] While Fromm's presentation of the entire movement toward independence from ties of every kind shows that he imputes positive value to rational authority, it is clear that he considers it a step that must be overcome as man moves toward independence. Even though ontogenetically and phylogenetically, rational authority has a critical function vis-à-vis irrational authority, it must itself be ultimately overcome.

Yet this view of rational authority in Fromm's work can be discovered only where he attempts to verify the totality of the dialectical process by ontogenetic and phylogenetic data. When he deals directly with things as they are, an evolutionary conceptual scheme emerges that allows for several phases in the dialectical process of man's development, and that can therefore confer a positive value on the role rational authority plays in this process.[72] But Fromm does not spend much time discussing this concession because it is his view that the claim of an authority to be rational has historically almost always represented the ideologizing and rationalizing of an irrational claim to authority and rule.[73] It is therefore legitimate in his view not to count on rational authority as a matter of principle and accordingly to reject any and all claims of any authority whatever. Thus it is that a dialectical mode of thought that admits only irrational authority and can therefore call itself revolutionary gains the upper hand.

Essential Nature and Function of Religion

Disregarding the etymology and conceptual history of the word "religion,"[74] and counter to our habit of associating a theistic system with the concept, Fromm enlarges the meaning of the word "religion" because there is no more suitable term and applies it to "any system of thought and action shared by a group which gives the individual a frame of orientation and an object of devotion."[75] Whether or not man *should* have a religion is not the decisive question, for as Fromm understands the matter, every man *must* have one. What counts is the kind of religion he has.[76]

Given this functional definition of religion based on the need for a frame of orientation and an object of worship, three points must be noted:

1. Religion here is understood as a broad spectrum of phenomena that are relatively independent of the original meaning of the word.

2. The nature of religion is understood wholly in terms of its significance as a response to a need, which means that religion is viewed only as a function.

3. This is the view of religion that predominates in Fromm, though it is not the only one. In his early study, "Die Entwicklung des Christusdogmas," he still advocates a concept of religion that is influenced by Freud. It is this early concept to which we now turn.

In Fromm's early writings, the primary task of religion is to prevent "any psychic independence on the part of the people, to intimidate them intellectually, to bring them into the socially necessary infantile docility toward the authorities."[77] Behind this judgment, we perceive the Freudian view of religious phenomena as satisfactions that are libidinous and imaginary.[78] The following assumptions led Freud to adopt this view of religious phenomena: In the religious attitude of the adult toward God, we find a repetition of the infantile attitude of the child toward the father. This at least explains how religion is possible psychologically. Why religion is necessary, or has been necessary thus far in history, has something to do with its narcotizing effect on feelings of impotence and helplessness. A belief in God offers consolation because it remobilizes the father's protection of the child and the libidinous tie of the child to his father. Belief in God therefore ends when man attains mastery over nature.[79]

As long as Fromm was an orthodox Freudian, he connected the character of religious phenomena—that is, that they are satisfactions occurring in the imagination and therefore not directly harmful—with society's demand that drives be renounced. "Man strives for a maximum of pleasure; social reality compels him to many renunciations of impulse, and society seeks to compensate the individual for these renunciations by other satisfactions harmless for the society—that is, for the dominant classes."[80] That is why religious phenomena as satisfactions of the imagination stabilize the social structure and social reality generally. Conversely, it is not only the psychic makeup but also the social reality that determines what the content and scope of these imaginary satisfactions will be.

In a society that is marked by class antagonisms, religion has a threefold function: "for all mankind, consolations for the privations exacted by life; for the great majority of men, encouragement to accept emotionally their class situation; and for the dominant minority relief from guilt feelings caused by the suffering of those whom they oppress."[81] As long as Fromm embraced this view of religion, which underlay his first major work after his dissertation, the treatise "Die Entwicklung des Christusdogmas" (1930), he saw no necessity for religion such as we find in his later formulation concerning the need for a frame of orientation and an object of worship. In the early work, religion is depicted as an opiate, an illusion that is becoming superfluous. And because he has not yet anchored religion in the structure of human needs where it would enjoy some true autonomy, he is able to reduce all its manifestations to the "external situation."[82] It is the "external situation" that brings about "psychic change" and one can analyze "how this psychic change found expression in new religious fantasies and satisfied certain unconscious impulses."[83] Any autonomous development of religious ideas that would be independent of the determining "external situation" and the "psychic change" it produces is unthinkable. The very equation "collective phantasies = certain dogmas"[84] indicates the totally reductionist concept of religion Fromm held while he followed Freud.

In view of his theoretical postulates, the result of Fromm's examination of the "development of the dogma of Christ" is predetermined: "The transformation of christological dogma, as well as that of the whole Christian religion, merely corresponded to the sociological function of religion in general, the maintenance of social stability by preserving the interests of the governing classes."[85] The following substantive change occurred: Early Christianity was hostile to authority and the state and satisfied the people's imagination with Jesus as the suffering human being who becomes God. When Christianity became the official religion of the Roman Empire three hundred years later, Jesus "eventually became God without overthrowing God because he was always God."[86] The Christological dogma merely reflects a Christian religion that had succeeded in integrating "the masses into the absolutist system of the Roman Empire."[87] But the cause of this change was the "change in the economic situation, i.e. the decline of productive forces and its social consequences."[88]

During the early thirties, Fromm's view of religion was a development of Freud's reductionist concept for Freud felt that religious phenomena "were nothing but" libidinous fantasy satisfactions. Fromm interpreted both religious phenomena and psychic structure as reflections of the economic and social situation. It was only when he abandoned the libido theory and interpreted man as a contradictory being who must satisfy certain indefeasible needs that his view of religion changed. Now, religion was no longer to be understood merely functionalistically as an epiphenomenon of certain economic and social conditions, but was derived from the definition of man's nature. In both cases, religion is functionalized, but as an answer to the need for orientation and for an object of worship, religion is now granted an autonomy it did not previously have. In other words, religion becomes necessary.[89]

With the new view of religion as response to an existential need, the critical question concerning religion is reformulated. While earlier it was asked whether or not there should be religion, and Freud answered that "religion was to be seen as an illusion that was becoming superfluous,"[90] the question that now arose was what religion ought to be if the concept of it was to comprehend all forms of response to the need for a framework of orientation and an object of devotion. Fromm's answer was simply that religion was either authoritarian or humanist. The reason we find only this single alternative throughout his work has something to do with his view of the history of the idea of God,[91] which rests on certain anterior judgments favoring a nontheistic humanism for which a functional concept of religion is legitimate and appropriate. This humanism can ultimately be concerned only with man.[92]

Authoritarian versus Humanistic Religion[93]

In his definition of authority and in his distinction between its rational and irrational forms, Fromm does not preclude the theoretical possibility that God might be declared a rational authority.[94] To the patriarchal God who is characterized by rational authority, he ascribes an important historical function in the development of the divine image.[95] Yet in a parallel to his antithesis between authoritarian and revolutionary character, he sees religion only as either authoritarian or humanistic. As with his distinction between rational and irrational authority, Fromm acknowledges that there may be a transcendent God who has the characteristics of love and justice. But when it comes to defining the kind of religion that meets the human need for a frame of orientation and an object of devotion, we see the same phenomenon as when he applied theoretical statements on rational and irrational authority to character types: just as he acknowledges nothing but the conflicting alternatives that are the "authoritarian" and the "revolutionary," so he confines himself to a mutually exclusive "authoritarian" and "humanistic" religion.

An authoritarian religion demands the recognition of a higher power. This demand for recognition does not lie "in the moral qualities of the deity, not in love or justice, but in the fact that it has control, i.e. has power over man. Furthermore, it shows that the higher power has a right to force man to worship him and that lack of reverence and obedience constitutes sin. The essential element in authoritarian religion and in the authoritarian religious experience is the surrender to a power transcending man."[96] In this definition of authoritarian religion, the consciousness of a difference between rational and irrational authority is still present. It is lost when Fromm deals with humanistic religion and identifies this kind of religion in theistic systems. "Humanistic religion, on the contrary, is centered around man and his strength. Man must develop the power of reason in order to understand himself, his relationship to his fellow man and his position in the universe. . . . He must develop his powers of love for others as well as for himself and experience the solidarity with all living beings. . . . Religious experience in this kind of religion is the experience of oneness with the All, based on one's relatedness to the world as it is grasped with thought and with love."[97]

The possibility of a religion based on a rational authority relation is no longer considered with reference to a humanistic religion,[98] and this leads to the creation of a specific conception of theism: "inasmuch as humanistic religions are theistic, God is a symbol for *man's own powers* which he tries to realize in his life, and is not a symbol of force and domination, *having power over man.*"[99] The following formulation states the same thing more simply: *"God is not a symbol of power over man but of man's own powers."*[100] For "while in humanistic religion, God is the image of man's higher self, a symbol of what man potentially is or ought to become, in authoritarian religion God becomes the sole possessor of what was originally man's: of his reason and his love."[101]

What Fromm calls "theistic" here has, from the point of view of theists, hardly anything in common with what is understood by theism in the philosophy of religion, for "theistic" has a specifiable meaning even before it is closely defined. It is true that theism as a concept in the philosophy of religion has no precise definition but takes on a meaning that varies with what it is contrasted with (such as atheism, monotheism, pantheism). Yet it would appear that the following definition is always applicable: " 'theism' is a doctrine that affirms God's existence in the sense that providence is also affirmed and that the latter includes God as person and as free."[102] That Fromm should believe that his definition of God could be called a theistic concept becomes understandable when one looks at his theory of the development of the image of God.[103]

For Fromm, "early Buddhism, Taoism, the teachings of Isaiah, Jesus, Socrates, Spinoza, certain trends in the Jewish and Christian religion (particularly mysticism), the religion of Reason of the

French Revolution" are examples of humanistic religion.[104] If one wished to show that these examples actually have the various characteristics of humanistic religion, certain qualifications would presumably have to be made. But Fromm's enumeration is intended merely for illustration, and it serves this purpose because all the examples have one thing in common: they stand in opposition to a prevailing current. The prophetic, the mystic, and the revolutionary stand in opposition to what is established. This characteristic also makes it clear that humanistic religion always defines itself by what is antithetical to it, though such opposition is not rebellious but revolutionary, for it attacks an ever-changing irrational authority without putting another in its place.[105]

To the extent that any religion is a response to the need for a framework of orientation and an object of worship, it deals with the question of meaning and the question concerning God. Especially as a reaction to an authoritarian religion, humanistic religion has a special relationship to the question about God, and in Fromm's works, it articulates itself in a particular interpretation of the history of the concept of God.

FROMM'S INTERPRETATION OF THE HISTORY OF THE CONCEPT OF GOD[106]

We must begin by identifying Fromm's methodological and religio-critical *parti pris* in this question: for him, the concept "God" is "only a historically determined one in which man has expressed the experience of his own higher powers, of his striving for truth and unity during a particular historical period."[107] The various forms the idea of God and the concept of God have taken are therefore analogies to the highest power in a given society and an expression of its social and political structure.[108] This approach means that the analysis of the concept of God must begin with the analysis of man's character structure, for the particular meaning God has always depends on what man takes to be the highest good.[109]

During the initial phase of human development, which can be understood as man's freeing himself from his primary ties to nature, mother, blood, and soil, man, no longer at one with nature because of his reason, yet tries to find security by clinging to these original ties. Many primitive religions testify to this phase in which totems—trees and animals, for example—are worshipped. As man develops his capacity for making things, he transforms the product of his hands into a god. This is the phase in which gods of earth, silver, and gold are worshipped and man projects his own powers and capacities onto the things he has made.

As man's sense of his own worth grows, his gods come to take on human form: "In this phase of anthropomorphic god worship we find a development in two dimensions. The one refers to the female or male nature of the gods, the other to the degree of maturity which man has achieved, and which determines the nature of his gods and the nature of his love of them."[110]

In many cultures, a matriarchal phase of religion preceded the patriarchal. In these matriarchically structured religions that have their counterpart in a matriarchal social structure, a goddess is the highest being and human beings are the equally valued and equally loved children of this goddess. The transition to the patriarchal phase involves both the primacy of the male in society and the dethroning of the mother goddess. Now the relation between man and divine being is no longer defined by equality among men but depends on the degree to which man complies with the demands of the father god. It is, therefore, its hierarchic structure that defines every patriarchal society.

A further development of the concept of God—and, along with it, of human powers and capacities that now extend to the application of the concept of God to man himself—can be traced in the course of patriarchal religion. Fromm shows, in considerable detail, this development in the Jewish concept of God. Throughout all the modifications of this concept, there persists one underlying idea: that "neither nature nor artifacts constitute the ultimate reality or the highest value but that there is only the ONE who represents the supreme value and the supreme goal for man: the goal of finding union with the world through full development of his specifically human capacities of love and reason."[111]

At the beginning of the Old Testament account of the concept of God, there stands a god who is represented as an absolute ruler. Having created all there is, he has the power to destroy that creation. His attributes are despotism and jealousy. Examples of this concept of God are the expulsion from Paradise, the Flood, the suggestion that Abraham kill his son Isaac.[112] Yet the absolute power of God over man is limited by the idea that man can become God's rival if he uses his reason: *Eritis sicut Deus scientes bonum et malum:* You shall be as Gods! For Fromm, the Fall is man's first act of self-liberation and the first realization of the human capacity to become God. "The whole further evolution of the concept of God diminishes God's role as man's owner."[113] The story of Noah, who makes an agreement with God because God feels remorseful for destroying creation, already makes manifest the evolution of the concept of the divinity: God ceases being the absolute ruler, his image changes from absolute to constitutional monarch who undertakes to respect all life. The idea of a covenant between God and mankind—for this is how Fromm understands the agreement between God and Noah—"constitutes, indeed, one of the most decisive steps in the religious development of Judaism, a step which prepares the way to the concept of the complete freedom of man, even freedom from God."[114] The promise to Abraham, and later the covenant with the Hebrews led by Moses, are a broadening of the idea of the compact. Here God obliges himself to observe those principles of justice and love that have made of man a free being, entitled to make demands. God, on the other hand, no longer has the right to refuse his help. The despotic ruler has become the loving father.

In a further phase, "the development . . . goes in the direction of transforming God from the figure of a father into a symbol of his principles, those of justice, truth and love. . . . In this development, God ceases to be a person, a man, a father; he becomes the symbol of the principle of unity behind the manifoldness of phenomena."[115] Though the story of God's self-revelation to Moses still has markedly anthropomorphic aspects, it lays the foundation for God's transformation into a symbol when God identifies himself as the nameless One. For Fromm interprets God's answer "I AM WHO I AM" as "My name is nameless," because in the imperfect tense, the grammatical form of the verb "to be" expresses a living process, a becoming. Only things that have attained their definitive form can have a name; God, therefore, cannot have one, his name is nameless.[116] "This God who manifests himself in history cannot be represented by any kind of image, neither by an image of sound—that is, a name—nor by an image of stone or wood."[117] It follows from this interpretation that positive statements about God cannot be made, and a negative theology such as Moses Maimonides' and mysticism do, in fact, take this position. Theology as talk about God is no longer possible: "God becomes what he potentially is in monotheistic theology, the nameless One, an inexpressible stammer, referring to the unity underlying the phenomenal universe, the ground of all existence; God becomes truth, love, justice, God is I, inasmuch as I am human."[118]

Although these comments on the history of the concept of God are necessarily concise,[119] and specific statements provoke contradictions, there is no room for a detailed critique. Instead, we will ask why this sketch of the history of the concept of God was set forth here.

In *The Art of Loving,* Fromm sets forth the history of the concept of God when he shows the parallel between love for God and love for parents and presents what he takes to be the mature human being in these two developments: "In the history of the human race we see—and anticipate—the same development: from the beginning of the love for God as the helpless attachment to a mother Goddess, through the obedient attachment to a fatherly God, to a mature stage where God ceases to be an outside power, where man has incorporated the principles of love and justice into himself, where he has become one with God, and eventually to a point where he speaks of God only in a poetic, symbolic sense."[120]

Fromm's primary interest in presenting this history is to show that it is the "mature" individual, the "humanistic" type, independent and free of all external determinants, who is the goal toward which history moves. This interest is nourished in equal measure by psychoanalytic practice and the social and political reality: what is at stake is making fixated and submissive people come into their own. The legitimacy of this goal as the highest possible one has been proved when in the history of the highest goal itself—which in our culture is traditionally called God—the dynamism toward this goal can be shown to be an internal historical principle. In other words, Fromm attempts to demonstrate that history as a development is meaningful and has a goal, and to do so through the course of history itself.

Fromm believes neither in revelation as God's action in history nor in any philosophical equivalent of such action. There are no principles that guarantee the origin, goal, and dynamism of history. There is only man—man who has an indefeasible need for a religion of whatever kind, which means that the answers given by atheism and materialism are inadequate and must be replaced by answers provided by nontheism and nonidealism. At the same time, however, the history of the highest goal—that is, the history of the concept of God—demonstrates that the goal of history is fully developed, universal man. Given a humanism for which ultimately only man exists, the history of the concept of God must always, and solely, have been a history of man.[121] All statements about God are fundamentally statements about man. Divine love and justice are symbols of man's own powers of love and justice, even though they are ascribed to God.

To the extent that the powers he has projected onto God are reclaimed by alienated man, the idea of God becomes unnecessary and man takes charge of himself and his powers. God becomes self-redeemed, universal man.[122] The process of the negation of God takes form in the history of a *theologia negativa,* though Fromm does not acknowledge that the classical *theologia negativa* is not synonymous with an *anthropologia positiva*, which is what his use of the negative theology presupposes.[123]

Fromm's interpretation of the history of the concept of God enables him to discern the goal of history: fully developed universal man who lives entirely through his own powers of love and reason. The inner dynamics of the history of the concept of God allow this human being to become visible so that statements about God pertain to man. Beyond that, the history of the concept of God also demonstrates the legitimacy of the interpretation according to which the history of the highest goal (God) actually shows the goal of history (man), for historical dynamics consist in the increasing negation of all statements about God. Fromm takes currents of the *theologia negativa,* of Jewish and Christian mysticism, as proof of all this.

The religio-critical "use" of the history of the concept of God throws light on the problem of the relation between theism and nontheistic humanism. If one applies Fromm's interpretation of the concept of God to a theistic concept of religion, the following nontheistic statements in theistic conceptual garb necessarily result: "The truly religious person,[124] if he follows the essence of the monotheistic idea,[125] does not pray for anything, does not expect anything from God; he does not love God as a child loves his father or his mother; he has acquired the humility of sensing his limitations, to the degree of knowing that he knows nothing about God. God becomes to him a symbol in which man, at an earlier stage of his evolution, has expressed the totality of that which man is striving for, the realm of the spiritual world, of love, truth and justice. . . . To love God, if he were going to use this word, would mean, then, to long for the attainment of the full capacity to love, for the realization of that which "God" stands for in oneself."[126] The particular quality of these statements is the result of using theistic concepts to express a nontheistic position.

Understanding the history of the highest goal, Fromm assumes, legitimizes the interpretation that the history of the highest goal (God) will allow one to recognize the highest goal of history (man). Along with this assumption, he postulates that it is precisely the analysis of the history of theistic concepts that shows that while these concepts are the result of historical conditions, they logically press toward their own replacement by a nontheistic conceptual scheme. Theistic systems exist only because they are not logically consistent: "We have seen that for historical reasons the Jews have given the name "God" to the X, which man should approximate in order to be fully man. . . . Although logically the next step in the Jewish development would be a system without "God," it is impossible for a theistic-religious system to take this step without losing its identity."[127] In opposition to Fromm's assumption that the history of theistic concepts and ideas legitimizes their nontheistic (humanistic) interpretation, the attempt was made above to show that such an interpretation can be legitimated through the history of the concept of God only if every theism has previously been viewed from a humanistic perspective. Without this humanistic *parti pris,* it is impossible either to interpret the history of the highest goal as the highest goal of history or to maintain that history itself legitimates such an interpretation.

Seen from Fromm's point of departure, such an interpretation and all its implications for the interpretation of the history of the concept of God are persuasive. But for the theist critic the argument is far from persuasive, for what the humanist sees as theism is nontheism as far as the theist is concerned. Here we can do no more than respect the differences in approach. A deeper examination of Fromm's humanist point of departure, which has been referred to here as a *"parti pris,"* will not be possible until we come to Part Four, but it should be noted that in spite of their differences, both positions are connected at one point. Anthropologically, both the theist and the humanist nontheist can speak of an experience of self-transcendence that is tied to the indefeasible human need for a frame of orientation and an object of worship. Everyone has this experience because everyone tries to find an answer to the unsolved problems of his existence, but the experience varies with every human being because it depends on the individual's particular situation and mode of expression. Thus the theist calls it the "experience of God," while Fromm speaks of a religious mood or the attitude of the X experience.

THE HUMANIST RELIGION AS THE REALIZATION OF THE X EXPERIENCE

The interpretation of the history of the concept of God reveals that the concept is only the finger that points at the moon, as it were. "This moon is not outside ourselves but is the human reality behind the words: what we call the *religious attitude* is an X that is expressible only in poetic and visual symbols."[128] Every human being experiences this X, though different cultures and social structures give it varying expressions. Behind the different religions, philosophies, and world views, there is the one experience that persists in all conceptual systems. Fromm calls it the X experience. "What differs is the conceptualizations of the experience, not the experiential substratum underlying various conceptualizations."[129]

There are two points of departure to the X experience as the experiential substrate of a humanistic religion and they determine the distinctiveness of the X experience. The first is the human being with indefeasible existential needs. In opposition to Freud's critique of religion as illusion, Fromm postulates a need for religion that is indefeasible and that articulates itself as X experience but to which one should only react humanistically. The other point of departure is the religious and philosophical assumption that the same question and experience X stand behind even the most widely differing systems of orientation. Which orientation best corresponds to human need can be clarified by the humanistic approach and the religio-critical interpretation of the history of the concept of God.[130] Fromm mentions the following psychological characteristics:

1. The X experience is the expression of a consciously felt disquiet about the existential dichotomies of life. Life is experienced as a "problem."

2. A human being who has the X experience has a definitive hierarchy of values whose highest is the optimal development of his capacities for reason, love, compassion, and courage.

3. For the human being who has had the X experience, man is never means but always end.

4. To realize the X experience means to surrender one's ego, one's greed, and to abandon one's fears in order to become "empty" and thus open to world and man. Seen from this perspective, the X experience can also be called the experience of transcendence, provided transcendence is not equated with a movement toward a transcendent God but refers rather to the transcendence of a narcissistic ego—that is, to a goal within man himself.[131]

The consequences of a realization of the X experience point toward mysticism. All precise statements concerning humanistic religion as the realization of the X experience refer back to Fromm's study of early Buddhism, which began during the twenties.[132] His acquaintance with Daisetz T. Suzuki led to his interest in Zen Buddhism.[133]

The realization of the X experience in humanistic religion as a nontheistic system does not mean, however, that this experience need be confined to Eastern mysticism. In the theistic conceptual system, the X experience is realized in the history of the concept of God: "The idea of the One God expresses a new answer for the solution of the dichotomies of human existence; man can find oneness with the world, not by regressing to the prehuman state, but by the full development of his specifically human qualities: love and reason."[134]

Before the realization of the X experience is presented in further detail, the presuppositions for Fromm's humanistic religion will be systematically sketched, using his humanistic point of departure and his interpretation of the history of the concept of God.[135]

The point of departure for every question regarding what it means to be human is man's contradictory existence, which causes him to search for a new identity as an answer. According to the humanist perspective on man and his world, (only) man is the starting point for an answer, although it is man in his historicalness. This dimension of historicalness reveals the idea of the One God that can become the principle of man's oneness with himself and his world under humanist presuppositions. For just as the idea of the One God means the negation of the power of many gods, so does this idea—when understood as principle of identity—mean the negation of all external determinations (heteronomy, authority). The new identity of man with himself and the entire human world is attained when man is wholly at home with himself and determines himself wholly through and by himself, and does so by fully developing his faculties of reason and love.

The transcendence of man is a coming-to-himself, which he attains to the degree that he transcends himself toward his own perfect form, in love and reason. In doing this, he goes beyond all alien or external determinations toward a new identity with himself, with others, and with his world. This humanistic concept of transcendence makes possible the identity of individual man with mankind, because in the human being who is wholly free of all external determinations, the oneness of all human beings is realized. For this reason, a new identity of man with himself and the human world is the real answer to the need for a frame of orientation and an object of worship. And this new identity is the goal of humanistic religion. It is the X that the humanist can experience only via the negation of all heteronomous determinations of man. To attain it, he must fully realize his capacities of reason and love.

Since man's new identity with himself and the world of man must be "experienced," it is useless to try to *think* identity. Whenever concepts and thoughts are deemed the highest good, an uncontested experience of identity cannot occur. Because they are the products of social and cultural conditions, concepts and thoughts express the variety among men and cultures.[136] In contrast, X stands for the experience that underlies all the various conceptual and intellectual elaborations, an experience that, by its very definition, must remain free of all alienating determinations. The humanistic approach demands that the experience of one's capacities for reason and love—the X experience—be realized only as the negation of all alien determinations.

The truth of humanistic religion is proved in its realization: when man mobilizes his own powers and thus seeks his new identity himself, he finds his identity. It is not a question of thinking in concepts, it is an experience based on productive activity; it is not theology considering how God is to be understood, but the right way (*halacha*) to experience "God" as X; it is not religion as the laying down of a particular experience of God in doctrine, but a religious ethos and the experience of the highest values: love and reason. Finally, it is a matter not of interpretation but of change: the experience of man's new identity with himself and the world "ultimately lies, not in thought, but in the act, in the experience of oneness."[137] The realization of the X experience means "conversion to a humanistic religiosity without religion, without dogma and institutions. . . ."[138]

These characteristics of the realization of the X experience determine the concept and function of religion in the humanistic sense. The point of departure is the fact that reason and love and other religious maxims and ideas are not—or are only inadequately—realized in social life, which means that man is determined heteronomously. As an established and socially relevant entity, religion has its *raison d'être* in antireligious practice. It is its task to realize religious ideas and to keep them alive for a better world. Because it is socially established, religion dissolves when religious ideas become social reality: "social life itself—in all its aspects in work, in leisure, in personal relations—will be the expression of the 'religious' spirit, and no separate religion will be necessary."[139]

These are the definitions by which humanistic religion orients itself and against which established religions must be measured if they are to satisfy the claim to be religions in the humanistic sense. For Fromm, "this demand for a new, non-theistic, non-institutionalized 'religiosity' is not an attack on the existing religions. It does mean, however, that the Roman Catholic Church, beginning with the Roman bureaucracy, must convert *itself* to the spirit of the gospel."[140] Whether any established religion is a religion in Fromm's humanistic sense is an open question.

With the demand that all heteronomous determinations be negated, it becomes possible to elevate the humanistic religion of the X experience to the status of a universal religion. By definition, the X experience precludes all attempts to link the nature of this experience to ideas and conceptual systems that are necessarily the product of a particular social structure and culture. Because it is grounded in those existential dichotomies that are common to all human beings, and because it limits itself to an experience accessible to everyone, the X experience is universally valid and definitive. It is the experience of the person who realizes his powers of reason and love and in this realization experiences his transcendence toward his perfect form, universal man. In the individual's identity with himself, he experiences his new oneness with universal man: as his own perfect form and as oneness with mankind.

The new identity of being human in a universal sense is the essence of humanistic religion as a universal religion. But it would be a mistake to assume that this universal humanistic religion is merely the result of the critique of religion. The negation of all heteronomous determinations becomes more than a critique of religion when it directs itself to the conceptualizations of the X experience in the historical religions and other objects of the nonproductive response (ideologies, doctrines, world views) to the need for a frame of orientation and an object of worship.

The external determination of man can be overcome only when those artificial needs (i.e., historical needs in contrast to existential ones) that produce the objects of a critique of religion in the first place are themselves overcome. It is useless to dethrone and negate an authoritarian god unless the artificial need for submission to authority is overcome at the same time.

The negation of external determinations identifies all kinds of greed and (irrational) passions as artificial needs to which man reacts with nonproductive character orientations. The critique of religion, as Fromm understands it, is the negation of heteronomous determination; it refers not only to conceptual systems and ideas and their corresponding social structures but also to the character of man. The X experience becomes possible only when, through strenuous effort, man dismantles his nonproductive orientations and makes his productive forces prevail instead of allowing himself to be governed by greed and irrational passions. In the negation of all external determination, man experiences himself as cause and goal of his belief in the universal man within himself.

ON THE PATH TOWARD THE HUMANISTIC X EXPERIENCE

Having presented the characteristics of the X experience in humanistic religion and indicated the conditions that make it possible, based on a consistent humanistic approach that negates all external determinations, we come to the following question: What leads to the X experience and what media facilitate this path toward self-redemption?

Fromm's epilogue to his book *You Shall Be as Gods* ends with this sentence: "What could take the place of religion in a world where the concept of God may be dead but in which the experiential reality behind it must live?"[141] It is the question about religious experience and practice, religiosity and spirituality in a nontheistic religion.

To begin with, the humanistic answer to the question concerning the forms of the X experience can be given in the form of a negation of the religious forms in theistic systems. To the degree that theistic religions understand God as transcendence with which man can enter into relations through certain religious practices, such practices are to be negated because they are the expression of authoritarian external determination. For "there is nothing they do, feel or think which is not somehow related to this power. They expect protection from 'him' (God), wish to be taken care of by 'him,' make 'him' also responsible for whatever may be the outcome of their own actions."[142] Such forms of religion are the expression of a submission to a "magic helper," and therefore forms of the X experience that enslave man,[143] for the same law that applies to the authoritarian and revolutionary character applies to these forms of religion: "The intensity of the relatedness to the magic helper is in reverse proportion to the ability to express spontaneously one's own intellectual, emotional and sensuous potentialities."[144]

In identifying humanistic forms of the X experience, one notices that their distinctiveness is defined by the distinctiveness of the object of the experience. If the X experience is characterized by the fact that X stands for the experience of the new oneness—the identity of universal man with all of humanity—and this X can be experienced to the degree to which external or heteronomous determinations are negated and man (re)gains *eo ipso* his own powers of reason and love, to experience his new identity in mobilizing these powers—if this is the case, a theoretical distinction can be drawn between (1) forms of experience whose task it is to negate external determinations so that the person may become aware of his own powers or capacities for oneness; and (2) the highest experience of identity itself, which eludes description but which is the goal of the previously mentioned forms of negation and which realizes itself in mysticism.[145]

All forms of experience whose task it is to negate those external and inner factors and influences that veil the immediate experience of the identity of universal man have this in common: they allow man to become aware of his capacities for a new oneness—that is, of his reason and his love. This "awareness," which is more than consciousness, thinking, or knowing,[146] has a negating component and, within that, a component of discovery. It is represented by the "radical awareness" of the small child in Andersen's fairy tale "The Emperor's New Clothes" that the emperor is not really wearing splendid garments but is naked. What is involved here is the awareness of both external determinations (idols, irrational authorities, etc.) and inner ones (greedy passions). As we become actively aware of our dependence, we experience the negation of external determinations as our self-liberation.

There are a number of exercises to promote consciousness as the experience of one's own faculties through the negation of all external determinations. Among them are the breathing and gymnastic exercises that help increase concentration.[147] There are also meditation exercises,[148] through which one can become optimally conscious of physical and intellectual processes in order to attain a higher degree of nonattachment (*Abgeschiedenheit* in the German mystic Meister Eckhart), nongreed, and nonillusion—in short, as optimal negation of external determinations and the awareness of one's own powers. In this endeavor, psychoanalytic self-analysis[149] plays a decisive role. Since it is a critical theory, it can serve to combat social rationalizations—that is, it can function as the critique of ideology,[150]—and it can also effectively counter individual rationalizations. Becoming conscious is the experience of man's liberation *from* himself, insofar as he has become alienated from his nature through idolatry and irrational passions, *to* himself, insofar as the negation of alienation permits a new identity.

"Becoming conscious" is a concept of self-redemption and thus the humanistic counterpart of "revelation," at least as understood in Christianity. The forms of experience that produce consciousness are the humanistic "means of salvation." Their justification is the aid they render man in attaining the experience of a new oneness of his life by experiencing within himself the identity between himself and the world. Yet they are not an extraneous aid or dependency, as is the Christian revealed religion, for example.

THE X EXPERIENCE AS THE MYSTICISM OF THE *ONE*

The experience of oneness eludes adequate description because it involves the negation of all dependence on what is external to oneself and the exclusive experience of identity.[151] When the attempt is made to articulate this experience, concepts that assert a paradoxical simultaneity of opposites are often used to indicate that the dichotomies of human existence are reconciled in the experience of identity.[152] Such an experience of identity in which the contradictions of human existence are sublated in a new oneness without resorting to a transcendent agency that creates oneness (a revealed God who brings reconciliation to human history, for example) or to some philosophical equivalent (like the identity of thinking and being in Idealism), and where there is therefore no need to transcend a humanistic position—such an experience can be found only in a nontheistic or a humanistically interpreted theistic mysticism. This kind of mysticism does justice to all that is demanded by the humanist view of the X experience as response to the need for a new oneness of man, for the decisive element in the mystical experience is "not . . . that the multiplicity of manifestations collapses into the one . . . but that in the one contemplating the act of contemplation is obliterated,"[153] and "that the most profound absorption, overcoming all multiplicity, also leads into the absolute oneness of things."[154]

Mysticism is legitimated by the fact that "man can perceive reality only in contradictions, and can never perceive in *thought* the ultimate reality-unity, the One itself."[155] For that reason, mysticism overcomes not only the aporias of philosophical speculation of whatever sort[156] but also a concept of God that is theologically explicable: "In mysticism, which is the consequent outcome of monotheism . . . the attempt is given up to know God by thought, and it is replaced by the experience of union with God in which there is no more room—and no need—for knowledge *about* God."[157] This kind of mysticism, which is understood nontheistically by Fromm, is the optimal realization of the experience of man's oneness with himself, his life, and his world.

The mystic experience of oneness was discovered and developed in the most diverse cultures and religions as *the vision of the ONE*. Fromm interprets the elaboration of the vision of the ONE from his religio-critical perspective. Just as he interprets the history of the concept of God as the history of the negation of God in favor of man and his capacities of reason and love, so the talk about the experience of the ONE must be seen as the verbalization of a nontheistic mysticism of identity.[158]

In the course of the development of mankind, when the individuation of man had reached a certain point, man responded to all his dichotomies by a vision of the ONE. Man arrived at the "vision of the one in opposition to the multiplicity of facts and phenomena outside himself but also in opposition to the multiplicity of drives and tendencies within himself."[159] The ONE is characterized by the fact that in the purest form of its experience, it reveals itself as devoid of any and all determinations. It is not a thing, neither does it have a name; it is neither quantifiable nor qualifiable. In this unconcealed form where the ONE is no longer understood as something but as a principle,[160] so that it can be experienced and verbalized only as the identity of opposites, it coincides with Nothingness. The ONE as NOTHINGNESS is a negation not only of all multiplicity but also of any and every phenomenal reality within and outside man.[161] The word NOTHINGNESS does not mean senselessness or nihilism; quite the contrary. Only where world and man are nothing and every form of desire ceases does man experience the oneness with himself and the world as identity. The mystic experience of the ONE is possible only when world and man are seen quite radically as NOTHINGNESS. This vision of the ONE was first elaborated in the religions of the East: in the Upanishads and Zen Buddhism.[162] Both of these forms of Eastern religion will now be considered more closely under this aspect.

In *Indian thought,* we encounter the vision of the ONE primarily in the Upanishads,[163] in exemplary fashion in Yajnavalkaya's teaching about Atman: "This self [Atman] is not this and not that. It is not palpable for it cannot be destroyed; it cannot hold anything together for nothing sticks to it; it is not tied down, it does not quiver, it suffers no harm."[164] This great unborn self that is free of aging and death, free of fear and immortal, is Brahman.[165] Brahman as encompassing divine power is Atman, for "The one being [is] experienced within and beyond the many as self [Atman] or divine power [Brahman]."[166] "The Brahman is this Atman: he is knowledge, voice, breath, eye, ear, ether, winds, heat, water, earth, wrath, non-wrath, joy, non-joy, right, non-right, he is everything."[167] And because the self is everything in the ONE and the ONE is in everything, someone who "knows" realizes that he is at one with the Atman: "He sees everyone as the self, everyone becomes the self for him, he becomes the self for everyone."[168]

The self is the principle of the ONE in contrast to all difference and multiplicity because it needs nothing, but exists wholly in and through itself. In the Upanishad from which the above quotations come, namely a conversation between Yajnavalkya and King Janaka, Yajnavalkya is asked what serves man as light. The first answer is, the sun. But when the sun has set, what serves as light? The answer is, the moon. But when the moon also has set, it is fire and finally the voice that serve as the light by which man sits, walks about, works and returns home. " 'But when the sun has set, when the moon has set, when the fire has gone out and the voice fallen silent, what then serves man as light?' 'The Self, great king, serves man as light,' he said, 'for it is by the light of the self that he sits, walks about, works and returns home.' "[169] The negation of all external determinations takes man wholly back to himself, to the experience of oneness with himself which proves simultaneously to be the transcendence toward the principle of the ONE that encompasses the all.

In the Upanishads, and especially in the case of Yajnavalkya, the ONE is clearly understood as the principle of negation so that the self (atman) is the 'it is not thus' above which 'nothing higher' exists.[170] In Buddhism also, there is a vision of the ONE that recognizes the ONE as a NOTHING. The Buddha, although a son of India, "attained the realm where the heat of the sun, rain, social or other distinctions between men, reincarnation, suffering, self-inflicted ascetic torment, things, philosophy and theoretical one-sidedness do not exist, where even every beginning, every end, and every existent vanish. He has attained genuine Nirvana and the truth that is beyond opposites."[171] Yet the Buddha has no concern with philosophy or speculation. Rather, he inquires of human existence why it creates suffering, and he understands that "man's greed leaves him perpetually unsatisfied and deprives his life of meaning," and that "this suffering can only be healed if greed is renounced."[172]

This approach, which asks questions concerning man's existence and its questionableness and then assigns the answers to the questions to man himself, shows, according to Fromm, Buddhism's radical humanistic view of man.[173] Such a statement touches on the difficult question of the extent to which the humanistic approach is peculiar to Buddhism or is merely the expression of a certain method called Zen, which has general validity independently of the religious and dogmatic views of Buddhism and can claim to be the only method to pass on Buddha's concern.[174] Fromm, who for many years was a friend of Daisetz T. Suzuki, the mediator of Zen in the West, sees the life and teaching of Buddha as humanistic to the highest degree.[175]

For Suzuki, Zen is "the quintessence and the spirit of Buddhism" and "the teaching of the heart of Buddha."[176] Zen is "not the destruction of the mind's activities but their fusion into the one, single power of concentrated vision."[177] "The final aim of Zen is the experience of enlightenment, called *Satori*."[178]

The experience of Satori means that one becomes conscious of a state of "perfect self-identity where all conceptual contradictions are effaced."[179] Satori is thus never knowledge in the usual sense of the term, for "to know means to set the object of knowledge against the knower. . . . but to know the thing really in the true sense of the term means to become the thing itself, to be identified with it in its totality, inwardly as well as outwardly."[180] Zen teaches a way that is opposed to the logical and philosophical method that prevails in the West. To attain a new oneness and to respond to our existential dichotomies, we have to reach a point that lies this side of all division—experiences that are not yet conditioned by logic, space, and time. This point "when our unconscious consciousness . . . comes to itself, is awakened to itself"[181] can only be reached if we withdraw into the inner self. "Satori may be defined as an intuitive looking into the nature of things in contradistinction to the analytical or logical understanding of it."[182]

"The fundamental object of Zen Buddhism is the penetration into the true nature of one's own mind or one's own soul."[183] To establish contact with the innermost powers of his nature, man must renounce all that is external and superfluous. "That is the reason Zen rejects everything that even remotely resembles an external authority. Zen has unconditional confidence in man's innermost nature. All authority in Zen comes from within."[184] Man's innermost being, his true nature, which only becomes the Satori experience when all intellectual understanding is transcended, is man's Buddha nature. Satori is the awakening of the Buddha nature in man. It means a "being at one with nature and the cosmos,"[185] which is attained when enlightened man wholly renounces all external authorities and also logical and spatio-temporal distinctions so that the contemplating subject and the object of its contemplation are identical. Suzuki calls this identity "self-identity," for in contrast to identity, "there is just one object or subject, one only, and this one identifies itself by going out of itself. . . . Self-identity is the logic of pure experience or of 'Emptiness.' In self-identity, there are no contradictions whatever."[186]

It is only through the experience of enlightenment that man experiences Prajna—unconscious consciousness. It is only through that enlightenment that he can wholly grasp reality and no longer limit himself to exploring the surrounding world.[187] "Our spiritual yearnings are never completely satisfied unless this Prajna or unconscious knowledge is awakened, whereby the whole field of consciousness is exposed, inside and outside, to our full view. Reality has now nothing to hide from us."[188] As the expression of an essentially different grasp of reality by the enlightened individual, Prajna can be called a special kind of intuition, "an immediately perceptible experience . . . that immediately grasps the totality and individuality of all things."[189] The enlightened one "thinks like the rain that falls from the sky; he thinks like the waves in the ocean, he thinks like the stars that shine in the nocturnal sky; like the green leaves that sprout when the spring wind is mild. In fact, he is himself the rain, the sea, the stars, the green."[190]

The vision of the ONE as articulated in the self-identity of Satori is mystical if mysticism is understood as the experience of oneness and of the ONE beyond, and in opposition to, philosophical speculation and logic.[191] At the same time, Zen is a nontheistic vision of the ONE because Zen has no interest in a dogmatic doctrine or a God to be worshipped or the logical question concerning the existence or nonexistence of God.[192] It has, to be sure, an affinity with Western humanism, but only those forms of humanism that are based on mystical experience.[193] More often than not, Western mysticism is strongly theistic, while Zen, at most, uses theistic terminology to make plain its humanistic position.[194] The nontheistic "confession" of Zen proposes to establish a humanism: "If it is maintained that Zen has no philosophy, that it rejects or denies the authority of any teacher, that it sweeps aside all so-called holy scriptures as if they were refuse, we must not forget that with this act of negation, Zen also sets up something extremely positive and eternally valid."[195]

Fromm believed that the vision of the ONE in the theistic Western religions is usually "distorted by the necessity to express this ONE in the categories of the society in question."[196] For example, the vision of the ONE articulates itself in the concept of God as a King of kings because, vis-à-vis the many gods, this gives relief to the principle of the ONE. But according to Fromm, such a monotheism has an inherent momentum that propels it toward a mysticism in which the vision of the ONE is increasingly purified of all socially and historically conditioned accidents until the concept of the ONE as a NOTHING appears in all its clarity.

It is again in the history of religion that Fromm sees a validation of his humanistic approach: "I believe that the history of religion can be seen . . . as the attempt to cleanse the concept of the ONE more and more of its accidental, historically conditioned residues."[197] The concept "God" is such a residue, a customary concept in the theistic religions of the West that symbolizes the necessity that man "see the ONE, that he concentrate on the ONE and thus give unity to his life—but also to his relations to his fellows."[198]

Fromm finds confirmation of his theory in a number of Western mystics whose understanding of the ONE is similar in its indeterminacy to the Eastern forms of vision of the ONE: Plotinus' philosophy of the "hen," the Sufism of Rumi, the vision of the ONE in the concept of the godhead in Eckhart, and the "cloud of unknowing." What is common to all these forms of mysticism,[199] and what distinguishes them from the theistic mystic trends in Judaism, Christianity, and Islam, is their total negation of the concept "God." These forms of mysticism do not seek a fusion with a transcendent God; for the sake of the totality of the experience, they understand the ONE as NOTHING. This NOTHING is not the opposite of being. It does not affirm anything because it wishes to be the negation of a negation but is a NOTHING beyond nonbeing and being. With this NOTHING, "every possibility of knowing the absolute by logical methods is denied. One thus looks into 'nothingness' but in this void the perfect Absolute is seized by a direct mystical intuition."[200]

The vision of the ONE as a NOTHING exists in Buddhism, and through the reception and development of Neoplatonic ideas, it seems to have found acceptance among a number of Western mystics.[201] Since in these forms of mysticism "Nothing as the other does not confront being but we see the dissolution of all particularity in the general, what is a fundamental distinction in Christian thought, the difference between creator and creature, and the basic presupposition of a personalistic God, are done away with."[202] The vision of the ONE is realized not as a mystic fusion with a transcendent being but as self-identity in NOTHINGNESS.

Fromm bases his humanistic understanding of theistic mysticism as the poetic expression of what is fundamentally a nontheistic experience of the ONE primarily on Meister Eckhart and his distinction between "god" and "godhead." The preceding reflections suggest that the West also developed a nontheistic vision of the ONE, which in Eckhart converges, especially linguistically, with a tradition of theistic mysticism. But this convergence does not necessarily mean that the "concept of the ONE is obscured" in a theistic mysticism,[203] and that therefore theistic mysticism is a historically and socially conditioned impure form of the always valid nontheistic vision of the ONE as NOTHINGNESS—and that this impure form must be overcome. Such an argument makes sense only if theistic mysticism is understood as the negation of a humanistic vision of the ONE, a negation that must be overcome.

If the religio-critical component in the underestimation of theistic mysticism is seen as a peculiarity of the humanistic approach, two types of the experience of the ONE can nevertheless be distinguished. Both may be called mysticism because they seek identity only in the experience of oneness and through the negation of all theological and philosophical speculation.

One type of mysticism can be characterized as theistic and/or humanistic in the sense that it seeks identity in oneness with God and/or with humanity. This is accomplished when all statements and intellectual constructs about God are recognized to be negations of the experiential reality "God" and are rejected for that reason. This type of mysticism is the consequence of a *theologia negativa* that, in becoming contentless, renounces all speculative philosophical and theological knowledge of God so that it may attain to a deeper understanding of God and/or man. Such experience of oneness as union obeys a dialectic: Theology as rational talk about God is understood as a negation of God's reality. This negation must, in turn, be negated in order to experience in the experience of oneness with God and/or *humanitas* what is positive in the experience of oneness with oneself, one's life, and one's fellow man. The mystic experience of the ONE must be called theistic and humanistic and is tied to union with God, if theism is not seen as a bar to the plenitude of humanness but rather as the condition of its possibility. It is to be called wholly humanistic (and nontheistic because of the religio-critical basis of humanism) when the negation of the reality of God becomes the condition for the possibility of the mystic experience of the ONE.

The other type of mysticism is called *nontheistic* because it wishes to experience its identity in the total negation of every possible nonidentity. It is only in total negation that man becomes free. In this type of mysticism, therefore, he experiences his self-identity beyond all consciousness, all thought, all reason, all being and nonbeing. Only NOTHINGNESS, which eludes all positive determination, is subject to no spatio-temporal specification, and is NOTHING as such, only this Nirvana makes possible the experience of a self-identity that overcomes all the barriers reason and its limitations and the experience of the world create, and that is both salvation of self and cosmic salvation. Man experiences himself as no longer separate or distinct from anything, as no longer drawn to anything. Greed is no more, and the passions that produce suffering are extinguished. Self-identity is transcendence within this world, without needs, without recourse to any authority whatever, and also without the need to act on behalf of others because "none of us can save anybody else's soul. One can only save oneself."[204]

Both types of mysticism have many formal characteristics in common. The most important is the demand of negation. But there are also common substantive elements such as the renunciation of externalities and desires and the negation of intellectual effort in favor of experience. Still, we have here two fundamentally different kinds of mystic experience of the ONE.

Although Fromm's humanistic interpretation of the mystical experience of the ONE was markedly influenced by his encounter with Buddhism, especially with Suzuki's Zen Buddhism, his understanding of the vision of the ONE really belongs to the first type, which is rooted in the Judaeo-Christian Western tradition. This is true especially because Eastern mysticism is fundamentally tragic and tends to express itself in a resigned view of reality that runs counter to the more optimistic tenor of Western humanism. Reason and love are the potentialities of man that make possible a humanistic view of reality, even when that reality is understood as a dialectical process of negation. Fromm's attempt to ground humanism in Zen Buddhism is not persuasive, for where Zen Buddhism assumes the transcendence of negation toward a NOTHING—where negation, in other words, is no longer dialectically sublated because it is necessary to dispense even with dialectics as a form of logic—Fromm no longer follows the Zen approach but interprets this negation dialectically.[205] Reason and love have no place in a process that breaks through all the barriers of reason and its limitations, and transcends relatedness and its specificity.[206]

Fromm is typically a dialectical thinker and it is on dialectics that he founds his humanism. The nontheistic vision of the ONE as elaborated in Zen Buddhism fulfills this purpose to only a very limited extent because Zen's Eastern mysticism knows no dialectical concept of negation. When Fromm says his humanism is based on a nontheistic vision of the ONE, he is really expressing his tie to the Western mystical tradition that sees in the process of negation of the mystic experience an element that is critical of theology and religion.[207]

5

THE HUMANISTIC ETHIC

"Psychoanalysis, in an attempt to establish psychology as a natural science, made the mistake of divorcing psychology from problems of philosophy and ethics. It ignored the fact that human personality can not be understood unless we look at man in his totality, which includes his need to find an answer to the question of the meaning of his existence and to discover norms according to which he ought to live."[1] With this statement, Fromm indicates his opposition to all monistic claims by any scientific discipline that it can "explain" man comprehensively. He also takes issue with the attempt to produce "value-free" knowledge only. A psychoanalysis that takes itself to be free of philosophical and religious presuppositions and that refuses to link its insights to an ethical demand must be assumed to be based on unreflected and therefore ideological premises. Fromm energetically opposes any kind of science that proposes merely to analyze, unmask, and relativize what was valid heretofore, without also having the courage to embark on the attempt to place what has been learned against a new horizon of understanding.

A COMPARISON BETWEEN HUMANISTIC ETHICS AS AN APPLIED SCIENCE OF THE ART OF LIFE AND OTHER SYSTEMS OF ETHICS

In Fromm's work, the word *ethic* means "a particular orientation that is rooted in man and therefore is valid not in relation to this or that person, this or that situation, but for all human beings."[2] This definition draws certain lines. To begin with, ethics is to be distinguished from custom (*Sitte*), even though there is an etymological relation between the two, because custom represents only what is generally acknowledged in a society. Nor is ethics the same thing as desirable forms of behavior or codices, as is implied by such terms as "medical ethics," "economic ethics," or "military ethics." Here the term "ethics" applies only to specific situations and does not do justice to the claim of universality. *Ethics* is used properly to refer to the one universal ethics that is applied to specific human situations, and without which all "ethics" degenerate into mere behavioral codes because their norms are not governed by the totality of man and what is appropriate to man. A further constitutive element of ethics is that it is rooted in man as a particular orientation. This means (among many other requirements) that the condition for the possibility of the comprehension as well as the object of ethics must be tied to human potentialities. To elucidate this demand, Fromm compares ethics with other applied sciences.[3]

Every art (in the sense of *technē*) relates to an applied science that is based in turn on insights of the "pure" sciences. What the art of teaching is, for example, is determined by pedagogy (an applied science) and its object, and pedagogy in turn is shaped by the insights of psychology, sociology, and so on. Ethics is the applied science of the "art"[4] of life, which is also its object. It is based on the science of man.[5] "Its object is not this or that specialized performance but the performance of living, the process of developing into that which one is potentially. In the art of living, *man is both artist and the object of his art.*"[6]

Humanistic ethics thus seen as the applied science of the art of life is clearly different from other systems of ethics.[7] To begin with, it differs from an *authoritarian ethics.*[8] In authoritarian ethics, not man but an authority that transcends him lays down what is good for him. "The norm-giver is always an authority transcending the individual. Such a system is based not on reason and knowledge but on awe of the authority and on the subject's feeling of weakness and dependence."[9] (Authority here is understood as irrational authority.[10]) An authoritarian ethic is based on what benefits the authority (this is true even when ethical action is understood as the glorification of God at the cost of one's own happiness). Obedience to the authority is the highest virtue, rebellion and disobedience the very essence of sin.

Closely related to the system of authoritarian ethics is the *absolute ethic* because it is usually found in an authoritarian system.[11] Its defining characteristic is the immutability and inviolability of the norms laid down by an absolute power. The validity of the norms is permanently beyond doubt because the authority is a superior and omniscient power. But to the extent that absolute truth is excluded as the goal of scientific thought, an absolute ethic disintegrates, usually into a system that is called a *relativistic ethic*. But such an ethic is as antithetical to a humanistic ethic as is an authoritarian or absolute one. A relativistic ethic rejects an objective, norm-giving power, whether such power be an irrational authority beyond man or the rational one of human reason: ". . . value judgment and ethical norms are exclusively matters of taste or arbitrary preference and . . . no objectively valid statement can be made in this realm."[12] Man is free to decide, and his activity the highest value as long as it is authentic.[13]

There is another kind of relativistic ethic, which replaces the subjective element with the survival of a society or a culture as its highest value. At the same time, it excludes the possibility of arriving at objectively valid norms and values for all men. Fromm calls this variety of relativistic ethic the socially immanent ethic: "by socially immanent ethic I refer to those norms in every culture which contain prohibitions and commands that are necessary only for the functioning and survival of that particular society."[14] In this system, the ethical norms are identical with the norms of the society—that is, the norms of those authorities that run the society. While the governing authorities will always endeavor to justify their claim to rule through these norms by saying that the norms are revealed by God or rooted in human nature, such attempts must be seen as ideologies and disguises of an ethical system that denies the presence of objectively and universally valid norms and denies as well that they can be known or considered binding.

The final example of ethical systems antithetical to a humanistic ethic is the *biologically immanent ethic*.[15] On the basis of the insights of comparative behavioral research, it does not seriously consider that there are specifically human capacities that can modify natural givens. Such an ethic considers the instincts behind animal behavioral mechanisms (such as aggression and care of the young) as the highest values and transfers them to an ethic valid for man. Here also, one cannot speak of objective norms that are valid for all men because not the whole man but only his animalistic and natural substructure (the mechanism of his drives that he shares with animal life) is made the starting—and end—point of the ethical system.

These other systems of ethics having been described, it now becomes possible to define *the characteristics of a humanistic ethic:*

1. Source: A humanistic ethic makes the fundamental assumption that man himself is the measure of all things, that "his value judgments like all other judgments and even perceptions are rooted in the peculiarities of his existence and are meaningful only with reference to it."[16]

2. Goal: Because a humanistic ethic can only base itself on man and his distinctive nature, man with his specifically human qualities rooted in the distinctiveness of his existence is the sole norm-giver and also the goal and object of all norms. "Good" therefore is everything that is good for man, "the sole criterion of ethical value being man's welfare."[17]

3. Object: It is in the specifically human quality of reason that a humanistic ethic sees the condition for the possibility of arriving at objectively valid norms and values that satisfy the demand for universality. Only these norms and values are binding on each human being because they have their origin in man's nature and can be recognized as such. ". . . moral norms are based upon man's inherent qualities."[18]

THE BASIS OF A HUMANISTIC ETHIC

The description of the source, goal, and object of a humanistic ethic makes clear that such an ethic must arrive at objective values that represent the basis for its norms. Fromm's thesis is that "values are rooted in the very conditions of human existence. Our knowledge of these conditions, that is of the 'human situation,' therefore leads us to establish values which have objective validity. This validity exists only with regard to the existence of man;

outside of him, there are no values."[19] The knowledge of the human situation, or, as Fromm usually puts it, of the "essence" or "nature" of man, is thus the basis and presupposition for the formulation of objectively valid norms and values. Such knowledge is acquired through the "science of man." Fromm's formulation, "objectively valid norms and values," is adopted here as we show how the humanistic ethic is grounded. To forestall any naturalistic misunderstanding, our critical examination[20] will note a rigorous distinction between the "natural values" that result from the knowledge of the human situation, and "ethical norms" as they relate to the process by which norms are discovered.

The "Science of Man" and Its Relation to the "Nature of Man"[21]

The science of man is the theoretical base for the applied science of ethics.[22] Of course, "science" does not mean here what it normally does—that is, a method of investigation patterned after the one used in physics, for example.[23] "Complete rational knowledge is possible only of things. Man is not a thing. He cannot be dissected without being destroyed."[24] Fromm's "science of man" is predicated on a more comprehensive concept of science than the one traditionally used in anthropology.[25] This becomes clear from both the object and the method of the science of man: "The subject of a science of man is human nature. But this science does not start out with a full and adequate picture of what human nature is; a satisfactory definition of its subject matter is its aim, not its premise. Its method is to observe the reactions of man to various individual and social conditions and from observation of these reactions to make inferences about man's nature."[26] Man's nature itself can never be observed but only its particular expressions in specific situations. A variety of individual disciplines such as history, cultural anthropology, social psychology, child psychology, and psychopathology do this observing. "Human nature . . . is a theoretical construction which can be inferred from empirical study of the behavior of man. In this respect, the science of man in constructing a 'model of human nature' is no different from other sciences which operate with concepts of entities based on, or controlled by, inferences from observed data and not directly observable themselves."[27] But precisely for this reason the science of man is not pure speculation: its task is to discover the core beneath man's various expressions and manifestations, and while this core is a theoretical construct, it can be shown to be man's nature that governs all expressions and modes of conduct. At the same time, this core represents a criterion that makes it possible to reveal that certain needs and qualities that are ostensibly part of human nature are artificially produced and are expressions of an alienated condition.[28]

The legitimacy of the method of the science of man ultimately derives from the distinctive character of its object. Pure science (meaning positivistic natural science) turns the object of its study into a thing. But man is not a thing, so an adequate understanding of the "object" man requires an engaged sketch of what man is, and at the same time proof and critique of this sketch by the observation of human expressions and modes of behavior. Behind this argument lies the conviction that complete knowledge is possible only in the experience of fusion. "The only way to full knowledge lies in the act of love; this act transcends thought, it transcends words."[29] For the scientific knowledge of man, this means that one must become speculatively engaged with the object of knowledge, that one discover what, as a being with projects, man truly is. The coincidence of speculative theory and of the observation of expression and modes of behavior will demonstrate that the insights obtained are correct.[30] "The concept of a science of man rests upon the premise that its object, man, exists and that there is a human nature characteristic of the human species."[31] Without such a presupposition, there can be no humanistic ethic, for "if ethics constitutes the body of norms for achieving excellence in performing the art of living, its most general principles must follow from the nature of life in general and human existence in particular."[32]

An indispensable condition for the possibility of a humanistic ethic is the assumption that man has a nature. Fromm's rejection of a relativism, of whatever description, where man is "nothing but" the product of cultural and other conditions that shape him is equally unambiguous. His remarks on man's nature[33] show that he believed that, strictly speaking, it is only the fact of contradiction and the correlative necessity of a desire for a solution that can be called the essence or nature of man. That the solution manifests itself in a variety of forms of human existence does not mean that these forms are the nature of man.[34] Rather, they are responses to the conflict that is man's nature.[35] It was only at a fairly late date that Fromm seems to have given such an unequivocal formulation to this assertion, which has an important bearing on the problem concerning the possibility of objectively binding values. In *Man for Himself*, he still maintained that "the drive to live is inherent in every organism"[36] and observed: "Existence and the unfolding of the specific powers of an organism are one and the same. All organisms have the tendency to actualize their specific potentialities. The aim of man's life, therefore, is to be understood as the unfolding of his powers according to the laws of his nature."[37]

In contrast to this substantive definition of the contradiction that characterizes man's nature and the urge to solve it,[38] Fromm later wrote: "Man has no innate 'drive for progress' but is driven by the need to solve his existential contradiction which arises again at every new level of development."[39] At the very least, this means that progress and the productive unfolding of man's inherent potentialities cannot necessarily be inferred directly from the observation of human expressions and modes of behavior and of the nature of man as revealed in them. Nor does the knowledge of man's nature thus understood make apparent what may be characterized as man's highest substantive value and what is to be defined as good and evil from the perspective of that value. Objectively valid norms thus do not simply result from man's nature.

In his later publications, Fromm defined his concept of man's essence or nature more precisely and showed its importance for the grounding of ethics. He did this by formulating human needs that proceed directly from man's nature and represent inalienable areas of responsibility.[40] Beyond that, the concept of human nature tells us something about the possibility of ethics in general, as it does about the creator of ethics. If man's essence or nature is understood as the contradiction between his existence in nature and his transcendence of nature (which is due to self-awareness, reason, and imagination) along with the necessity of answering this contradiction, then ethics is grounded in man's nature and the human being with self-awareness, reason, and imagination is capable of producing an ethics. That man can make ethical statements is thus given with his nature.

The how—that is, how man must respond to the contradiction he experiences—has its basis in human nature only in a formal sense: the formulation of the construct of the "how"[41] is possible only by a human being who possesses consciousness of self, reason, and imagination. It is in the real world that this construct must prove its validity. But the definition of man's nature alone does not enough guarantee the correctness of this construct.[42] Although man's nature can only be shown to be man's dichotomy between nature and reason and is therefore the concept of an aim,[43] man's nature can also be described as a core that persists through all manifestations and forms of behavior. The tension between these two ways of understanding man's nature must be maintained if a "science of man" in Fromm's sense is to be possible. Formally, the "how" therefore has its basis in man's nature in the sense that the specifically human qualities constitute the distinctiveness of human nature and are simultaneously the condition for the possibility of assuming that creative responsibility that is man's because of his specific human qualities.

The Path Toward the Knowledge of Objectively Valid Norms and Values

Since Fromm in his later publications takes a more nuanced view of the way norms and values are grounded, he can no longer simply write "that our knowledge of man's nature . . . leads to the conviction that the sources of norms for ethical conduct are to be found in man's nature itself."[44] Yet he continues to maintain that objectively valid values can be discovered. An essential presupposition for this discovery is the comprehensive knowledge of man. What is also needed is the adoption of a highest value by which all other data and values would be judged.

It should be stated here that "objectively valid" is not the same thing as "absolute."[45] Rather, objective validity means the maximal congruence of the model (theory, hypothesis, "rational vision") and its verification by observable facts.[46] It is precisely this path that Fromm takes as he searches for a general principle of value[47] by which all observable expressions and modes of behavior can be judged and whose objective validity will be proved when an answer that is adequate to man's nature is discovered. For Fromm, the supposition "that it is desirable that a living system should grow and produce the maximum of vitality and intrinsic harmony, that is, subjectively, of well-being"[48] is such a general principle of value—the sole premise that must be posited to arrive at objectively valid norms. The actual principle of value in this premise is growth and unfolding that lead to the goal, inner harmony or well-being. This goal is not the necessary content of the premise, but is directly given with the definition of man's nature as contradictory being.

In Fromm's other formulations also, it is the unfolding and growth of man's potentialities and capacities that is the general principle of value by which the phenomena of life can be judged and objectively valid norms and values found. "Valuable or good is all that which contributes to the greater unfolding of man's specific faculties and furthers life."[49] All the responses man makes to his needs that can be qualified as good "have in common that they are consistent with the very nature of life, which is continuous birth and growth."[50] And to the question concerning man's well-being: "What is the optimal functioning of the system 'man?'" Fromm answers, "It means the optimal development of all his faculties, minimal friction and waste of energy within man, between man and man, and between man and his environment."[51]

Fromm knows that the value he ascribes to the growth and unfolding of man's potentialities places him squarely in the tradition of all the great humanistic religions (he names Buddhism, Judaism, Christianity, and Islam[52]) and of the humanist philosophers from the pre-Socratics to the present (he refers to Aristotle, Spinoza, and John Dewey[53]). At the same time, he takes a strong stand against all attempts to make what is technically possible the general principle of value. Such attempts supplant "man and the unfolding of all of man's potentialities" as a principle of value with one according to which "one ought to do whatever it is technically possible to do,"[54] and the goal is no longer the well-being of man but technical realizability.[55] The rightness of the humanistic principle of value as compared to the technical, for example—both being premises initially—only becomes clear in the application of these principles to the goal of any ethic, the art of life. That means that the validity of the posited general principle of value is proved when these norms enable man to lead an optimal life. Fromm undertook to prove the objective validity of norms and values and of the general principle of value that determines them when he recognized that man's modes of conduct are the expression of specific orientations of the character structure.[56] His analysis of the modes of response to existential needs showed that there are two fundamental orientations and character structures that constitute two utterly different possible answers—the productive and the nonproductive orientation—and two kinds of syndrome—the syndrome of growth and the syndrome of decay, which are characterized by biophilia and necrophilia, respectively. Both possibilities determine individual and social health and sickness, suffering and joy, regression and progression, life and death, function and dysfunction of the system "man." The objective validity of the value "productive love," for example, and of the ethical norms derived from it, according to which man must establish a productive and loving relationship to his fellow man, is proved by the fact that only the productive orientation does optimal justice to the need for relatedness because it optimally develops human potentialities. This proof through the need for a relatedness that stems from man's nature simultaneously justifies the general principle of value that is not contained in a statement about that nature and according to which the good is defined as that which brings about and guarantees the growth and the unfolding of human capacities. Therefore it is possible to arrive at objectively valid norms and values as one advances toward this proof, and "to design a model of character structure that is conducive to optimal functioning and minimal waste of energy."[57] With his characterology, Fromm satisfied this demand of a humanistic ethic. The result of his research was that humanistic ethics is identical with a "biophilic ethics."[58]

MAN'S CAPACITY FOR THE MORAL

Fromm defines man's nature as contradiction from which the various human needs result. It is therefore part of man's nature to respond to these needs. The analysis of the various responses has shown that, fundamentally, two antithetical responses are possible, both of which express the corresponding character structure. It can be demonstrated that the response whose content is the growth and unfolding of man's possibilities can be considered good and therefore ethically normative.

Far from all human beings have subscribed to this general principle of the value of growth and unfolding. They have decided, or were urged to decide, in favor of a different answer. Therefore the question remains whether man truly has the capacity to shape his life in accordance with the principles of a humanistic ethic, or whether he is determined by facts or factors that exclude this possibility either in principle or accidentally. This raises the question concerning man's freedom. The answer to the question concerning man's capacity to act morally is of decisive import for the future of mankind, as well as for the justification of *any* ethic, and a humanistic ethic in particular.

The Question Concerning Man's Potential Goodness

Our analyses of the various character orientations, and even more, their coordination with character structures, have shown that there are fundamentally two categories of response to human needs, a progressive and a regressive one, and that the degree of progressiveness or regressiveness can vary.[59] In the regressive response, "man attempts to find again harmony with nature by regressing to a prehuman form of existence, eliminating his specifically human qualities of reason and love."[60] In the progressive response, "his goal is the full development of his human powers until he reaches a new harmony with his fellow man and with nature."[61] Man is capable of both responses, as the multiplicity of human character orientations and their mixtures show. This multiplicity also makes it apparent that the degree of progressive or regressive orientation of the character structure varies among individuals and within each individual, depending on whether his specifically human qualities unfold or atrophy. According to the general principle of value that good is defined as what serves growth and the unfolding of human potentialities, and evil as what prevents this, man has the choice between good and evil to the extent that he is capable of progression and regression. "Man is inclined to regress *and* to move forward; this is another way of saying he is inclined to good *and* to evil."[62]

The question that has been debated for centuries in Western philosophy and theology—is man basically evil and corrupt or good and perfect?[63]—is rejected by Fromm as a false alternative if it means to address itself to man's nature; for "the essence of man is neither the good nor the evil, neither love nor hate, but a contradiction which demands the search for new solutions—either in a regressive or a progressive way."[64] The real question is what factors, determinants, and conditions can be held responsible for one man's reacting progressively and another's negatively to the contradiction of his life, and to what extent are these givens unmodifiable so that they determine man's capacity for the moral?

The Determinants of Man's Capacity for the Moral

Against the background of the classical distinctions "makeup vs. environment" or "constitutional vs. acquired," and using his knowledge of the extent to which man can be molded, Fromm makes the following judgment: "I believe that only exceptionally is a man born as a saint or as a criminal. Most of us have dispositions for good and for evil, although the respective weight of these dispositions varies with individuals. Hence, our fate is largely determined by those influences which mold and form the given dispositions."[65] "Dispositions" refer to temperament, talent, and other constitutional givens.[66] The justification for Fromm's judgment that these psychological givens are relatively insignificant in determining an individual's choice of good or evil stems from his insight into man's incomparably stronger conditioning by factors that only become effective in the course of his psychic development and thus make him what he is. Under the concept "character,"[67] Fromm subsumes all those psychic qualities that, though rooted in the soil of constitutional dispositions, derive their specific orientation from particular influences that mold them. A discussion of the determinants of the capacity for the moral, therefore, involves a more narrow question: What significance does character, its dependence on influences, and its structure have for the capacity for the moral?

The family has the most important influence on character molding. "But the family itself is mainly an agent of society, the transmission belt for those values and norms which a society wants to impress on its members. Hence, the most important factor for the development of the individual is the structure and the values of the society into which he has been born."[68] However, the importance of socioeconomic conditions in shaping character becomes apparent only through particular character dynamics and because character functions as a substitute for instinct.[69] For if character is "the (relatively permanent) form in which human energy is channeled in the process of assimilation and socialization,"[70] it is this character that accounts for the decisions every individual has to make because of his nature. Fromm therefore speaks of character structure's governing man's decisions in the sense that man always prefers those values that correspond to his character structure. "The biophilous, life-loving person will decide for biophilous values, and the necrophilous person for necrophilous ones. Those who are in between will try to avoid a clear choice, or eventually make a choice according to the dominant forces in their character structure."[71]

If character structure is thus determinative of man's decisions but a specific character orientation is by definition something man has acquired, both good and evil are potentialities. Man is capable of both. In accordance with the premise that good is the growth and unfolding of man's capacities of reason and love and it is only in and through the development of those capacities that man attains full humanity, the regressive response to the contradiction in man's nature emerges as a possibility only when the progressive response is not or cannot be given.[72] For that reason, only man can be evil: "Evil is man's loss of himself in the tragic attempt to escape the burden of his humanity."[73]

If good or evil stems from a corresponding character structure and orientation, and human energy is therefore channeled into a good or an evil (i.e., progressive or regressive) form, an individual may commit himself to so regressive a use of his energy that eventually a progressive (biophilic) response is no longer possible. While such a person cannot be called nonhuman, he is profoundly unhuman in his decisions and reactions.[74] An individual who has realized his capacities for reason and love to the highest degree, on the other hand, will no longer be capable of reacting destructively, narcissistically, necrophilically, or in some other regressive fashion. He also is governed by his character structure to the extent that he can hardly respond except progressively.[75] Such a person is closest to the goal of a humanistic ethic and therefore the goal of human development itself because, through the unfolding of his specifically human qualities, he realizes in the best possible way man's new harmony with nature.

Character or Instinct as Determinant of Man's Capacity for the Moral: The Dispute with Konrad Lorenz

Fromm's understanding of character as a substitute for (animal) instinct[76] and as the decisive determinant of man's capacity for the moral stands in sharp opposition to two current views that derive from biologistic thought. One is the Freudian theory that character is shaped by an instinctlike libido organization and that there are two equally fundamental instincts, Eros and the death instinct, that are in conflict with each other. The other is the view of human behavior that starts off from instinctual behavioral mechanisms that can be observed in the animal world and transfers those mechanisms to man. We have already dealt with Fromm's opposition to Freudian theory.[77] Now we will take up his dispute with behavioral research, specifically with the opinions of Konrad Lorenz.[78]

"For Lorenz, as for Freud, human aggressiveness is an instinct fed by an ever-flowing fountain of energy and not necessarily the result of a *reaction* to outside stimuli."[79] Aggression is understood by Lorenz as a drive that, in its destructive orientation, is "a spontaneously arising and growing quantity of excitement whose goal is the destruction of objects, that increases more and more even when controlled and that must ultimately lead to an explosion."[80] In analogy to the pressure created by water or steam in a closed container that eventually causes overflow or rupture, Lorenz' model of aggression has been called "hydraulic." In the animal kingdom, this aggressive drive serves life positively, as intraspecific aggression, because it assures the survival of the individual or the species. It serves life all the more insofar as in the evolutionary process deadly aggression is transformed into a behavior made up of symbolic and ritual threats that fulfill the same function.

This aggressive drive—which is to be positively valued—is the origin of human aggression. According to Lorenz, there is no destructive instinct that was passed on from animal to man because there is no reason to believe that such an instinct exists in the animal kingdom.[81] The reason for human destructiveness must therefore lie in a distinctive development of the human species that transformed the life-preserving aggressive drive into destructive aggression. Lorenz hypothesizes that this occurred in the early Stone Age when the improvement of weapons and clothing and the growth of social organization reduced the importance of those natural factors that influence selection (hunger, cold, wild beasts). A negative intraspecific selection whose principal ingredient was war between hostile neighboring tribes now set in.[82]

Lorenz' thesis combines two elements: "The first is that animals as well as men are innately endowed with aggression, serving the survival of the individual and the species. . . . The other element, the hydraulic character of dammed-up aggression, is used to explain the murderous and cruel impulses of man (but little supporting evidence is presented)."[83] Lorenz assumes a transformation of the originally defensive and life-preserving aggression in man into a destructive one that expresses itself as an innate destructive drive even when there are no external conditions to stimulate it. "The so-called evil in animals becomes a real evil in man, even though, according to Lorenz, its roots are not evil."[84] To give rein to this inherent destructiveness, man creates conditions in which he can satisfy his innate and ever-increasing destructiveness.[85]

The consequences of such a view of human destructiveness for a humanistic ethic and for the future of mankind are obvious, so it is not surprising that Fromm should have turned quite decisively against it. To begin with, he criticizes the fact that the concept of aggression is inadequately nuanced and points to the fundamental difference between kinds of destructive human behavior. Aggression can be either reactive, or sadomasochistic or necrophilic.[86] However, it is Lorenz's hypothesis of an instinctive destructiveness that Fromm subjects to decisive criticism. The opposite hypothesis, held principally by American behaviorists, is that destructiveness is always either the consequence of frustration or learned. In their view, destructiveness can be explained by social or environmental influences and is not part of man's organism.

Neurophysiological knowledge renders both positions untenable.[87] "The solution lies in the assumption that a readiness to be aggressive is inherent in human physiology but that this aggression does not express itself spontaneously or that it constantly intensifies like sexuality but that it must be mobilized by specific stimuli. When such stimuli are not present, aggression does not manifest itself at all because it is always being kept in check by the simultaneously operating inhibiting tendency that has its own center in the brain, neurophysiologically speaking."[88] Therefore neither the thesis that proposes spontaneous self-stimulation nor the one that postulates growing excitement (hydraulic model) is acceptable. The mere fact that the degree of destructiveness varies from one individual to the next, and between cultures, should make one skeptical about the hydraulic model. The important question here concerns stimuli or occasions.[89] In the case of the animal, stimuli are the preservation of its own life or that of its species, concern for its young, access to animals of the opposite sex, access to sources of food—all vital interests. When these interests are directly threatened, defensive aggression sets in. Man responds aggressively to the same basic stimuli, except that observation shows he reacts incomparably more aggressively and destructively. The reasons he does so lie in his specific situation and specific human qualities.[90] Man can foresee dangers, which means that not just direct but also foreseeable future threats prompt his reactive or defensive aggression. A second characteristic is man's capacity to create symbols and values with which he identifies to such a degree that a threat to them becomes a threat to his vital interests. A third is man's capacity for idolatry, which becomes a necessity in certain phases of development if he wishes to survive spiritually; when such idolatry is questioned, he experiences this as an attack on his vital interests. Finally, various kinds of education and ideologies, using methods that range all the way down to brainwashing, can suggest vital interests to man. This all goes to show that the real problems of reactive aggression are psychological, social, and economic: "The real psychological problems here are: the problem of man's dependence on his idol, a missing critical attitude, suggestibility and all that is connected with a lack of full spiritual development. But all these factors are themselves the result of earlier social structures that were based on the principle of exploitation and force, that continue to be so based and had to be so based because the productive forces were underdeveloped."[91]

A second kind of aggression is peculiar to man. Fromm calls this aggression sadomasochistic to distinguish it from reactive aggression, which, while it takes its own form in man, is nonetheless identical in principal with animal aggression.[92] Sadomasochistic destructiveness is rooted in the feeling of impotence that results from the specific human situation, and articulates itself as the need for transcendence to which the individual reacts nonproductively when he sets out to acquire power over others through sadistic and cruel means.

Finally, there is necrophilic destructiveness, which, like sadomasochistic aggression, is observed only in human beings.[93] A person with this orientation is fascinated by nonlife, decay, disease; by what is dead. His goal is not power or omnipotence but destruction for its own sake. Necrophilic destructiveness is the precise opposite of all biophilic strivings, and also of that aggression that is directed toward the preservation of vital interests.

For the question being discussed here, it is important to note that there are specific forms and kinds of human destructiveness whose conditions lie in man's situation. These must be understood as differently oriented responses to human needs. Since the kind of response that finds expression in a given character orientation can be explained by the factors that mold the character structure, it is unnecessary to hypothesize a destructive drive peculiar to man.[94] Precisely because character is a substitute for (animal) instinct in the sense of molding man toward certain character orientations and a specific character structure, by a habitualization of stimulus and response, the distinctively human types of sadomasochistic and necrophilic destructiveness must be understood as pathological deficiencies in man's powers that owe their existence to certain shaping influences.

This understanding of the etiology of human destructiveness offers the possibility of overcoming these deficient forms because it shows that neither instinct nor a distinctively human destructive drive determines man's actions, but rather a character that is acquired and shaped and for whose shaping man is therefore responsible.

Man's Capacity for Making Choices: Freedom as the Ability to Act in Alternative Ways[95]

If we understand character as the decisive determinant in man's choice between good and evil, and if we realize that character is shaped by factors that usually lie beyond the responsibility of the particular individual, we may well ask to what extent can one even speak of man's capacity and freedom for the moral at all? In traditional treatments of the problem, freedom is usually discussed only as a general or abstract concept, without paying sufficient attention to those determining factors that become relevant in a concrete decision. "The will is not an abstract power of man which he possesses apart from his character. On the contrary, the will is nothing but the expression of his character."[96] Our impression that we have freedom of the will comes from knowing our desires. But the decisive question is not what we consciously will, but what are the mostly unconscious motives that determine this or that wish. "Our motives are an outcome of the particular blend of forces operating in our character."[97] If that is true, can there be such a thing as freedom of the will, or is determinism the only possible position?

The knowledge that motivations are determined by character must not blind us to the fact that inclinations vary in strength. "The problem of freedom versus determinism is really one of conflict of inclinations and their respective intensities."[98] There are individuals who have lost the capacity for choosing the good (growth, unfolding of one's powers) because their character structure has forfeited the capacity to act in harmony with the good. Such individuals are exclusively determined by inclinations that Fromm calls irrational passions because they represent character traits of nonproductive orientations. The opposite case is a person who can no longer choose evil because his character structure has so dominant a biophilous and productive orientation that he has lost all greed for evil. "In these two extreme cases we may say that both are determined to act as they do because the balance of forces in their character leaves them no choice."[99] If freedom is understood as choice between alternatives, both these individuals are unfree. But in the majority of people, who find themselves between these two extremes, a conflict of inclinations is possible. In them, what actually takes place is the outcome of the differing strengths of their conflicting inclinations: "it is precisely the average man with contradictory inclinations, for whom the problem of freedom of choice exists."[100]

There is another sense in which the concept of freedom is used, and it has nothing to do with freedom of the will or the freedom of choice. Just as one can speak of a loving or independent individual, one can also speak of a free one. What is meant here is a mature, fully developed, productive person. "Freedom in this sense has no reference to a special choice between two possible actions, but to the character structure of the person involved and in this sense the person who 'is not free to choose evil' is the completely free person."[101]

Within the framework of questions concerning the capacity and freedom of man to make moral choices, there arises the question as to the factors this freedom depends on, especially when the irrational inclination is stronger. "Man, while like all other creatures subject to forces which determine him, is the only creature endowed with reason, the only being who is capable of understanding the very forces which he is subjected to and who by his understanding can take an active part in his own fate and strengthen those elements which strive for the good."[102] This specifically human quality of reason is the "decisive" factor in the choice of the good; it can be called consciousness or "awareness,"[103] and means these things:

1. "Awareness" of what constitutes good and evil.
2. "Awareness" of what correct action to take in a concrete situation as the suitable means for attaining a desired goal.
3. "Awareness" of the unconscious desire behind the obvious one.
4. "Awareness" of the real possibilities among which one can choose.
5. "Awareness" of the consequences of one's choice.
6. "Awareness" of the fact that all "awareness" is effective only when it is accompanied by the will to act, and "awareness" that one must be prepared to accept the pain of frustration if one acts against one's passions.

Every realization of this specifically human capacity of "awareness" takes us one step further into the freedom to choose good instead of evil. Failure to act on such awareness, on the other hand, means a "hardening" of the irrational passions that can ultimately result in their total sway.[104] The power of "awareness" is never omnipotence, however, for it has "decisive" power only within a limited number of "real possibilities" in the sense of alternatives.[105] "The real possibility is one that can materialize, considering the total structure of forces that interact in an individual or a society."[106] This means that the real possibilities are "determined" by the overall situation and that "the possibility of freedom lies precisely in recognizing which are the real possibilities between which we can choose, and which are the 'unreal possibilities' that constitute our wishful thoughts whereby we seek to spare ourselves the unpleasant task of making a decision between alternatives that are real but unpopular (individually or socially)."[107]

Fromm summarizes his understanding of freedom and the freedom to choose in the following sentences: "man's actions are always caused by inclinations rooted in (usually unconscious) forces operating in his personality. If these forces have reached a certain intensity they may be so strong that they not only incline man but determine him—hence he has no freedom of choice. In those cases where contradictory inclinations effectively operate within the personality there is freedom of choice. This freedom is limited by the existing real possibilities. These real possibilities are determined by the total situation. Man's freedom lies in his possibility to choose between the existing real possibilities (alternatives). Freedom in this sense can be defined not as 'acting in the awareness of necessity' but as acting *on the basis of the awareness of alternatives and their consequences*. There is never indeterminism; there is sometimes determinism, and sometimes alternativism based on the uniquely human phenomenon, awareness."[108]

Authoritarian and Humanistic Conscience

Freud "explained" both the genesis and the content of an assumption that has persisted throughout Western culture and that tells us that something in man guides him as he chooses between good and evil.[109] The superego comes into existence when the male child, compelled to renounce his oedipal strivings, identifies with the internalized commands and prohibitions of the father. This "explanation" of conscience as the internalized authority of the father deprives it of all objective validity. And because the essential part of the father's norms is merely the "personal mode of social norms," the upshot is a relativization of all morality. "Each norm has its significance, not because of the validity of its contents but on the basis of the psychological mechanisms by which it is accepted."[110]

How unsatisfactory this view of conscience is becomes apparent in a variety of ways. Investigations of matriarchically structured societies by cultural anthropologists especially have shown that not only the father figure but also the mother figure is essential for the growth and content of conscience. "There is a voice which tells us to do our duty, and a voice which tells us to love and to forgive—others as well as ourselves."[111] Both the fatherly and the motherly conscience are present in the adult human being as its own father and mother, and both are there as opposing voices. "In contrast to Freud's concept of the superego, however, he [the adult] has built them inside not by incorporating mother and father, but by building a motherly conscience on his own capacity for love, and a fatherly conscience on his reason and judgment. Furthermore, the mature person loves with both the motherly and the fatherly conscience, in spite of the fact that they seem to contradict each other. If he would only retain his fatherly conscience, he would become harsh and inhuman. If he would only retain his motherly conscience, he would be apt to lose judgment. . . ."[112]

Beyond the critique of Freud's concept of conscience, it is primarily the relativism implicit in this "explanation" that provokes Fromm's opposition. What is at issue is the question "whether there are any norms whose contents transcend a given social structure and correspond better to the demands of human nature and the laws of human growth."[113] It is true nonetheless that with the assumption of a superego, Freud identified a form of conscience that exists in man. Fromm calls it "authoritarian conscience" and sometimes "heteronomous conscience."[114] Authoritarian conscience is the voice of an internalized external authority (parents, state, public opinion, etc.) that, because it is internalized, is a considerably more effective regulator of conduct, for although man can hide from an external authority, he cannot escape his conscience, which is part of himself. The characteristic aspect of authoritarian conscience (the superego) is that its "prescriptions . . . are not determined by one's own value judgments but exclusively by the fact that its commands and tabus are pronounced by authority."[115] In other words, the prescriptions of conscience have validity not because they are good but because they are laid down by authorities. For this reason, they are a function of the accidents of social structure, of traditions and cultural peculiarities.

Authoritarian conscience is rooted in feelings of fear and admiration of authority. "Good conscience is the consciousness of pleasing (external and internalized) authority."[116] The strength of the authoritarian conscience depends on the character structure: the more symbiotically tied to authorities a person is, the more markedly is his conduct determined by a superego conscience; the more someone has developed his own productive capacities and attained independence, the less he listens to the voice of his authoritarian conscience.

There are certain peculiarities of the contents and hierarchy of values of the authoritarian conscience. "The prime offense in the authoritarian situation is rebellion against the authority's rule. Thus disobedience becomes the 'cardinal sin,' obedience, the 'cardinal virtue.' "[117] For the authoritarian conscience, all disobedience is disobedience toward the authority because the authority alone decides what is good, and what is evil.[118]

Consequently, the person who seeks independence from his symbiotic fixation in order to become productive and self-reliant has a bad conscience, at least until he manages to reduce his symbiotic relatedness to the point where it is no longer the authoritarian conscience that determines his moral feelings but the value of his individuality and integrity that governs his conduct.

This consideration introduces a second kind of conscience, which Fromm calls "humanistic conscience" or "autonomous conscience."[119] "This conscience is an inner voice that calls us back to ourselves. By this 'ourselves' is meant the human core common to all men, that is, certain basic characteristics of man which cannot be violated or negated without serious consequences."[120] The more precise meaning of this "core" was indicated in the comments on man's nature and needs—that is, man is to react productively to the dichotomies of his life by unfolding all his powers and potentialities. "The humanistic conscience is the voice of our self which summons us back to ourselves, to become what we potentially are."[121]

In contrast to the authoritarian conscience, for which good is everything that is obedience to authority, the humanistic conscience sees everything that promotes growth, unfolding, and life as good, and everything that runs counter to this as evil. The criterion for good and evil is man's nature itself, in which the general principle of value, growth, and unfolding proves its validity. The humanistic conscience depends on the degree of development of specifically human powers. The relationship of conscience "to one's own productiveness is one of interaction. The more productively one lives, the stronger is one's conscience and, in turn, the more it furthers one's productiveness. The less productively one lives, the weaker becomes one's conscience; the paradoxical—and tragic—situation of man is that his conscience is weakest when he needs it most."[122]

The forms of expression of a bad humanistic conscience are usually unclear because it "speaks" only indirectly: through a feeling of depression, fatigue, apathy, a vague sense of guilt, an unease that can turn into intense fear, and physical and psychological illnesses. In many people, dreams are the only chance for the (humanistic) conscience to express itself, for "the dream is the language of universal man"[123] and the place "where we think and feel what we think and feel."[124]

The distinction between authoritarian and humanistic conscience is fully justified, yet in the (average) individual, both are always present at one and the same time; they do not exclude each other. The decisive question, therefore, is their relative strength and interaction. Feelings of guilt often find expression in concepts of the authoritarian conscience (a failure to act, for example), although their dynamics are rooted in the humanistic conscience (the incapacity to free oneself from a symbiotic tie, for example). To attribute guilt feelings to the authoritarian conscience in such a case is to rationalize the claim of the humanistic conscience.[125]

The closeness of the authoritarian and the humanistic conscience is also due to the fact that the contents of norms in the two are often identical, the difference being merely the motives that prompt conscience to speak. Such motives can themselves be subject to an evolutionary process during the course of which the humanistic conscience develops out of the authoritarian one as an individual or a society finds itself and unfolds its productive powers. The possibility for the development of the humanistic conscience then depends on the strength of individual and social authorities. But development will be almost wholly arrested if the conscience reverts to a strict and unshakable irrational authority such as certain religions postulate. "No power transcending man can make a moral claim upon him," Fromm writes from his humanistic perspective. "Man is responsible to himself for gaining or losing his life."[126] All decisions are his. They rest "upon his courage to be himself and for himself."[127] Man for himself!

THE MEANING OF THE HUMANISTIC ETHIC FOR THE DISCOVERY OF NORMS IN A THEOLOGICAL ETHIC

To set forth the meaning of Fromm's humanistic ethic one needs a comprehensive understanding of his concept of humanism. Such an understanding can only be acquired by analyzing the sources and forms of Fromm's thought, which we will do in the latter part of this study. Although we cannot do justice to his concept of humanism here, what we have said about his humanistic ethic up to this point suffices to relate that ethic to a theological ethic and to make some tentative critical judgments about it. A sketch of the self-understanding of theological ethics as understood by present-day Catholic moral theologians will introduce these considerations.

On the Present Self-Understanding of Theological Ethics

Theoretical reflections suggest that ethics is a science that goes beyond research in the natural sciences because it necessarily has to do with meaning.[128] For this reason, ethics can be called a "hermeneutic science."[129] Its "meaning is not made, it is found, and always presupposed in every decision."[130] To reflect on already existing or emerging norms is an essential task of a scientific ethic. But although scientific ethics is principally concerned with what is already there, its interest extends beyond reflection on the factual validity of norms because the postulate that calls for responsibility and obedience vis-à-vis already existing norms is not all there is. Scientific ethics aims at the grounding of norms and of normativeness through an inquiry into the rationality of norms ("normative reason").[131] Showing how norms are grounded involves the discovery and the rationale of norms.[132]

Norms are human creations, which means that man is responsible for them. It must be possible to advance valid reasons for norms, that is, "the rationality of the grounds on which normative decisions, valuations and convictions rest must be demonstrable."[133] It is only on this premise that "normative reason can be thought of as reason, that normative procedures are possible as scientific procedures, and that ethics is possible as science."[134] On the basis of this scientific and theoretical self-understanding of ethics as a science of meaning, the following constitutive elements may be noted: Ethics as a science begins with the unreflected anterior understanding of what morality is and "initially sets forth moral demands and how they are grounded in a historical nexus of meaning in what is essentially a fact-finding process."[135] Ethics attempts to show that the prescientific understanding of the moral is rational, and to justify that understanding scientifically. This occurs in a "continuing collaboration between ethics and the human and social sciences on the one hand, and philosophical anthropology on the other."[136] The goal is the awareness of those positive and normative criteria that operate in moral demands. As a science, finally, ethics proposes to confront the meanings, values, and structures of the world (normative potency)[137] that it has discovered in its collaboration with the other disciplines with the "normative explications"[138] in existing moral demands, and to develop out of that confrontation a critical distance from the moral norms as articulated in any anterior understanding.

All this can be accomplished by ethics as a science where the discovery of norms is concerned. But where it is a matter of the ultimate grounding of the meaning of ethical norms and where their claim to bindingness is to be established, the limitations of such a nontheological ethics become apparent and the task of a theological ethics emerges. For an ethics that excludes the dimension of faith cannot "go beyond logical and ethical criteria of validity and identify some ultimate and absolute order that applies to all action."[139] It is precisely a theological ethics that seeks an ultimate meaning-conferring ground for all being and action.[140] The assumption of such a "meta-empirical, meta-logical, theonomous meaning"[141] is constitutive when "definitive conditions, ways and goals of what human beings can and should be"[142] are articulated. But theonomy must not be understood as even the final material norm, and is therefore not heteronomous. Theological ethics does not contradict the autonomy of ethics but is simply concerned with the conditions under which ethics is possible.

The scientific and theoretical postulates of ethics and theological ethics lead to a specific *understanding of the moral* that, under the concept "autonomous morality," is currently the subject of animated discussion, at least in the theological ethics of Catholic provenance.[143] The question is how the moral in a theological ethic becomes binding. In contrast to a position that stipulates that the bindingness of the moral is solely grounded in faith, and therefore postulates specifically Christian norms that can only be understood and realized in and through faith,[144] the exponents of an "autonomous morality" follow Thomas Aquinas[145] and view the moral as constituted in human reason. Moral norms must be accessible to rational reflection if their content is to be morally binding. For this reason, the exponents of "autonomous morality" view the content of morality "as autonomous in the sense that the specifically Christian does not originally and authentically determine, modify or add to it."[146]

According to Alfons Auer, the moral can be defined as yea-saying to the claim that reality makes on the individual.[147] The concept "reality" (*realitas*) means "a being that presses toward unfolding and perfection";[148] thus it implies a dynamics of self-realization. To the extent that it is perceived by man, reality is personal, social, and material. And because it can only be experienced within the horizon of history, it is always historical.[149] If the moral is understood as yea-saying to the given historical reality, the moral has a dynamic character and "concrete ethical norms cannot be seen as immutable but are subject to historical change."[150]

With his reason, man has been given the capacity to perceive the claim of reality, its values, meanings, and structures. The rationality and intentionality of reality enable the *animal rationale* to perceive the claim of reality. The moral as yea-saying to the claim of reality thus has a "rational structure"[151] and the bindingness of the moral does not derive from the demand of an irrational authority but from its own rationality. The rationality of reality—that is, of both the reality of the perceiving subject and the reality of its object that makes possible the rationality of the moral—is possible only as historical rationality. This entails a necessary "perspectivism of moral insight" and "varied forms of the moral."[152] "The rationality of the moral also means its autonomy."[153] If the moral does not have its ground and its reason (*principium*) in belief in God but rather in that rationality of the real that also governs man's reason, the moral is autonomous because it is posited by reason and grounded in it.[154]

The postulate of the autonomy of the moral affects the understanding of the process by which norms are discovered. The rationality of the real in the moral can be articulated only if the following three constitutive elements are taken into account: (1) without a base in the human sciences and (2) anthropological integration, there can be (3) no ethical norms.[155]

From the point of view of Christian and theological ethics, the autonomy of the moral in the process of the discovery of norms means that there is nothing uniquely and distinctively Christian in concrete ethical statements precisely because what is moral is determined by the rationality of the real.[156]

When people speak of the autonomy of the moral, it must be made clear that they cannot refer to the absolute autonomy of the world and of morality. The autonomy of the moral is implicit in the autonomy of reality, but this autonomy "is possible because of certain transcendent relations. . . . These relations do not adversely affect the self-subsistence of the world although they ground it."[157] When autonomous morality is discussed, what is meant is always a "relational autonomy,"[158] not a secularist understanding of autonomy. On the basis of such an understanding of autonomy, the specific characteristic of a theological ethics turns out to be a horizon of meaning that is grounded in faith and relevant in both the discovery and the grounding of norms.

Although what is specifically Christian is morality should not be looked for in concrete ethical injunctions, it is true nonetheless that a specific horizon of meaning that is grounded in the faith prompts the Christian to adopt a specific ethical position. And his ethical conduct also is motivated by this horizon. Regarding the process of discovery of ethical norms, the "autonomous morality" speaks of a critical, stimulating, and integrating effect of the new horizon of meaning that Jesus' life and teaching opened up for the Christian.[159] Jesus' call for conversion (Mark 1, 15), for example, is "primarily motivated by the divine compassion that becomes manifest in Jesus himself"[160] and leads to his fundamental criticism of the prevailing morality because that morality is marked by legalistic rigidity, cultic self-assurance, hypocrisy and self-righteousness, excessive preoccupation with material well-being, and a hardened attitude toward social concerns.[161] The critical effect of Jesus' message here consists in a new attitude toward the norms that may mean both a critique of the Torah and greater rigor in its application.

For "autonomous morality," what is uniquely and distinctively Christian in morality does not lie "in concrete ethical instructions that are developed from an understanding of the faith"[162] but in a specific horizon of meaning peculiar to the faith that motivates the Christian in his concrete ethical acts and therefore prompts a different attitude toward autonomously developed demands.

The distinctive quality of a theological ethic becomes apparent when the autonomy of the moral is given its ultimate ground. "The autonomous human rationality that guides action is ultimately theonomously grounded,"[163] not to establish a heteronomous claim over man and his world but, on the contrary, to create the conditions for the possibility of man's belief in man, in his autonomy, and in his intrinsic worth.

As understood by Christians, theonomy is precisely not heteronomy but the condition for the possibility of autonomy.[164] But the compatibility of theonomy and autonomy is not only the precondition for the Christian attempt to ground the rationality of the autonomy of the moral in something ultimate, for it is only the theonomous relation that creates the "unconditional ethical dignity"[165] of human autonomy. It is true that man's reason has an inherent dynamics of self-affirmation and self-determination. But the conviction that human life is an unconditional value and that human dignity is inviolable does not suffice to ground an unconditional moral demand. To find the unconditionality of autonomous morality convincing "requires grounds that are anterior to anthropological reason and ground it. These grounds reveal themselves to man only in that transcending faith through which he recognizes God as the ultimate ground of meaning and as the God who became incarnate so that humanness might participate in his own absolute meaning."[166]

Thomas Aquinas was the first to make a comprehensive attempt at "autonomous morality in the Christian context,"[167] at theonomously grounding man's dignity and the autonomy of the moral in an ultimate rationality.[168] In his teaching on the law (*lex*), he presents an ethical system in which "human normativeness in its logical grounding is understood theologically and ethically in such a way that God is recognized and preserved as the ground and the goal of this normativeness on the one hand, and man as a being that gives norms to itself on the other."[169] The presupposition for this system is the insight that reason is required if the natural order is to be seen as making a moral demand.[170]

The rational character of the moral implies the autonomy of the moral.[171] But this autonomy requires grounding in God's reason, which itself is not grounded but is the ultimate ground. Both the rational character of the moral and God's reason, which ultimately grounds this reason—that is, both the autonomy of the moral and the theonomous ground that makes it possible—are conceived of by Thomas Aquinas as "law" (*lex*). Because the phenomenon of the law includes both grounding and being grounded, it can serve as an interpretive key that "reflects all normativeness in its validity, its basis and its operation as stemming from the one, encompassing reason of God that alone can create validity since God is both creator and perfector."[172]

A law must always articulate normative reason. In so doing, it mediates "the reason of its author with the reason of those to whom it addresses itself."[173] But although the concept of the law mediates divine and human reason so that all human reason has its ultimate ground in divine reason, the relation of the two remains an analogous one. Divine reason is not simply given to man as law; rather, it is given to his rational understanding. This makes the autonomy of the moral possible and preserves man as a being that gives himself norms.[174]

Theologians are increasingly arguing against the assumption of "autonomous morality" according to which moral norms are discovered autonomously by the Christian as well as by everyone else because they are grounded in man's reason. Their contrary belief has been termed *Glaubensethik* (ethics of faith),[175] although the meaning of this term must be inferred from their critique of "autonomous morality" because a systematic exposition of the *Glaubensethische* position that could claim to be taken seriously as an alternative to "autonomous morality" does not yet exist. Besides, a great many of the arguments advanced by the *Glaubensethiker* against autonomous morality stem from misunderstandings and incomprehensions.[176]

The controversy between *Glaubensethik* and "autonomous morality" is sparked by the question "whether living up to moral demands and discovering and implementing those ethical norms that are decisive for the preservation of humanness necessarily require [Christian] belief. . . ."[177] The *glaubensethische* position ultimately defines the relation between Christian message and moral reason by saying that Christian morality goes counter to human reason: "The Christian ethos must be capable of avowing a position that human reason will consider paradoxical."[178] A "theonomous ethic" is set against the autonomy of the moral, and the incompatibility of theonomy and autonomy of the moral is noted.[179] The assumption that Christian faith is required to make the moral binding shows scant respect for human "reason as a principle and yardstick of the moral."[180] "Because it lives by the faith, the Christian ethos gives moral action a degree of certainty that can never be attained by purely rational argument."[181]

In their estimate of the relevance of Christian belief to a Christian ethos and a theological ethic, the representatives of *Glaubensethik* differ in principle from the upholders of an "autonomous morality." The theological ethicist of the two camps agree that there are specifically Christian orientations (of belief, hope, and love) that have their basis in Christ's redemptive action, and that the Bible contains a number of concrete moral demands. What they do not agree on is whether the commands and demands that accompany the manifestation of God's redemptive intent in Jesus Christ are recognizable by, and binding on, the faithful only, or are accessible to the same degree to nonreligious, rational moral reflection, and whether they must indeed be so accessible if their content is to be morally binding.[182]

It is the *glaubensethische* position that the content of a Christian ethic is determined by a specific assessment of man or of humanness. The question concerning the content of the Christian ethic is therefore the same as the "question concerning those relationships between God and man, and between the saved among each other, that are the effects of the spirit of God or of love and not the result of any objective conditions but transcend those conditions in favor of the new man that God intends."[183] Regarding the relationships that obtain among men, it is not objective principle—that is, urgencies, values, and meanings deriving from man's physical nature and intersubjectivity—that apply. What is relevant is that the Christian "view of man that establishes a positive moral relation between him and his fellow as a matter of principle, i.e. a relation of mutual help or of being-there-for others."[184]

The dichotomy of autonomous reason and Christian rational faith that the *Glaubensethik* postulates is the expression of a fundamental mistrust of the power of scientifically discoverable urgencies and laws. Whenever in discussing man it is asked what is objectively given and what the normative relevance of these givens is, *Glaubensethik* suspects that man himself is being betrayed.[185] In the name of a total image of man, it takes the moral reason of the Christian as the expression of a specifically Christian concept of God, and this is why the reason of faith with an autonomous, innerworldly reason must be contrasted with it.

For the *Glaubensethiker*, the moral reason of the Christian is indissolubly tied to his faith and can neither be understood nor realized without it. According to Joseph Ratzinger, it is Christ himself who furnished the model: "in saying who would be admitted to, who excluded from, God's Kingdom, he established an indissoluble link between this central theme of his sermons and the fundamental moral decisions that flow from the image of God and are an intimate part of it."[186] To speak of an autonomy of the moral in the Christian sense, therefore, means surrendering the reason of faith to the spirit of the times. Only when the moral "is an indissoluble element in the fundamental concept of what is Christian"[187] is a distinctively Christian ethic preserved. That is why, in moral matters, belief "includes fundamental decisions that are substantive in nature."[188]

Preliminary Critical Examination of Fromm's Humanistic Ethic

Now that we have sketched the background of the questions raised by a theological ethic, we can undertake a preliminary critical appraisal of Fromm's humanistic ethic. The above section on the self-understanding of contemporary theological ethics suggests that the distinction between the discovery of norms and the grounding of meaning should be retained, but that attention should be focused on the discovery of norms. The problem of the ultimate grounding of normativeness and moral norms raises the question how a humanism that understands itself as the negation of any and every theonomy can be grounded. We refer to the comments on "humanistic religion," especially the "mysticism of the ONE"[189] and the reflections on Fromm's understanding of humanism and the grounding of it, in Part Three of this study.[190]

*The Search for a Natural "Unbeliebigkeit"**
of Human Normativeness

Despite decisively different approaches to the question of the ultimate grounding of the moral, there is a wide area of agreement between a theological ethic in the sense of "autonomous morality" and a humanistic ethic as Fromm understands it. The autonomy of the moral is the point of departure for both ethics, and both reject authoritarian and absolute ethics, be they fundamentalist or decisionist, be they inaugurated by ecclesiastical, social, or political entities.[191] Both ethics also agree that the cultural and ethnic diversity of ethics does not justify ethical relativism, that the factual validity of norms and convictions does not guarantee that the norms in question are moral ("socially immanent ethics"[192]), and that the natural substructure man shares with all other living beings does not imply moral normativeness ("biologically immanent ethics").[193]

In considering how moral norms can be found—Fromm speaks somewhat imprecisely of "objectively valid norms and values"—the theological and the humanistic ethic premise man's right and capacity to discover norms through his reason.[194] But they can do this "rationally" only if they view man's reason itself as a "part and function of a human nature"[195] to which human reason must address itself. Human nature is something with which reason must deal; it is also anterior to it. Yet reason interprets, orders, and shapes this nature. As a reason that discovers and decides, it is a normative principle.[196]

* non-optionality, non-arbitrariness; *unbeliebig*: not left to discretion, in some sense compulsory. See also n. 198.—ED.

The fact that reason is tied to human nature means that in the discovery of norms, it is the human and social sciences[197] that must be made the starting point for a discovery of the "natural *Unbeliebigkeit*"[198] of human normativeness. The significance of these empirical sciences is not so much that they can demonstrate the natural nonarbitrariness of an individual and singular norm, but rather that they provide those data and materials through which it becomes possible to arrive at "laws of human normativeness that are general by virtue of the logic of their claim."[199] Such an ultimate natural *Unbeliebigkeit* that is anterior to all concrete material forms of normativeness and grounds these must hold for all men. It cannot be discretionary, and the claim to being a determinant that lies in its *Unbeliebigkeit* notwithstanding, it can have no more than a predisposing role as regards possible forms of humanness, moral norms, and possible moralities.[200] Finally, it must be applicable when one attempts to understand either an individual personality or social entities and their reciprocal dependence.[201]

Fromm's humanistic ethic presupposes the knowledge of an ultimate natural *Unbeliebigkeit*, a knowledge that comes from investigating the possibilities and the specific conditions of human existence ("*conditio humana*"). With his definition of the "nature of man" as that of a contradictory being who has inalienable human needs, and with his identification of certain character orientations, he has demonstrated an *Unbeliebigkeit* that is universally applicable and that exerts a binding and decisive claim on all persons in regard to the kinds of existence they can lead, their potential for development, the elaboration of moralities and their realizability. It is the peculiarity of human needs that they must be responded to, and it is the task of character to structure the response to these needs in a particular way. Needs and character orientations match each other and represent laws of human normativeness that have a generally predisposing function.[202]

Character as the Principle of the Methodological Unity of Empirical Data, Philosophical-Anthropological Reflection, and the Creation of Ethical Norms

The significance of Fromm's attempt to define the natural *Unbeliebigkeit* of man's being and acting lies first in the way he arrives at its definition. His method must be distinguished from "phenomenological" analyses of human existence that have their basis primarily in reflection on the *conditio humana* or some human essence that is posited *a priori*, and not in the diverse possibilities of humanness that can be discovered with the help of the empirical sciences.[203] Fromm's method also differs from the many attempts to formulate a psychological, sociological, ethological, biological, or other kind of anthropology that relies on the various sciences and their findings.[204] These attempts are unsatisfactory. Where they use empirical data, their contribution is from the perspective of a particular science and employs the insights of a particular science (e.g., psychoanalysis) to investigate phenomena that come under the purview of another scientific discipline (e.g., conflicts between social groups). Although the aim of such anthropologies is the formulation of a more complex understanding of man, they attain this goal only by universalizing a particular perspective—the sociological one, for example. Such an anthropology does not develop a method that does justice to the various aspects of the object under study.

The difficulty that attends the discovery of a method that will do justice to the various aspects of an object relates principally to the twofold aspect of man, as individual personality and as social entity. From the point of view of the sciences that investigate this twofold aspect of man, the primary task is to combine a psychological and a sociological approach in a method that will do justice to both aspects. Fromm, however, developed a method that takes seriously the unity of man as individual and as social being. The principle that connects both aspects is man's character, which unfolds in accordance with man's aspects as both individual and social character. Seen ideal-typically, character may be defined in terms of various character orientations. In contrast to Freud's concept of character as instinctual, Fromm believes a person's dominant character orientation is the result of the shaping influence of socioeconomic conditions. The character orientation that prevails in a society molds the individual's character through the family, which is the psychic agency of society. Consequently, man's unity as individual and as part of society is guaranteed in the entity called character, which combines both aspects.

This functional view of character as a substitute for animal instinct permits Fromm to do justice in yet another respect to the variety of perspectives under which man may be seen. Behavioral research, which is based on comparisons between man and animal, nonetheless offers no precise definition for the relationship between the two. Since it postulates a merely analogous relationship, it is not really prepared to think about the specific differences that distinguish man as a culture-creating being. But when character is understood as a substitute for the animal's instinctual apparatus that is adequate to the possibilities and limitations of the human species, the unity of man is preserved and the method of the scientific investigation of man has its unified ground in the concept of character.

Fromm developed a specific view of the empirical human and social sciences as perspectives on man according to which these sciences are unified in a sociopsychological method based on the concept of character. Before we evaluate his philosophical and anthropological reflections that are based on his empirical insights, we will examine the significance of some of his findings for a theological ethic.

The Empirical Data and Their Significance for an Ethical Perspective

The discovery of character as a dynamic entity is the achievement of Freud. The term *dynamic character* means that it is character that predisposes and determines human behavior. Although this insight is part of the very foundation of psychoanalysis and analytic psychotherapy, it has hardly been considered in theological ethics, partly because of the strong influence American behaviorism has had on European thought, and partly because of academic psychology's aversion to psychoanalysis. Behind both phenomena lies a positivistic concept of science that cannot penetrate beyond the behavior of the individual. While behavior is seen as motivated and directed, inquiry does not address itself to a character that orients behavior. If character were an object of scientific interest, man would no longer be observed, measured, and judged exclusively by his behavior. Instead, behavior would be understood as the expression of a character that has been shaped in a particular way. Identical or similar forms of behavior (such as the readiness to help others) would then have to be seen as qualities of altogether different characters (loving or domineering, for example), while quite divergent forms of behavior (loving and hating, e.g.) could be viewed as expressions of one and the same (i.e., the authoritarian) character. Only the attempt to investigate the character of an individual and a society can lead to a better understanding of their behavior. Knowledge of character makes plausible the most widely divergent forms of behavior of an identical subject because all behavior is grounded in character.

The understanding of human behavior as the expression of a specific character can already be found in the theological and philosophical and ethical tradition, specifically in Aristotle's doctrine of the moral virtues and, more importantly, in Thomas Aquinas' theory of the virtues that are the result of training.[205] Especially where human behavior was evaluated morally, and moral and pedagogic criteria and contents were needed, the doctrine of the virtues could convey a deeper understanding of man, without an expressly empirical method. In contrast to the doctrine of virtues and its understanding of man, casuistics is not interested in the habits that determine behavior. Its reduction of man to his behavior is also characteristic of positivistic behaviorism in psychology and social psychology and in so-called analytic ethics.[206]

Fromm's theory of character can be seen as an attempt to use the modern human and social sciences to provide a new foundation for the traditional doctrine of virtues. There is an obvious affinity between Fromm's and Aquinas' understanding of man. It is Fromm's achievement to have provided a scientific explication of this understanding, and to have done so by utilizing his sociopsychological method: he adopts Freud's dynamic concept of character and the insight that the various character traits of an individual are structured, but he takes the concept out of the framework of the instinctivist libido theory. In this way, Fromm arrives at a new definition of character orientations that does justice to man's unity as individual and social being. At the same time, he introduces a principle of classification of the various character orientations, according to which they are judged as either life-promoting or life-inhibiting.

In a theological ethics, the ideal-typically formulated orientations in man's relation to his natural and social environment represent empirical data by which the causes, motivations, and goals of human behavior can be interpreted comprehensively.

Since character orientations also represent economic conditions and production processes and the social and political structures and concepts of value that are their function, they are concentrations or condensations of the world in which—and of the human beings among whom—they exist. In their specific orientation, they can therefore serve as keys to a detailed understanding of human behavior. Specifying an individual's character orientation makes possible an inclusive interpretation of his behavior because in a given character orientation the various determinants of human behavior are understood as a unity.

An example of the relevance of these comments for a theological ethic follows:

A child is given money by his parents to buy a friend a birthday present. Instead of spending the entire sum on the present, the child secretly saves half of it.

A casuistic morality of whatever description will attempt to measure the moral quality of this act by what the child actually did. It will also consider certain circumstances in order to mitigate or avoid the severity of a statement that the child's act is intrinsically good or bad. Finally it may be content with the observation that a truly serious moral conflict is not involved here.[207] An ethical consideration that makes use of the human and social sciences to examine the child's behavior will attempt to discover its determinants. This means that it will try first to understand that behavior, and then to make a moral judgment based on insights into the conditions of that behavior.

In the effort to show the logic of the child's behavior, Fromm would go back to character as the dispositive and determinant entity. For if the behavior can be shown to be the expression of a particular character orientation, the other social, cultural, political, religious, and economic determinants that are represented in a given character orientation will become apparent and a comprehensive understanding of the child's behavior will be possible.

In our example, it seems plausible to interpret the child's behavior as avarice. "Avarice" is a character trait that probably, though not necessarily, belongs to Fromm's hoarding orientation (the degree of certainty with which a form of behavior can be ascribed to a character orientation depends on how precise the description is). The fact that the child did not use the money he kept to buy candy or something else he wanted but put it aside, and the fact that he acted surreptitiously, support the classification "hoarding." Assuming that the child's behavior can be determined to flow from the strong dominance of a hoarding character orientation, inferences can be drawn about the social situation of the child's family, the educational maxims he has been exposed to, the nature of the parent-child relation, the family's bourgeois response to the capitalist economic order, the importance of money in interpersonal relations, the social order in which rank is determined by the magnitude of one's fortune, concepts of value according to which the accumulation and saving of money are seen as ways to achieve happiness, and so on. And all this makes possible further inferences about other forms of behavior and character traits that are also typical of a hoarding orientation. Beyond that, certain boundary lines can be predicted within which, given certain demands, the child's behavior will run its course.

From this example, it becomes apparent that man's behavior is the expression of a character orientation that has a typical structure. It follows that behavior is not a matter of choice: ascribing behavior to a character orientation makes the child's actions plausible. But this example also shows that the attempt to understand behavior brings to light the whole complexity of an individual's aspects and their interconnectedness. This makes moral judgment considerably more difficult, yet no ethics can renounce the effort to understand human behavior before pronouncing judgment.

Fromm's attempt to use the character concept to understand man in his totality affects both ethical perspective and moral pedagogy. It is only within the field defined by the character orientation that governs behavior that an individual's actions can be judged or changed. Where a given orientation such as the hoarding one is clearly dominant and behavioristic methods are used to promote a better adaptation to social, professional, or other demands through stimulus-response techniques, behavioral changes can only be expected within this hoarding orientation. This conclusion also applies to moral pedagogy that believes it can change man through his consciousness (by information, sermonizing, catechism, etc.) without taking him seriously in his manifold dependencies and entanglements (two thousand years of Christian moral education are eloquent testimony to the failure of the attempt to change man by piecemeal adaptation). A genuine change of behavior becomes possible only when, along with personal and intellectual effort, an effort is also made to change the factors that shape character so that a shift in the dominance of the character orientation occurs.

The fact that behavior is determined by the orientation of the character structure also affects the moral judgment of behavior. That character governs behavior means that the factors that mold character must be included in the moral judgment. Man has a creative responsibility that always extends to the economic, social, political, and cultural spheres, since these all have a share in the molding of character. Thus moral judgment can never be reduced to the moral judgment of concrete instances of behavior.

In questions concerning individual guilt, it is not possible to abstract from existing dispositive factors. Here it is not a matter of asking how an immoral act can be explained, and thereby excused, and substituting this approach for an inquiry into personal culpability. To distinguish between subjective guilt and objective conditions, and to excuse subjective error by citing objective factors that cause culpability, is no more acceptable. If flawed objective conditions are not seen as the responsibility of the subject, the concept of guilt will be reduced to subjective behavior and a process that will cause the perpetuation of subjective misconduct will be institutionalized. To give the question of personal responsibility for flawed behavior its correct place value, two things are necessary. One, the fact that socioeconomic factors shape the character structure and are dispositive and determinative of behavior must be taken seriously; and two, it must be realized that man has a decisive responsibility for these forces and can therefore be culpable. Of course, this makes the problem of guilt and the moral judgment of behavior more difficult. On the other hand, to distinguish between varying degrees of guilt and to make behavior the only yardstick is questionable when the relevant moral entity is the character and the forces that conditioned it, not the actual behavior in question. The understanding of man in his totality and on the basis of an insight into the complexity of conditions that predispose his behavior is something we owe to the human and social sciences. In Fromm's concept of character, the conditions are given a unity that brings the various influences together in a single entity: the character structure with a particular dominant orientation.

The significance of the empirical data in Fromm's social psychology is not limited to the understanding of character and the formulation of specific orientations of the character structure. The observation of the various character orientations with reference to their total functionality or dysfunctionality yields *an evaluation of character structures* that remains empirical and does not yet imply an ethical judgment, although it is relevant to one. The origin of the idea of evaluating character orientations must be looked for in Fromm's psychotherapeutic practice. He observed that certain kinds of relatedness to the world and to others occur with greater frequency among persons who suffer neurotic symptoms, and that an analytical therapy is successful when the nature of the relatedness to the environment changes. The change in the kind of relatedness is an expression of the fact that the dominance of the orientation of the character structure has altered. Orientations that become clear in psychoanalytic therapy and can be called "sick" or "healthy" apply generally to every individual human being and to the character of social entities. There are dominances in character orientations that further both the individual and society, and therefore promote a well-being and happiness based on the freedom to realize one's own life. There are others that enslave men and turn them into cripples, and admit of human well-being only on the basis of unfreedom and the surrender of one's independence—cases where, in line with what is dominant, apparent well-being turns into illness and unhappiness.

During the course of his life, Fromm provided a number of reformulations of the distinctive qualities of character orientations, partly because he wished to emphasize aspects he had not emphasized previously and partly because he wanted to arrive at the most comprehensive understanding possible. They are always expressed as opposites, the fundamental antithetical character orientations being almost always present simultaneously and in a mixture so that the only question to be settled is whether a nonproductive or a productive orientation is dominant. The paired opposites are: productive/nonproductive; active/passive; biophilic/necrophilic (or syndrome of growth/syndrome of decay); mode of having/mode of being. Whatever aspect the character orientations are viewed under, one orientation always inhibits unfolding and the other always furthers it. If the character structure is productive and biophilic and thus oriented toward growth, man lives in the mode of being—that is, he lives from within himself, rationally, immediately, related in love: he lives by being himself. But if the character structure is nonproductive and necrophilic and therefore oriented toward decay, man lives in the mode of having—that is, he *is* only to the extent that he *has*, be it property, education, family, honor, children, laws, others who control him or whom he can control: he lives only to the extent that he owns things.

Fromm's evaluation of the character orientations in terms of two opposing, fundamental possibilities of living one's life was the result of observations he carried out with the aid of the empirical human and social sciences, and of his assumption that the concept of character is to be understood as a principle that gives coherence to all observations. The evaluations express man's fundamental intentions, according to which he can conduct himself. In the concept of the orientation of a character structure, the intentionality of the reality that is man is thus interpreted with reference to two alternative potentialities. But this definition of the character orientation does not imply a moral judgment. The question as to which orientations are to be preferred, which are morally good, cannot be answered merely by understanding the intentionality of the character structure toward unfolding or inhibition. The ethical question transcends the sphere of the empirical, of the data of the human and social sciences, because empirical knowledge does not unambiguously tell us what is morally good and what is morally evil. Even so, the furthering and unfolding of life is a definition that results from the very intentionality of character and therefore makes a dispositive normative claim.

This distinction between the evaluation of the character orientations and the question of moral judgment—that is, between the normative claim of empirical data and a moral norm that transcends empirical knowledge—demonstrates the *critical contribution that Fromm's insight based on empirical data* can make to an ethical perspective. Because character orientations can be defined as "life promoting" or "life inhibiting" within the sociopsychological context without its therefore being possible to decide what is morally good, empirical data can be used to criticize existing ethics and the convictions by which people live. On the basis of his empirical concept of character, Fromm is in a position to criticize an economic order whose only concern is maximizing the gross national product, and to oppose a philosophical and anthropological view that postulates the *homo homini lupus* thesis or the notion of the *bellum omnium contra omnes*. Again on the basis of empirical data, he can criticize a traditional natural law ethic for incorrectly identifying natural and moral value. Fromm's concept of character thus has a threefold critical function: it evaluates other empirical data, other philosophical-anthropological assumptions, and other ethical arguments. Beyond its critical function, the concept of character has a constructive use for philosophical-anthropological reflection and the creation of ethical norms.

The Philosophical-Anthropological Reflections and Their Significance for an Ethical Point of View

Ethics is a hermeneutic discipline that arrives at moral judgment by way of a philosophical-anthropological interpretation of empirical data. In this process, the philosophical-anthropological interpretation has its own scientific place value. Rather than simply interpreting empirical data to achieve a more comprehensive understanding of man, it begins with the fundamental fact that man is endowed with reason and then takes this fact into account as it confronts empirical data. Not just empirical insights are decisive in the explication of philosophical-anthropological reflections but also certain preferred forms of thought and conceptual models that are rooted in the thinker's own philosophical and religious traditions.[208]

Fromm's philosophical-anthropological reflections are thematized in *the question concerning man's nature or being*. Two elements form the starting point of his thought: the gift of reason by which man differs from the animals; and the character of man, which represents the principle of unity of individual and society, of economic, political, social, cultural, religious, and other shaping factors, and in which all behavior insofar as it expresses relatedness to the surrounding world has its base. Both elements come together in Fromm's definition of character as a substitute for animal instinct. In man, character takes on the functions that are discharged by instinct in animals *and* it is the expression of man's reason. This definition of character legitimizes philosophical-anthropological reflection—namely, as reflection about the changes that occur in man as the security instinct gives is lost.

The comparison between man and animal that is based on the premise that human character replaces animal instinct is amplified by Fromm into a question about the unity or harmony of animal and man and their environment ("nature"). Viewed formally, he examines the original sociopsychological situation that obtains as man is born (both individual man and the species mankind, whose birth continues to this day) in order to determine what general biological and particular (socio)psychological relevance the gift of reason and the formation of character, accompanied by the concurrent loss of instinct, may have. Thought about the specifically human situation leads to the insight that man must be defined as a contradictory being. The contradiction that defines his nature is grounded in reason itself, for reason is the counterprinciple to the instinct that governs autoplastic behavior. Endowment with reason means that humanness, in contrast to animal existence, is not a given but a task. There are solutions to the contradictoriness of human existence, but no resolution of the contradictoriness itself. Character represents the specifically human agency that mediates the task of humanness. Its orientations are types of possible reaction to this contradictoriness.

The relevance for ethics of the philosophical-anthropological definition of human nature only becomes apparent when the fact that human existence is a task is interpreted with references to certain inalienable existential needs. In contrast to anthropologies that define man's being ethologically and with reference to his animal ancestors, and discover in the parallelism between animal behavior and patterns of human interaction ultimate inescapable structures of the species man,[209] Fromm views the existential needs as ultimately not-optional (*unbeliebig*). An understanding of these needs is stimulated by empirical data but born of reflection about man as a contradictory being, and then confirmed, in turn, by empirical data. It can be said very generally that character is the human reaction to man as contradictory being, and that the various character orientations represent the answers (both productive and nonproductive) that can be given to this contradiction at a particular moment. The orientations of the character relate to the explications of man's contradictory existence. They are kinds of reaction to various questions that are understood as needs and that interpret the one contradiction. Fromm's postulate of existential needs is the fruit of his philosophical-anthropological reflection about an empirical concept of character that initially provokes, and later confirms, philosophical-anthropological reflection.

Since man always and everywhere has existential needs, renouncing their satisfaction is as impossible in the long run as not satisfying physical hunger or thirst. These needs inescapably shape human life and action, not by how they are satisfied, but by the fact that they must be satisfied. For this reason, every human being is primordially related to his natural and human environment and must remain so throughout his life. This is true even of the narcissistic or psychotic individual who has a wholly disrupted relation to his environment. "According to nature"—that is, to the extent that he reacts with his reason to the contradiction between nature and reason—man is a social being (*homo socialis*). His existential needs for the experience of identity are inescapable, as are his needs for rootedness, transcendence, and a frame of orientation and an object of devotion. Every act and every form of behavior is a certain kind of reaction to these needs. The fact that every human being always and necessarily reacts to existential needs signifies an ultimate natural *Unbeliebigkeit* about what humanness is and what it ought to be. It is here that the existential needs have direct relevance for an ethical perspective. Existential needs are normative, for although they do not decide whether an individual will react morally or immorally in a given instance, they do point up the natural constraints within which moral action becomes possible. Thus they are the natural ground for human, moral action. The fact that existential needs must be met becomes obvious whenever changes in the process of production or the social order, for example, in the hierarchy of values or the structure of meanings, limit or altogether suppress the possibility of reaction to existential needs. Dehumanization and psychological and physical death are the consequences. In such a situation, man will normally attempt to find substitute objects to satisfy his needs. A living religion, for instance, can never be "abolished" by decree or by the threat of reprisals unless the world view that functions as a substitute religion (or a party ideology) at least comes close to substituting for the many-sided religious phenomenon. Where no such substitute for a frame of orientation and an object of devotion is created or permitted, interest in life is paralyzed, and this paralysis is expressed in psychic and psychosomatic illnesses, even widespread suicide and the decline of civilization.[210]

To recapitulate: Existential needs are the direct result of man's nature as a contradiction. Because they must be satisfied, they represent ultimate constraints on human normativeness. While the manner of their satisfaction does not necessarily derive from reflection on human nature, observations made when the factors affecting the satisfaction of needs undergo change clearly show that there are only two fundamental possibilities for the satisfaction of needs and that these are alternatives. They correspond to the valuations of the character orientations, which are nothing other than ideal-typical answers to the whole question of the contradictory being that is man: the reaction to existential needs is necessarily either productive and biophilous, or nonproductive and necrophilous.

As regards an ethical perspective, it should be noted that it is not only the necessity to satisfy needs that grounds human-moral action in nature but also the fact that man must always react in either/or fashion to his existential needs. Wherever man reacts to his existential needs, he necessarily satisfies them either productively or nonproductively, and this alternative forms part of the conditions under which human action as moral action first becomes possible.[211]

Formally stated, man's freedom to react to his needs can be reduced to the freedom of choice between a productive and a nonproductive satisfaction. But such a definition does not mean that the productive reaction is morally good. The question concerning moral norms is answered neither by demonstrating the natural *Unbeliebigkeit* of human normativeness nor by recognizing the natural value that productive satisfaction is life promoting. The productive satisfaction of needs can become a moral norm only when man decides to affirm as morally good natural values that are life promoting. Of course, the ability to affirm them is predicated on the insight into the ultimate, naturally given *Unbeliebigkeit* of being a creature of need that is part and parcel of man's specific situation. It also hinges on the investigations of natural values by the human and social sciences. The natural *Unbeliebigkeit* of being a creature of need constitutes the ultimate natural ground of human, moral action as such. The various existential needs and the necessarily alternative reaction to them are therefore ultimate natural grounds of moral action, grounds on which those natural values that are dispositive and determinative of moral action are based.

The critical contribution of philosophical-anthropological reflection is threefold. First, the claim to autonomy of philosophical-anthropological reflection grounds a criticism of such empirical research that refuses in principle to go beyond empirical data and to inquire into a certain understanding of man. From the perspective of the theory of science, such a positivist reduction to "empiricism" is an attempt to veil the fact that certain prior, mostly unreflected, understandings underlie all research in the human and social sciences. The demand to reflect on these prior understandings is tantamount to the postulate that philosophical-anthropological reflection is autonomous.

When, because of a certain view of man, communication between empirical research and reflection is neglected or rejected in principle as unscientific, empirical research evades evaluation of its scientific program and of certain specific presuppositions and consequences of research. A critique of a research project that wishes to discover, for example, how to improve the mechanisms of persuasion through which certain consumer needs might be more effectively stimulated so that these artificially produced needs enjoy the same claim to satisfaction as inalienable physiological and existential needs—such a critique is possible only when the intrinsic value of philosophical and anthropological reflection is first acknowledged and its significance for empirical research not denied.

The critical function of philosophical-anthropological reflection for the empirical human and social sciences embraces more than a critique of the position that empirical research is not influenced by the question concerning the image of man. As the above example makes clear, Fromm's philosophical and anthropological reflections criticize any understanding of the human and social sciences that excludes all ethical questions *a priori*. Beyond this, the formulation of existential needs yields a substantive critique that can be used to examine empirical data and research to discover whether their effect is dehumanizing or furthers the unfolding of human potentialities. The analysis of man as a contradictory being with defined existential needs thus implies a criticism of the insights of the human and social sciences in their entirety when they set ethical questions aside, and of their individual insights when they contribute to preventing the satisfaction of existential needs.

Fromm's philosophical and anthropological reflections provide a further critical contribution. In contrast to other philosophical and anthropological definitions of man, his statements are coordinated with empirical data and have a principle of methodical unity, the concept of character. They can thus criticize ways of understanding man that do not include an empirically tangible entity (such as character) in which the most widely divergent aspects of human existence come together. Their critique addresses itself principally to anthropologies whose point of departure is either an underived definition of being, which they interpret, or whose basis is some ascertainable aspect (such as the biological or psychological; or man's *natura physica, homo faber, homo oeconomicus, homo ludens,* etc.), which they universalize. Substantively, they criticize either the missing relation to the empirical or the claim to an encompassing definition that shows no methodical unity of aspects and therefore fails to overcome a substantive perspectivism.

Finally, the philosophical-anthropological reflections are capable of criticizing attempts at ethical normativeness that either elevate a natural value to a moral norm and favor a casuistic natural law, or that represent an ethical relativism that denies the possibility of binding natural values. Ethical norms are not the arbitrary creations of a situation, culture, or period, but are grounded in ultimate natural *Unbeliebigkeiten* that can be defined as particular existential needs and their alternative satisfactions. It is only because they have intrinsic value that the philosophical-anthropological reflections can make a contribution to the problem of hom ethical norms are created. Philosophical-anthropological reflections are not empirical data, but a constructive interpretive frame that has its ground in empirical data. Neither are they moral norms, but rather their natural ground.

Summary: Ethical Norms as Based on a Human-Natural "Unbeliebigkeit"

Whether a humanistic ethic can contribute to the discovery of norms in a theological ethic depends in part on the self-understanding of theological ethics. If theological ethics understands itself as "autonomous morality within the Christian context,"[212] it must have recourse to empirical data and philosophical and anthropological reflection because where decisions of moral reason are involved, it depends on the knowledge of natural *Unbeliebigkeiten* as generally dispositive laws. In the process of discovery of norms, however, metaphysics and faith make no claim to determine the content of ethical norms.[213] Both a theological and a humanistic ethic demand that the moral be autonomous.[214] Consequently, the problem of the discovery of norms and of ethical normativeness is the same for both ethics. Therefore one may justifiably ask what contribution Fromm's humanistic ethic makes to the process of discovery of norms in a theological ethic.

Both ethics follow Thomas Aquinas in seeing the principle and the criterion of the moral in man's reason: actions are called "human or moral insofar as they are determined by reason."[215] This identification of humanity, morality, and reason demands the rejection of any heteronomy in the definition of the content of the moral. Neither God nor society, nor an idea nor nature (as in the stoic "living according to nature"), nor the empirical data of the modern human and social sciences, but only human reason can be the principle of moral action. "What is proper for man lies in *'secundum rationem esse,'* in the orientation toward reason which is the real principle of human action. That is why we call those manners and morals good that agree with reason, and bad those that contradict it."[216]

It has already been shown that reason as the reason that cognizes and decides can be a normative principle only if it is understood as a component of a human nature that is antecedent to reason and something with which reason must deal. The reason that makes moral decisions is thus part of a complex network of natural conditions and must respect these natural structures and mechanisms as nonarbitrary.[217] When reason takes cognizance of natural structures and mechanisms, it discovers "that the rationality of natural ends (*inclinationes naturales*) points in the same direction as human reason."[218] Although it is true that reason as the agency of moral decisions alone determines what is good and what is evil, reason itself rests on what an antecedent nature intends. And although it is also true that it is not the empirical or nature but reason that is the principle of the moral, the substantive definition of moral norms and values is nonetheless tied to the knowledge of natural values and norms.

Any attempt to establish ethical norms in which reason is the principle of the moral must be able by its method to do justice to the interdependence of reason and nature in man. Fromm's achievement and his contribution to a theological ethic are to have defined the character of this interdependence on the basis of man's empirically ascertainable rational nature, and to have introduced the concept of character to give systematic unity to his idea. This assertion will now be explained.

If reason as the principle in establishing norms must refer to human nature and its fundamental intentionalities when it defines the contents of the moral, an *Unbeliebigkeit* of natural structures and mechanisms that is relevant to moral action can be discovered only where this human nature is addressed as governed by reason. Already in the formulation of the problem human nature must not be defined "biologically," as if man's biological or physiological nature were complemented by a psychological and intellectual one. From the very beginning, human nature must be understood as determined by reason and therefore as inquiring and modifiable. In questions involving man and his nature, this human nature must always be antecedently defined as rational nature. Fromm succeeds in this approach because both in his research in the human and social sciences and in his philosophical and anthropological reflection he starts with a primary understanding of human nature whose defining characteristic is the substitution for instinct.[219]

The assumption that human nature is guided by instinct or that it is quasi-instinctual turns out to be false because in the genesis of man there is a cause-and-effect relationship between the gift of reason and the loss of instinct. The situation that results from the presence of reason is seen by Fromm as the *conditio humana*, and he makes use of his knowledge of the human and social sciences to reflect on this birth of man. Reflection leads to the insight that it is not instinctual needs but certain rational and therefore "human" or "existential" needs that express man's natural *Unbeliebigkeit*. The fact that these human needs are rooted in man's reason and that their adequate satisfaction is possible only through reason justifies Fromm's assertion that character is the substitute for animal instinct, for it is only in and through character that man's nature can be appropriately appreciated. Character makes it possible to take man seriously in his relatedness to his surrounding world and to refuse to reduce his biological nature to the sociological. Only in character is the psychic quality of human nature respected and not limited to the merely physiological (instinct).

Fromm's characterological definition of human nature does justice to two facts: that human nature is determined by reason, and that human reason is governed by nature. In man, nature is always characterologically mediated rational nature. Because man is preserved in his wholeness, ultimate natural conditions and laws represent ultimate human-natural *Unbeliebigkeit*.

It is initially in the empirical concept of character as a substitute for animal instinct that the interdependence of man's reason and nature is respected. But the empirical concept of character entails that of human needs, a concept that is also significant in philosophical and anthropological reflection. Methodologically, therefore, empirical insights guide philosophical-anthropological reflection. Because "character" and "need" have been defined as rational, not only the empirical but also the philosophical-anthropological insights are legitimated as scientific insights. A positivism that limits itself to purely empirical research and disputes the cognitive value of philosophical and anthropological reflection must be viewed as a truncated and falsified version of the very idea of science.

Fromm's proposal can serve as a model for a theological ethic that confronts the problem of mediating empirical and philosophical-anthropological forms of thought and knowledge by attempting, for example, to "integrate" the findings of the human and social sciences philosophically and anthropologically. In his work, both levels, the empirical and the philosophical-anthropological, are brought into relation as the problem is formulated, and the concepts of "need" and "character" enable him to do justice to both levels. It should also be noted that a theological ethic whose distinctive characteristic is its grounding of the meaning of human normativeness will find useful a model for the discovery of ethical norms that takes seriously the autonomy of the moral, yet does not reject a grounding of the meaning of human normativeness that is independent of—though not without significance for—the discovery of norms. Fromm's model for the discovery of norms can accomplish this because in the task of discovering ethical norms, he recurs to a human and natural *Unbeliebigkeit* that is itself marked by this openness: human needs, especially the need for a frame of orientation and an object of devotion, imply the task of establishing a meaning that cannot be solved by the methods of empirical science or of philosophical-anthropological reflection alone. It is here that Fromm points to religion, even though he understands religion humanistically and nontheistically.

Finally, it is necessary to emphasize that the identification of what is ultimate human-natural *Unbeliebigkeit* is an important contribution to the problem of ethical normativeness. The determination of individual human needs is the result of reflection on man's situation that makes use of empirical, especially psychological and sociopsychological, findings. The distinctive rational quality of human nature means that man has certain needs that differ from physiological ones in that they represent an ultimate human-natural *Unbeliebigkeit* with respect to what man can and should be. Needs inescapably mold human normativeness because they must be reacted to either productively or nonproductively. This necessity to react in one of two ways becomes truly significant only when one examines individual needs, for in previous ethical models it cannot always be taken for granted that the need for relatedness and rootedness, or for a frame of orientation and an object of devotion was recognized as a natural *Unbeliebigkeit*.[220]

It is in problems of sexual ethics that the difference between the two perspectives becomes very clear. While the need for the preservation of the species in the form of sexual need cannot lay claim to making human normativeness generally choiceless, the need for relatedness is universal and inalienable and therefore the expression of an ultimate human and natural *Unbeliebigkeit.* Man must always react to this need. Sexual need has no universality, which means that it, in contrast, does not put constraints on what humans are and should be. Consequently, it must be subordinate to the need for relatedness. Sexuality can have a certain role as the need for relatedness is reacted to, but man's love (as a reaction to his need for relatedness) is not determined by his sexual need. This difference in the two needs as regards their claim to determine human normativeness is decisive and makes itself felt in specific problems of sexual and marital morality.

This example shows the significance of identifying and designating human needs as naturally *unbeliebig* and generally dispositive of human normativeness. The kind of reaction to such needs must still be determined, but the mere fact of identifying these needs is of decisive importance for the setting of ethical norms because that very identification entails a claim to shape normativeness not-optionally (*unbeliebig*).

Fromm's contribution to the problem of ethical norms goes beyond the designation of human needs to the insight that reaction to these needs must always be either productive or nonproductive, and that only a productive (biophilic) reaction does justice to human needs in the sense that it prevents the dysfunction of the system "man" and thus furthers man's unfolding. With the help of Fromm's theory of character, the productive reaction can be defined more precisely: Fundamentally, human beings and social entities can react to any human need in countless different ways. But the reactions in all their variety and distinctiveness still express either a dominant productive or a dominant nonproductive character orientation. The conduct of every individual and social entity is the expression of a character orientation. Therefore the moral quality of a form of behavior is defined by whether it expresses a productive or a nonproductive reaction to a human need. Consequently, there is a correspondence between, on the one hand, the ultimate and natural *Unbeliebigkeit* of reacting to needs, be it productively or nonproductively; and on the other hand, the distinctive quality of character orientations that shape human reactions not-optionally (*unbeliebig*), by qualifying them as productive or nonproductive.[221]

Part Three

SOURCES AND FORMS OF THE THOUGHT OF ERICH FROMM

6

SOURCES OF FROMM'S THOUGHT

MOSES MAIMONIDES: THE JEWISH TRADITION OF THE NEGATIVE KNOWLEDGE OF GOD

Fromm interprets God's revelation of his name to Moses (Exodus 3:14) as the expression of the idea of the nameless God.[1] Without entering into the exegetical problem in any detail, one can only see the interpretation of the revelation "I am who I am" as "my name is nameless"[2] as the extension of the ban on images to the "acoustic image," that is, the name, especially since, according to the Old Testament, name expresses being and the person who knows another's name has power over him.[3] Subsequently, the ban on images is an important source for the negative attitude of Judaism toward all theology as a "speaking about God." In contrast to Christianity, the Jewish tradition has incomparably stronger reservations about all dogmatic theology. The insistence on the doctrine of negative attributes—that is, on negative theology and ethics as the essence of religion—is correspondingly more marked. Jewish negative theology leads to the mysticism of the kabbala and Hasidism, on the one hand, and to a more or less rationalist philosophy of religion on the other.

Maimonides (Moses ben Maimon, 1135–1204) occupies a key position in these developments, for he not only offers a negative theology that was developed from Neoplatonism and influenced Meister Eckhart's mysticism but, through his study of Aristotle, he also became one of the principal representatives of medieval Jewish rationalism. Beyond that, history paradoxically (?) made him the guarantor of Jewish orthodoxy because he formulated the thirteen articles of the Jewish faith that are valid to this day.[4]

Fromm sees in Maimonides' formulation of the doctrine of God's negative attributes the logical development of the Old Testament concept of God and its negative interpretation. This place value of Maimonides in Fromm's critique of religion and in the self-representation of the Jewish understanding of religion calls for some scrutiny of Maimonides' negative theology.[5]

The starting point of Maimonides' Jewish *theologia negativa* is the question concerning God's attributes and the possibility of knowing them: Are there attributes that can describe God's nature—as Scripture does, for example, when it states that God is faithful, compassionate, and long-suffering, or jealous and wrathful—or do such attributes violate the ban on images that is meant to guarantee God's transcendence and unknowability? The answer is that God can only be assigned negative attributes.[6] For "with every application of a positive definition to God, he is made similar to the creatures, which means that a step is taken away from the knowledge of his true nature while with every additional negation that is proved necessary, the knowledge of God becomes more perfect."[7] The reasons for the impossibility of making a positive statement about God's nature derive from a philosophical and "theological" concept of God that cannot be conveyed by any kind of analogical thinking. Every positive statement about the nature of God is subject to the ambiguity of definition that requires *genus* and *differentia specifica.* "Such a difference that is based on the connection between genus and species must not exist between God and all that being that is not divine."[8] Maimonides' critique of an analogical mode of thought that makes positive statements about God's nature is aimed at those who include God's essential attributes and those of other beings in a single definition: "Similarity is based on a certain relation between two things; if between two things no relation can be found, there can be no similarity between them, and there is no relation between two things that have no similarity to each other."[9]

If it is impossible to make positive statements about God's nature, it would seem plausible to renounce any and every kind of knowledge of God. But Maimonides had to find a way toward the knowledge of God because the true knowledge of God is the foundation for his entire system. The way he finds is that of negation. Of course he could not advance his enterprise simply by negating

God's positive attributes, assuming there were legitimate positive attributes to begin with. His solution to the problem of negative attributes is to combine negation and privation: "It is not the positive attributes that are negated but those of privation."[10] For if attributes "merely negate imperfections but do not claim perfections,"[11] God's nature remains unaffected. "In order to pronounce the negative attributes without any qualms, it is necessary to connect with them the idea that they deny an imperfection in God which his very nature excludes."[12]

Man's knowledge of God grows "the more man succeeds in keeping false, inappropriate definitions away from him and understands his difference from any and every other kind of being. The specific function of this negative knowledge is that it banishes all imperfections from the idea of God."[13] This applies down to ultimate philosophical concepts: if it is asserted about God that he exists, this is not an attribution of being but a denial of nonbeing.[14] It is precisely this example that makes it clear that with his doctrine of negative attributes Maimonides teaches a *theologia negativa* that is not necessarily intent on dissolving theology.[15] Instead, he proposes that the understanding of the negation of attributes as the negation of privations makes possible a knowledge of God that "is based on a content of highest positivity."[16]

In his doctrine of attributes, Maimonides arrives at the conclusion "that there is no possibility of obtaining a knowledge of the true essence of God, and since it has also been proved that the only thing that man can apprehend of Him is the fact that He exists, all possible attributes are inadmissible."[17] Yet Scripture contains an abundance of statements that appear to be about God's nature. "Here, Maimonides . . . takes the same path as his Jewish and Muslim precursors when he understands the positive biblical statements about God in part as positive forms of statements that are actually negative, in part as statements not about the nature but about the workings of God."[18] To the extent that with the fact of God's existence, God is recognized as the supreme cause of being, positive statements can be made about the effects that emanate from him.[19] Maimonides connects this doctrine with Moses' request of God: "Now therefore, I pray thee, if I have found favor in thy sight, show me now thy ways, that I may know thee and find favor in thy sight . . ." (Exodus 33:13). God's answer,

Maimonides writes, is twofold: The petition "show me thy ways" is answered by God as follows: "I will make all my goodness pass before you" (Exodus 33:19); while he responds to the second petition by saying: "You cannot see my face" (Exodus 33:20).[20] Maimonides writes: "Consequently the knowledge of the works of God is the knowledge of His attributes, by which He can be known. The fact that God promised Moses to give him a knowledge of His works, may be inferred from the circumstance that God taught him such attributes as refer exclusively to His works, 'merciful and gracious, long-suffering and abundant in goodness etc.' "[21]

The Jewish tradition knows thirteen qualities of God's action that can be summarized in two attributes: "love and justice."[22] The meaning of such qualities of action, however, is not "that God really possesses qualities but that He performs actions similar to such of our actions as originate in certain qualities, i.e. in certain psychical dispositions; not that God really has such dispositions."[23] Qualities of action only seem to be statements about God, for the qualities ascribed to God are actually only descriptions of his effects, whose purpose it is to lead man to perfection: "for the chief aim of man should be to make himself as far as possible, similar to God: that is to say, to make his acts similar to the acts of God, or as our Sages express it in explaining the verse, 'Ye shall be holy': 'He is gracious, so be you also gracious; He is merciful, so be you also merciful.' "[24]

It must be noted that "every attribute predicated of God either denies the quality of an action, or—when the attribute is intended to convey some idea of the Divine Being itself, and not of His actions—the negation of the opposite."[25] The meaning of this doctrine of attributes is the pure knowledge of God, though that knowledge is realized only to the extent that God is denied attributes. "It will not be clear to you, that every time you establish by proof the negation of a thing in reference to God, you become more perfect, while with every additional positive assertion you follow your imagination and recede from the true knowledge of God . . . by affirming anything of God, you are removed from Him in two respects; first, whatever you affirm, is only a perfection in relation to us; secondly, He does not possess any thing superadded to the essence."[26]

According to Maimonides, it is actually "dangerous" to assign positive attributes to God because such assignment leads to polytheism[27] and furthers idol worship: "when we say that that essence which is called 'God' is a substance with many properties by which it can be described, we apply that name to an object which does not at all exist."[28] When man ascribes attributes to such an imaginary being, he projects his own positive attributes (which Maimonides considers capacities) onto the God he himself has created, and at the same time moves further and further away from his own being.[29] The strict observation of the ban on images in the sense of the negative knowledge of God prevents idol worship and *eo ipso* man's alienation. Of course, this negative theology can be effective only where the existence of an unknowable God is uncontested, for every attempt to name him also means the alienation of man as Maimonides understands it. Maimonides' application of the Neoplatonic *via negationis* to the Jewish concept of God produces a *theologia negativa* that proposes to return man from his alienation to himself and his own capacities, and can only accomplish this when—and to the extent that—it clings to the existence of this unknowable God. The true—negative—knowledge of God is not only the guarantee but also the condition that must be met if man is to be able to achieve his own perfection.[30]

The interpretation of the positive biblical statements about God's nature as statements about qualities of God's actions that are intended to induce man to take such action makes clear once again what this understanding of negative theology is. At the same time, it leads to a specifically "ethical" concept of God and religion that is characteristic of the Jewish philosophy of religion. Maimonides' *theologia negativa* disputes "those attributes of the divine being that cannot serve as model concepts for human actions."[31] This statement logically entails the demand that only "those of God's attributes may become the object of human and religious knowledge that define God's nature as the primordial image of morality."[32] God's nature can therefore be conceived only as the ideal of human action.[33] God does not even mean "the power from which man may derive his morality but merely the model, the pattern by which he is to guide his actions. The Jewish concept of God is thus exclusively one of the ethical meaning of the idea of God."[34] If the knowledge of God thus becomes knowledge of the laws of human action on the basis of which human acts become moral ones,[35] then every attempt to make positive statements about God's nature must be judged as the alienation of man in favor of an idolatry. But here also, it holds true that the alienation of man can only be prevented, and human acts only become moral ones, when a negative knowledge of God is the condition of their possibility.[36] "Without the 'He is gracious,' there is no 'Be you also gracious.' "[37]

Positive statements about God's nature are actually statements about what man ought to be, but only to the extent that statements about God's nature are statements about his effects. Clinging to the existence of God is an expression of negative theology and at the same time the condition for the possibility of affirmative and ethical statements about man.[38]

HERMANN COHEN: THE RELATIONSHIP OF ETHICS AND RELIGION IN THE JEWISH PHILOSOPHY OF RELIGION

In the history of the Jewish faith, the prophets play a central role because they interpret the knowledge of God as the ways of God that man is to walk. They are not concerned with the revelation of God's nature, for the knowledge of God teaches what man is to be. "The revelation of God and the revelation of what is moral in man come together in this way. . . . To search God means to strive for the good; to find God means to do the good."[39] This affinity of religion and morality found its most telling expression in the prophets. It is true of the Jewish faith in general and raises the question regarding the relationship between religion and ethics.[40]

Since the question concerning the relation of religion and ethics was reformulated by Kant, and since Hermann Cohen (1842–1918) was one of the most distinguished representatives not only of Neo-Kantianism but also of the enlightened "science of Judaism," and since, moreover, Fromm quotes Cohen time and again in his interpretation of what is Jewish, this relation will be demonstrated by showing how Hermann Cohen dealt with it.[41]

The prophetic tradition and the doctrine of negative attributes in Maimonides create a specifically Jewish concept of religion that cannot dispense with morality. "For religion also is morality, and it is only as morality that it is religion."[42] While in Christianity, knowledge of God as the belief "in the nature of God and in divine salvation" is the essence of religion and this belief "is elevated to the fundamental condition of human morality,"[43] it is ethos that is the essence of Jewish religion. Jewish knowledge of God means that only moral attributes may be predicated of him so that they may serve as a model for man's actions: "God's essence is morality and only morality."[44] The difference "between the only God and the many gods lies in the idea of morality"[45] because every positive statement about God's nature that does not relate to man's morality leads to idolatry.[46]

This understanding of God involves "his being turned into an idea that demands both the surrender of his metaphysical claims and the renunciation of all elaboration of him as a person. The transcendence of God can only be the transcendence of the idea. . . ."[47] "Idea" means that God has no actuality, "for actuality is a concept relating thought to sensation." Yet God is an ethical reality insofar as "ideas are archetypes of action."[48] God is the primordial image of morality and the real meaning of the idea of God is that "true morality can become real, will become real."[49] Where God is understood as idea, he is suprasensuous: something not to be described, reckoned, or understood; "neither a thing nor a lawful nexus nor a concept. But one can say what would not be if there were no God or, differently expressed: for what God 'lays the ground.' "[50] "God's being suprasensuous is the true precondition for moral effectiveness: namely, to serve as the basis for the moral state of mankind and of world history."[51] How religion and ethos (morality) become interchangeable in this concept of God is clearly stated by Hermann Cohen: "Ethics would be demeaned and religion obscured if God's significance were to be found beyond the realm of morality. The ethics intrinsic to God's nature, and that alone, constitutes religion in Judaism."[52]

God's functional transcendence[53]—which means that the idea of God becomes the principle of morality, and morality the essence of religion—makes one ask about the concept of religion and its relation to ethics as the science of morality. For Cohen, the Jewish self-understanding of religion is determined by the efforts of the prophets "to first turn the interest of men away from their worry about the gods. . . . But as this caused them to be seized by the thought of the good, they discovered the real meaning of the only

God."[54] (The concept of the "only" God stands for the distinctiveness of the "idea" of God as transcendence mentioned above.) But because the idea of God became the principle of morality and morality is religion, this concept of religion has a universal validity, and religion becomes justifiably a "religion of reason."[55]

According to Cohen, the question concerning the relation between ethics and religion must therefore start from a concept of religion in which religion as the religion of reason is turned into "a general function of human consciousness."[56] If ethics as the science of morality and the reflection of the ethos is determined by reason, then the answer to the question concerning the relation between an ethic governed by reason and a religion of reason is suggested. What is at stake here is nothing less than the question whether ethics is able "to master the entire content of the concept of man [or, if not, whether] religion on its part is able to fill this gap."[57]

For a long time, Cohen believed that in the relation between religion and ethics, "the introduction of Jewish-religious concepts into ethics had made religion superfluous."[58] Religion is only a historical presupposition, since ethics "takes the ideas created by the naïveté of the creative religious consciousness . . . beyond the religious stage . . . and gives them the certainty of autonomous moral insight. For the fully developed cultural consciousness, systematic ethics takes over the moral task of religion."[59] It is only in his late work[60] that Cohen discovers a distinctive quality of religion that, though it does not make it autonomous vis-à-vis ethics, yet signifies that religion adds something to ethics.[61] Ethics, which he saw as "wholly defined by the idea of the universal validity of the moral principle and which develops the moral idea of man exclusively from this perspective, therefore defines man as part of the All and sets for him the task of rising to the idea of the All."[62]

If religion is to have a place in ethics, it must have an idea of God that corresponds to the God of ethics. But the God of ethics knows only the idea of the universality (*Allheit*) of man, the idea of humanity. Religion, on the other hand, also knows a God of the individual who is significant for the moral problems of the individual, for sinful and suffering man.[63] Thus the distinctive character of religion vs. ethics is found precisely in its view of the relation between God and man. And the only God's distinctive character is no longer that "He emerges from the relation between man and man, from the idea of morality,"[64] and thus confronts messianic mankind as the only God. Instead, it is in compassion with one's fellow human and in the recognition of man's weakness and sin that a new meaning of God's uniqueness arises. "He is unique for the human being insofar as man must be thought of as unique."[65] This meaning of God is not posited by moral reason but derives from the distinctiveness of religion, although this distinctiveness does not necessarily mean that there is an autonomous reason within the system of philosophy.

Cohen attempts to do justice to this new relation between man and God in his concept of "correlation," a concept that goes beyond mere relation and indicates "that a reciprocal relation exists between man and God."[66] Reason here "is the condition by virtue of which God can come into correlation with man"[67] and reveal himself to him.[68] And it is only through reason "that man can come into correlation with God." "Thus, reason is made the root of the content of revelation. And no offense should be taken because the correlation of God and man, this correlation of the divine spirit to the human, has as an unavoidable consequence a kind of identity of logical reason in both."[69]

The concept of correlation has special significance for the specifically religious relation between God and man, for it may be understood neither as mediation by a man-god, as in Christianity, nor as mystical unity or pantheistic identification of God and man (and nature). What is involved is the unification of the uniqueness of God and that of man as individual, though "God and man have to remain separated, insofar as they are to be united."[70] The pure monotheism of Judaism can be a religion of reason and maintain a distinctive quality vis-à-vis ethics only if it upholds the clear separation between the "individual in its isolation and God in His uniqueness."[71] Religion is to enter into this correlation of God and man in its distinctiveness, but its moral effort and its moral goals are to be the same.[72]

If religion and ethical (or moral) reason become one, the meaning of God in the correlation of God and man is merely "to guarantee the goal, the success, the victory and the ethical self-improvement of man. . . . This transcendence of God means that man can preserve his humanness unaided."[73] But because the correlation between God and man is "the fundamental equation of religion, man in this correlation must first of all be thought of as fellow-man."[74] Respect for the moral dignity of the other as ethics knows it is thus transformed into love of one's fellow man through compassion.[75] The distinctive quality of religion becomes even clearer in the experience of guilt, for guilty man asks for a God who is not only a God of mankind but also a God of the individual. Yet this distinctive quality does not imply a *deus ex machina*, for the experience is possible only in the correlation of God and man: "the work of liberation is wholly man's. But the result of the liberation is something remote from his nature, his profession, his concept, for that result is salvation. It lies wholly in God's hands. . . . Man and God remain separate, like striving and success, like struggle and victory prize."[76]

Despite this difference between religion and ethics, it must not be overlooked that moral reason can also make these statements. The concept of correlation clearly shows that Cohen is concerned with showing that the Jewish religion is a religion of reason.[77] In the correlation of the unique God and man in his isolation, religion makes a contribution to moral reason, but that contribution does not signal any deficiency of reason. The relation of ethos (morality), ethics, and religion (as religion of reason) should be defined once again: "theoretically, morality constitutes the content of ethics and practically it is the content of man's self-education. This self-education appears in the light of religion as the divine education of mankind. Hence morality and religion are conceptually distinguished. If, however, religion has its own share in the spirit of man . . . then the concepts of God and man meet again."[78] Even in the religious language of Cohen's late work, God remains "idea," though religious ideas (such as God's love, fellow man, reconciliation) enter into Cohen's idea of God. "The turn to religion has changed the content of the idea of God, not its methodical character."[79] The Jewish doctrine of negative attributes, reinterpreted as moral reason, governs Cohen's thought throughout. "The love of God must be interpreted as love of the moral ideal, and the idea of God's love for man is justified only as an exemplar for pure moral action."[80] Cohen's religion of reason places him in a certain tradition of Jewish intellectual history, which had an outstanding medieval representative in Maimonides and which is frequently labeled "rationalism." But it is a rationalism that seeks to show that moral demands necessarily follow from a prophetically understood monotheism.[81] "The religious experience here is that of God as the power of the good"[82] because his unknowability makes him the model of morality. Consequently, there is no conflict between God's revelation and reason as moral reason. Human reason can recognize revelation because revelation reveals morality.[83] In this Jewish tradition of rationalism, the purpose of revelation lies not in the speculative but in the moral sphere.[84] Since the substantive definition of what religion is corresponds to the purpose of revelation, religion has its purpose in morality.

Still, the difference between the medieval concept of rationalist religion as represented by Maimonides and the modern one as represented by Cohen cannot be overlooked: while revelation as understood by reason is the source of religion for Maimonides, Cohen, who follows Kant, sees reason itself as the source of religion and can therefore speak of a "religion of reason."[85] "Cohen proposes to construct true religion as the religion of reason and to reveal the doctrine of the religion of reason in the historical religion of Judaism."[86] The detailed comments here on Maimonides' negative knowledge of God and on the relation between ethics and religion in Cohen—both of whom illuminated a specifically Jewish tradition of rationalist understanding of religion as moral reason—were intended to show both their closeness to, and their difference from, Fromm's thought. Especially with reference to Cohen's religion of reason, this matter can be summarized as follows:

At the beginning of his "radical interpretation of the Old Testament and its tradition,"[87] Fromm observes that his own method of understanding the Bible has been profoundly influenced by Cohen's mode "of viewing the Old Testament and the later Jewish tradition as a whole."[88] While Cohen understood the Bible in the spirit of Kant, Fromm writes,[89] he, Fromm, interprets it from the standpoint of a radical humanism.[90] If this reinterpretation is to indicate more than a purely formal similarity in method, there must be something that Bible, tradition, and reinterpreter's point of view have in common. In Cohen's attempt, this common element is the thread that runs from the prophets' negative knowledge of God to the view of the attributes as God's workings or effects to the identity of the religion of reason and moral reason—a thread that was identified here as a specifically Jewish rationalism.

Fromm takes up this thread of development but proposes to continue it from his own humanistic perspective. He also looks for the common element in the negative theology of the prophets, Maimonides, and Cohen, but his aim is to negate God in favor of man. This means that he reinterprets the prophets, Maimonides, and Cohen humanistically, although they themselves were not interested in the negation of God but in a rationalistic interpretation of God as the condition for the possibility (as guarantor, in Cohen's case) of morality. Their concern was not to negate the concept of God in religion but to preserve ethical monotheism from idolatry and to solidify that monotheism as moral reason.[91]

Cohen's and Fromm's common interest is man and his future, the liberation from all powers that hinder his moral capacity of reason and love. Cohen's struggle against the myth of religion[92] corresponds to Fromm's struggle against all irrational authority. The two men share an antipathy to religion as dogma and plead for a religion that is the essence of morality. Both want man to develop his powers of reason, justice, and love, and thus to usher in the messianic age. Yet their fundamental differences must not be overlooked. In Cohen's work, man's existence and his future are assured only if the uniqueness of God as negative theology understands it is asserted and maintained, for only "God's transcendence means that man can maintain his humanness unaided."[93] Fromm, on the other hand, wishes to preserve man and assure his future by negating the "idea" of God for the sake of humanism. According to the logic of negative theology up to Cohen's religion of reason, to negate God is, in effect, to affirm him. At the very point where the attempt is made to derive humanism from monotheism by taking recourse to a concept of negative theology that proposes to subvert monotheism itself, the irreconcilability between "ethical monotheism"[94] and radical humanism becomes apparent.

The fundamental question of every religion, including Fromm's humanistic one, concerns the relation between God and man. By definition, this is a relation of difference that presses toward unity. Within the Jewish tradition, there is a wide stream that understands this unity as the "experience" of unity, and that is Jewish mysticism. During the years the socialist Schneur Salman Rabinkov tutored him in the Talmud, Fromm became acquainted with such a tradition, namely Habad Hasidism.

SHNEUR ZALMAN: ETHOS BECOME MYSTICISM

If Gershom Scholem is correct, religion in its classical form does not emerge from the world of myth that fills nature with gods and makes it "the scene of man's relation to God" until man is torn out of "the dream-harmony of Man, Universe and God"[95] and made aware of a duality. "The great monotheistic religions live and unfold in the ever-present consciousness of this bipolarity. . . . To them, the scene of religion is no longer Nature, but the moral and religious action of man and the community of man. . . ."[96] All their offers to bridge this abyss notwithstanding, religions cling to the polarity of God and man; it is their very lifeblood. In contrast to this function of separation, mysticism proposes to make experienceable a new unity in the soul of man.[97]

This general notion of mysticism includes the following characteristic elements:

1. Every mysticism develops within a religion and, depending on the historical distinctiveness of that religion, attains a greater or lesser degree of autonomy.[98] Insistence on autonomy vis-à-vis the prevailing religion can lead mysticism to negate religion. "Every mysticism stands above a ground that it vigorously rejects and from which it nonetheless receives its distinctive quality that is never identical with mysticisms grown elsewhere."[99]

2. What distinguishes mysticism is the immediacy of the individual's contact with God, and the possibility of a direct experience of unity. "Mystical religion seeks to transform the God whom it encounters in the peculiar religious consciousness of its own environment from an object of dogmatic knowledge into a novel and living experience and intuition."[100]

3. Mysticism seeks unity on a level meant to be definitive, so that mystical knowledge is eschatological: "The Mystic . . . forestalls the process of history by anticipating in his own life the enjoyment of the last age."[101]

These characteristics apply generally *cum grano salis* to Jewish mysticism. Here it is especially religio-philosophical rationalism that develops in a reciprocal relation to mysticism, especially the Kabbala.[102] In contrast to the classical Jewish theology of the Middle Ages and the modern period as represented, respectively, by Maimonides and Hermann Cohen, men whose concern was the struggle against all forms of pantheism and myth, Jewish mysticism proposes to preserve the vitality of the religious experience of unity.[103] It accomplishes this task by a mystical "interpretation of the attributes and the unity of God in the so-called doctrine of the 'Sefiroth,' "[104] and by a mystical view of the Torah as revelation, "the living incarnation of the divine wisdom which eternally sends out new rays of light."[105] The various Jewish mysticisms understand the unity of God and the meaning of the Torah differently. Our interest here is the last historical form of Jewish mysticism, modern Hasidism,[106] specifically Habad Hasidism.[107]

Our interest in Habad Hasidism is both objective and subjective. Our discussion of the humanistic concept of religion pointed to mysticism, and our attempt to better understand Fromm's humanistic elaborations against the background of Jewish traditions suggests an examination of this particular form of Jewish mysticism, especially since Habad Hasidism emphasizes the rational aspect more strongly than Hasidism and mediates that rationalism with the tradition of Jewish rationalism.[108] Our subjective interest in Habad Hasidism is that while Fromm was a student in Heidelberg, his teacher of the Talmud was Schneur Salman Baruch Rabinkov, a Habadnik—that is, a follower of Habad Hasidism, which was founded by Rabbi Shneur Zalman. Since Habad Hasidism is a modification of Hasidism, it cannot be understood without a glance at fundamental Hasidic tenets.

Hasidism was established by Israel Baal-Shem-Tov. Up to the middle of the eighteenth century it spread from Podolsk and Volhynia and also flowered in Poland and Galicia. It had emerged from the ruins of Sabbatianism, a chiliastic and messianic movement centered around Sabbatai Z'vi, which, though in the tradition of late medieval Jewish mysticism, perverted this tradition with an apocalyptical and personified messianism.[109] Hasidism can be seen as the attempt "to preserve those elements of Kabbalism which were capable of evoking a popular response, but stripped of their Messianic flavor to which they owed their chief successes during the preceding period."[110]

During the first fifty years[111] Hasidism was marked by a "spirit of enthusiasm which expressed and at the same time justified itself by stressing the old idea of the immanence of God in all that exists."[112] This immanence is not to be understood pantheistically but rather as the divine emanations that entered nature at the "breaking of the vessels": "A divine spark dwells in beings and things."[113] "Things are important as the exile of divine being. . . . By concerning himself with them in the right way, man comes into contact with the destiny of divine being in the world and helps in the redemption."[114] The sparks represent the scattered divine light, the divine glory (*Shekhina*) that went into exile at the breaking of the vessels.[115] These divine sparks can be "raised" by man when he acts with "Kavvana," "in the inwardness of his soul's concentration."[116] "The task of man is seen to consist in the direction of his whole inner purpose toward the restoration of the original harmony which was disturbed by the original defect—the Breaking of the Vessels—and those powers of evil and sin which date from that time."[117]

These views, which are taken from the Kabbala of Isaac Luria,[118] made it possible for Hasidism to offer a direct form of religiosity for everyone without its being necessary to deny the fundamental tenets of Jewish monotheism. The knowledge of God means a searching for God, but this search occurs in the midst of life "in order to unite all things of this world with his thoughts, his speech and his act, and all that only in the name of God in truth and simplicity, for nothing in the world stands outside of God's unity, and whoever does a thing not in the name of God separates that thing from God's unity."[119] It is man who effects salvation through his moral action and everyone who does his work with *Kavvana* "works on the redemption of the world, on its conquest for God."[120]

"The sparks doctrine of the later Kabbala has become in the hands of the Baal Shem Tov an ethical teaching, and has been amplified into a precept embracing the whole life of man"[121] because "it rests with man to purge the sparks of things and beings which are met with every day."[122] The Zaddik, the "devout individual,"[123] brings salvation because "in his entire thought, feeling and acting, he unites what seems to be separate and independent with the root, with God, and brings the light of God into it."[124] In this way, all difference between the sacred and the profane is abolished. The profane now becomes merely a preliminary stage of the sacred, it is "what has not been sanctified as yet."[125]

With the Hasidic principle of "man's responsibility for the fate of God in the world"[126] the ethical and the religious spheres are brought into unity by man's sanctification, which is based on the idea that it is through man's action that creation is perfected: "The final goal of piety is to unify the divine sparks in the universe with God, to unite creation with its creator."[127] The Zaddik is like "the patriarch Enoch" who was a cobbler; "with each stitch of his awl as it sewed the upper leather and the sole together, he joined together God and his Shekhina."[128] Because "it is man's duty to do all that he does with the purpose of uniting the highest divine Essence with its Shekhina which dwells in the world,"[129] he unites God and world so that the world is redeemed and he finds his unity with God in it. In Hasidism, according to Buber, an event unique in the history of mankind occurred, and it is that "mysticism has become ethos. Here the original mystical unity, to which the soul desires to ascend, is no other form of God than the demander of the demand, and the mystical soul cannot become real, if it is not one with the moral soul."[130] This distinctive quality of Hasidism as mysticism turned ethos[131] is given special significance in Shneur Zalman's Habad Hasidism.[132] Generally speaking, there are no profound differences between Habad Hasidism and Hasidism, but the Habad school represents the first attempt to systematically verbalize the lived mysticism of Hasidism: "study becomes as important as, and sometimes more important than, 'service of the heart.' "[133] The function of the Zaddik as mediator between God and man is also rejected. In addition, Habad Hasidism and its systematization makes clear that unlike the Kabbala, Hasidism is interested in giving "a new emphasis to psychology, instead of theosophy."[134] "With every one of the endless stages of the theosophical world corresponding to a given state of the soul—actual or potential but at any rate capable of being perceived—Kabbalism becomes an instrument of psychological analysis and self-knowledge."[135] This is the point of view under which kabbalistic ideals remain valid and are chosen: "What has really become important is the direction, the mysticism of the personal life."[136]

Shneur Zalman's principal work, which was published under the title *Liqqutei Amarim* in 1796 and as *Tanya* in 1798, characteristically begins with the "Book of the Intermediates," "so-called after the type of personality on which the book centers attention, that is, the intermediate type whose moral position is between the Zaddik ('righteous man') and the rasha ('wicked man')."[137] How this intermediate man comes about, what elements define him, and what powers he has are all explained by kabbalistic ideas. The doctrine of the (negative) attributes of God as statements about his effects that was influenced by the ban on images found expression in the Sefirot doctrine of the En Sof, who is to be understood as the divinity. The *sefirot* are aspects or manifestations of a divinity that is unknowable in principle. Shneur Zalman gives the traditional understanding of God's attributes as archetypes and exemplars for man's morality a new meaning: while he views the kabbalistic speculations about God as archetypes of statements about the manifestations of the human soul, he also understands the manifestations of the soul as the struggle between the various faculties and potencies of an animal soul and a divine soul, and correspondingly places the capacity for morality in the divine soul.

The *benoni* (average man) is possible because "in every Jew, whether righteous or wicked, there are two souls. . . . There is one soul which originates in the qelipah and sitra ahra. . . . From it stem all the evil characteristics deriving from the four evil elements which are contained in it. . . . From this soul stem also the good characteristics which are to be found in the innate nature of all Israel. For example, mercy and benevolence are derived from it."[138] In addition to this "animal" soul, every Jew has another, "which is truly a part of God above"[139] and can therefore be called "divine." The divine soul manifests itself[140] in ten faculties "corresponding to the supernal Ten Sefirot [divine manifestations], from which they have descended. . . ."[141] These ten faculties are subdivided into the three powers of reason [*sechel*] and the seven attributes [*middot*] of love of God, fear, honor, and so on, that have their source in the powers of reason.

The three powers of reason are wisdom (*hokhma*), understanding (*bina*), and knowledge (*da'at*). In Luria's Kabbala, they represent the first three *sefirot* of the En Sof and, as "the core of the divine soul,"[142] constitute the essence of Shneur Zalman's **HaBaD**

Hasidism. The first element of the acrostic represents "*hokhma* ('the potentiality of what is'),[143] that which is not yet comprehended and understood, or grasped intellectually; consequently, there is vested in it the light of the En Sof, blessed be He, Who can in no way be comprehended by any thought."[144] When this power is brought from potentiality to actuality, that is, "when a person cogitates with his intellect in order to understand a thing truly and profoundly as it evolves from the concept which he has conceived in his intellect, this is called bina,"[145] the second element in the acrostic. Etymologically, *bina* means to separate, to distinguish between two opposites.[146] "Metaphorically, it also means 'to perceive' and in the so-called causative form, it primarily means 'to distinguish, to understand.' "[147]

The third aspect of reason (and the third element in the acrostic) is *da'at,* "the etymology of which is to be found in the verse: 'And Adam *knew* Eve.' "[148] The closeness of *da'at* to what Fromm calls "radical knowledge" is apparent even though Fromm interprets the object of knowledge humanistically.[149] *Da'at* means "that people should know the greatness of God from authors and books; but the essential thing is to immerse one's mind deeply into the greatness of God and fix one's thought on God with all the strength and vigor of the heart and mind. . . ."[150] "Da'at implies attachment and union."[151] Since every *sefira* is the source for the next lower *sefirot, da'at,* in this mystical sense of "radical knowledge," is the "basis of the middot[152] and the source of their vitality."[153]

The three potencies of reason are to be understood as three emanations of a self-unfolding divinity. But one must also see them as the three stages of development that represent the principle of development of all beings. All beings "are initially hidden in the divine wisdom. They become manifest in understanding and recognizable in the knowledge of God."[154] Since in Hasidic thought it is the intrapsychic events that are emphasized in parallelism with intradivine events, the Habad principle takes on a special significance for processes within the human soul, especially when it is understood as the coincidence of the divine and the animal soul.[155]

The Habad reason and the *middot* are the inner faculties of the divine soul and express themselves only in the three external faculties of the soul: speech, thought, and action.[156] When the divine soul is seen in this totality of its inner and outer faculties, the totality of the 613 Torah precepts appears in them. For "the faculties of Habad in his soul are clothed in the comprehension of the Torah. . . . And the middot, namely, fear and love, together with their offshoots and ramifications, are clothed in the fulfillment of the commandments in deed and in word, namely, in the study of Torah which is 'the equivalent of all the commandments.' "[157] Love is the root of the Torah's 248 commands, while fear is the root of its 365 prohibitions.

The "divine" element of man's divine soul has its basis in this relatedness to the Torah. The optimal realization of the faculties of the divine soul by the optimal fulfillment of the commands of the Torah means at the same time the mystical knowledge of God: "For the essence of the Holy One, blessed be He, no thought can apprehend Him at all, except when it apprehends, and is clothed in the Torah and its Middot, only then does it truly apprehend, and is clothed in, the Holy One, blessed be He, inasmuch as the Torah and the Holy One, blessed be He, are one and the same."[158] This identification of the good with the holy becomes clearer when the distinctiveness of the animal soul and its polarity to the divine soul in man are perceived.

Just as the divine soul manifests itself in ten holy *sefirot* and is clothed in three garments, so the animal soul manifests itself in ten "crowns of uncleanliness"—namely, the seven evil *middot* and threefold reason—and these ten unclean "categories" cause the garments of thought, speech, and action to be unclean.[159] The animal soul comes from the *sitra ahra,* "the other side," the side that is the opposite of holiness and belongs to the world of the *qelipot.*[160] Without discussing in detail the complicated kabbalistic theories about the coming into existence of the world of the *qelipot* as forces of evil,[161] it should be noted that evil is seen as a secondary phenomenon of the creation *ex nihilo* that does not exist for its own sake and can be overcome.[162]

Among the evil powers of the *qelipot* that are represented by materiality, Shneur Zalman distinguishes two kinds: "the qelipot are subdivided into two grades, one lower than the other. The lower grade consists of the three qelipot which are altogether unclean and evil, containing no good whatever."[163] The second grade is found only among Jews and kosher animals and plants. It is called *qelipat noga* and "is an intermediate category between the three completely unclean *qelipot* and the category and order of holiness."[164] While the unclean *qelipot* are the cause of evil desires and bad qualities, the *qelipat noga* is the source of natural physical needs that can be influenced by reason. Because in the *qelipat noga,* which is found in Jews alone, good and evil are mixed, one must postulate that compassion and kindness are innate Jewish qualities.[165]

The decisive question revolves around the divine and animal soul in man. According to kabbalistic opinion, every soul has an "abode" in man, a place, that is, where it tends to manifest itself.[166] These "abodes" for the animal soul are "the left ventricle that is filled with blood" and from which all bad qualities spread throughout the body. The divine soul, on the other hand, is concentrated in the brain and spreads over the body, principally into the right ventricle. From here, the holy feelings (*middot* of the divine soul) that have their origin in the brain, the seat of Habad reason, make their effects felt. Since both souls in man strive to "rule the body and all its limbs, they wage war against each other."[167] "Just as two kings wage war over a town, which each wishes to capture and rule, that is to say, to dominate its inhabitants according to his will, so that they obey him in all that he decrees for them, so do the two souls—the divine and the vital animal soul that comes from the qelipah—wage war against each other over the body and all its limbs. It is the desire and will of the divine soul that she alone rule over the person and direct him, so that all his limbs should obey her and surrender themselves completely to her. . . ."[168] The object of the war is not the destruction of evil, but rather that "the evil is converted into, and becomes, completely good, like the good nature itself, through the shedding of the soiled garments, the pleasures of this world, in which it had been clothed."[169] The only weapons in this war are the mobilization of Habad reason (and its *middot*) in their garments of thought, speech, and action.[170] Because this divine reason is clothed in the Torah and its commands,[171] the encompassing fulfillment of the Torah precepts on the basis of a profound study of the Torah is the only effective weapon if the divine soul is to be dominant over the animal one.

The degree of superiority of the divine over the animal soul corresponds to the realization of Habad reason in the fulfillment of the precepts of the Torah. "When a person fortifies his divine soul and wages war against his animal soul to such an extent that he expels and eradicates its evil from the left part . . . he is called 'incompletely righteous' or 'a righteous man who suffers.' "[172] To be a completely righteous individual, a Zaddik, requires that one have "completely divested himself of the garments of evil," renounce the pleasures of this world, and devote himself wholly to his love for God.[173] When the animal soul dominates in man, the goodness of the divine soul is subservient to the evil of the *qelipa* and destroyed by it. Depending on the degree of dominance of evil, one speaks of "the wicked man who prospers" and the "wicked who suffers."[174] Both extremes, the Zaddik and the wicked, are relatively rare, which means that it is the intermediate forms that hold the greatest interest. The *benoni,* "intermediate man," is an individual "in whom evil never attains enough power to capture the 'small city' so as to clothe itself in the body and make it sin. That is to say, the three 'garments' of the animal soul, namely, thought, speech and act, originating in the qelipah, do not prevail within him over the divine soul to the extent of clothing themselves in the body. . . ."[175]

Intermediate man is not a goal of the moral and religious life. Yet the dominance of the good (= divine) within him is the presupposition for his sanctification, which means *eo ipso* a strengthening of his good faculties: "The essential thing is to govern and rule the nature that is in the left ventricle of the heart[176] by means of the Divine light that irradiates the divine soul in the mind."[177] But the heart can only be governed by Habad reason when, through meditation on the greatness of the En Sof, a spirit of radical knowledge and fear of God are developed in the right ventricle. This love of God consists in the desire "to cleave to Him through the fulfillment of the precepts of the Torah and of the Rabbis, and through the study of the Torah which is equivalent to them all."[178]

This outline of the "Kabbala turned ethos"[179] and "presented in the guise of mystical psychology"[180] suffices to show the parallels between the ideas of Habad Hasidism and Fromm's humanistic view of man. Although Fromm never drew on this Jewish mysticism for his concept of a humanistic religion,[181] his work shows conspicuous parallels with Habad Hasidism of both a philosophical-anthropological and a concrete psychological-ethical kind, parallels that go beyond the similarities in patterns of thought that exist between him and Maimonides and Cohen. The conflict between divine and animal soul has a counterpart in Fromm's alternative of productive and nonproductive character orientations, and the parallel becomes more marked in Fromm's understanding of the various character structures as syndromes of growth and decay whose extreme forms are the saint and the criminal, respectively. The identification of the good and the holy in the divine soul recurs in humanistic inversion when the productive and the ethical are posited as identical. To an extent, the Sefirot doctrine is a model for the dynamic view of character in which character trait represents the expression of an underlying character structure, for in their psychological interpretation, the *sefirot* are manifestations of the divine or animal soul and emanate from them. The view of the character structure as a mixture of productive and nonproductive orientations and the dominance of some quality can be found under the "crust" of the kabbalistic conceptual apparatus in the struggle of Habad reason against the *qelipat noga*. And it is obvious that the kabbalistic struggle between divine and animal soul for the "small city" gave birth to Fromm's "alternativism" doctrine.

Even though the view that man is to unfold his productive powers of reason and love is considered self-evident, it presupposes something that is anything but that—that man is potentially good by nature. From a theistic point of view, both elements are present in the Hasidic doctrine of creation and its purpose. Fromm adopts them in their humanistic inversion: the study of the Torah that constitutes the basis for the fulfillment of the Torah in Shneur Zalman becomes the reason of scientific knowledge,[182] and the realization of the precepts in the love of God becomes the realization of the capacity for productive love. As the Habad reason of the divine soul finds its expression in the study of the Torah and the fulfillment of its precepts of love, the productive character finds its expression in the realization of the powers of reason and love. Still, the difference between the two views is enormous, and lies in the way they are grounded. In Shneur Zalman's Hasidism, the Habad reason of the divine soul guarantees the capacity for holiness. In Fromm's humanism, it is the experience of one's capacity for humanness in reason and love that must guarantee the capacity to become universal man.

KARL MARX: MAN AS THE MAKER OF HIS HISTORY[183]

Our analysis of humanistic religion revealed the religio-critical aspect of Fromm's humanism concept: "humanistic" is the dialectical counterconcept of "theistic." When one looks for the figure in intellectual history who set Fromm on this path of religio-critical understanding of humanism, one finds that Fromm himself points to Karl Marx (1818–1883).[184] "Marx was capable of connecting a spiritual heritage of the Enlightenment humanism and German idealism with the reality of economic and social facts, and thus to lay the foundations for a new science of man and society which is empirical and at the same time filled with the spirit of the Western humanistic tradition."[185]

According to Fromm, it is characteristic of Marx's understanding of humanism that he enlarges on the belief shared by all humanists that man can perfect himself unaided, and that he maintains against the theists among them that man makes his own history and is his own creator.[186] "Marx fought against religion exactly because it is alienated, and does not satisfy the true needs of man. Marx's fight against God is, in reality, a fight against the idol that is called God."[187] Marx's influence on Fromm's thought, especially on his religio-critical humanism concept, is obvious. But to evaluate this influence critically in the context of today's exegesis of Marx is difficult because there is such an enormous number of frequently conflicting interpretations. Statements Fromm himself made permit an initial orientation as one investigates his understanding of Marx in the context of Marx interpretation. According to these statements, historically and politically important Marxisms can hardly claim to be legitimate heirs of Marx, for to them, "socialism is not a society humanly different from capitalism, but rather, a form of capitalism in which the working class has achieved a higher status."[188]

In face of such an understanding of man in communist and socialist systems,[189] Fromm believes that Marx is interpreted correctly only if his humanistic concern is understood. This concern is articulated principally in the writings of the young Marx, especially in the *Economic and Philosophical Manuscripts* (Paris 1844 manuscripts). Fromm's view of Marx is therefore close to the so-called humanistic or anthropological interpretation of Marx,[190] which assumes that these early writings are the key to understanding him[191] and underlines the continuity of Marx's thought up to the "mature" Marx of *Capital.*[192] Against this humanistic interpretation is the group of Marx interpreters who see *Capital* as the central work and the early humanism as no more than a residue of youthful idealism.[193]

For Fromm, however, Marx's entire *oeuvre* constitutes an explication of the humanistic approach. "The Marxist theory, as well as the socialist movement, was radical and humanistic—radical in the above-mentioned sense of going to the roots, and the roots being man; humanistic in the sense that it is man who is the measure of all things, and his full unfolding must be the aim and the criterion of all social efforts. The liberation of man from the stranglehold of economic conditions which prevented his full development was the aim of all of Marx's thought and efforts."[194] Fromm believed that this interpretation placed him in the same camp as Marxists and critics of Marxism of a great many different persuasions such as the Yugoslav philosophers associated with the journal *Praxis,*[195] the Pole Adam Schaff,[196] Ernst Bloch,[197] and the Christian scholar of Marxism Jean-Yves Calvez.[198] All of these men agree that Marx's ultimate aim was human, not economic, change. The difference between their interpretation and the one that proposes to grasp Marx by way of his economic interests is the result of a different understanding of the methodical approach of Marx's view of reality. Reflection about this makes it possible to understand the significance the critique of religion has for the self-emancipation of man.

Hegel's attempt to make thinking and being coincide provoked Marx's criticism because the tension between an interpretation of reality and the actual structures of that reality was intolerable for him in the long run.[199] He noted, "To Hegel, the life-process of the human brain, i.e. the process of thinking which, under the name of 'the idea,' he even transforms into an independent subject, is the demiurgos of the real world, and the real world is only the external, phenomenal form of the 'the Idea.' With me, on the contrary, the idea is nothing else than the material world reflected by the human mind, and translated into forms of thought."[200] Marx criticizes the Hegelian philosophy of history because its exclusive interest is pure thought; it eschews real interests, even political ones.[201] Therefore, he believed, Idealistic philosophy itself must be questioned: "Because Hegel puts self-consciousness where man ought to be, the most divergent human reality appears merely as a certain form, a determination of self-consciousness. . . . Hegel makes man the man of self-consciousness, instead of making self-consciousness the self-consciousness of man, of real man, of the man who lives in the real world and is conditioned by it. He sets the world on its head and can therefore do away with all limitations in his head though this means that they remain in force for bad sensuousness, for real man."[202]

The world must be put back on its feet. As a formal principle, this "materialistic" seizing of reality persists throughout Marx's work. "Materialism . . . means that it is the political, social and economic praxis that primarily determines the life of man, and therefore history."[203] The materialist concept of history is a "socio-economic theory of history."[204] The materialist view of reality places man as active subject "into the center of history and development, and this must be the point of departure for every further statement."[205] Materialism thus means "that all aspects of the historical process depend on how man fashions his existence."[206] The correctness of this materialist view of man and history according to which the possibility of change lies wholly with the capacity of the subject of history, man, to effect it becomes apparent when the critique of existing conditions reveals the alienation of reality and the liberation of man restores him as the subject of history: "All emancipation is the reduction of the human world and of relationships to man himself."[207]

The methodical principle for man's self-emancipation is a "critical dialectic of theory and praxis"[208] as a "philosophy of history with practical intent."[209] "Marx's dialectic of theory and praxis consists in deriving a theory from the empirical analysis of social and economic conditions that criticizes and changes undesirable states of affairs. But change cannot be effected by a theory unless it be one that passes back into praxis."[210]

Marx's interpreters differ in their view of the application of the methodological principle of the critical dialectic of theory and praxis. A good many students of Marx do not limit his dialectic to the social process as determined by economic factors, but see it as universal, as the dialectic of man and nature in history. In the birth of man as man, these interpreters see the emergence of the unavoidable conflict between man and nature that is subsequently articulated in the alienation of man from his work, his fellow man, and himself, and that is manifested as capitalistic class society. To abolish the alienated situation by abolishing private property,[211] then, means not only "the emancipation from economic constraints and a humane reordering of the social organization of work";[212] it means a new unity of man and nature as a realm of freedom and the beginning of man's true history. The new unity is positive communism: "This communism, as fully developed naturalism, equals humanism, and as fully developed humanism equals naturalism; it is the genuine resolution of the conflict between man and nature, and between man and man, the true resolution of the conflict between existence and being. . . . It is the solution of the riddle of history and knows itself to be the solution."[213]

The various camps of Marx interpreters are distinguished by their differing applications of the methodical principle of the critical dialectic of theory and praxis. When, as in Fromm, the dialectic is also applied to the universal relationship of man and nature, it is primarily the Marx of the "Paris Manuscripts of 1844" who is being interpreted. Commentators who apply the dialectic only to the social process as determined by economic factors view its wider application as an erroneous interpretation that Marx himself refutes "in part in his early writings, and altogether in his late work."[214] These differing applications of the dialectic lead to conflicting views of important Marxist concepts. Since Fromm's application can serve as an example of the wider application of the dialectic and has already been discussed in some detail,[215] the following brief comments are confined to the narrower application of the dialectic.[216]

By "history," Marx means neither an anarchic piling up of facts nor a unified process as Hegel understands it.[217] "The materialistic dialectic is non-teleological. . . . While it is true that the lawful succession of social formations introduces something like an overarching structure into human history, we are not dealing with a pervasive 'teleology.' . . . Because Marx does not start off from a total meaning that predates man, history becomes the sequence of ever-new individual processes, a phenomenon that can only be understood by a philosophy of universal discontinuities that consciously renounces the claim that it can provide an unbroken deduction from principle."[218] According to this interpretation, the "middle" and the "mature" Marx rejected Feuerbach's "true man." The disappearance of talk about "man" and "the nature of man" in his work is taken as an indication that Marx abandoned the Feuerbachian idols "man" and "nature" as he acquired a more precise knowledge of economic history.[219] Concurrently, Marx discarded the use of "estrangement" and "alienation" because he discovered in the meantime that men are never wholly at home with the objects of their production. While everything must be done to end man's enslavement by capitalist relations, the "realm of freedom" is not free of work, nor does communism mean "the true resolution of the conflict between man and nature."[220] "Marx's equation humanism = naturalism is no more correct than he took Hegel's equation subject = object to be."[221] The "realm of necessity" remains "because even in a world that has become genuinely human, the complete reconciliation of subject and object cannot occur."[222] "Men cannot ultimately free themselves of natural necessities."[223]

The variety in the way the methodological principle of the critical dialectic of theory and praxis is applied, either to social and economic processes only or, following the early Marx, to the universal relation between man and nature in history not only explains the various views of Marx but also affects Marx's own understanding of religion and its critique. That critique initially derived from Feuerbach,[224] who developed it in confrontation with Hegel and for whom "religion represents the most ominous consequence of the abstraction from sensuous and material reality"[225] and puts man at odds with his own nature. "All of man's qualities and values are hypostasized as a transcendent being."[226] This thesis, which has an inner relation to the theistic doctrine of God's negative attributes,[227] identifies the core idea of the critique of religion: If "man affirms . . . in God what he denies in himself,"[228] then the true nature of religion is anthropology and it becomes the aim of all critiques of religion to emancipate man from religion so that his own being may be restored to him and he become his own God.[229]

Initially, Marx adopted Feuerbach's critical position and joined him in criticizing Hegel: "And to you, speculative theologians and philosophers, I give this piece of advice: free yourselves of the concepts and prejudices of traditional speculative philosophy if you wish to arrive at things as they are, i.e. at truth. For you, there is no other way to truth and freedom except through Feuerbach. Feuerbach is the purgatory* of our time."[230] But Feuerbach's critique of religion turned out to be only a passing purgatory, for Marx came to believe that it is not religion that causes man's self-alienation; religion is merely "the general theory of this world . . . its logic in popular form . . . its universal basis of consolation and justification."[231] Therefore a critique of religion alone cannot restore his perfection to man, for "man is no abstract being squatting outside the world, Man is the world of man, the state, society. This state, this society, produce religion, which is an inverted world-consciousness, because they are an inverted world. Religion . . . is the fantastic realization of the human being because the human being has attained no true reality."[232] The very existence of religion suggests that man demands an illusory happiness because real happiness eludes him. The abolition of religion involves the demand that man surrender all illusions about his condition. This means, in turn, the abandonment of "a condition which requires illusions. Thus, the critique of religion is the critique in embryo of the vale of tears of which religion is the halo."[233]

The critique of religion points to man's true reality, which must be defined more closely against the background of conflicting interpretations of Marx. But first the task of the critique of religion in Marx's work should be indicated in summary fashion. Marx does not share Feuerbach's view regarding the function of the critique of religion because he feels that religion refers us away from the religious individual and to a differently understood, true reality of the human being.[234] "The true critique of religion and of religious alienation thus presupposes the critique of the secular world. But what is at first a purely intellectual critique of religion is necessary so that man's attention may be called to the phenomenon of self-alienation and alienation, to this cause of all his misery."[235]

Through the critique of religion, both Feuerbach and Marx at-

* There is a pun here on Feuerbach's name, which literally means "fiery brook."—TRANS.

tempt to make man the creator and actor of his history. for the intention of the critique is to disillusion man and make him realize he is the center of reality: "The critique of religion disillusions man so that he will think, act, and fashion his reality as a man who has lost his illusions and regained his reason, so that he will revolve about himself as his own true sun. Religion is only the illusory sun about which man revolves so long as he does not revolve about himself."[236] Thus the critique of religion has no less a function than to usher in the Copernican revolution from God to man, from theism to humanism, and to make Prometheus the model for man.[237] *Man's true reality* becomes visible when he is understood materialistically. This happens when he is taken seriously in his concrete situation and it is understood that he is enmeshed in a variety of empirically accessible conditions. For Marx, man's ultimate and greatest dependency lies in his being a part of economic conditions and of the social conditions that are shaped by them. If the true human being is to be known, his enmeshment in economic and social conditions must be investigated. But because the critique of heaven has become that of earth, man must be seen in the critical dialectic of theory and praxis. Man's alienated dependence on alienated processes of production that create alienated social conditions and philosophy and religion as alienations of man, in turn, calls for a true reality of man in which he is free of the chains of economic alienation and creates his history himself in "free, conscious activity."[238]

At this point, the controversial application of the methodological principle of the critical dialectic of theory and praxis again becomes noticeable because the idea of liberated man—of man in his true reality—will differ according to the *kind* of application. Those interpreters who judge Marx by his mature economic work believe that liberated man will come into existence when he has become the master of economic conditions because those conditions will then no longer dominate him as incalculable natural forces. These interpreters also take a more modest view of the degree of freedom that will be achieved because, in contrast to Engels,[239] Marx continued to believe "that the true realm of freedom can only flower on the realm of necessity as its base."[240] In the realm of natural necessity, freedom "can only consist in socialized man, the associated producers, regulating their metabolism with nature rationally, subjecting it to their common control instead of being ruled by it as by a blind power."[241]

In contrast to this view of man's true reality, which limits itself to the perception of the "real possibilities" in socioeconomic processes, the application of the critical dialectic to the universal nexus between man and nature in history allows a more encompassing view of man's true reality. In this view, it is man's perfection that is of interest—in other words, his capacity to exhaust all his possibilities in a complete unity with nature. The insights into socioeconomic relations and laws as preconditions for a revolutionary praxis and the realization of socialism are means to an end: "a fully developed humanism that equals naturalism . . . the true resolution of the conflict between existence and being—between freedom and necessity."[242]

If the question concerning the meaning of history is part of man's true reality, man in his concrete situation is taken seriously only if he is also understood in his conformation to a certain perfection and in his capacity to realize it. In his early writings, Marx formulated this task,[243] although he lacked the apparatus for its empirical investigation and consequently shifted his analytic interests increasingly to the area of socioeconomic processes.[244] Yet he set forth important psychological insights about man's true reality[245]—for example, in the concept of "passion" and "alienated passion"; in the distinctions between "constant" and "variable" drives, between "the real needs of man" and his "artificially produced" ones,[246] between "ideas" that, as ideologies, have the function of rationalizations and "real ideas" that are rooted in human and social reality.[247] There is, besides, the concept of a "human nature" as a "human nature in general" and a "modifiable human nature"[248]; the concept of "love"; and finally the concept of "productive life" as "free conscious activity," which is man's true wealth[249] because it makes him biophilous and turns him against the domination of dead matter over him.[250]

It is Fromm's achievement to have taken up the question the young Marx asked, and to have juxtaposed it with the insights of psychoanalysis. The concept of character that Fromm took from Freud and developed can serve to identify the psychic preconditions for the realization of man's true reality.[251] At the same time, he postulated an interdependence between socioeconomic conditions and psychic needs and introduced the concept of "social character" that mediates between the two entities.[252] Fromm's Marx reception represents a logical development of the investigation of man's true reality as a universal humanism = naturalism. It is a development in the sense that it attempts to take seriously the discovery of man's enmeshment in his psychic needs. Fromm revealed this enmeshment as the psychic dependence on a variety of human needs, which means that man cannot but react to these needs. One of these needs is for a frame of orientation and an object of devotion, to which, according to Fromm, humanistic religion reacts optimally. The following comparison of this concept of religion with Marx's critique will also describe the concept of humanism more precisely.

Fromm's concept of a humanistic religion and Marx's critique of religion initially appear to have little in common. Marx was never seriously interested in theology or religion, and certainly not in an analysis and discussion of the contents of religion.[253] The consequence is that there exists no genuine Marxist atheism,[254] the atheistic interpretation of religion as "the opium of the people"[255] being primarily an expression of anti-Marxist apologetics. Marx's interest in religion was inspired by Feuerbach's and the left Hegelians' critique and his own insight "that religion is exhaustively defined as a function of bad social conditions."[256] Religion is of interest as a social phenomenon and tells us something about man's alienation. Once alienation has been done away with, religion will no longer be necessary.

In spite of this difference in what they take religion to be, the two men give the same treatment to important aspects of the concept of religion. It must first be noted that what Marx called "religion" is largely its social manifestation as church and state church, and he translates religious values into nontheological language.[257] And Fromm's humanistic religion is called "religion" only because its underlying experience ("X experience") articulates itself in the historical religions. The aim of humanistic religion is the dissolution of the historical, socially established religions.[258] When these terminological differences are taken note of and the difficulties of nomenclature attending a nontheistic standpoint in a linguistic universe stamped by theism are allowed for, it turns out that what both concepts of religion have in common is more significant than what divides them.

The common features of Marx's and Fromm's concepts of religion stand out even more clearly when they are seen against the background that shaped their critiques of religion, namely the Enlightenment idea that man is not truly himself when he owes himself to someone other than himself. Independence and freedom are the preconditions for the birth of man as man come of age. The possibility of a reconciliation between man and a reality beyond him is unacceptable to this free thinking because it would be counter to the autonomy postulate. Both theonomy and heteronomy are *a priori* contradictions of man's self-creation, and because the claim of theonomy has always been articulated as a claim to rule by ecclesiastical and social groups, every theonomy always also means heteronomy.[259] For both Marx and Fromm, only a concept of autonomy that excludes any sense that one's existence is owed to something other than oneself is valid: "A being sees himself as independent only when he stands on his own feet, and he only stands on his own feet when he owes his existence to himself. A man who lives by the grace of another regards himself as a dependent being."[260] For both, autonomy can only be attained in opposition to heteronomous = authoritarian structures. But both also agree (and herein they differ from Feuerbach) that this opposition is not to direct itself primarily against the contents and manifestations of the established religions[261] but against those conditions that allow such narcotizing religions to come into existence. "Enlightenment will bring genuine liberation only . . . when the conditions that give rise to religion are also changed in such a way that the need for approval and consolation disappears. . . ."[262] A critique of the various established religions becomes unnecessary once man and his world are understood humanistically.[263]

The critique of heaven must become the critique of earth. The goal toward which all criticism strives is the knowledge of man's true reality, "the essentiality of man and of nature."[264] The combative quality of the opposition to all heteronomy disappears the moment heteronomy is dismissed as the opposite of autonomy, and one can therefore dispense with all discussion of the contents of religion, indeed with all critiques of it. Confrontation becomes unnecessary because in the active understanding of man's true reality—that is, of man in his nature as socialism perfects him—all heteronomous determinations dissolve. Then "the question of an alien being, a being above nature and man—a question which implies an admission of the unreality of nature and of man—has become impossible in practice. Atheism, which is a denial of this unreality, no longer has any meaning, for atheism is a negation of God, through which negation it asserts the existence of man. But socialism as such no longer needs such mediation. Its starting-point is the theoretically and practically sensuous consciousness of man and of nature as essential beings."[265]

This quotation from the *Economic and Philosophical Manuscripts of 1844* also defines Fromm's concept of religious humanism. But it also makes clear the difference between his concept of humanistic religion and Marx's concept of religion. Fromm's understanding of humanism coincides with the early Marx's critique of religion in that the negation of God "which eo ipso makes possible and posits man's existence is to be viewed as a historical process of enlightenment that reaches its goal with the materialistic view of man."[266] It is therefore no longer necessary to deal with theistic religions[267] unless humanistic values and insights "in theologic garb" can be discovered there and utilized for the humanistic understanding of man and reality.[268] Because the birth of that man who no longer owes his existence to any alien being has become historical fact in the process of enlightenment, all attempts regarding "the essentiality of man in nature"[269] articulate themselves as "science of man."[270] In the case of Marx, this science is primarily determined by man's enmeshment in socioeconomic conditions, while Fromm believes that "man's true reality" can only be perceived when his psychic needs are taken seriously as human needs.

By humanism, Fromm means science. But humanism is also a religious concept for him, although only to the extent that he believes that the traditional religions have come to an end in humanism. Anyone who wishes to take seriously man in his true reality as a creature of needs must note man's need for a frame of orientation and an object of devotion, a need that has manifested itself historically in the major religions. If humanism is the ultimate form of man's religious need, a humanistic self- and world-understanding and the humanistic experience of the ONE necessarily form part of man's productive unfolding.[271] Fromm calls the productive reaction to this need the X experience or humanistic religion; the concept "religion" here is to be understood "humanistically."

As to the question of what Marx's and Fromm's concepts of religion have in common, only a nuanced answer is possible. Fromm himself attempts to show an objective continuity when he interprets Marx's struggle against religion merely as the socially adapted expression of one who in reality was a very religious, prophetic person opposed to the authoritarian and idolatrous realizations of religion in church and state because they offended against profound religious interests: "Marx's atheism is the most advanced form of rational mysticism, closer to Meister Eckhardt or to Zen Buddhism than are most of those fighters for God and religion who accuse him of 'godlessness.' "[272] For Fromm, the religious element in Marx lies primarily in the fact that he opposed all idolatry, particularly the idolatry that turns man into god.[273] Man is to become true man: such is Fromm's view of Marx's understanding of religion.

As long as only the religio-critical humanism concept that is common to, and binding on, both men is considered, no objection can be raised to this interpretation of Marx's criticism of religion. But Marx believed that man has already become true man when he views religion materialistically. In Marx, the critique of religion has the function of defining religion as illusory. When man, having stood on his head, returns to his feet, religion loses its claim to existence. Because religion is merely "the sigh of the oppressed creature . . . the call to abandon illusions about the people's condition is the call to abandon a condition that requires illusions."[274] The critique of religion has done this job of disillusionment once and for all, which means that all interest is now focused on man's true reality. As far as Marx is concerned, this reality does not include a human need for a frame of orientation and an object of devotion. His understanding of materialism implies the dissolution of religion because religion is no more than a function of bad social conditions.[275] He knows that "for Germany, the critique of religion is essentially completed; and the critique of religion is the prerequisite of every critique."[276]

This claim has important consequences for a judgment of Marx's understanding of history and man, and those consequences make clear why Marx interpreters who are interested in Marx the economist and want to limit the application of the methodical principle of the critical dialectic of theory and praxis to social processes as shaped by economic factors refuse to accept the early Marx as the true one. Denying that religion has any claim means that one anticipates a condition that can only be worked for in the revolutionary struggle to change socioeconomic conditions. The Marx criticism that is based on Marx the economist objects to adopting the contents of a theistic religion in the critique of religion and to interpreting them humanistically. It therefore also refuses to interpret humanistically and as an event in history the eschatological and messianic ideas according to which the unification and unity of God and man will be accomplished in the days of the Messiah.[277] When religion is unmasked as a historically outdated epiphenomenon, no substantive statements can be made about what man in his perfection will be.

For Marx, it is a historical fact that religion has been overcome: man's eschatological true reality has already been achieved. With the postulate of an existential need for a frame of orientation and an object of devotion, Fromm necessarily revises the merely functional aspect the critique of religion has in Marx. If man is taken seriously in his existential needs, and the need for a frame of orientation and an object of devotion is defined as an existential need and not merely as a historical and therefore artificial one that must be overcome, then religion is an essential part of man and everything depends on how the religion that optimally corresponds to this existential need for a frame of orientation and an object of devotion can be more closely defined.[278]

The difficulties that result when the materialistic approach is applied to psychic needs and an existential need for a frame of orientation and an object of devotion is postulated are not merely difficulties of nomenclature. Along with Marx, Fromm takes the established, authoritarian religions as his starting point and criticizes their ideological and idolatrous character.[279] For both, religions are historical phenomena that were overcome by religio-critical humanism, and it is only as a result that humanism attained its rightful place. When this humanism is taken seriously and the materialistic approach is applied to man's psychic structure of needs, the necessity to deal with religion arises once again, and the critique of religion again becomes necessary if a productive reaction to this existential need is to be made possible.[280]

Because the critique of religion remains an essential part of humanistic religion, religio-critical humanism can no longer simply be grounded by asserting that the Enlightenment has put an end to religion. Marx could announce that history had invalidated the claim of religion because he declared religion to be ultimately a product of economic alienation and the critique of religion unnecessary as man's real dependencies were understood.[281] In this respect, Marx's thought is stringent. But it is also shortsighted, as Fromm's application of the materialistic approach to man's psychic needs makes clear. Conversely, Fromm's concept of religion can no longer simply legitimize the humanistic approach as deriving from a critique of religion whose historical role has already ended, because in the religio-critical confrontation, the humanistic reaction to the need for a frame of orientation and an object of devotion must always prove itself anew.

Both humanism and humanistic religion need constant religio-critical grounding: they are not simply facts of scientific credulity but the object of a trusting belief in man because he is man. By elevating man to the role of originator and actor of his history in opposition to any heteronomous determination of him by authoritarian religion, Fromm, along with Marx, grounds humanism religio-critically. Yet in Fromm's case, humanism remains belief and tied to the possibility and experience of humanistic religion. Still, this difference from Marx's concept of religion merely represents a variation of the two men's common fundamental belief that "the question of an alien being, a being above nature and man . . ." is redundant insofar as their concept of autonomy, derived from the Enlightenment, implies an *a priori* dialectical contradiction between any theonomy and man as the creator and actor of his history.

7

FORMS OF FROMM'S THOUGHT

Having identified some sources of Fromm's sociopsychological discoveries and philosophical-anthopological views and of his understanding of humanistic religion and ethics, we will now attempt to define more closely certain forms and conceptual constructs that underlie and persist throughout his work. First, we seek to establish a link between Fromm's insights and views and a conceptual model and certain forms of thought, and to discover their roots in intellectual history. The difference in the forms of thought that were noted, especially in the comments on humanistic religion, will then be thematized and shown to result from a competition between interpretive models. Finally, by identifying the forms of thought, we attempt to make it easier to differentiate between Fromm's empirical and scientific thought, and his philosophical and anthropological reflections.

THE ECSTATIC-CATHARTIC CONCEPTUAL MODEL AND ITS FORMS OF THOUGHT OR CONTENTLESS FORMULAE (*LEERFORMELN*)

Fromm's contrapositioning of authoritarian and revolutionary character and authoritarian and humanistic religion, and his particular understanding of a *theologia negativa,* only become comprehensible against the background of a form of thought that is dialectical in nature. Ernst Topitsch ascribed such a form of thought, for which dialectics is always a process of negation and contradiction, to an intellectual model or construct that uses this form of dialectic as its most important form of thought. Because of its origin in divination and gnosis, but also because of its character and function, he calls this construct "ecstatic-cathartic." Before the ecstatic-cathartic model can be discussed in its distinctive character and development, the concern that caused Ernst Topitsch to call such forms of thought "contentless" will be critically evaluated.

The Concept and Function of Contentless Formulae According to Ernst Topitsch, and Their Critique[1]

If a positivistic concept of science is adopted as the point of view from which to understand man and world, an explanation is needed for the fact "that through the centuries, certain linguistic formulae have been recognized as relevant insights or even as fundamental principles of being, cognition and valuation, and that they continue to be so recognized to this day, and this not in spite of the fact but precisely because, and insofar as, they have no factual or normative content or none that can be more closely specified."[2] On the presupposition that scientific statements about man and his world[3] must be falsifiable, all statements that cannot be falsified by simple empirical data because they elude a direct test become pseudo-statements: they are contentless assertions.

The origin of such contentless formulations lies in archaic, mythic, and religious ideas in which "a differentiation among the various forms of human orientation in the world does not yet exist and what is articulated later as religion, philosophy, science, art, morality, law and politics is still found in undifferentiated unity."[4] On this primitive level, man attempts to make the world and his own self (the soul) comprehensible by "viewing the more remote and unknown in analogy to what is closer at hand and known, and this principally by taking certain fundamental situations of the social production and reproduction of life as models."[5] The world is thus seen in analogy to a social structure such as the family, the clan, or the state, so that reflection about and interpretations of the world, man, and soul correspond to a sociomorphous conceptual model. At a higher stage of cultural development, the world and the self are interpreted by analogy to the products of human skill: under these conditions, thinking occurs in accordance with a technomorphous model or construct.[6] In addition to technique and social structure, nature and particularly the processlike character of life provide the basis for yet another model, the biomorphous. Finally, there are the doctrines concerning the soul and those interpretations of the world that are inspired by ecstatic-cathartic motifs and have their origin "in the belief that there is a soul that can be separated from the body, a state in which it becomes capable of superhuman achievements."[7]

At the time they prevailed, conceptual models had a variety of functions and enabled man to orient himself comprehensively in regard to himself and his environment. More specifically, models can have the following functions: "Information about important events, especially about the consequences of certain forms of conduct, and control over the environment and one's own body were expected of them. They also seemed to instill confidence in a course of action for they sanctioned norms and decisions, made unavoidable suffering easier to bear, and offered compensations for real renunciations."[8]

Topitsch's interest in these constructs and forms of thought is the result of an ideology-critical concern: the "critique of mythical and metaphysical interpretations of world and self by their historical, sociological and psychological analysis."[9] In this undertaking, Topitsch traces a variety of conceptual constructs through the history of philosophy and theology, and formulates a number of conclusions:

The history of philosophy shows a process of rationalization leading from myth to philosophy.[10] Philosophy must limit itself to that sphere of the factual that can be described in "contexts of falsifiable statements,"[11] and every statement that is part of a conceptual construct or a form of thought should be based on falsifiable experiential knowledge. If traditional constructs and patterns do not satisfy this requirement, they do not constitute knowledge but are contentless formulae—empty in the sense that they do not tell us anything about man's experiential knowledge.[12] If, nonetheless, such formulations are used to interpret reality, they are inadmissibly given a content and what results is an ideological understanding of man and world.[13]

Whether traditional forms of thought and constructs are contentless formulae that have the character of pseudo-statements and ideologies hinges on a certain understanding of science. Topitsch's concept of science is close to that of the Neopositivists of the Vienna circle,[14] and a general critique of positivism[15] applies to his ideology-critical understanding of contentless formulae. It is not a matter of disputing that the traditional models of the understanding of self and the world can be ideologies and contentless, but of criticizing an approach that asserts that a Neopositivistic concept of science generates the only valid criterion for a critique of ideology. This would be true only if a definitive interpretation of man and history could be advanced, and if man and all his possibilities could be scientifically "understood." The analysis of forms of thought and constructs as practiced in the sociology of knowledge can explain the mechanism by which significant insights are passed on over centuries. It can also show why significant insights without definable substantive and normative content can be passed on, and what function such contentless formulations have. But such a sociology bars a comprehensive understanding of the significance of forms of thought and conceptual models if it excludes *a priori* the possibility of some further-reaching significance simply on the basis of a Neopositivist decision about what science is. To limit oneself to a concept of science that extends no further than to the description of sets of falsifiable statements in the realm of the factual[16] reduces the reality of man[17] to areas of falsifiable experiential knowledge. How little justice such a reductionist concept of science and reality does to man and his history is obvious when it is compared with Fromm's attempt to understand man as a being with imperative psychic needs. For this reason, Fromm's more comprehensive concept of science[18] is given preference here over Topitsch's Neopositivist one.

The following comments are based on the historical and sociological insights and research of Ernst Topitsch and should be read with this reservation about his positivistic approach in mind. The decision to speak of a contentless formulation rather than of a form of thought is governed by the relation of a form of thought and an ideational construct to the comprehensively understood reality of man.

In opposition to Topitsch, it is argued here that reality comprehends more than the circumscribed and circumscribable sphere of the factual, that it transcends what can be described in contexts of falsifiable statements.

The History of the Ecstatic-Cathartic Conceptual Model and of Its Forms of Thought

Of the significant models that were developed during the course of intellectual history—the models by which man interpreted his world, himself, and his history—the one Topitsch calls "ecstatic-cathartic" is especially revelatory of Fromm's thought, particularly of his dialectic.

The origins of the ecstatic-cathartic model or construct must be looked for in the gnostic myths, which, in turn, were molded by shamanistic magic and divination. These myths were formed on the basis of experiences "of superiority over the pressure of the environing world that occur in states of trance or under the influence of drugs, and either set in spontaneously or—in the majority of cases—are induced artificially by chanting and rhythmic dances, vigils, fasting, breathing exercises and other ascetic practices."[19] Such experiences form the background for the beginnings of an ideational construct central to which is the possibility of an ecstatic superiority over the limitations imposed by space and time and one's own corporality. While in Greek philosophy from Parmenides to Aristotle, and especially in Plato, mystical ideas were increasingly transformed into the conviction that the soul[20] that was freed of its body enjoyed a contemplative superiority over the world,[21] and true philosophy was viewed as an important means of the catharsis of the soul, renewed contact with magic and ecstatic salvation doctrines of Oriental provenance subsequently led to the rise of gnostic and Neoplatonic speculation.[22] "The basic gnostic motif is the pressure of reality that is experienced with cutting incisiveness and its result, the need for salvation that seeks satisfaction in a corresponding interpretation of the human self and of the entire world process."[23] The gnostic interpretation of the human self sees in men souls of light that have fallen away from a divinity conceived as unknowable. Since they lost the knowledge of their divine origin in their fall, they can either become completely estranged from that origin or recover knowledge of it (gnosis) by becoming aware of their divine character.[24] This gnostic "knowledge" is a "process of redemption that transforms man by reawakening his consciousness of divinity."[25] Man's salvation is gnosis, a becoming aware of "the divinity of his own 'true' self."[26]

This idea of the estrangement of the human soul from its divine origin and its salvation through gnosis subsequently became the model for an interpretation of the entire world process. The world emanates from God, and God and world thus become distinct. From this estranged state, the world returns to unity with the world ground or God. This model of *próodos* (emanation) and *epistrophē* (return) gives rise to the "alexandrine world schema and its fundamental idea of God's descent into matter which also means the creation of the world and a return of man to God by which he is redeemed."[27] The assessment of any given present as a time of necessary estrangement and calamity explains the attraction this ecstatic-cathartic construct of Gnosticism and Neoplatonism had for Judaeo-Christian apocalypticism. Both the apocalyptic and the gnostic traditions see "the present, pressing evil as a necessary negative stage on the way toward ultimate salvation."[28] During the course of the intellectual history of the West, especially after this three-phase model of salvation was received by Dionysus the Aeropagite, both traditions repeatedly fused and had particular influence on the history of Jewish and Christian mysticism.

Topitsch traces the ecstatic-cathartic construct through history all the way down to the concept of dialectics in Hegel and Marx. He proves the presence of this form of thought in Isaac Luria's Kabbala[29] and demonstrates that a tradition runs from there to Friedrich Christoph Oetinger,[30] the Tübinger Stift, and on to Hegel and Schelling. Swabian pietism, an intense Christian eschatological consciousness that attained its fullest development in Johannes Albrecht Bengel, Oetinger's teacher, can also be noted.[31]

Topitsch draws on the concept of alienation in Hegel's philosophy of history and his theory of work[32] for a convincing illustration of these summarily sketched developments, for we see here an application of the pattern of a "three-phase rhythm of original state, *próodos* and *epistrophē* negation and negation of the negation, etc."[33] In his concept of the dialectic, Hegel reflects this form of thought.

The Concept of Dialectics as Form of Thought and Contentless Formula as Rooted in the Ecstatic-Cathartic Model

The concept of dialectics is as old and polymorphous as Occidental philosophy.[34] Hegel's understanding of it takes a specific form that adopts the substance of the ecstatic-cathartic tradition.[35] "Dialectics manifests itself in the dialectical and process-like development of his philosophy."[36] This philosophy carries out the process of "life"[37] in which "the elements of separation and opposition or negation are as effective and indispensable as those of reunification and reconciliation or negation of the negation."[38] The dialectics of being takes place within the dialectics of knowledge because "the world process in its totality is conceived as the dialectical self-realization and the coming to consciousness of spirit which means that . . . the laws of reality . . . are necessarily also those of thought."[39] Such an "idealism" is grounded in an Absolute that, as identity and nonidentity, finds its true unity only in the sublation of its own nonidentity. "Hegel's dialectic presupposes the concept of the Absolute; it cannot do without it."[40]

Dialectical thought becomes problematical when it is made a general principle of knowledge and order, and this is true whether or not an absolute is premised. When Karl R. Popper notes, for example, that for Hegel "dialectics is a theory that maintains that something—particularly human thought—develops in a way that is characterized by the so-called dialectical triad of thesis, antithesis and synthesis,"[41] he is really no longer talking about Hegel's understanding of dialectics. In such formulations, there is indeed the danger that dialectics will be seen as contentless. In his critique of Hegel, Topitsch emphasizes two circumstances that make the concept of dialectics contentless. First, in Hegel, the dialectical triad is transposed "from the realm of unverifiable theosophical speculation to that of verifiable facts"[42] so that a conflict between dialectics and formal logic and the methods of the sciences develops.[43] And second, by the application of dialectics to all areas of reality, the concept of dialectics becomes nebulous[44] and that of negation totally empty. Dialectics is given general validity, and the concept of negation comes to comprehend all kinds of nonidentity such as logical contradiction, scientific refutation, evaluative rejection, social conflict, the sequence of developmental stages, and finally, mere difference. When all of these areas are subsumed under this concept and integrated in the dialectical rhythm as negation or negation of the negation, dialectics as a form of thought becomes an arbitrarily manipulable contentless formula.[45] Whether this critique of dialectics is also a justifiable critique of Hegel cannot be decided here. But it is true that by extending the application of the dialectical triad, Topitsch has made us aware that there is a line that separates scientific from nonscientific thought and that also defines the boundary between form of thought and contentless formula.[46] Dialectics as a concept becomes contentless in the sciences when a dialectical triad is asserted even though it has no relation to what is empirically given or can actually be falsified by experiential fact.[47] This means "that dialectics cannot really be used to make empirical predictions."[48] But Topitsch's claim[49] that we are already dealing with contentless formulae and nonscientific thought whenever falsification is impossible is the outgrowth of a Neopositivistic concept of science to which we do not assent.[50]

In the work of Marx, dialectics as a form of thought took on a distinctive cast. It is being considered here because Marx's thought had a particular influence on Fromm's. Marx transferred the ecstatic-cathartic model of Gnosticism into this world: "Just as in gnosticism, the world emanates from God or he estranges himself from it and attains his perfection through a painful self-estrangement, so working man estranges himself from the product of his labor and is to find salvation from his self-estrangement in a higher being, i.e. true humanity in socialist society."[51]

How dialectics and empirical data relate to each other is a question that arises anew when the idealistic basis of the concept of dialectics is abandoned in an "inversion." For "the best argument in favor of dialectics lies in its applicability to the development of thought, especially of philosophical thought,"[52] so that for Hegel, for example, history is the history of ideas. Marx opposed Idealism but retained Hegel's doctrine that "the dialectical 'contradictions,' 'negations' and 'negations of negations' represent dynamic forces of historical development."[53] But Marx's materialistic reformulation does not mean that dialectics is identical with the essence and the law of natural and historical movement, that it is a procedure of empirical research, a method for systematic and deductive presentation, or a method for presenting social history or the history of ideology.[54] Marx uses dialectics merely as a "procedure to reconstruct the categorical system of a class-related social science, as a method in the critique of political economy, and as a form of ideology critique."[55]

Although a number of misunderstandings of statements by Marx—especially of his early writings, which propose a *Realdialektik*[56] (dialectic of the real)—are thus excluded, it is precisely when dialectics is understood as a form of ideology critique that the danger that it will degenerate into a contentless formula arises.

Marx judges what exists and is given at any particular time, not by philosophical reflection, but by a critique of such reflection as an ideology, though he cannot advance grounds for this decision that lie beyond the criticism itself. As a consequence, dialectics as a form of thought falls under the suspicion of being a substitute for a comprehensive theory. Negation can become arbitrary and dialectics itself a contentless formula—that is, ideological—and this is the decisive weakness of the concept of dialectics in a Marxism that neither can nor wants to dispense with a comprehensive theory. This reproach also applies to Fromm's reception of Marx and his understanding of dialectics.

As a process of *positio, negatio,* and *negatio negationis* in the three-fold sense of sublation as *tollere, elevare,* and *conservare* (the way Hegel and Marx used it), dialectics is a form of thought derived from the ecstatic-cathartic construct that is rooted in a gnostic-apocalyptic tradition. A number of concepts and elements in Marx's theory make it possible to clarify this assertion.[57] The extent to which his self-proclaimed this-worldly and scientific view of man actually follows the ideas and forms of thought of gnostic and apocalyptic doctrines of salvation "becomes perfectly apparent in the Marxist interpretation of the historical and social process and especially of economic development as a drama of man's self-realization by way of his self-estrangement."[58] If it is true that man creates himself through work, "the product of his labor . . . begins to confront him as an autonomous power."[59] Not only the parallel to cosmological ideas in gnostic or kabbalistic traditions emerges here, but the gnostic and apocalyptic notion of an apocalyptic increase and intensification of negative forces has its counterpart in the role Marx assigns to the proletariat when revolution ushers in socialism.[60]

More generally, one may say that the power of the negative can be seen as the key to an understanding of theories about apocalypse, Gnosticism, the Kabbala, mysticism, pietism, and other forms of ecstatic-cathartic ideas all the way down to Hegel's and

Marx's systems. This is why a particular view of history becomes necessary: "If the present time of the world in which the self lives is not its home, some event must have caused this questionable condition. That God and world are estranged from each other becomes meaningful only on the presupposition that history is identical with the eon of sin that lies embedded between creation and salvation. . . . Gnostically, salvation means abolition of the distance from the origin. And distance is estrangement."[61] This approach gives force to Marx's demand that a theory of history not content itself with statements about the here and now but develop overarching ideas.[62] It also shows that the topos of a negative view of the present is necessary, and that what is negative in the present must be emphasized for the sake of a future good. In addition, we see here the grounding of the claim to have a concept of criticism whose premise is that the critique of what exists is always necessary and legitimate.[63]

In Marx's case, more than gnostic knowledge—that is, gnosis as contemplation—is employed to overcome the negative. This is precisely the basis for his critique of Hegel and of Hegel's assessment of philosophy. Yet Marx does not abandon the tradition of the ecstatic-cathartic construct; he merely chooses its markedly apocalyptic and practical form in which transfiguration involves the practical and active transformation of man.[64] The "power of evil and of suffering, in short of the 'negative,' is the real motif of both Hegel's and Marx's thought. They seek a solution that will make this power appear as both necessary and as destined to be abolished by man."[65]

DIALECTICS IN FROMM'S WORK

Defining the ecstatic-cathartic conceptual model in the dialectics of Hegel and Marx allows us to see that with his philosophical-anthropological, religio-critical, and ethical views, Fromm stands in the tradition of this model. Although he explicitly traces the most important concepts to Marx, he makes, apart from some reflections on "paradoxical logic,"[66] no comments on dialectics, let alone any sociological reflection about dialectics as the form of thought of a particular conceptual model. Nonetheless, it is obvious that his roots are in this tradition. It can also be shown that Marx was not the primary mediator of this model.

Fromm's Thought in the Tradition of the Ecstatic-Cathartic Model

Fromm grew up in a Jewish spiritual and social milieu and was influenced by the cathartic element of this religion, which orthodoxy especially emphasizes. As a young man, he was much influenced by his Talmud teacher, Schneur Salman Rabinkov, who was both a Habadnik and a socialist and responsible for Fromm's interest in socialist thought. One may plausibly assume that it was primarily Rabinkov and the mysticism of Habad Hasidism, and only secondarily Marx's religio-critical modification of the conceptual model, that shaped Fromm's thought.

Hasidism is primarily a development of the Lurianic Kabbala and its apocalyptic version in Sabbatianism[67] and shares the concerns of Jewish mysticism with these.[68] Gershom Scholem sees the origin of Jewish mysticism in the fact that "Gnosticism, one of the last great manifestations of mythology in religious thought . . . lent figures of speech to the Jewish mystic,"[69] and he demonstrates this in his discussion of Merkabah mysticism, the precursor of the Kabbala.[70] It is not surprising that Jewish mysticism should be a stimulus for an ecstatic-cathartic construct: "To most Kabbalists, as true seal-bearers of the world of myth, the existence of evil is, at any rate , one of the most pressing problems, and one which keeps them continuously occupied with attempts to solve it."[71]

It is principally with the Zohar and on the basis of the Sefirot doctrine that Jewish mysticism was elaborated in Spanish Kabbalism. The Sefirot doctrine represents a theosophical speculation that synthesizes various gnostic, Neoplatonic, and apocalyptic traditions in a typical ecstatic-cathartic construct, the kabbalistic one.[72] In the "breaking of the vessels," the gnostic doctrine concerning the sparks became the kabbalistic cosmogony that included all those details that are characteristic of an ecstatic-cathartic construct.[73] While the tradition of the ecstatic-cathartic model that runs from the Lurianic Kabbala to the Christian Kabbala and Swabian pietism and on to Hegel and Marx is relatively hazy, the link to Hasidism and the Habad Hasidism of Shneur Zalman is clear and direct: the most important source for the

Habad doctrine is the Zohar and Luria's Kabbala. The Habad doctrine itself can be seen as a transformation of theosophical speculation into "an instrument of psychological analysis and self-knowledge"[74] in which, that transformation notwithstanding, the ecstatic-cathartic construct retains its validity. The process by which mysticism becomes ethos, which accompanies the transformation, and the emphasis on the "way" this entails[75] opens up an understanding of many philosophical-anthropological and psychological and ethical views of Fromm,[76] and also facilitates access to ecstatic-cathartic constructs in the mysticisms of Asia. So Fromm's thought was given a specific turn by Habad Hasidism, and his most important interests during the twenties—Freud's doctrines, Karl Marx, and Buddhism—were reinforcements of already existing forms of thought within an ecstatic-cathartic conceptual construct.

Freud himself clearly expressed the conviction on which his movement was founded: "Where Id was, there shall Ego be."[77] In this process of "enlightenment," reason plays a decisive role, but it is a reason that governs the unconscious and irrational passions and frees man of the power of the unconscious. Psychoanalysis is primarily interested in the cathartic aspect of reason, and catharsis is therefore a central concept in Freud. Even after Fromm's break with Jewish orthodoxy, both Buddhism and his study of Marx contributed, each in its own particular way, to his retaining the forms of thought of the ecstatic-cathartic construct in which he had been rooted up to that point. The study of Marx played a greater role as he critically distanced himself from theistic positions: Marx's critique of religion grounded Fromm's humanism,[78] while Marx's socialism provided him with a secular theory of history.[79] The encounter with Buddhism, and later with Zen, led to the concept of a nontheistic religion as a mysticism of the ONE.[80]

As one surveys the various phenomena in Western intellectual history and other cultures that stimulated Fromm's interest, one notices that they are primarily thinkers, movements, and facts that can be classified as belonging to the ecstatic-cathartic construct insofar as their understanding of man, his world, and his history is concerned. What is invariably involved is a "radical knowledge," a "becoming aware" of man's innermost productive capacities,[81] an "illumination,"[82] the awakening of *"humani-*

tas"[83]—in short, gnosis that not only does without mysticism[84] but actively combats it as irrationality.[85]

Before sketching how Fromm's thought is rooted in the cathartic construct by examining his views on man and man's history, we will turn our attention to his reflections on paradoxical logic. The purpose of these comments is not to critically investigate the correctness of his statements but rather to allow elements of his ecstatic-cathartic thought to emerge from what he subsumes under the concept of "paradoxical logic."[86]

Besides Aristotelian logic, which is based on identity, contradiction, and the excluded middle, there exists, according to Fromm,[87] another mode of thought whose existence in the West can be traced to Heraclitus and which later shows up as "dialectics" in the thought of Hegel and Marx. The principal home of this mode of thought, however, is the East—China and India. It can be called paradoxical logic and is a form of thought that assumes, as Heraclitus did, that "the conflict between opposites is the basis of all existence."[88] In contrast to Aristotelian logic, paradoxical logic, such as Taoism or Brahmanic philosophy, attempts to find a solution beyond all dualism: "The harmony (unity) consists in the conflicting positions from which it is made up."[89]

What thinking within an ecstatic-cathartic construct means can be recognized most clearly when one examines the consequences of the summary concept "paradoxical logic." An example would be Fromm's emphasis on the meaning paradoxical logic has for a negative concept of God and his assertion that the philosophy that follows the Veda contains the idea that God is the extreme form of ignorance. Fromm writes: "We see here the connection with the namelessness of the Tao, the nameless name of the God who reveals himself to Moses, of the 'absolute Nothing' of Meister Eckhart."[90] According to Fromm, another consequence of paradoxical logic is that man can never grasp unity intellectually but only in the "experience of oneness,"[91] so that the mystical experience of the ONE becomes the only adequate form of religion. This means that doctrinal contents and science are not of primary importance; rather, the emphasis is on transforming man and knowing "the right way" (*halacha,* Tao).[92] "Paradoxical logic . . . led to tolerance . . . the paradoxical standpoint . . . to the emphasis on transforming man."[93] It is impossible to overlook the closeness of what is here called "paradoxical thinking" to the ecstatic-cathartic construct, even though the concept "paradoxical logic" is ultimately unclear. The construct emerges with greater clarity in Fromm's view of man and his history, however. The following comments will sketch the affinity between the two by comparing Fromm's statements on man's nature and history and the typology of the ecstatic-cathartic construct.

In the question concerning man's self-understanding, the point of departure is the difference between man and animal, which has been established by abundant empirical research. Not only a comparison between this point of departure and traditional definitions of man's nature[94] but also a glance at other contemporary philosophical anthropologies[95] shows that the definition of man as a contradictory being is not a necessary inference from empirical data. It is merely a possible, and perhaps optimal, interpretation. To see man's nature in his contradictoriness is consonant with the ecstatic-cathartic construct, whose basic motif is the pressure of reality that expresses itself in various dichotomies and is to be overcome. Gnosticism sees men as light souls[96] that have fallen out of a primordial unity and become estranged from their origin. Fromm believes that man's dichotomy derives from a break[97] with the harmony of nature. The contradictoriness results from the fact that man is both part of, and more than, nature. In transcending nature through the consciousness of what he is, and through his reason and imagination, man expresses the ecstatic as well as his need for salvation.

In Gnosticism, the fate of the fallen light souls is either total estrangement or the becoming aware of their divine character and the abolition of the estrangement through gnosis. In Fromm's thought, man's reason, which is responsible for his having "fallen out of" harmony with nature and for the demand that he resolve his dichotomies and the specific human needs in which they result, makes possible two answers: either man can react nonproductively and become increasingly estranged; or he can react productively, by mobilizing his powers of reason and love and by attempting to establish a new unity of himself, world, and nature.

The ecstatic-cathartic construct and Fromm's philosophical-anthropological observations also agree that a positive definition of man's nature or essence will be possible only when the "divinity of his own 'true self' "[98] has been recognized, or when an optimal unfolding of his biophilic capacities has caused him to attain a new unity.

This also indicates the parallel between the two philosophies of history. Apocalypticism is a form of the messianic idea and significantly influenced gnostic cosmogony and theory of history. Fromm sees his view of history as a development of prophetic messianism, so the formal similarity between the ideas is not surprising. It is true, of course, that he applies the cosmogonic model of the original state, *próodos* and *epistrophē*, only to man as humanity and does not reflect on the development of the cosmos. It is different with the assessment of the present historical period as one of necessary estrangement and inescapable evil: in Fromm's theory of history, estrangement is required, and the supposition of a necessary estrangement is consonant with both a gnostic and a humanistic position that does not care to burden man with responsibility for estrangement but does charge him with responsibility for overcoming it. In gnostic-kabbalistic cosmogonies, the "fall of the sparks" is the necessary precondition if their positive meaning is to be understood. In Fromm, the fall of man is the condition for the possibility of his discovering his productive capacities of reason and love. In view of Fromm's interpretation of socialism as a secularized messianism, the notion that his socialism has its home in the ecstatic-cathartic model requires no further proof.[99]

The rootedness of Fromm's thought in the ecstatic-cathartic model also becomes apparent when one looks at questions and answers that persist throughout his work. The first fundamental problem, the relation between individual and society, reflects the profound problematics of the sociological autonomy of Jewish groups in society as a whole, and is related to Fromm's own background. The answer to this basic question comprises his entire sociopsychological work, especially the linkage of sociology and psychoanalysis in an original sociopsychological method, the development of the concept "social character," and the view of man as primarily a social being. But Fromm's social psychology is more than an answer to the question regarding the relation between individual and society. It must be seen within the framework of the more encompassing question concerning unity in multiplicity and a principle of unity that can bring together the multiplicity of phenomena. It is here that Fromm's rootedness in an ecstatic-cathartic construct becomes apparent, for in such a construct, multiplicity is the emanation of the ONE, and the return to the ONE is salvation from exile, Diaspora, estrangement, dispersal.

A second fundamental question that persists throughout Fromm's work concerns man's capacity for the moral as a capacity for unity in mankind. It was provoked by the brutality of two world wars, the murder of millions of Jews, and the possibility of man's nuclear self-destruction. Fromm's humanistic ethics provides the answer to the fundamental question regarding man's capacity for the moral. It deals with the way, the *halacha,* and the preconditions for taking it. The preconditions lie in a humanism that sees itself as salvation through man's own efforts. Man's self-assertion in his potential goodness is part of this humanism. This self-assertion corresponds to man's potential divinity on the basis of gnostic knowledge or Hasidic self-sanctification. Therefore humanistic ethics has the task of grounding man's capacity for unity against all opposing theories of aggression, and of showing the way to unity. Its general principle of value is man's unfolding to *humanitas,* which, as humanity, represents man's unity, and, as humanness, defines the condition for the possibility of unity.

A third fundamental question that persists and most clearly points to the origin of his thought in the ecstatic-cathartic construct regards the experience of a meaning that encompasses man and his world. Fromm's answer to the fundamental question of an encompassing experience of meaning is humanistic religion as the mystical experience of the ONE. Just as humanistic ethics can name the goal and the path to that goal, so humanistic religion can name the way the ONE is experienced insofar as it means man's oneness with himself and with his human and natural environing world. The experience of the ONE is possible only when man renounces all heteronomous influences, negates his dependencies, and thereby becomes aware of his own true, inner self. Only in this self-limitation ("emptiness," "nothingness") does the ecstatic quality of the experience of the ONE become possible: the mystic experiences his oneness with his human and natural world as an anticipation of his perfection.[100] Belief and faith in man and his future find support in this encompassing experience of meaning, so that humanistic religion as the mysticism of the ONE makes possible a humanistic ethos through this encompassing experience of meaning.[101] For mysticism means the experience of the reconciliation of contradictions and the unity of difference and diversity, grounds the capacity for the moral in that experience, and directs man's moral striving toward a goal. Similarly, salvation according to the ecstatic-cathartic construct cannot do without the mystical experience of the ONE in oneness.[102]

Dialectics as Form of Thought and Contentless Formulae

The words "dialectics" and "dialectical" occur infrequently in Fromm's work. He never commented on "dialectics" as a form of thought or a method. Yet dialectics as a form of thought plays an eminent role in his work, and it is precisely the understanding of dialectics that we find in Hegel and Marx and that has its home in the ecstatic-cathartic construct.

By dialectics is meant a form of thought, "a three-phase rhythm of original state estrangement and return negation and negation of the negation, etc."[103] It is asserted that it is legitimate to interpret reality dialectically as long as such an interpretation cannot be falsified in the sphere of the empirical sciences. Beyond this limit, dialectics becomes contentless formula.[104] The distinctiveness of dialectics lies in its concept of negation, which means that dialectics proceeds by the negation of the given. It thus implies a particular kind of criticism.[105] The detailed demonstration of the presence of dialectical thought in Fromm's work will be limited largely to his critique of religion because it is here that the line dividing it from the use of dialectics as a contentless formula can be easily demonstrated.

In his grounding of humanistic religion, Fromm's point of departure is that humanistic religion is the negation of authoritarian religion. Therefore only a revolutionary character—the dialectical counterconcept of the authoritarian character—can do justice to the concern of humanistic religion. The dialectical conjunction of humanistic religion and revolutionary character, and of authoritarian religion and authoritarian character, means that the antithetical entities contradict each other and are therefore incompatible. This dialectical conjunction also means that humanistic religion and revolutionary character are possible only in the process that negates authoritarian religion and the authoritarian character.[106] Understanding dialectics as a process implies a historico-theoretical aspect that, in Fromm, takes the form of a theory of the history of the concept of God.

Within the dialectical process, the epithets "humanistic" and "revolutionary" have an antiauthoritarian function, for it is only the principle of disobedience that can break the dominance of obedience to irrational authorities in the long run.[107] This dialectical view of man's dependence on authority results from an investigation of irrational authority relations and has its justification insofar as such irrational relations can in fact be dissolved only by opposition (or contradiction). Dialectics as a form of thought is thus perfectly valid where irrational authority relations can be diagnosed. But doubts about the validity of dialectical thinking arise when rational authority relations are no longer considered possible and dialectics is used pervasively. It could be shown[108] that while Fromm distinguishes between rational and irrational authority relations and maintains that the former do in fact exist because they are postulates of everyday life, his systematic discussion of the revolutionary character and humanistic religion entirely ignores the possibility of rational authority and argues that authoritarian character and authoritarian religion, and revolutionary character and humanistic religion, are always dialectically conjoined. The daily experience of rational authority notwithstanding, he thus maintains the validity of a dialectic that is really the constraint and dictate of a form of thought. The result is that dialectics becomes a manipulable contentless formula when it is applied to phenomena of rational authority.

If dialectics as a form of thought is applied to all authority relations without exception, it will degenerate into a contentless formula. This observation becomes a criticism of Fromm in all those instances where he no longer has faith in the possibility of rational authority relations, yet fails to prove that they are impossible. The following paired opposites, all of which derive from the problem of authority relations and which Fromm unjustifiably sees exclusively as dialectical contradictions, could be named: authoritarian : revolutionary character; authoritarian : humanistic religion; theism : nontheism; theonomy : autonomy.

The criticism here is not of the contrasts as such, but rather of the definition of the contradiction as necessarily a dialectical one. It is not disputed that an irrational authority relation can very often be discovered behind the first concept of the pair of opposites. It is disputed, however, that the pairs of opposites are incompatible *a priori*: obedience is not invariably submission to an irrational authority, nor are theism and theonomy always the same as heteronomy. With his postulate of a rational authority relation, Fromm himself indicates a line that separates a certain form of thought as a means of interpreting reality, and the claim of a reality that can be experienced and is subject to scientific scrutiny. This reality represents a line beyond which the validity of the form of thought used up to that point cannot extend. If it is not respected, the form of thought degenerates into a contentless formula.

A second line that separates form of thought and dialectics as contentless formula emerges in the application of dialectics to the understanding of the history of the concept of God.[109] For Fromm, the history of that concept is a history in which man increasingly learns to understand himself as ultimate reality and highest value. Man's progressive self-knowledge goes along with a process of negation: to the extent that every statement about God is negated, man understands that he himself is God insofar as he is a genuinely human being.[110] This idea has its origin in the ban on images in Judaism; it is given greater depth in the Jewish philosophy of religion and especially in the doctrine of negative attributes.[111] Fromm uses it in a religio-critical sense: the recognition that statements about God are impossible, and the critique of any idea about God that transcends man ground the humanistic view of man and his world as a reality that exists wholly through and of itself. The relation between God and man must therefore be expressed dialectically. The goal is the freedom and independence of man from a God whose *a priori* meaning is unfreedom and dependence. In the case of free and independent man, this process of negation does away with the contradiction. A critique of this view coincides with the critique of Fromm's concept of authority, but this is not to say that his conviction that history legitimizes the process of negation has already been addressed.[112]

The humanistic view of man and world in history is grounded in a critique of religion that can be inferred from the history of the concept of God. The line Fromm traces in the history of the concept is no more than a presentation of the development of a negative theology, and makes visible a process by which the concept of God becomes increasingly less meaningful. An interpretation of this religio-critical development as a process of negation within a dialectical triad seems plausible and is judged correct and valid by Fromm, for he interprets this line of development in religion as the development of religion generally. The religio-critical and humanistic interpretation of the history of negative theology therefore becomes legitimate only if the general course of religion is understood as a dialectical process and the development of negative theology up to nontheistic mysticism is seen as a process of negation within the dialectical triad.

Apart from important critical questions concerning the function of the process of negation in the history of negative theology,[113] the view of the history of the concept of God as a process of negation must be taken exception to because no dialectical triad can be demonstrated. Dialectics as a form of thought that makes it possible to interpret the history of the concept of God as that of a process of negation implies an original state that can neither be postulated nor proven. The *Urgeschichte* of religion as Fromm himself outlines it[114] knows neither an original state that might correspond in some respects to a final one, nor such a thing as a falling out of this original state. There is only the history of the concept of God in which certain developmental phases and tendencies are recognizable, but these cannot be subsumed under one heading. What one can observe is that the concept of God and its critique depend on biological, economic, political, and sociocultural factors. And in the history of the concept of God and in the history of the critique of religion, one can certainly discover a tendency toward "demystification," "desacralization," "demythologization," and other forms of man's claim to reason as he seeks to reach intellectual maturity. For Fromm, this tendency is the point of departure for an interpretation of the history of the concept of God. But a tendency that can be documented historically neither allows the kind of unambiguous inference that would be necessary to ground a theory of history nor justifies the interpretation of the history of the concept of God as a process of negation. An interpretation of this history as a process of negation becomes possible only if that process can be shown to be part of a dialectical triad. It is precisely here that Fromm fails, for he does not see man's earliest development according to the ecstatic-cathartic model, as an original state and *proodos,* but philo- and ontogenetically, in accordance with a biomorphous[115] conceptual construct,[116] as a continuing process of developing consciousness. This model is based on discoveries in those sciences that investigate man's origins and see the development of man and of mankind as a gradual detachment from ties to nature and mother. In line with this biomorphous approach, the goal of development is judged to be total freedom and independence. Because Fromm interprets this process dialectically, he combines two irreconcilable conceptual constructs, for the dialectical interpretation is necessarily tied to the ecstatic-cathartic construct. And in the interpretation of the history of the concept of God as a process of negation, dialectics becomes a contentless formula—that is, a method of interpreting history that has no genuine basis. If, however, the history of the concept of God cannot be interpreted dialectically, a humanistic interpretation of the critique of religion loses its justification, for then the critique of religion does not necessarily imply a negation of the concept of God. Theism is not a contradiction of humanism, nor can there be an *a priori* humanistic interpretation of it.[117]

The Universal Claim of Dialectical Thinking and Its Critique

An individual's life from birth to death represents a development that takes place in accordance with certain rules. A fundamental rule whose existence can be demonstrated empirically, especially by psychology, states that development is possible only as a permanent process of detachment. Accordingly, independence and freedom can only be achieved if a previous condition of security is given up and an identification that was possible hitherto is lost. If man does not accomplish this permanent exodus, or if it is prevented, developmental malfunctioning and physical and psychic illnesses set in. Man's life rule accordingly states that the unfolding of human life is possible only where what prevailed hitherto is negated and left behind. The process of growth implies a process of negation. This fundamental rule of all human development, the knowledge of which is shared by all cultures, forms the empirical basis of a biomorphous conceptual construct that helps Fromm interpret his sociopsychological data in particular. In his investigation of individual productive and nonproductive character orientations in the process of assimilation and socialization, the biomorphous construct was clearly influential. The distinction between a syndrome of growth and one of decay can be traced to it, and it is also used in the interpretation of historical developments: the history of mankind is interpreted not only dialectically but also biomorphously, as a process of the increasing unfolding of his gift of reason, which distinguishes man from animal. The same holds for developments in intellectual history, as the understanding of the history of the concept of God illustrates. Because the biomorphous construct also implies a process of negation, its affinity with the ecstatic-cathartic construct and its form of thought, dialectics, becomes understandable. But the difference between the two must not be overlooked, for while the process of negation is part of the triad of original state, *proodos* and *epistrophē,* the biomorphous construct knows no such movement. It has a more or less direct development (which may have an internal dialectical structure) whose peculiarity is that the process of evolution is also always a process in which what was valid heretofore is negated.

The absence of the dialectical triad in the biomorphous construct results in an even more important difference in the understanding of the process of negation. In the biomorphous construct, negation means the negation of what gave rise to the following stage, whether this development is understood as circular (the rhythm of nature and the seasons) or evolutionary (the orthogenetic view of the development of prehuman life, for example). In both a detailed examination of the individual developmental stages and the global perspective on the entire course from its beginnings to its final state, negation in the biomorphous construct always means that the new negates the beginning or what precedes, and that the development can be understood both as a process of unfolding and one of negation. In dialectical thought, the process of negation is something different. Here negation ultimately always means the negation of a negation. When a development is understood dialectically, what exists is always and necessarily estranged and to be seen as the negation of an original condition. Interpreting a development dialectically as a process of negation means negating what existed before and exists now as a negation of an original state, and to abolish with this negation of the negation the negation of the original state. In contrast to the biomorphous construct, the dialectical interpretation makes possible an encompassing interpretation of the process of negation because that is the only interpretation that can interpret the present as a negation of the original state, a negation that must be negated in turn.

A dialectical interpretation of the process of negation must always be in line with, and legitimized by, empirically discoverable data, and the competing interpretation of the process of negation according to the biomorphous construct must be taken into account. The few attempts in Fromm's work to demonstrate processes of negation in and through empirical data suggest that the processes of negation should be interpreted biomorphously rather than dialectically. This applies both to the demonstration of man's historical development as a process during which irrational ties and irrational authorities are negated in favor of freedom and independence,[118] and to the setting forth of the history of the concept of God,[119] for in both of these historical developments, the empirical data do not indicate that the processes of negation should be understood dialectically. Instead, the data invite an understanding of the historical lines of development as a process of negation according to a biomorphous construct. Fromm interprets these two historical developments[120] and all processes of negation dialectically because his thought is anchored in a conceptual construct that interprets man, his history, and his world ecstatically-cathartically. We have shown that this interpretive approach and its form of thought, dialectics, differ from the interpretation of sociopsychological findings that flows from the data themselves—namely, a biomorphous understanding.

The difference in the interpretive possibilities is not the same as the difference between the empirical findings of social psychology on the one hand, and the philosophical-anthropological reflections and views on humanistic religion and ethics on the other. The question regarding the significance and validity of Fromm's insights and thoughts is not decided along the line that separates these two kinds of scientific statements. Instead, it is necessary always to inquire critically in both areas what the nexus between form of thought or conceptual construct and empirically discoverable data may be. A criticism of certain interpretations of philosophical-anthropological assumptions does not mean that these assumptions are necessarily false. First, the interpretations of the assumptions must be viewed critically, from the perspective of the forms of thought that underlie them. It must be asked whether the interpretations in question optimally correspond to the empirical data that are relevant to the assumptions, or whether they must be revised by a conceptual construct that is more adequate to the data. That it is easier to criticize in the area of humanistic ethics and religion than in the field of sociopsychological findings is obvious, but such an observation does not imply a separation in principle of the two areas of discourse. Neither a positivistic, self-imposed limitation to "value-free" insights nor the view that evaluative and interpretive statements about empirical findings are independent does justice to the question being asked here.

The critique here set forth applies to all dialectical thought that derives from an ecstatic-cathartic conceptual construct and claims universal validity. In conclusion, it raises the question of the extent to which the claim to universality of dialectical thought is a presupposition or a consequence of Fromm's religio-critical concept of humanism. What function does dialectics have in grounding humanism? The further question of the extent to which dialectically interpreted findings can also be relevant to a Christian understanding of man and world, especially to a theological ethics, hinges on the answer that is given to that question.

In Fromm's work, dialectics not only has the task of interpreting, ordering, and evaluating empirically discoverable data. His primary object in setting forth his critique of religion was to ground an encompassing theory of man and his history. This is especially true of the interpretation of the history of the concept of God as a dialectical process of negation. When dialectics is turned into a universally valid principle of all being and becoming, the questions and problems of man are given an answer that man could not provide on his own—that is, in the absence of dialectics as a theory that encompasses all reality. But because dialectics grasps all that exists as the negation of an original state, and because what exists, being the negation of an original state, can only be sublated and brought to a new identity if this negation is negated in turn, there is posited a theory that is universal because it encompasses all reality, in which an entity that transcends this reality does not exist, and where such an entity is not required for a solution. Universalizing dialectics as a form of thought thus satisfies the concern of Gnosticism from which it derives and which wishes to allow man to become aware of his divine nature as a task that he sets and must accomplish himself. Understood as a universal theory, dialectics grounds a humanism that is religio-critical *a priori*. Fromm's humanism is essentially tied to dialectical thought.

A further question regards the significance Fromm's dialectical thinking has for a Christian theology and ethics if dialectics is indispensable to the grounding of his religio-critical humanism concept. From a formal point of view, the following observation can be made: Fromm's religio-critical humanism concept is incompatible with a theistic-Christian perspective, to the extent dialectics is used universally. A theological critique of Fromm's religio-critical humanism concept would therefore set in at the point where the universalizing of dialectics encounters the resistance of empirical data (as in the case of the concept of authority or the history of the concept of God) and causes dialectics to degenerate into a contentless formula. Theological criticism, on the other hand, has its limit where givens (such as the overcoming of an irrational authority relation) call for a dialectical interpretation.

Fromm's significance, and that of his sociopsychological insights, his philosophical-anthropological reflections, and his religio-critical and ethical views for a Christian theology and a theological ethics have their limit where his form of thought, dialectics, becomes the universal theory of an ecstatic-cathartic understanding of man and world that is rooted in gnosis and in which the negation of the negation represents, as a critical theory, the principle of self-redemption. Such a universally dialectical view can be contrasted with an understanding of man and world that is oriented according to a biomorphous construct that sees not merely estrangement and negation but also creation and affirmation in what exists, and in which redemption means not only critique and negation but also healing and being healed. The final part of this book will show in some detail the line along which these two views touch on each other.

Part Four

HUMANISM AS SCIENCE AND AS RELIGIOUS ETHOS IN FROMM'S WORK

In Part One, Fromm's discoveries in psychoanalysis, social psychology, and philosophical-anthropological reflection were presented. Using his understanding of religion and ethics as an example, we then set forth and critically evaluated his concept of humanism in Part Two. Part Three identified some of the intellectual sources and antecedents to which Fromm, his thought, and his discoveries owe their peculiar stamp.

Part Four is not simply a summation of what preceded it. Our interest here focuses on the alternative of "having" and "being" as Fromm explicated it in his last major work, *To Have or to Be?* This alternative should first be seen as an ultimate abstraction from empirical findings in the context of the character doctrine: all human thinking, feeling, and acting occur either in the mode of having or in the mode of being. Beyond that, this alternative is a key to understanding human reality generally, including religious and ethical reality, so that the words "having or being" point to that line along which humanism as science and humanism as religion—or, better, humanism as religious ethos—become one.

8

THE ART OF LIVING: TO HAVE OR TO BE?

THE MODES OF HAVING AND BEING AS CHARACTEROLOGICAL CONCEPTS

Having and Being as Ultimate Assessments of Human Reality

The sociopsychological concept of character that is to be understood comprehensively lies at the center of Fromm's scientific view of man. Character is structured, which means that depending on the way it has been shaped, it has a distinctive quality that can be understood ideal-typically as the orientation of the character, and characterized as functional or dysfunctional for the development of man as a system. It is dispositive and determinative of human energy so that man's behavior vis-à-vis his natural and human environment corresponds to the quality and orientation of the character structure.[1] The various character orientations can enter into a variety of mixtures. Of primary scientific interest is which character orientation is dominant and whether this dominant orientation is productive or nonproductive.

The question as to the degree of intensity the dominance of a productive or nonproductive orientation has in the character structure led Fromm to the insight that one can speak of two character syndromes, the biophilically oriented syndrome of growth, and the necrophilically oriented syndrome of decay.[2] The setting up of syndromes takes into account the specific quality of character, namely, that a biophilic-productive or a necrophilic/nonproductive orientation is accompanied by certain components that converge as the orientation becomes increasingly defined. The more marked the convergence, the more clearly the growth or decay syndrome develops, and the more the alternative orientations exclude each other.[3] In other words, if an orientation develops and becomes a syndrome, the biophilic or necrophilic qualities intensify. These insights and ideas about character syndromes also apply to the discovery that human life is always oriented either toward having or toward being.[4]

Fromm's use of the concepts "having" and "being" derives from the nomenclature of the critique of capitalism found in Marx's *Economic and Philosophical Manuscripts* (1844): "Political economy, this science of wealth, is therefore at the same time the science of denial, of starvation, of saving, and it actually goes so far as to save man the need for fresh air or physical exercise. This science of the marvels of industry is at the same time the science of asceticism, and its true ideal is the ascetic but rapacious skinflint and the ascetic but productive slave. Its moral ideal is the worker who puts a part of his wages into savings. . . . Self-denial, the denial of life and of all human needs, is its principal doctrine. The less you eat, drink, love, theorize, sing, paint, fence, etc., the more you save and the greater will become that treasure which neither moths nor maggots can consume—your capital. The less you are, the less you give expression to your life, the more you have, the greater is your alienated life and the more you store up of your estranged life."[5]

Fromm attempts to find an empirical basis for the distinction between having and being that lies behind Marx's equation of having more and being less. And he acknowledges: "What I saw led me to conclude that this distinction, together with that between love of life and love of the dead, represents the most crucial problem of existence; that empirical anthropological and psychoanalytic data tend to demonstrate that having and being are two fundamental modes of experience, the respective strengths of which determine the differences between the characters of individuals and various types of social character."[6] Having and being are thus not character orientations in the sense mentioned above—like the receptive or hoarding orientations, for example.[7] They are modes of experience, as Fromm writes in this passage, or modes of human existence, as he usually calls them.

Like the concepts biophilia and necrophilia, having and being are ultimate judgments that antedate the individual character orientations and designate two fundamentally different tendencies, attitudes, or strivings of man and his character.[8] The judgment that someone lives in the mode of having or in the mode of being thus extends the previously discussed distinction into productive and nonproductive character orientations, but differs in (like biophilia and necrophilia) seeing character as a syndrome. The definitions "mode of having" or "mode of being" are more encompassing that the judgments "biophilia" or "necrophilia." Their use permits one to define and understand all levels of reality in terms of their value. Compared to the other alternative, the having/being alternative is an ultimate abstraction by which to evaluate human reality. The following description of these modes will show that despite its generality, this distinction most aptly defines human reality in terms of its quality. It can thus apply to any reality to which man can relate, and with these definitions every such reality can be more than adequately judged in regard to its value for the functioning of man as a system. By the ascription of a human reality to either the mode of having or of being, the most encompassing, aptest, and therefore the most definitive, judgment is rendered.

Definition of the Two Modes

The findings of psychoanalytic theory and psychotherapeutic practice, his sociopsychological insights and discoveries, his study of "radical" thinkers and personalities in the history of philosophy and religion, and finally his personal, untiring efforts to disillusion his own and the social pseudo-world with its rationalizations and ideologies—all these things enabled Fromm to give a very precise definition to the two modes. It is in the nature of things that it is easier to define the mode of having in all its variants and manifestations, that the definition of the mode of being is more difficult and therefore occurs, in part, *e contrario*. In contrast to the mode of having, the mode of being is an experience that cannot be precisely defined.[9]

The easiest access to what Fromm means by the "having mode of existence" can be had through his view of private property. In the having mode, "all that matters is my acquisition of property and my unlimited right to keep what I have acquired."[10] There is almost nothing that cannot be owned or become the object of acquisitive striving: material objects of every kind, some of which are acquired by a passion to collect; individuals one is responsible for but of whom one also has the right to dispose, such as children, marriage partners, the sick, the crippled, the ignorant. Virtues and values can become possessions (to have prestige, an image, courage, health, beauty); convictions of a religious, philosophical, and political nature are acquired like possessions and stubbornly defended. Truth and right can be taken possession of through legal proceedings or war, if need be. And through marriage, we also acquire the right to be loved. The methods by which things are acquired or the ways in which they are owned are also multifarious. They extend from acquisition through payment to illegal appropriation, and are called incorporation, interiorization, internalization, introjection, identification, and include all varieties of consumption.[11]

The desire to own something and to therefore have power over it is characteristic of the relation between subject and object in the mode of having: ". . . the statement 'I (subject) have O' (object) expresses a definition of I through my possession of O. The subject is not myself but I am what I have. My property constitutes myself and my identity. The underlying thought in the statement 'I am I' is "I am I because I have X'—X equalling all natural objects and persons to whom I relate myself through my power to control them, to make them permanently mine."[12] This way of defining existence by what one has or can have means nothing other than that the subject is no longer the source of human existence. Instead, it is determined by the object: "it has me, because my sense of identity, i.e. of sanity, rests upon my having it (and as many things as possible)."[13] The subject-object relation is reified in the mode of having; the well-being and happiness of the individual are determined by possession and the superiority over others and other things.[14]

In the mode of being, well-being and happiness can be experienced when man loves, shares, and gives.[15] This presupposes that man is independent and free and has critical reason, for these presuppositions are required if the most important characteristic of the being mode is to be present, and that is being active.[16] However, activism or busyness is the very thing that is not meant here. "What is meant is to renew oneself, to grow, to flow out, to love, to transcend the prison of one's isolated ego, to be interested, to 'incline,' to give."[17] All these verbs merely circumscribe an experience and an act that ultimately cannot be described but only lived.[18] In his activity, man experiences himself as source and subject of his human existence. The contrast to the mode of having thus becomes apparent. In the subject-object relation, the subject remains the actor and the center of existence, irrespective of what occurs or has occurred inside this relation. Unity is preserved: "I and my activity and the result of my activity are one."[19]

Characteristics of the Two Modes

There are certain characteristics that will bring out the differences between the two modes with greater clarity.[20] These characteristics distinguish the realizations of the modes of being and having because they result from the way the subject-object relation is shaped even when they are not in the foreground of behavior. Knowledge of these characteristics makes it easier to ascribe behavior to one or the other mode and makes the idea of the two modes more palpable.

In the attempt to give a very general definition of the mode of being, a central characteristic of that mode was named: (productive) activity. The corresponding characteristic in the mode of having is passivity. When man is in the state of passivity, he is not himself in what he does or doesn't do, in what he thinks, feels, and experiences. He "is lived" by inner and outer circumstances, constraints, needs, and passions that "have him" and determine him. For this reason, activism and busyness are really forms in which passivity expresses itself, while meditation and concentration exercises can be forms of the most intense activity.[21]

A further, central characteristic of the two modes can be suggested by the concepts "security" and "insecurity." The human being whose dominant orientation is the value of having is always marked by a specific anxiety and insecurity that are induced by the permanent danger that he may lose what he owns. Such an individual is constantly obliged to mobilize all his energy to cling to and secure what he has. The compulsive need for security, which also characterizes all forms of obsessional neurosis, generally applies where the attempt is made to orient oneself through having.

But the development of human life depends on man's not clinging to what he has. A small child has its body and its mother's breast. In time, it discovers that it has a mother, a father, brothers, sisters, and toys. For a child, this having is a necessity because it is helpless without it. As the individual becomes older and independent, however, progress is possible only through an attitude that enables him to desist from seeking security by clutching his possessions. This developmental law also applies to the having of such things as profession, knowledge, children, social position, and life itself. Where the attitude toward these things is such that one makes oneself and the meaning of one's life depend on them or their possession, constant fear and insecurity necessarily result. Such a life harbors a permanent doubt: "If I am what I have, and if what I have is lost, who then am I?"[22] The answer must necessarily be, "Nobody but a defeated, deflated, pathetic testimony to a wrong way of living."[23] The fact that I can lose what I have creates the unceasing anxiety that this loss may in fact occur. A life in the having mode is therefore always an anxiety-ridden life. This anxiety can attach itself to any and everything. It is fear of thieves, of economic change, of revolutions, illnesses, death, and it is fear of love, of freedom, growth, change, of the unknown.[24]

This kind of anxiety and insecurity do not exist in a life lived in the being mode. "If I am who I am and not what I have, nobody can deprive me of or threaten my security and my sense of identity. My center is within myself; my capacity for being and for expressing my essential powers is part of my character structure and depends on me."[25] Such powers in man are his reason, his love, his artistic and intellectual creativity. All of them grow by use. In opposition to all those things that are important in the having mode, it can be said of the powers that are essentially man's: "What is spent is not lost, but on the contrary, what is kept is lost."[26]

With the concepts "solidarity" or "greed" and "antagonism," two other characteristics that always mark the modes of being and having can be named.[27] In the having mode, man defines himself by what he has or can have. This definition implies that man is insatiable: he would like to have, have a great deal, have more, most. Thus greed is intrinsic to having. "It can be the greed of the miser or the greed of the profit hunter or the greed of the womanizer or the man chaser."[28] Greed is insatiable in the two senses: a greedy individual will always have an excessive desire and boundless wishes, and all the satisfactions of his greed notwithstanding, he will never have enough because having cannot truly satisfy his human needs and therefore he will not overcome his inner emptiness and boredom, his loneliness and depression.

Greed is part of the mode of having and creates a permanent antagonism among men. "If everyone wants to have more, everyone must fear one's neighbor's aggressive intention to take away what one has. To prevent such attack one must become more powerful and preventively aggressive oneself."[29] And greed causes everyone to seek to have more than anyone else so "there must be competition and antagonism among individuals in the struggle for getting the most."[30] The antagonism among men that sets in with the mode of having becomes dangerous where it is not just competition and struggle for consumer goods and property but where the right to life and the chance for survival of nations and social groups are at stake. The antagonism among military and political power blocs in the form of the nuclear arms race will necessarily bring destruction over the longer term.[31]

The greedy mode of having necessarily tends to separate human beings, create class opposition, and set up distinctions because it privatizes those objects and values that make life attractive, fulfilled, and worth living, and makes them means of self-assertion. Such striving for private possession has very subordinate affective meaning in the being mode, for here man need not own to experience pleasure or to use an object. "In the being mode, more than one person—in fact millions of people—can share in the enjoyment of the same object, since none need—or want—to have it, as a condition of enjoying it."[32] Sharing the values of this world because the greed to own does not exist means that the separation and division of the having mode will be replaced by unity and solidarity. "Nothing unites people more (without restricting their individuality) than sharing their admiration and love for a person; sharing an idea, a piece of music, a painting, a symbol; sharing in a ritual—and sharing sorrow."[33] It is the wisdom of all great religious, political, and philosophical movements that only the experience of sharing sustains relations between human beings. Solidarity is therefore the alternative to the antagonistic principle of strife and competition in the having mode.[34]

From this perspective, it is understandable that the problem of sin and forgiveness should receive an interpretation and a solution that is specific to each mode.[35] In the having mode, the religious concept of sin[36] means that man resists God in what is called "disobedience" because the individual infringes on God's right as laid down in his laws and commandments. When man sins, he resists God because he wants to do as he thinks best. This disobedience is forgiven only when there is renewed submission.[37] The concepts "disobedience" and "submission" characterize the relation sin:forgiveness in the having mode. "Separation" and "atonement" are the corresponding terms in the being mode. When it is not the having more or less and the being more or less right, or the differences and structures of order, that are the guiding values in life, but solidarity, unity, love, sharing, and communicating, sin is to be understood as separation that can be ended only when a new "becoming one" (at-one-ment) between persons occurs.[38] In the being mode, sin is not seen as disobedience but as separateness and the consciousness of it. "This sin is rooted in our very human existence . . . it does not need to be forgiven. But it does need to be healed; and love, not acceptance of punishment, is the healing factor."[39] Sin in the being mode thus means "unresolved estrangement, and it is overcome by the full unfolding of reason and love, by at-onement."[40]

Still another alternative that can serve to define the difference between the modes of having and being is identified by the concepts "joy" and "pleasure."[41] Pleasure, which defines the mode of having, is "the satisfaction of a desire that does not require activity (in the sense of aliveness) to be satisfied."[42] This applies to all kinds of pleasure and amusement. Fromm mentions the pleasure of social success, of making more money, winning in the lottery, sexual pleasure, the pleasure of eating one's fill, of winning a race, the "state of elation brought about by drinking, trance, drugs; the pleasure in satisfying one's sadism, or one's passion to kill or dismember what is alive."[43] In the case of all these pleasures, man is very busy but never really productive. Characteristically, pleasure has a "peak" but that peak does not cure the inner instability; at best it obscures it temporarily, after which it reemerges all the more clearly.[44] A further characteristic of pleasure is the need to intensify the excitement. To feel satisfied, man needs more and more pleasure—the insatiability of the having mode manifests itself with special force in pleasure.

Since we live in a world of "joyless pleasures,"[45] it is not easy to illustrate the joy characteristic of the being mode with equal clarity. "Joy is the concomitant of productive activity. It is not a 'peak experience' which culminates and ends suddenly but rather a plateau, a feeling state that accompanies the productive expression of one's essential human faculties. Joy is not the ecstatic fire of the moment. Joy is the glow that accompanies being."[46]

Though joy, in contrast to pleasure, is something inconspicuous and more inward, this does not mean that it did not strike many masters of living as the criterion of a happy and accomplished life. Buddhism rejects pleasure so that man can enter Nirvana in a state of joy that is free of greed. The New Testament warns against the pleasures of this world and wants to be Glad Tidings. The Sabbath is a day of joy and anticipates the messianic time in this regard. The experience of inner joy motivates the mystics and masters of spiritual renewal of the most widely differing persuasions. A life in the being mode is directed toward the optimal unfolding of man's powers: "Joy is . . . what we experience in the process of growing nearer to the goal of becoming ourself."[47]

Aging, dying, and death are the events that most seriously call into question human existence. This fact could be used as an argument against the humanistic belief in a positive and biophilic sense of life: the fear of death could be set against joy in life. Actually, however, the fear of dying and the affirmation of living are not strivings that compete in man. Rather, they are expressions of the fact that man lives and gives form to his life in the having or the being mode.[48] The more someone lives in the being mode, the less he will fear aging, dying, and death, because even as his physical, emotional, intellectual, and spiritual powers decline, his attitude toward this fact of human existence will be an affirmative one.

The antithetical experiences of fear of dying and the affirmation of life are characteristics of the orientation of human existence. They become plausible as such when we consider that in the having mode, one makes a constant effort to make one's own life the object of possession and of the insatiable desire for more. In that case, fear of dying is not the justified fear of the suffering and pain that precedes death, but rather the fear "of losing what I have: the fear of losing my body, my ego, my possessions, and my identity: the fear of facing the abyss of non-identity, of 'being lost.'"[49]

The fear of death as of a loss of possession has its counterpart in the being mode, where it is the affirmation of life as a productive and active process. A life in that mode is the task of life itself. When a person concentrates on what is alive, the problem of existence as a "being toward death" does not arise.[50] For "the more we rid ourselves of the craving for possession in all its forms . . . the less strong is the fear of dying, since there is nothing to lose."[51]

A further characteristic that distinguishes the modes of being and having becomes apparent in an examination of the relation to time. The having mode is bound to time. Past, present, and future are determining factors of the life to which having gives direction. In contrast, timelessness is a striking aspect of the being mode: productive activity occurs here and now, is accomplishment of the *kairos,* and means immediacy.

"In the having mode we are bound to what we have amassed in the past: money, land, fame, social status, knowledge, children, memories."[52] Nostalgia, sentimentality, the desire to deck oneself out in traditional costumes or to preserve historical monuments, historicism, and the like are expressions of a being bound to the past in the having mode. This being bound to time becomes especially conspicuous when rituals, customs, conventions, and routines are involved, for they convey the experience of identity through the time-boundness of having. A change in routine or ritual—eating fifteen minutes later than usual, for example, or the change in a religious ceremony that results from liturgical reform—these changes can completely unsettle people because the shock of the unaccustomed disrupts their sense of identity. A change in social customs has a similar effect, as when men begin to wear their hair long. New ideas do not have as revolutionary an impact as changes in habitual behavior. Time-boundness in the having mode also affects the attitude toward future events. The perspective is that of having: how many things, and what sort of things, someone will have or will have had. "The future is the anticipation of what will become the past."[53] The present can only be understood as the borderline between past and future.

The statement that timelessness is characteristic of the being mode does not mean that life in that mode necessarily realizes itself outside of time. The mere fact that human life is limited to a certain number of years shows clearly enough that man cannot escape the temporal dimension. He therefore has no choice but to respect time, "but this respect for time becomes submission when the having mode predominates."[54] "Timelessness," therefore, means that the temporal dimension does not dominate man in all he does.[55] Significant events such as the artist's creative act or the experience of an idea or vision occur in the timelessness of the moment. "The experience of loving, of joy, of grasping truth does not occur in time, but in the here and now."[56] The here and now is eternity as timelessness, while the understanding of eternity as an indefinitely extended duration is the expression of a conception of time according to the having mode. Whereas in that mode, the past is something dead to which man clings and over which he can dispose, there is a re-creation of the past in the being mode so that what is dead awakens to new life. "To the extent that one does so, the past ceases to be the past; it is the here and now."[57] The future can similarly be experienced as a here and now in the being mode. "This occurs when a future state is so fully anticipated in one's own experience that it is only the future objectively, i.e. as external fact, but not in the subjective experience."[58] Fromm considers "genuine utopian thought,"[59] which he contrasts with utopian daydreams, as one such possibility.

Exemplifications of the Modes in Human Action

The various characteristics of the two modes make it clear that there are differences in principle in the experience, interpretation, and shaping of human reality. All these characteristics reflect the alternative of being and having, and all ways of living and expressing one's life are formed by these two fundamental tendencies and orientations. The following examples are meant to illustrate the different forms that are given to human action in the two modes. They have been selected from the chapter "Having and Being in Daily Experience."[60]

The first example is conversing as discussing. In the having mode, the relation to the world and oneself is such that "I want to make everybody and everything, including myself, my property."[61]

When two individuals whose character structure is strongly oriented toward having converse with each other, each of them has his own opinion and identifies with it. The discussion may be "heated" and take place at a high scientific or philosophical level but no real exchange occurs. The only thing that counts for either participant is to put forward the most telling argument by which to defend his property—his opinion. Actually, neither has any interest in changing either his own opinion or that of the other: "Each is afraid of changing his own opinion, precisely because it is one of his possessions, and hence its loss would mean an impoverishment."[62]

A conversation between two persons who have no need to cling to their opinions, their knowledge, their image, takes an entirely different course. Because their egos do not stand in their way, mutual engagement, spontaneity, and creativity are possible. "While the having persons rely on what they have, the being persons rely on the fact that they are, that they are alive and that something new will be born if only they have the courage to let go and to respond."[63] Such a conversation is not a trading of arguments and information but a living and enlivening dialogue in which it no longer matters who has the truth because the truth lies in the act of conversing.

Another example that also gives us a better understanding of Fromm's religio-critical position is the experience of faith.[64] Religious, political, and personal convictions always involve faith, but faith in the having mode differs in principle from faith in the being mode. "Faith in the having mode is the possession of an answer for which one has no rational proof."[65] Such possession usually is one of many articles of faith that were formulated by others and adopted because they are administered by an authority (the church as bureaucracy in the widest sense). Such a faith makes one's own thinking and deciding, but particularly one's own experience, unnecessary and gives certainty despite, or precisely because of, that fact.[66]

When the content of a faith becomes a possession that gives security, the relation between the subject and the object of faith is changed in such a way that the object as a reified possession determines the subject. When this occurs, faith in the having mode becomes idolatry: "While I can have the idol because it is a thing, by my submission to it, it, simultaneously, has me."[67] Faith in the having mode guarantees security at the price of the self's surrender.

Faith in the being mode is primarily an inner attitude. What is involved here is less the having of a faith than a being in it. What is important is not specific ideas or articles that must be believed, although faith in the being mode can certainly be belief in convictions, values, and hopes. But it is a precondition that the person who has faith really be the subject of that faith so that it may be said of him that he is "in faith toward" himself or others and, in the case of a theistic belief, in faith toward God.[68] "My faith in myself, in another, in humankind, in our capacity to become fully human also implies certainty, but certainty based on my own experience and not on my submission to an authority that dictates a certain belief."[69] Of course, the certainty such a faith, which is a direct product of one's own experience, can offer depends directly on the extent to which the believer realizes his life in the being mode and can recognize himself and the world without the rationalizations and ideologies that are characteristic of the having mode.[70]

The experience of love will provide a final illustration of the two modes.[71] The characteristic expression "to have love" makes it clear that the act of love can be reified so that loving becomes an object one can have and possess. In actuality, however, loving is a productive activity and one can only adequately speak of love when someone loves in the being mode. Such love can be described as "caring for, knowing, responding, affirming, enjoying: the person, the tree, the painting, the idea. It means bringing to life, increasing his/her/its aliveness."[72] Loving in the being mode can only be understood as a process in which man renews and strengthens his self through love.

Where the having mode is dominant, the word "love" is usually misused; it is meant to veil the absence of love. For in the having mode, it is not the experience of love but the possessing, capturing, and controlling of the love object that is involved. This taking hold of and having another for the purpose of securing and affirming the self that generally passes for "love" finds expression in the observation that with marriage, love often ends. While two individuals court each other and one seeks to win the other, all the marks of love are there: both are alive, attractive, interesting, and beautiful. But with marriage or soon thereafter, the situation often changes fundamentally. "The marriage contract gives each partner the exclusive possession of the other's body, feelings, and care. Nobody has to be won over any more, because love has become something one has, a property . . . the error that one can have love has led them to cease loving."[73] The real purpose of love is to make one's own life safer through the possession of the partner. And there is a particular kind of marriage that corresponds to this goal: it changes into "a friendly ownership, a corporation in which the two egotisms are pooled into one: that of the 'family.' "[74] In this community of interests, the partners can possess jointly what they have: money, prestige and standing, a home, children, relations, and so forth. That love can develop into a pure community of goods does not militate against marriage as such, but shows that a life in the having mode makes people incapable of true love. Neither a (new) marriage nor group marriage, nor group sex, nor switching partners can deal with this shortcoming,[75] for it has its base in a character structure that having orients.

Having and Being as Fundamental Orientations of the Character Structure

The preceding examples illustrated the relevance of the having and being modes to a few fundamental experiences of human life. Their key function in the concrete diagnosis, evaluation, change, critique, and reorientation of life also became clear. The reason the having/being alternative applies to all these functions is that it designates fundamental orientations of the character structure. The judgments that are made when we speak of an orientation around having or being have this encompassing significance only because they are connected with the empirical key concept "character." They have a share in the discovery that it is in character that the individual in his totality, with all his limitations and possibilities, becomes an object of empirical experience; that the methodical unity of all the discoveries of the human and social sciences can be found in the concept of character; and finally, that it is in character that we find the sphere that is dispositive of the thinking, feeling, and acting of both the individual and of social entities, and that it can be understood ideal-typically. Even though it may sound speculative to speak of the "having or being" alternative, the fact remains that it is always characterological entities that are being referred to: fundamental orientations of the character structure that represent ultimate assessments of the human reality in all its manifestations, according to Fromm's view of character.

When it is said that the having and being modes shape human life alternatively, this does not mean that only one mode can be present. On the contrary, in the majority of cases, the presence of both modes can be demonstrated, and there is usually a mixture of the two, although one of them will be dominant. The more one controls, of course, the less important the other will be: the two extremes are the exclusive dominance of one of them. Because both modes are real possibilities for the majority of individuals and societies, dominance is decided by socioeconomic structures and the ethical norms that prevail in them. "Cultures that foster the greed for possession, and thus the having mode of existence, are rooted in one human potential; cultures that foster being and sharing are rooted in the other potential. We must decide which of these two potentials we want to cultivate, realizing however, that our decision is largely determined by the socio-economic structure of our given society that inclines us toward one or the other solution."[76] That character structures are shaped by economic and social structures and demands makes it understandable why it is in the industrialized and highly civilized cultures that the character structure that is oriented around having dominates. All of these are societies whose principles are increase, profit, and wealth, for which reason they foster a social character that is oriented to having. And as soon as such a social character becomes dominant, no one wants to remain an outsider, so one simply follows the majority, all of whom have nothing in common but mutual antagonism.[77]

The pull of a social character oriented around having does not imply that the fundamental orientation of the individual character is totally determined. Just as socioeconomic conditions do not altogether determine the character structure, so the fundamental orientation of the society does not mean that the individual has no choice.[78] But the greater the dominance of the having mode in a society, the more personal effort, religious experience of what is humane, and critical reason are required if life is to be led in the being mode. To wrest dominance from the social character that is oriented around having, the economic conditions and the political and social structures, as well as the ideas concerning the meaning and goal of man and the corresponding ethical norms and religious convictions, would have to be fundamentally changed.[79] Thus we come to the conclusion that "social change interacts with a change in the social character; that 'religious' impulses contribute the energy necessary to move men and women to accomplish drastic social change, and hence, that a new society can be brought about only if a profound change occurs in the human heart—if a new object of devotion takes the place of the present one."[80]

HAVING AND BEING AS RELIGIOUS CONCEPTS

From the Characterological to the Religious Understanding of the Having/Being Alternative

With the having/being alternative, Fromm refers to "two fundamental modes of existence, to two different kinds of orientation toward self and the world, to two different kinds of character structure the respective predominance of which determines the totality of a person's thinking, feeling and acting."[81] From our comments up to this point, it is clear how encompassing this definition is. Every human expression, every feeling, every form of conduct toward others, nature, the self—in short, every manifestation of human existence is governed by the having/being alternative. The reason for this claim to universality lies in Fromm's view of character: character directs every expression of human existence. And for this character, he can identify two competing fundamental orientations that apply to every expression of human existence: every human reality can be ascribed to a character structure that is oriented either around having or being. It is true, however, that the unambiguousness of this ascription depends on the strength of the fundamental orientation in question.[82]

For Fromm, the having/being alternative with its universal validity and applicability to all levels of human reality is always a characterological magnitude that is defined by his sociopsychological experiences and insights. But what is really surprising in the study of the having/being alternative is that the great masters of life throughout human history, especially the founders of religious movements, were also persuaded of the existence of this having/being alternative.[83] The reason for their historical impact lies precisely in the fact that they called on man to live in the mode of being rather than in that of having, and that they took this step themselves. This is true of Buddha's teaching: arriving at the highest level of human development precludes the craving for possessions.[84] An experience of the world that proposes to wholly renounce having in order simply to be is practiced in Zen Buddhism.[85] The prophetic oratory of the Old Testament testifies to the having/being alternative, as do the *logia* in Christ's Sermon on the Mount. The poverty movement of the Middle Ages, Francis of Assisi, and Meister Eckhart are examples from the Christian tradition. Spinoza expressed it in philosophical ethics,[86] Goethe in the language of the poet.[87] In Karl Marx, having and being are not only concepts of economics but the essence of a secularized messianism as well.[88] And Albert Schweitzer is an example in our century of the determinative power of a life lived in the being mode.[89]

That the having/being alternative is also at the center of religious questions and problems and that having and being are "at the same time fundamental 'religious' categories"[90] will be demonstrated in the following discussion of that alternative in the Old and New Testaments and in Meister Eckhart. The demonstration from the New Testament goes far beyond Fromm's comments.[91]

The Having/Being Alternative as the Essence of a Religious Ethos

A central theme in the Old Testament that pervades both the theology of history and the prophetic speeches is the symbolism of the exodus. "Abraham is to leave what he has—land and family—and go to the unknown."[92] The departure from Egypt is considered the historical exodus, but it gets its religious and liturgical meaning primarily from the inherent symbolism: on the one hand, we see the abandonment of a way of life that guarantees safety and a home in which there are fleshpots and drink, but that way of life also makes man dependent and enslaves him so that the loss of a home and security becomes the freedom for a new way of life. The promised land as the goal of a new way of life, on the other hand, means true fulfillment, though the promise cannot be taken as assurance. The symbol of the new life is the desert: "The desert is no home: it has no cities; it has no riches; it is the place of nomads who own what they need, and what they need are the necessities of life, not possessions."[93] The desert makes it impossible to lead a life of having and holding. It yields no food or drink, allows no settling down. The nomad is a traveler.

Because the desert is the symbol of a form of existence that renounces all having, it is the place where man encounters God, where God acts. Only in the mode of being is that immediacy which Israel speaks of as God's action in history experienced. The relevation of God's name must be seen under this aspect of not having. The dance around the golden calf and the ban on images represent the two modes of belief in God. Settling in the land of Canaan meant the end of the direct way of life in the being mode, but the knowledge of this way finds a new form in the critique of the prophets: "These revolutionary thinkers, the Hebrew prophets, renewed the vision of human freedom—of being unfettered of things—and the protest against submitting to idols—the work of the people's own hands."[94] The prophets' criticism of the cult and the laws is always a critique of attempts and temptations of man to make himself secure by possession.

The destruction of the Temple, the Babylonian exile, the rebuilding of the Temple, and the destruction of Jerusalem by the Romans, the centuries of persecution during the Diaspora and the establishment of the state of Israel in this century, reflect the changing dominants in the way of life of the Jewish people. For Fromm, the richness of the Jewish religion becomes visible only when it renounces state, temple, a priestly and military bureaucracy, animal sacrifice and ritual, where all that remains is "the ideal of being."[95]

The New Testament gospels demonstrate that Jesus adopts and carries on the prophetic tradition in many respects. The prophetic quality in his sermons becomes very clear when historical-critical methods are used to attempt to get at the oldest layer of the Christian tradition. That the so-called second source, *Q*, which predates the gospels of Matthew and Luke, must be given special attention here is due to the fact that before Jesus' teaching was written down, it was passed on orally for a considerable time. For mnemotechnical reasons, if for no other, this oral tradition preferred parables and images and easily remembered (because sometimes offensive) *logia*.[96] The earliest *Q* texts are individual utterances that come from the oral tradition of a Judaeo-Christian community in the Palestinian-Syrian border region. All of the texts have the literary form of prophetic sayings and are usually introduced by an appropriate formula. As one surveys this material, one is struck first by the fact that most of it is part of the so-called ethical demands Jesus made. There is the rigorous ban on divorce (Matthew 5:32; Luke 16:18) that becomes comprehensible when one knows that according to the law of the time, the wife was part of a man's possessions so that divorce for the sake of remarriage was necessarily prompted by the motive of having. The statement that one should turn the other cheek when struck (Matthew 5:39; Luke 6:29) and the command to love one's enemies (Matthew 5:44–48; Luke 6:27f; 32–36), only become plausible when they are seen as the radical renunciation of having the right on one's side. That one should give to everyone who asks and not demand that what is taken be returned (Matthew 5:42; Luke 6:30) is possible only where possessions no longer exert power over man.

To have the right on one's side and to have possessions as forms of a life in the having mode are also warned against by Christ: "Do not lay up for yourselves treasures on earth, where moth and rust consume and where thieves break in and steal. . . . For where your treasure is, there will your heart be also" (Matthew 6:19, 21; cf. Luke 12:33f). "Judge not, and you will not be judged" (Luke 6:37; cf. Matthew 7:1). And the comment about the mote and the beam (Matthew 7:3–5; Luke 6:41f) only takes on concrete meaning when one realizes that the person who is nothing in his own right is always tempted to see the injustice in what others do because he wants to be in the right. The "golden rule" (Matthew 7:12; Luke 6:31) formulates the same insight positively.

Food and clothing can be significant expressions of the having mode. Where they are vital concerns because it is believed that existence depends on having them, Christ's warning against "being anxious" applies (Matthew 6:25–33; Luke 12:22–31). And finally, the fundamental orientation around having for the purpose of assuring and securing one's existence is itself the object of a warning by Christ: Men should fear the one who can not only kill the body but also the soul or, as Matthew puts it: "fear him who can destroy both soul and body in hell" (Matthew 10:28). That this dangerous power is life in the having mode is shown by the discourse about the two sparrows that can be had for a farthing—which have practically no commercial value, in other words, yet do not fall to the ground. The following observation that even the hairs on the head are numbered has the same meaning. And in conclusion, there is the positive statement of what counts. The string of sayings ends with the phrase: "Fear not; you are of more value than many sparrows" (Luke 12:7; cf. Matthew 10:28–31), which means that it is not the (market) value of a person that is important, but that he experience himself as value, and live accordingly.

In all these *logia* that belong to the oldest layer of *Q*, we note that their common denominator is the renunciation of having and the demand to be, so that the having/being alternative can in fact be considered a key to the understanding of these sayings. Still, it must not be overlooked that these commands, prohibitions, and warnings relate to something that is not simply called "mode of being" or "unfolding of one's powers of reason and love." Regarding concrete ethical and religious living, Christ's prophetic speech becomes reality in the individual just as it does in the person who obeys the humanistic call to a life in the being mode. But the fact remains that Jesus' call is tied to belief in him and God as father, and to his message about the Kingdom of God (or "heaven" in Matthew) as an event that refers to the future and that is already being realized in following Christ.

That the call to renounce a life in the having mode is linked to Christ's message concerning the Kingdom of God is the reason that the Kingdom of God itself (now and in the future), belief in Christ or the Father, following Christ and other central concepts of the New Testament, become the essence and symbol of a life that is oriented around the being mode. Entities such as hell, damnation, the Pharisees, the devil, and the demons, on the other hand, stand for a life in the having mode. The claim to truth that the various theological (and also mythological) concepts and the realities they wish to make comprehensible have for modern man cannot be examined here.[97] But it should be kept in mind that Christ's message is profoundly determined by the having/being alternative and that its center is an ethos that is oriented around being but remains tied to a theist faith. A life in the being mode does not only mean the optimal unfolding of man's productive powers, and the renunciation of all desire to have. In the biblical sense, this ethos remains tied to the religious commitment to the person of Christ and is realized only in following him.

Against the background of the specific New Testament understanding of the having/being alternative, the other texts that are part of the oldest layer of the *Q* tradition also become plausible. The prophetic statement about the confessing and denying of Christ (Matthew 10:32f; Luke 12:8f) is valid precisely because Christ lives wholly in the being mode. The Beatitudes (Matthew 5:3f; Luke 6:20b f) speak for themselves when we read: "Blessed are you poor, for yours is the kingdom of God" (Luke 6:20). The petitions of the Lord's Prayer (Matthew 7:7–11; Luke 11:9–13) are the expression of a knowledge about a life in the being mode that comes from community with God. And the condemnations of the Pharisees (Matthew 23:25; 27:29–31; Luke 11:39, 42–44, 46–48, 52) require no special explanation after what has been said so far: "Woe to you, scribes and Pharisees, hypocrites! for you cleanse the outside of the cup and of the plate, but inside they are full of extortion and rapacity" (Matthew 23:25). The necrophilous quality of a life in the having mode could hardly be expressed more pointedly: "Woe to you, scribes and Pharisees, hypocrites! for you are like whitewashed tombs, which outwardly appear beautiful, but within they are full of dead men's bones and all uncleanness" (Matthew 23:27).

It is not just in the oldest traditions that the closeness of Christ's message to the having/being alternative can be shown, although it is especially clear here. Once one sees the connection between the religious ideas and statements of biblical man and the having/being alternative, one notices at every step that this alternative is the key to these texts.[98] The following considerations are therefore meant to serve as examples.

Among the parables that are intended to illustrate the distinctiveness of God's Kingdom, those that make clear that what is quantitatively wholly inconsequential can yet attain a never suspected fullness, provided one is willing to renounce an orientation around the quantitative (=the measurable and ownable) and to allow the seemingly insignificant within oneself to grow. Such parables include the one about the sower (Mark 4:3–8; Matthew 13:3–8; Luke 8:5–8), about the mustard seed (Mark 4:30–32; Matthew 13:31f; Luke 13:18f), and about the leaven (Matthew 13:33; Luke 13:20f). The parables about the treasure in the field (Matthew 13:44) and the precious pearl (Matthew 13:45f) show with particular clarity that it is necessary to renounce much for the sake of a single thing.

The meal as an image for the being mode is utilized in all its aspects: in the parable about the feast (Matthew 22:1–10; Luke 14:16–24), in the stories about the miracle of the feeding of the multitude (Mark 6:32–44; 8:1–10; Matthew 14:13–21; 15:32–39; Luke 9:10–17; John 6:1–15), in the discourse on the loaves (John 6:26–59), and in the establishment of the Lord's Supper before Christ's death (Mark 14:22–25; Matthew 26:26–29; Luke 22:15–20).

The harsh sermons about wealth require no explanation. One should mention what is said about the "laying up" of treasure (Matthew 6:19–21; Luke 12:33f), the warning against covetousness: "Take heed, and beware of all covetousness; for a man's life does not consist in the abundance of his possessions" (Luke 12:15); the parable about the rich fool (Luke 12:16–21); the parable about the rich man and poor Lazarus (Luke 16:19–31); the rich youth (Mark 10:17–22; Matthew 19:16–22; Luke 18:18–23); the danger of wealth: "It is easier for a camel to go through the eye of a needle than for a rich man to enter the kingdom of God." (Mark 10:23–31; Matthew 19:23–30; Luke 18:24–30); the observation about the widow's farthing (Mark 12:41–44; Luke 21:1–4).

Close to the question of wealth is another peculiarity that is part of Christ's gospel and life, and that is his turning to the poor, the despised, the lost, the outcasts for whom a number of miracles are performed. Christ's traffic with public sinners, publicans (perhaps also with Samaritans and heathens), and the simple folk—that is, people who are insignificant in a religious and social sense—is not the expression of a revolutionary pathos or a desire for political upheaval but the realization of a religious ethos that recognizes institutionalized structures of the having mode in religious, cultic, and social classifications.

From this perspective, Christ's curiously ambivalent attitude toward the law becomes understandable. On the one hand, not even a tittle of it must be changed (Matthew 5:18; Luke 16:17), and sometimes it is even made more stringent or reduced to its original meaning, as in the question of divorce (Mark 10:2–12; Matthew 5:27f, 31f; 19:3–12; Luke 16:18). On the other hand, Christ criticizes the law, and he and his disciples violate it, as when Jesus heals on the Sabbath (the withered hand, Mark 3:16; Matthew 12:9–14; Luke 6:6–11; the infirm woman: Luke 13:10–16; and the man with dropsy: Luke 14:1–6), or when he uses the occasion of the plucking of the ears of corns by his disciples to make a fundamental criticism of it: "The sabbath was made for man, not man for the sabbath" (Mark 2:27). The paradox of a more stringent application of the Torah and a simultaneous critique and violation of it is resolved when the having/being alternative becomes the decisive criterion for determining the meaning of the injunctions.

A choice between a life in the having or the being mode is articulated in the many calls to follow Christ. Rejection of all ties and assent to a life for others after the model of Christ are demanded. Who follows him must abandon father and mother, son and daughter (Matthew 10:37–39; Luke 14:26f; cf. Mark 3:31–35; Matthew 12:46–50; Luke 8:19–21), and agree to the conditions of such a decision ("For what will it profit a man, if he gains the whole world and forfeits his life? Or what shall a man give in return for his life?" [Matthew 16:25f; cf. Mark 8:34–38; Luke 9:23–26]). Following Christ means a life of watchfulness *in statu viatoris* after the model of Israel's march through the desert. This expresses itself in Christ's own wandering and in his pitilessness toward everything "settled," or in his instructions as he sends out his disciples: "Foxes have holes, and birds of the air have nests; but the Son of man has nowhere to lay his head. . . . Leave the dead to bury their own dead, but as for you, go and proclaim the kingdom of God." . . . No one who puts his hand to the plow and looks back is fit for the kingdom of God" (Luke 9:58,60,62; cf. Matthew 8:20–22). The disciples are allowed neither purse nor shoes and are to ask for food and drink where they enter (cf. Luke 10:3–12; Matthew 10:5–16; Mark 6:7–13).

The evangelists, finally, describe the life of Christ as a life in the mode of being. Thus Jesus is born in a manger because there is no room for the family in the inn, and he is first discovered by the shepherds (cf. Luke 2:4–20). Christ's self-understanding is verified in the story of the temptation (cf. Matthew 4:1–11; Mark 1:12f; Luke 4:1–13): after forty days of fasting, he is to prove to the devil(!) in the desert(!) that he "is" someone because he "has" power over nature—that is, power to turn stones into bread(!) and to suspend gravity. When he refuses, the devil offers him power over all men so that he would be the greatest and strongest, though on the condition that he submit to the devil. Christ rejects this devilish offer to "be" through "having" power over men.

The realization of a life in the being mode and the renunciation of all desire to have reaches its climax in Christ's suffering and death. He understands himself as a "corn of wheat" that will bear fruit for many (cf. John 12:24). The total renunciation of having leads to the goal of a life in the being mode. This is the content of his statement about his resurrection. The stories about encounters with the resurrected one therefore testify to his being and life, but emphasize at the same time when they talk of his being a spirit that he can no longer be encountered in the having mode. For this reason, the spirit is the essence of life, reason and love, efficacy and being, for Christians.

Depending on the addressee and the situation-in-life of the writing, the Acts of the Apostles, and especially Paul's letters, reflect the having/being alternative more or less clearly. And even though the "early Christian communism" of the Acts cannot be taken so literally as to mean that the Jerusalem community was always of the same mind, it is undeniable that the first communities were wholly shaped by the religious ethos of Christ's life and gospel, and that people were capable of a total renunciation of all having. It was this renunciation that made them share and distribute everything they owned, that made them willing to roam the land as wandering prophets, and that made them ready for martyrdom.[99] The radicalism in matters of property survived for a relatively long period in the history of the church, as the statements by a number of church fathers on the question of property and the development of monasticism and the poverty movement demonstrate.

The Pauline handling of traditions that were not part of the Jesus tradition is especially illuminating as regards the sensitivity of men to the having/being alternative in the Hellenistic and Judaeo-Christian cultural sphere around the beginning of our era. In addition to the catalogues of vices and virtues that characterize the modes of being and having, it is especially the statements about love in I Corinthians 13:1–7 that are typical. What is said here (in I Corinthians 13:4, e.g.: "love is patient and kind; love is not jealous or boastful; love is not arrogant or rude") is equally true of a life in the being mode. The lines have a number of Greek and Jewish parallels. It can be shown that Paul took them from the Jewish tradition, which had adopted Greek motifs, and transformed them into the style of Jewish wisdom.[100] Although I Corinthians 13:1–7 does not come from the Jesus tradition, it is impossible to overlook the relation between the statements made in I Corinthians 13 and Christ's religious and ethical message about a life in the being mode.

Another affinity shows up in the reception of gnostic ideas by John. This is true of central concepts of the Gospel According to John (such as light, world, *pneuma*), of theological statements (such as his so-called realized eschatology concerning the raising of the dead and the final judgment, which illustrate the problem of time-boundness and timelessness in the having and being modes, respectively), and of the theological and religious and ethical statements in the Epistles of John: "No one who abides in him sins; no one who sins has either seen him or known him. . . . No one born of God commits sin; for God's nature abides in him, and he cannot sin, because he is born of God. . . . He who does not love abides in death. Any one who hates his brother is a murderer" (I John 3:6, 9, 14, 15). Here also, love and God are interchangeable concepts, and in its religious and ethical relevance, love is identical with a life in the being mode: "Love is of God; and he who loves is born of God and knows God. He who does not love does not know God; for God is love. . . . There is no fear in love, but perfect love casts out fear. For fear has to do with punishment, and he who fears is not perfected in love" (I John 4:7–8, 18).

The having/being alternative as the essence of a religious ethos can also be demonstrated in Eastern and Western mysticism. Since Fromm read Meister Eckhart for decades, his mysticism can serve as an example of that alternative. What Meister Eckhart means by being and having becomes clear in his sermon on Matthew 5:3: "Blessed are the poor in spirit, for theirs is the kingdom of heaven."[101] He asks himself what this poverty can mean, and arrives at this answer: "A poor person is one who wills nothing, knows nothing, and has nothing."[102] To have no will can mean very different things. For Meister Eckhart, it means neither that one should be will-less or weak-willed, nor that one should fulfill God's will rather than one's own. Instead, "the person who wants nothing is the person who is not greedy for anything: this is the essence of Eckhart's concept of non-attachment."[103]

Nor does the person who knows nothing mean someone without education or culture, for by knowledge, Eckhart does not mean the object of knowledge—that is, knowledge as a having—but the act of abstraction from all knowledge: someone who knows nothing "must be so completely free of all knowledge that he does not know, recognize or feel that God lives within him; even more: he is to be free of all knowledge that is alive within him."[104] It follows that what is involved here is a forgetting of what one knows. "In the mode of being, knowledge is nothing but the penetrating activity of thought—without ever becoming an invitation to stand still in order to find certainty."[105] Finally, it is only the person who has nothing who is truly poor in spirit. Meister Eckhart radicalizes this idea when he asks whether man should be so poor that God cannot even find a place in him to be active. His answer is of ultimate stringency and involves the identification of the concepts of God and soul: "that [only] is being poor in spirit when man is so utterly free of God and all his works that God, if He wished to be active within the soul, would himself be the place wherein He wished to be active. . . ."[106] And a little later, he adds: "Therefore I ask of God that he rid me of God."[107]

These and similar formulations have always been the objects of conflicting Eckhart interpretations. Some feel that they confirm Meister Eckhart as an atheist who uses religious language, while others interpret these statements that dissolve God's transcendence from the perspective of Meister Eckhart's theological interest and take them for the most radical expression of his belief in God. The interpretation of Diemar Mieth[108] probably gets to the core of what Eckhart's wishes to say: "The father-sonship of the human being is taken so seriously that man in God is really God's deputy. His willing of God, his knowing of God, his having of God does not take grace seriously enough, because it makes God its intention rather than making the intention of God, which is man, its own." A true belief in God and a life genuinely lived through God's grace are realized only when man renounces God, for it is only in renouncing God that he can make God's intent—perfect man—his own. For Meister Eckhart, the imputation that he denies God is merely a confession by which the person making that imputation proves his unbelief—his wanting to have God. But that this argument is correct will be plausible only to the person who, for the sake of God's grace—and for Eckhart, this means for perfected man's sake—renounces all willing, knowing, and having of God, and is therefore poor. Because the truth of his belief in God is wholly dependent on the realized experience of such belief, Meister Eckhart can close his sermon with these words: "Those who do not understand this sermon should not be troubled in their hearts. For as long as man does not resemble this truth, he will not understand this speech. May God grant us that we live so as to eternally experience it. Amen."[109]

Eckhart sees in poverty the freedom from any and every possible object of having, and this even includes the concept of God. Only when man is radically poor is he himself, and free, and at one with things. Only where he is wholly free of God can God be entirely within him, only then are he and God truly he and God, the only way they can be one.

THE FUNCTION OF HUMANISTIC RELIGION IN THE GROUNDING OF A HUMANISTIC UNDERSTANDING OF MAN

Meister Eckhart's application of the idea of poverty to the concept of God makes it clear that it is only through the having/being alternative that the answer mysticism gives to the question about man's innermost and ultimate destiny becomes plausible. And it is only through it that the relevance of humanistic religion to Fromm's understanding of man becomes apparent. If the being mode is understood as the total renunciation of every form of having, it is the condition and the possibility of a mystical experience of the ONE.

For the self-understanding of humanistic religion, it follows that the question concerning the validity and dogmatic truth of the concept of God is irrelevant[110] because it is still rooted in the having mode, the very thing that must be overcome. The experience of God is possible only if one resolves not to make a distinction between man (soul) and God. But it is also true that one's own self can be experienced only if it renounces all autonomy. God and man (soul) can only become one and be experienced as one if there is mutual renunciation.[111] Where God and man are involved and both are to be known—that is, where the truth of religion and the truth of an empirical knowledge of man are at stake—knowledge is possible only as the experience of the ONE that is both man and God at the same time. The truth content of both realms of reality and truth must be negated if the truth that connects both is to be attained. But this truth is real only as the mystical experience of the ONE.

The mystical experience of the ONE is the experience of a life that is lived wholly in the being mode. Because it is a "pure" experience, its concrete realization occurs only when all possible experiences of having are renounced. Such an experience of being becomes accessible through breathing-concentration and meditation exercises[112] whose aim is to rid man of every concrete experience so that he can experience the totality of man and God in one, that is, the totality of man in his humanity.

This self-understanding of humanistic religion gives access to an understanding of the function of humanistic religion in the ultimate grounding of scientific knowledge and of man's meaning and end. With the postulate of the mystical experience of the ONE as an experience of life in the being mode, that base has been found in which both empirical, anthropological, and ethical knowledge and religious statements are ultimately grounded and which also grounds their claim to truth and general validity. In its claim to be both science and religion, Fromm's humanism has its ultimate ground, which is the same for both claims in the experience of the ONE. For both scientific humanism, which rejects a theistic belief even as its ultimate ground and therefore does not require a theonomous grounding of its autonomy concept, and religious humanism, which sees a form of having in every dogmatic concept of God and for which religion is therefore identical with the experience of a life in the being mode, are views that have their warrant and legitimation in the mystical experience of the ONE.

The experience of the ONE is the point at which the two aspects of the humanism concept, the empirical and the religious, come together. The characterological findings are these: Man attains an optimal unfolding if he is oriented toward renouncing all reification of the experience of self and world and develops his powers of reason and love instead. The religious-critical reflections produced the demand that any and every concept of God be negated because the experience of the ONE is possible only through the dialectical abolition of every distinction between God and man. The results in the two cases can be formulated as follows: The insight into man and his end is grounded in the experience he has of himself. This experience is total—that is, the experience of the oneness of world, man, and God—to the extent that man renounces the possibility of reifying his being by a form of having.

In contrast to philosophical attempts that define reason as the ultimate principle of being,[113] and also in contrast to theological and philosophical views that make God as person and/or reason the guarantor of reality, Fromm's grounding provides a different "solution." Here the mystical experience of the ONE is the ultimate ground for the reality of the world and of man and the ultimate warrant for trust in this reality. This solution will always be criticized by representatives of the other two positions because the mystical experience of the ONE cannot be objectified, which is why its persuasive power is always tied to subjective experience (even if the reasonableness of this mystical "solution" can be shown). But the person who acknowledges the mystical experience of the ONE as the only true warrant of the experience of self and world will reject every attempt to ground human existence in an entity that controls man heteronomously. For the mystic, every religion and philosophy that is centered around concepts, words, doctrines, beliefs, logical laws, and so on hinders the experience of the immediacy of the ONE. Where such entities as God, being, the Church, and reason exist, they, being negations of the ONE, must be negated in the experience of the ONE if man is to be rid of all knowing, willing, and having. They are of no positive significance for the experience of the ONE.

No statements about the *unio mystica* can be made, but something can be said about the way to it. Humanistic religion as experience of the ONE is about the way, the *halacha,* the eight paths, *mondo* and *koan,* concentration and meditation exercises. All of them are based on the religious ethos of a renunciation of all having and aim at the experience of man in his totality.

Fromm's postulate that the claim to the truth and bindingness of human reality be grounded in a mystical experience does not mean that the ultimate grounding in the mystical experience of the ONE is any less stringent. Even from the perspective of a philosophy and/or religion that is wholly oriented around reason, it has to be conceded that the mystical experience of the ONE fulfills the function of an ultimate ground of human existence and of what human existence should be. It is true, of course, that the communicability of this postulate is tied to subjective experience: only for the person who enters into the mystic experience of the ONE can that experience lay claim to ultimately ground existence. Fromm gave stringency and objective validity to this experience by making the transcendental experience of the ONE—the *unio mystica* being the experience of the total negation of the objects of experience, that is, of empirical entities—the goal of the perfectly palpable experience of the renunciation of having. And not only is this experience palpable, it can be demonstrated by empirical methods. This means that man is, develops, is healthy and happy, to the extent that he renounces having as a means of defining his existence. Both kinds of experience, the empirical experience of world and self and the religious, mystical experience of the ONE, are based on the having/being alternative, which is itself an experiential value that is demonstrable in both an empirical and a religious sense. This makes it apparent that the mystical experience of the ONE is the negation of all objects of experience—that it consequently renounces all having—and thus grounds itself, and becomes the ground for, any and every empirical experience of the having/being alternative.

Just as God's reason is recognized as the ultimate ground of all empirical and moral reason in Aquinas' philosophical thought, and as the grounding reason of God and the grounded reason of man and his world are mediated in analogous fashion through the concept of law,[114] so the having/being alternative serves in Fromm's "solution" as an "interpretive key"[115] that grounds the truth, validity, and bindingness of all empirical and moral experience in the all-encompassing mystical experience of the ONE. Because it is not man's reason and the reason of God that both grounds and transcends it, but rather experiences that have their base in the mystical experience of the ONE, the following differences result:

1. To the extent that they mean the renunciation of having, experiences of being admittedly have no objective or logical stringency. They are, however, tied to a subjective experience that is immediately persuasive and effective in and of itself; experiences have a transforming power.

2. The mystic experience of the ONE as the ultimate ground of the experience that it is only being and not having that has a transforming power is not transcendent in the sense of that transcendence that can be spoken of only by way of analogy. It is the concrete and historical individual who experiences within himself his ultimate ground as he experiences the ONE. But this ultimate ground is not understood as transcendence: rather, it is that endpoint of the empirically experienceable dialectic that man has being to the degree he negates manifestations of willing, knowing, and having as negations of his humanness. To a view of man that is oriented around having, the experience of the ONE must seem something "altogether different," a NOTHING, and transcendent for that reason. In reality, it is the experience of the totality of man in the full unfolding of his reason and love.

The experience of the ONE grounds what human existence is, and should be. The having/being alternative plays the role of a key that interprets how empirical and mystical experience are grounded. The understanding of the having/being alternative corresponds to the dialectic that is rooted in what we have called the tradition of the ecstatic-cathartic model. Where what exists is functionalized and made to serve as a means for securing one's existence, this orientation is recognized as the having mode and judged to be the negation of "true" or "genuine" humanness. The demand that the having mode be renounced and the being mode become dominant can only be met when the having/being alternative is used in the sense of a critical theory: the having mode is a negation of human existence and human potential and can be sublated by negation. The substantive definition of this dialectical process is this: negation of everything man has, the object and goal being the experience of his totality in the mystical experience of the ONE.

9

FROMM'S HUMANISM AS A CHALLENGE FOR A CHRISTIAN THEOLOGY

REFLECTIONS ON A FRUITFUL DISCUSSION BETWEEN CHRISTIAN THEOLOGIANS AND THE HUMANIST FROMM

The having/being alternative develops the earlier distinctions "productive/nonproductive" and "biophilic/necrophilic." As a characterological concept, it has empirical validity and is the quintessence of religious experience. The encompassing meaning of the experience of the having/being alternative makes it possible to postulate a nexus in the grounding of the is and the ought of human existence where the experience of the having/being alternative is itself the interpretive key by which man ultimately grounds himself in what he is and in what he ought to be. The grounding of the individual in the mystical experience of the ONE represents a challenge for any theology that grounds man theonomously. Such a challenge can lead to a fruitful exchange between Christian theologians and the humanist Fromm[1] if what applies to every challenge by modern humanisms applies here as well: "The challenging modern humanisms are themselves being challenged."[2]

First, the self-understanding of the discussion partners must be clarified. The theologian who wants to show that his talk about God is rational is not used to seeing man's existence, meaning, and obligation grounded in experience, although he knows that his talk about God is possible only when there is experience of God's speech, and that it is consequently grounded in such experience. He also knows that theology only attains its goal when it furthers the belief that man experiences his life, his meaning, and his existence as grounded. Theology mediates religious experience but cannot itself be the experience of God while confining itself to talk about him.

Mysticism is different[3] because it is concerned with experiential value and because, by representing a negative theology, it usually overcomes the inability of theology to be direct religious experience. Negative theology is due to the insight that thinking about God with the object of arriving at substantive knowledge of him conflicts with the experience of God himself as a matter of principle. Religious experience is possible only in the experience of one's own not-knowing. Every knowledge of God is recognized as a heteronomous determination and must therefore be done away with. Theology attempts, of course, to reflect and transcend this position when it attempts to show and ground the rationality of religious experience. To be able to advance grounds for the rationality of religious experience, theology needs transcendence. Pointing to transcendence, it also claims that it transcends the level of religious experience by thought. It aims at an ultimate ground beyond man and postulates a theonomous grounding of every human reality, including the religious experience of the mystic. This goal contradicts that of mysticism, for it is precisely the demonstration of some ultimate reason or a theonomous grounding of religious experience that mysticism is not interested in. Mysticism sees itself as an ultimate grounding because only the experience of the ultimate ground can be an ultimate ground.

Although this is merely a synopsis of theology and mysticism, it is indispensable to set forth self-understanding and goals if a discussion between Christian theology and Fromm's humanism is to take place. For Fromm's position differs from that of the theologian. Because of his Jewish ancestry and because of the way he dealt with the problem of religion throughout his life, he is more appropriately referred to as a "mystic." The question of the theologian interests him only where theology could become an obstacle to mystical experience. This does not mean, however, that he wishes to dispute theology's right to exist. Whether it should or should not exist is decided, as far as he is concerned, by whether or not it furthers the mystical experience of the ONE. What counts is the religious experience, not rational demonstration by complicated theological reflection. For him, truth is not decided by whether a conviction can survive rational scrutiny but in the experience of truth, which is itself experienced truth. This is also the reason he can claim that belief in God is of secondary import. Theism or nontheism is not ultimately decisive for the religious experience. The experience of the ONE as the negation of all knowing, willing, and having does not need to be demonstrated by rational thought; it is true and rational in itself.

It is in *the attempt to ground his humanism in mysticism* that Fromm's contribution to the discussion between theology and mysticism must be seen. By using the characterological finding that being is possible and real to the extent that it is free of having, as he interprets the mystical experience of the ONE, and by making this plausible, he answers those questions regarding the grounding of the religious that theology is normally concerned with. The having/being alternative reveals the condition for the possibility of religious experience generally and creates a nexus between the grounding of religious and empirical experience. The unity of empirical experience, when aided by characterology, and of religious experience in the mysticism of the ONE is guaranteed by the having/being alternative, which is valid for both experiences.

The nexus in the grounding of empirical and religious experience that the having/being alternative makes possible defines Fromm's concept of humanism and the discussion between Christianity and humanism along with it. Fromm's humanism not only combines scientific knowledge and religious experience but can also ground both concepts in such a way that the truth and bindingness of scientific knowledge and confidence in them have their ultimate ground in religious experience on the one hand, and religious experience has its ground in the empirical experience that science makes possible on the other. For that reason, the mystical experience of the ONE is not a leap into some sort of transcendence or irrationality; neither is it a mystification of reality (mysticism is the very opposite of mystification) but represents the consistent, if not continuous, realization of the experience that man is to the degree that he negates the determination of his life by what he has and can have. The experience of the ONE gives an answer to the question and the questionableness "man" without leaving the sphere of the human. For it discovers that with the negation of all possible having determinations of human existence, unity with oneself and with the natural and human environing world becomes possible, and that it is only in the freedom from all heteronomy that reason and love unfold.

A productive exchange between Christian theologians and Fromm's humanism must respect this distinctiveness of his humanism concept, which is both scientific and religious. It must be acknowledged that:

1. Fromm's scientific humanism is grounded in the mystical experience of the ONE.

2. With the help of the having/being alternative, the truth and bindingness of what man is and should be are ultimately grounded in the mystical experience of the ONE.

3. This ONE can be experienced by man.

4. The grounding nexus that mystical experience creates lays claim to autonomy vis-à-vis theological attempts to ground religious experience.

If these implications of Fromm's concept of humanism are respected, the interpretive key, the "having/being alternative," can serve as a critical theory for a variety of problems and questions of Christian theology. From the perspective of Fromm's humanism, the question of the grounding of the autonomy of human existence and obligation (of what man is and ought to be) can be answered by the assertion that a Christian theology can ground man's autonomy theonomously, provided belief in God does not mean heteronomy in the definition of human existence. The Christian faith is certainly open to such a possibility of theonomous grounding: the more radically the idea of the man-god as son of man is understood and realized, the closer the answer of the Christian theologian and the Christian mystic will come to the answer of the humanist. The experience and definition of man, of his being and his obligation, are then tied to the understanding of Christ's life and the following of Christ, because in Christ's total humanity, God's essence reveals itself. Such a theonomous grounding of man's autonomy can be found in theology.[4] Examples would be the Father-Son relationship of the Gospel According to John, the theologies of Christian mystics, and the ascription of the *lex nova* and the *lex naturalis* in Thomas Aquinas. All these theologians wish to ground human existence and obligation theonomously in such a way that the condition for the possibility of humanness, that is, God—God's will and reason as they became manifest in the life of Christ—corresponds to those potentialities for the unfolding and realization of human existence that are grounded in man.[5] Of course, the realization of such a humanism that is "willed by God" and grounded in him is tied existentially to the life of Christ. For in Christ, the confidence in one's own *humanitas* is ultimately grounded, which means that autonomy and the experience of man's powers is relational: their validity is ultimately grounded in, and guaranteed by, the experience of following Christ. Like the humanistic attempt, the Christian realization of humanness is grounded in the experience of man's own powers. But for the Christian, the possibility of this experience lies in adherence to Christ, because in the life of Christ, God's will regarding man's perfect form—that is, his will regarding eschatological *humanitas*—expressed itself in a way that is valid for all time.

The endeavor of Christian theologians to ground the autonomy of man (and of the moral) theonomously does not necessarily imply a heteronomous claim in the theological definition of what man is and should be, nor does such theological reflection and the demand that Christ be followed necessarily reduce the possibility of experiencing and realizing human and humanizing potentials. But in view of the criticism Fromm's scientific and mystical humanism entails, such theonomous grounding is a possibility only for those Christian theologies that do not insist on heteronomy in the theonomous grounding of human existence and human obligation. There is no requirement here to prove in detail that official theology especially succumbs to the temptation to define man heteronomously. A belief that is institutionally protected and supported must always combat the institution's tendency to tie the truth of religious experience to commitment to itself, which means that the problems of self-preservation become a priority for the institution.

Independently of this problem (an important one in theological and ecclesiastical practice) that a relational autonomy concept is a restricted one—and this applies both to theologies that view theonomy as heteronomy and to claims to authority by church and faculties of theology—Fromm's understanding of humanism calls into question theological thought altogether. While it is true that he does not exclude the possibility of a theological grounding of human existence provided this entails no heteronomous claim on man,[6] he decided in favor of a grounding that dispenses with all theology as talk about God and as reflection about theonomy. The possibility of the mystical experience of the ONE even makes the effort to establish a relational autonomy redundant. His critical question can be formulated in these terms: Why should theology and the theological grounding of the relational autonomy of the human be necessary or meaningful if man is humanized in the religious experience of (eschatological) *humanitas*, and when this religious experience occurs in the most concentrated and effective form in the mystical experience?

Presumably, this question cannot be settled definitively because thinking and talking about God (theology) and experiencing God or the ONE (mysticism) are distinct possibilities for man that are not mutually exclusive and neither of which can be shown to be subordinate to the other. While theology is based on the experience of God's speech and has man's experience of God as its goal, mysticism in Fromm's understanding makes the claim that it can attain to a direct religious experience through the negation of every kind of theological knowledge and therefore believes it can also judge theology. But even this claim that mysticism makes will not prevent man from reflecting on his religious and mystical experience or from making it communicable through language. Verbalization, however, is already theology, even as negative theology.

Yet the legitimation of theology does not do away with the critical questioning of every (Christian) theology by mysticism, especially by humanistic mysticism. There is the further fact that the criticism that humanistic mysticism makes belongs to a tradition of dispute that theology and mysticism have carried on inside the Christian religion. The fight of the Church and its theological authorities against alleged gnostics, theosophists, and mystics, and against conversion and reform movements, too often is (or has been) a fight of those who believed they possessed the faith as they battled others who were (or are) inspired by the transforming power of religious and mystical experience. Inquisition and the suspicion of heresy threaten every religious renewal. Whenever religious experience and theological and ecclesiastical doctrine reached some kind of accommodation in the history of the Church and of theology, reflection on and verbalization of the religious and mystical experience became an impulse for theological and ecclesiastical reassessments. Mysticism, being critique, has both a destructive and a constructive function in theology.[7]

Although Fromm's humanistic mysticism calls into question every theology, the religious experience of the having/being alternative and its grounding in characterology nonetheless can have significance as a critical theory for a Christian theology, especially for a theology that is administered by the Church. This is all the more true since the having/being alternative has proved to be a suitable interpretive key to Jesus' religious and ethical message and, oddly enough, precisely to those elements in his gospel that would be difficult to understand otherwise and have found little application for that reason. A Christian theology that has its basis in the testimony to Christ's gospel and ethics by those who followed him, and whose goal is to follow Christ now, itself engages in a critical function vis-à-vis differently grounded historical and contemporary theologies and forms of the discipleship of Christ then and now. The having/being alternative can aid in this critical function. By bringing the most diverse statements and demands into a horizon of understanding and by showing the congruence of Jesus' teaching and life, the having/being alternative can facilitate the understanding of Jesus' religious and ethical message. And the interpretive reduction of the substance of Jesus' teaching and life to the having/being alternative makes possible the use of that alternative as a critical theory for the critical function of Christian theology. Finally, because the having/being alternative is not only the quintessence of religious experience and of the theological and ethical verbalizations of that experience but also an ultimate evaluation of fundamental orientations of the character structure and thus a characterological entity, the humane and humanizing qualities of all kinds of theological, ecclesiastical, and religious phenomena can be judged with its aid. For these reasons, Christian theologians should not overlook Fromm's constructive contribution, even though they differ in approach and there is a clearly perceptible difference in principle in the grounding of human existence and obligation. There is an impulse in Christian belief that is critical of religion, of church and theology. Fromm's humanism which, thanks to the having/being alternative, is both religious and scientific, contributes to the realization of that impulse insofar as it follows and takes hold of Jesus' teaching.

In conclusion, a discussion of the question regarding the specifically Christian in a theological ethic will illustrate this possibility. The opposition to an "autonomous morality in a Christian context" by the so-called ethics of belief (*Glaubensethik*)[8] would like to postulate a specifically Christian quality in the content of ethical norms. *Glaubensethik* not only believes that Jesus' ethos constitutes a specific horizon for the Christian that motivates his ethical behavior in a particular way ("autonomous morality" makes the same assumption), but also feels that there are substantive demands that derive only from the devout discipleship of Christ and whose fulfillment requires a strong faith.

Such an attempt to define Christianity as distinct from other religions, and especially from modern humanisms, must be judged as rather apologetic and naïve against Fromm's humanistic ethic. The explication of the religious ethos by the having/being alternative has shown that a humanistic ethic can also contain those radical ethical demands that characterize Jesus' message, and that it can ground the bindingness and realizability of such an ethos. From the humanistic perspective, the substance of Jesus' ethos is not necessarily grounded in revelation, nor is belief in the god-man a necessary condition for understanding and realizing it. The having/being alternative adequately explains the rationality of Jesus' ethos. To the extent that alternative is a characterological magnitude, it can ground normativeness in characterological—that is, empirically verifiable—knowledge.

If the having/being alternative can be shown to be an interpretive key to all elements of Jesus' message, the following observation applies to the function of Jesus' ethos in the grounding of a theological ethic, the differing views of the *Glaubensethiker* notwithstanding: Jesus' ethical message does not represent a compendium of Christian norms. Instead, the various moral demands can be understood as exemplifications of that ethical demand that is intrinsic to the promise of the Kingdom of God and that can be made plausible by the having/being alternative. Since that alternative does not present a norm for action but a metanorm, it has an essentially critical function for normative behavior.[9] This is the reason Jesus' warning about wealth, for example, addresses itself to the attitude, the behavior, and fundamental character orientation of securing existence by wealth. Such a demand can take concrete form in the renunciation of wealth, but its direct target is the attitude. How the attitude that is demanded can be optimally realized in any given instance is decided by the place value that wealth, for example, has in an individual's life.[10]

In contrast to the *Glaubensethik,* "autonomous morality" sees what is distinctively Christian in moral matters "not in concrete ethical injunctions that can be developed from an understanding of the faith,"[11] but in a specific horizon of meaning that motivates the Christian in his concrete ethical conduct in a particular way and therefore urges upon him a different attitude toward moral demands. In contrast to "autonomous morality," a humanistic perspective on Jesus' religious and ethical message asserts that even this specific horizon of meaning produces no effects that differ from those that would result from a humanistic interpretation of Jesus' proclamation of the Kingdom of God. Whether the horizon of meaning is understood theistically—in Christian terms, as the beginning of God's Kingdom in Jesus Christ and as a giftlike offer of revelation—or as the ethos of the renunciation of having that has its "gracelike" liberating effect in the gamble that is the renunciation of having, Fromm believes that in renouncing the having mode, man experiences that liberated and redeemed humanness that he can interpret as given him, as transcending him, and as revealed to him because it is not a result of his knowing, willing, and having.

Christian theologians will resist such an interpretation of the specifically Christian horizon of meaning. When "autonomous morality" anchors the distinctively Christian quality of morality in the critical, stimulating, and integrating effects of Jesus' message, it calls for a theistic horizon of meaning: the gracelike offer of a divine will to salvation that antedates all human action. If a Christian accepts God's will to salvation as revealed in Jesus Christ, this new horizon of meaning motivates him to adopt a new ethical attitude. Since the new horizon became incarnate in Jesus, the ethical relevance of this horizon of meaning becomes recognizable in Jesus' life and teaching as his ethos. This ethos, however, is not itself the specifically Christian quality of the moral but a result of it. It can be understood as the consequence of a particular Christian horizon of meaning, but need not be so understood. Interpreting Jesus' ethos by the having/being alternative has demonstrated that the rationality of that ethos does not necessarily lie in a theistic horizon of meaning. While it is true that from a theological perspective, the specifically Christian horizon of meaning is constitutive for Jesus' ethos, Fromm's humanistic perspective sees the reason of Jesus' ethos as grounded in the practice that renounces having. The ultimate ground for this practice of renunciation is the mystical experience of the ONE.

Having drawn a line that marks off the humanistic ethic, and having demonstrated that the having/being alternative serves as a key to the understanding of Jesus' ethos, it now becomes necessary to argue for the understanding that autonomous morality has of the specifically Christian in a theological ethic. For only the adoption of human reason as the principle of all morality can guarantee the communicability and bindingness of norms. This concern coincides with Jesus' ethos because through the having/being alternative, the reason of that ethos can be understood as the expression of the rationality of reality, provided that reality itself is interpreted through the having/being alternative, as Fromm interprets it. Representatives of an ethic of belief are therefore incorrect in thinking that where the discovery of norms is concerned, there are real differences between a Christian and a humanistic reason as here described. What difference there is must be looked for where an ethics adapts to the demands of a culture and society that is oriented around having and therefore puts forward a conception of the rationality of reality and of the moral that is no longer either Christ's or humanistic because it no longer follows the reason of the having/being alternative. Both Christian ethics and Fromm's humanistic ethic have a characteristic in common that distinguishes them from other ethics, and that is that the having/being alternative furnishes them with a criterion that is better suited than any other to discover ethical norms that are humane and have a humanizing effect.

Independently of the question concerning the discovery of norms, Fromm's humanism calls in question the conviction (which not only *Glaubensethiker* hold) that only a Christian theology can ultimately ground and guarantee the meaning of normativeness. The mystical experience of the ONE must be viewed as a distinctive and valid attempt to ground the meaning of what man ought to be. It is the religious experience of a humanistic ethos whose effects are powerful and which, by its renunciation of all determinations through having, gives direct experience of man's perfect form. The experience of the ONE thus ultimately grounds and guarantees the ethos of the having/being alternative. The ethos of the having/being alternative is therefore the condition for the possibility of the religious experience of the ONE and at the same time that religious experience itself. A humanistic ethic is grounded in the experience of this religious ethos, for humanistic ethics is concerned with strengthening the dominance of the being mode. But because a life in the being mode is only an interchangeable term for humanistic ethos, a life in that mode is *eo ipso* "ethical," that is, morally good. Humanistic ethics aims at the practice of an ethos of being that is ultimately grounded in the mystical experience of the ONE as the negation of all forms of having.

QUESTIONS CHRISTIAN THEOLOGIANS MIGHT ADDRESS TO THE HUMANIST FROMM

Humanism both enriches a Christian theology and calls all of it into question. The preceding considerations regarding a productive dialogue between Christian theologians and Fromm should serve primarily to deepen the understanding of his humanism and to forestall a premature judgment of it by a self-assured theology. Such caution has its deeper reason in the claim Fromm's humanism makes: it is based on experience that, even when religious, finds expression in the serious consideration and realization of humanness, and that becomes evident in that act of realization. Fromm attempted to live this humanism. The talk about being as based on the negation of all determinations by having represents the conceptualization of his scientific and religious experience and the daily practice of his religious ethos. The power of his lived humanism, however, does not mean that there are no questions that Christian theologians might address to him. But because humanism takes up the religious problem and gives it a coherent development that leads to a nontheistic mysticism, this dialogue would have to include an inquiry into the claim that mysticism has vis-à-vis theology and, most importantly, the claim that theology might raise vis-à-vis mysticism. The following questions and problems provide points of departure for this sort of definition of the function and place of theology and mysticism:

How can a lived religious ethos and the concomitant experiences be conveyed without the verbalization of the experiences becoming a substitute for the religious experience itself? Why does mysticism usually develop as a countermovement to an established faith that is primarily or wholly oriented around the avowal of certain dogmas and ecclesiastical structures? To what extent does theology have its legitimation in the necessity to give a philosophical answer to the questions life poses, particularly when theology understands itself as a communicable, rational reflection about empirical and religious experience? More specifically, don't such experiential facts as suffering, fear, sadness, guilt, death, unhappiness, and illness justify theological thought that goes beyond the undoubtedly accurate observation that it is principally the attitude toward these phenomena that decides their existential place value, not the philosophical or theological awareness of their problematical character?

To what extent does the human need for communication and the necessity that experiences be communicable make theology and a communion that is defined by theology and tied to a particular church community indispensable?

Can the relationship between theology and mysticism actually be grasped dialectically in such a way that religious experience can be had only if a theological knowledge that is necessarily an alienation of religious experience is negated? Or isn't it rather the case that in the process of religious experience, a constructive share must be conceded to theology if mystical experience is possible only through the radical realization of a religious ethos, yet this ethos must be thought about, taught, and learned? Where will the critical function of distinguishing between an orgiastic experience of unity and the mystical experience of the ONE be performed unless it be in the rational reflection of religious experience and in the religious and ethical demand that having be renounced?

Isn't it true that where theology is seen only as negative theology, it is overlooked that mystical experience is always discontinuous experience whose interpretation and verbalization are themselves theology, so that theology and mysticism necessarily quicken and criticize each other? As long as mystical experience can only be discontinuous, must the developing awareness and knowledge of the unity of the religious experience—that is, "positive" theology—not be a constructive precondition for a mystical experience of the ONE? In terms of personal experience and psychological preconditions, it may be asked: Doesn't a person who has the mystical experience of the ONE as a discontinuous experience of his life wholly in the being mode use this experience he has had as a form of knowledge that prompts him to have further religious experiences, so that reflection about the experience and its interpretation constitute a necessary and positive mediating function for religious experience? Doesn't this mean that religious experience necessarily depends on theology, and must one not concede to theological knowledge and reflection that functional significance that may accrue to all objects of having? The fact of having itself does not tell us whether this having is functional or a mode of existence. Precisely where theology mediates religious experience, theological knowledge means a functional having.

When this mediating function of theology is denied, is there not the attempt to ignore both the admission of finiteness and the acknowledgment that there is a necessary mixture of the fundamental orientations of being and having in the character structure because all one wants to see is the possibility of the religious experience in a punctual life that is lived wholly in the being mode? Doesn't the view that concentrates entirely on the end point of a negative dialectic and that envisages only the punctually possible experience of this end point in the mystical experience of the ONE neglect the concrete dealing with reality by a character structure that, even when the being mode is dominant, is always also determined by the having mode? Doesn't this mean that life succumbs to the temptations of religious enthusiasm and certain gnosticisms that assert, at the price of a practical, rationally governed sense of reality, that messianism and eschatology are at hand?

If it is true at the level of characterology that human existence is marked in principle by a mixture of the two modes even though punctually, the experience of a life wholly in the being mode is possible, why should the peculiarity that human life is fundamentally mediated and determined by having not be relevant to the application of the having/being alternative to the problem of religious experience? Why should what is true of life in general not be true of the mystical experience: namely, that the mystical experience calls for theological reflection so that the religious—including the religious ethos—is mediated and determined in principle by theological reflection, that is, in and through a communion?

That theology necessarily hinders or prevents the religious and mystical experience cannot be proved until theology surrenders its functional distinctiveness and replaces the religious experience. But why should "positive" theology be *a priori* a having determination and therefore hinder or prevent a religious experience if it is true that human life is fundamentally mediated by having and this does not automatically bring the dominance of having with it?

Since the religious experience is discontinuous and not the same thing as a life in the being mode, must the necessity of a mediation not be taken seriously and does it not become necessary to demand a mediation whose goal is the experience of immediacy?

All these questions notwithstanding, we will conclude with the following reflection: The mystical experience of the ONE is the discontinuous experience of a life lived wholly in the being mode. This experience itself is not mediated but results from the negation of every kind of mediation. The phrase "man for himself" applies here. Every belief, every hope, and every love of oneself, of man, the world and *humanitas* is grounded in this experience. It presupposes that man experience himself as totally free and independent, for it is only then that his life, his action, his love, his reason, compassion, willingness to sacrifice, his selflessness, his sharing, his forgiving, and his joy can be grounded in him. And only when they are grounded in him is it he that loves, thinks, works, shares, sorrows, delights.

Theistic religion and theology wish to mediate. Christian theology presents itself as a mediator and therefore requires the imitation of Jesus. The decisive question is this: What is being mediated, and to what end? If redeemed man is the goal, then here also, what is mediated is that *humanitas* that is experienced as man's capacity for immediacy. If religion, the Church, and theology can make possible such experiences of immediacy, then these institutions have a mediating function and define themselves by the task of making the immediacy of human life possible. Whether the Christian religion, theology, and the Church actually do justice to this task will not be decided here.

It can be said, however, that the writings of the New Testament testify to the fact that Jesus' life had such a mediating function, a function whose aim is the immediacy of the religious experience of God in man. Under these conditions, the question concerning the identity and the difference of Christianity and humanism is decided by a personal decision to risk the experience of immediacy. Here the ethos of Jesus and the ethos of humanism make an identical avowal: The Courage to Be Human.

Postscript by Erich Fromm: RELIGION AND SOCIETY

Religion is a system of ideas, norms, and rites that satisfy a need that is rooted in human existence, the need for a system of orientation and an object of devotion. This definition applies to all religions, whether they worship idols, pray to an invisible God, or have no concept of a "god," like Buddhism, for example. Man's idea of a "sacred" being depends on social structure and cultural tradition. In most societies, religion and social structure form a coherent whole. Since man's character is determined by the social structure, its religion, being an expression of psychological needs that are anchored in existential conditions, is also socially determined.

Capitalist industrial society (like the "socialist" state-capitalist societies) is profoundly irreligious. Its norms are maximal production, ruthless egoism, exploitation. Man's "salvation" is maximal material success, his duty good "functioning."

But man cannot stop dreaming. He longs for a world in which love, freedom, and justice are rooted, and since such a world does not exist, he creates a separate institution alongside society: religion. In it, he finds consolation, encouragement, hope, but also many illusions. And these illusions are necessary, for religion has made its peace with irreligious society. God and Mammon: to each his own. This compromise and the illusions it produces may be effective for a long time, but man always awakens again, notices that he is merely dreaming, and demands real salvation. Only a changed reality, a society that realizes the principles of love and human autonomy throughout its structure, can satisfy this demand. In such a society, a separate religion would no longer be needed, for the society would have made the religious principles its own and would thereby have "sublated" them as separate religious principles.

These comments also sketch what is essential in Karl Marx's position on religion. For him, religion was an opiate for man because it tries to satisfy his profoundest needs by illusions instead of allowing him to pluck the living flower. Marx was not antireligious. He was a profoundly religious person and an enemy of "religion" for that very reason.

Notes

INTRODUCTION: ERICH FROMM'S LIFE AND WORK

1. J. S. Glen, "Erich Fromm: A Protestant Critique," p. 11. Computer technology now makes it possible to arrive at a proximate judgment about an author's popularity because it can provide lists of all the reviews of a new book. Cf. G. C. Tarbert, ed., *Book Review Index*. There are also large-scale indexes that list all those passages in which one author quotes another. Cf. the *Social Sciences Citation Index*, 1970.

2. E. Z. Friedenberg, "Neo-Freudianism and Erich Fromm," p. 305.

3. J. H. Schaar, *Escape from Authority*, p. 3.

4. See the titles designated by the letter M in the bibliography. Most of these are dissertations. Even in the Soviet Union, interest in Fromm has recently increased, although the material is largely apologetic. An example would be V. I. Dobren'kov's study, *Neo-Freudianism and the Search for Truth: Erich Fromm's errors and illusions*.

5. The biographical information comes from E. Fromm, *Beyond the Chains of Illusion* (1962a), pp. 3–12; "Im Namen des Lebens" (1974b); Fromm and R. I. Evans, *Dialogue with Erich Fromm* (1966f); B. Landis and E. S. Tauber, eds., *In the Name of Life*, pp. x–xiv; E. Z. Friedenberg, "Neo-Freudianism and Erich Fromm," pp. 306f; M. Birnbach, *Neo-Freudian Social Philosophy*, p. 234; Munzinger-Archiv. Internationales Biographisches Archiv. H. J. Schultz, *Humanist ohne Illusionen*.

6. E. Fromm and R. I. Evans, *Dialogue with Erich Fromm* (1966f), p. 56.

7. Cf. E. Fromm, *Beyond the Chains of Illusion* (1962a), p. 4.

8. Ibid., p. 9.

9. B. Landis and E. S. Tauber, eds., *In the Name of Life*, p. xi.

10. E. Fromm, *Das jüdische Gesetz* (1922a).

11. The important role Fromm played as a member of the Frankfurt Institute for Social Research seems to have been deliberately ignored after he left it toward the end of the thirties, especially by Max Horkheimer. Setting this record straight would be a much appreciated piece of historical research. Horkheimer was so reluctant to acknowledge Fromm's membership that when Oskar Hersche asked him in 1969 who the members of the institute had been around 1930 (M. Horkheimer, *Verwaltete Welt*, p. 11), he could answer: "There were a number of people. I should begin by mentioning Friedrich Pollock, Franz Borkenau, Henryk Grossmann, Karl August Wittfogel, Leo Löwenthal, Karl Korsch, Gerhard Meyer, Kurt Mandelbaum, all of whom except Löwenthal had been hired by Grünberg. All of them published books in the Institute series. There were also some psychoana-

lysts who belonged to the Institute for we realized that sociology and psychoanalysis would have to work together. But their association was less close. Karl Landauer, Heinrich Meng and Erich Fromm and some others were members of this group. They held seminars on psychoanalysis, though not at the University but at the Institute." But it is not true that Fromm's association was "less close," nor was he just one among a number of others. In 1930, Horkheimer had invited him, as an expert on psychoanalysis, to become one of the four members of the core group of the institute, and to become an associate for life. Fromm accepted and spent the following years working on his study of the authoritarian character structure of German workers and employees before Hitler (Cf. Fromm, *Arbeiter und Angestellte am Vorabend des Dritten Reiches. Eine sozialpsychologische Untersuchung,* 1980a). That Fromm's scholarly work in the "Frankfurt School" was forgotten may have been due to the odd treatment of dissidents by those institute members who were in charge at the time. But the desire to have people forget Fromm and his work must also have been connected with the intent to disavow the Marxist methods and psychoanalytic discoveries of the study on the authoritarian character structure of German workers and employees on the eve of the Third Reich. Especially in the case of Horkheimer, there are indications that he abandoned his Marxist beliefs and turned (or returned?) to bourgeois convictions as early as during his stay in the United States, quite simply because he was afraid of being considered a leftist or a Marxist where this was inopportune. (This is also the reason the expression "Marxist theory," for example, was replaced by "critical theory," and "capitalist society" by "alienated society.")

In his introduction to the reprint of the *Zeitschrift für Sozialforschung,* Alfred Schmidt is somewhat fairer in his assessment of Fromm's scientific contributions while he was a member of the Frankfurt Institute, although he offers nothing more than an analysis of a Fromm essay. On the "Frankfurt School," cf. M. Jay, *The Dialectical Imagination: A History of the Frankfurt School and the Institute of Social Research 1923–1950;* P. V. Zima, *L'Ecole de Francfort.*

12. Fromm, *Beyond the Chains of Illusion* (1962a).

13. Cf. M. R. Green, *Her Life,* pp. 358f.

14. H. Marcuse, *Eros and Civilization,* p. 238. The critique of Neo-Freudian revisionism has recently been published as an epilogue in *Triebstruktur und Gesellschaft. Ein philosophischer Beitrag zu Sigmund Freud,* pp. 234–269. The dispute between Marcuse and Fromm was quite violent and found expression in a variety of publications. Cf. Fromm, "The Human Implications of Instinctivistic 'Radicalism' " (1955b); "A Counter-Rebuttal to Herbert Marcuse" (1956b); *The Crisis of Psychoanalysis* (1970a), pp. 25–31; O. Schatz, ed., *Der Friede im nuklearen Zeitalter,* pp. 227f.; E. Fromm, *The Anatomy of Human Destructiveness* (1973a), pp. 463f, n.24; *To Have or to Be?* (1976a), p. 75.

15. On the now extensive literature on "Neo-Freudians," cf. especially C. Thompson, *Die Psychoanalyse;* and also *Interpersonal Psychoanalysis,* esp. pp. 95–99, 361–366; M. Birnbach, *Neo-Freudian Social Philosophy;* E. Z. Friedenberg, *Neo-Freudianism and Erich Fromm;* W. Herberg, *Freud, the Revisionists and Social Reality;* J. Rattner, *Psychologie der zwischenmenschlichen Beziehungen;* R. Wiegand, *Gesellschaft und Charakter;* Th. W. Adorno, "Die revidierte Psychoanalyse."

16. E. Fromm, *The Crisis of Psychoanalysis* (1970a), p. 21, fn.; "Although Horney, Sullivan, and I are usually classified together as a 'culturalist' or 'Neo-Freudian' school, this classification hardly seems justified. In spite of the fact that we were friends, worked together and had certain views in common—particularly a critical

attitude toward the libido theory—the differences between us were greater than the similarities, especially in the 'cultural' viewpoint. Horney and Sullivan thought of cultural patterns in the traditional anthropological sense, while my approach looked toward a dynamic analysis of the economic, political, and psychological forces that form the basis of society." Cf. Fromm, *The Heart of Man* (1964a), p. 14; and Fromm and Evans, *Dialogue with Erich Fromm* (1966f), pp. 58f. The reserve, especially vis-à-vis Karen Horney, is due to disputes within the psychoanalytic movement in the United States during the war years. While in 1941, Fromm and Horney, among others, opposed the New York Psychoanalytic Institute and contributed significantly to the establishment of the American Association for the Advancement of Psychoanalysis, personal reasons lead Fromm to break with Horney in 1943. Together with Clara Thompson, Harry Stack Sullivan, and others, he then formed a New York branch of the Washington School of Psychiatry that was supported by the William Alanson White Psychiatric Foundation. On this, see M. R. Green, *Her Life*, pp. 361–366.

17. Cf. M. Norell et al., *Reminiscences of Supervision with Erich Fromm.*

18. Cf. E. Fromm, *Let Man Prevail—A Socialist Manifesto and Program* (1960b).

19. This effort found expression especially in *May Man Prevail? An Inquiry into the Facts and Fictions of Foreign Policy* (1961a), in which Fromm unmasks fear of Russian aggression as a fiction by analyzing the Communist social structure at the time. As late as 1974, Fromm, acting on the suggestion of Senator William Fulbright, wrote a paper on the policy of détente for a hearing held by the U.S. Senate Committee for Foreign Relations which deals with American relations with Communist states; cf. Fromm, "Remarks on the Policy of Détente" (1975a).

20. On the concept of socialism in the work of Fromm, cf. especially E. Fromm, ed., *Socialist Humanism* (1965a).

21. Cf. E. Fromm, "The Case for Unilateral Disarmament" (1960c); "Afterword" (1961c); *May Man Prevail?* (1961a); Fromm and M. Maccoby, "A Debate on the Question of Civil Defense" (1962b); E. Fromm, "Zur Theorie und Strategie des Friedens" (1970h); "Epilogue" (1970g).

22. H. J. Schultz, *Humanist ohne Illusionen*, p. 37.

23. Cf. the preface to the German edition of *The Revolution of Hope* (1971a).

24. E. Fromm, *Das jüdische Gesetz* (1922a), p. 237. On the following discussion, see the chronologically arranged Fromm bibliography of this study.

25. This becomes very clear in the short essay "Dauernde Nachwirkung eines Erziehungsfehlers" (1926a).

26. Cf. especially E. Fromm, "Über Methode und Aufgabe einer Analytischen Sozialpsychologie" (1932a).

27. Cf. E. Fromm, "Sozialpsychologischer Teil" (1936a), and note 11.

28. Cf. especially the reviews by T. H. Gill, A. T. Boisen, L. B. Hill, P. Mullahy, M. F. A. Montagu, L. Wirth, and E. E. Hadley in the journal *Psychiatry.*

29. E. Fromm, *The Forgotten Language* (1951a); see also Fromm, "Der Traum ist die Sprache des universalen Menschen" (1971a).

30. *Sigmund Freud's Mission* (1959a); *Marx's Concept of Man* (1961b); *Beyond the Chains of Illusion* (1962a).

31. This is the subtitle of *You Shall Be as Gods* (1966a).

32. On the final statements concerning the function of "religion," see Fromm, "Einige post-marxsche und post-freudsche Gedanken über Religion und Religiosität (1972b); and the concluding part of *To Have or to Be?* (1976a).

33. See note 21.

34. As, for example in B. M. McGrath, *An Examination of Erich Fromm's Ethics with Implications for Philosophy of Education,* pp. 59f. M. Birnbach says in *Neo-Freudian Social Philosophy,* pp. 191f: "One is left with the feeling that in the constructive parts of his writings, he verbalizes more than he analyzes; the voice he speaks with is that of the prophet rather than that of the scientist. . . ." On this judgment, see also B. R. Betz, *An Analysis of the Prophetic Character of the Dialectical Rhetoric of Erich Fromm.*

35. E. Fromm. *Beyond the Chains of Illusion* (1962a), p. 10.

36. E. Fromm and M. Maccoby, *Social Character in a Mexican Village* (1970b). There is a correspondence in method between this piece of fieldwork and Fromm's major sociopsychological study from the thirties, *Arbeiter und Angestellte am Vorabend des Dritten Reiches. Eine sozialpsychologische Untersuchung* (1980a).

PART ONE: The Sociopsychological Insights and Philosophical-Anthropological Ideas of Erich Fromm

CHAPTER I. SOCIAL PSYCHOLOGY

1. E. Fromm, *Beyond the Chains of Illusion* (1962a), p. 12. For the perspective of psychoanalysts on Fromm's reception and critique of Freud, see especially the studies by R. G. Mandolini Guardo, *De Freud a Fromm, Historia generale del Psiconanalisis,* pp. 418–466; D. Wyss, *Die tiefenpsychologischen Schulen von den Anfängen bis zur Gegenwart,* pp. 188–195; E. Wiesenhütter, *Freud und seine Kritiker,* pp. 53–58; F. Heigl, *Die humanistische Psychoanalyse Erich Fromms.*

2. E. Fromm, "Über Methode und Aufgabe einer analytischen Sozialpsychologie" (1932a), p. 28.

3. Though Freud later developed a different polarity of drives, namely, Eros and Destrudo, this change in his doctrine of drives can be ignored for the purposes of our discussion here. But see the discussion on the death instinct on p. 49f.

4. E. Fromm, *Beyond the Chains of Illusion* (1962a), pp. 31f. See also Fromm, *The Anatomy of Human Destructiveness* (1973a), pp. 443–445.

5. See E. Fromm, *Beyond the Chains of Illusion* (1962a), pp. 31f; and Fromm, "Über Methode und Aufgabe einer analytischen Sozialpsychologie (1932a), p. 29.

6. "Methode und Aufgabe," (1932a), p. 31.

7. See especially *The Future of an Illusion* and *Civilization and Its Discontents.*

8. It is only toward contemporary sexual morality that Freud's position is truly critical. See E. Fromm, "The Human Implications of Instinctivistic 'Radicalism' " (1955b), esp. p. 344.

9. See especially E. Fromm, "Sozialpsychologischer Teil" (1936a), pp. 88f; and Fromm, "Über Methode und Aufgabe einer analytischen Sozialpsychologie" (1932a), pp. 35f.

10. "Methode und Aufgabe," (1932a), p. 39.

11. Cf. ibid., pp. 37f.

12. On the following, see E. Fromm, "Oedipus in Innsbruck" (1930d); Fromm, "Introduction," in P. Mullahy, *Oedipus: Myth and Complex* (1948a); and the writings of P. Mullahy; E. Fromm, "The Oedipus Complex and the Oedipus Myth" (1949b); *The Forgotten Language* (1951a), pp. 196–231; R. de la Fuente-Muniz, "Fromm's Approach to the Study of Personality," pp. 13f; E. Fromm, *Sigmund Freud's Mission* (1951a), pp. 10–18; M. Birnbach, *Neo-Freudian Social Philosophy,* pp. 46–48; E.

Fromm et al., "The Oedipus Complex: Comments in 'The Case of Little Hans' " (1966k); E. Fromm, *The Anatomy of Human Destructiveness* (1973a), pp. 358–365.

13. Cf. S. Freud, *Totem and Tabu.*

14. E. Fromm, "Über Methode und Aufgabe einer analytischen Sozialpsychologie" (1932a), p. 38.

15. J. J. Bachofen, *Mother Right.* Cf. the studies by L. H. Morgan, *Systems of Consanguinity and Affinity*, and *Ancient Society;* R. Briffault, *The Mothers.* See also E. Fromm, "Robert Briffaults Werk über das Mutterrecht" (1933a); "Die sozialpsychologische Bedeutung der Mutterrechtstheorie" (1934a); "The Significance of the Theory of Mother Right for Today" (1970f); A. Turel, *Bachofen-Freud. Zur Emanzipation des Mannes vom Reich der Mütter.* On the history of the influence of Bachofen's *Mother Right,* see H.-J. Heinrichs, ed., *Materialien zu Bachofens 'Das Mutterrecht.'*

16. Extensively in E. Fromm, "The Oedipus Complex and the Oedipus Myth" (1949b).

17. Ibid., p. 338.

18. By Bronislaw Malinowski, Ruth Benedict, and Margaret Mead, for example.

19. In his "Die sozialpsychologische Bedeutung der Mutterrechtstheorie" (1934a), p. 221, Fromm writes as follows: "The patricentric type is characterized by a complex in which a rigorous superego, guilt feelings, docile love toward paternal authority, the desire to dominate weaker individuals, the acceptance of suffering as punishment for one's own feelings and an incapacity for happiness are dominant. The matricentric complex, on the other hand, is characterized by a feeling of optimistic confidence in an unconditional maternal love, minor guilt feelings, reduced strength of the superego and greater capacity for happiness and pleasure. At the same time, the development of the motherly qualities of compassion and love for the weaker and those in need of help is seen as an ideal."

20. On Fromm's critique of Sigmund Freud's ontogenetic interpretation of the Oedipus complex, see E. Fromm, "The Oedipus Complex and the Oedipus Myth" (1949b), pp. 356–358; and P. Mullahy, *Oedipus Myth and Complex*, p. 277f. This view of Fromm's has important consequences for therapy. In "The Oedipus Complex and the Oedipus Myth" (1949b), p. 358, Fromm emphasizes: "While Freud assumes that the conflict arising from the child's incestuous strivings is rooted in his nature and thus unavoidable, we believe that in a cultural situation in which respect for the integrity of every individual—hence of every child—is realized the Oedipus complex will belong to the past." There is a further consequence for self-understanding and the reciprocal attribution of sexual roles by man and woman. On this matter, see Rainer Funk's essay "Der Fluch, kein Mann zu sein, Psychoanalyse im Widerstreit," which states Fromm's views.

21. E. Fromm, "Über Methode und Aufgabe einer analytischen Sozialpsychologie" (1932a), pp. 39f.

22. E. Fromm, "Sozialpsychologischer Teil" (1936a), p. 92.

23. E. Fromm, *Man for Himself* (1947a), p. 57.

24. Ibid.

25. On the following, cf. especially E. Fromm, "Psychoanalytic Characterology and Its Application to the Understanding of Culture," (1949c).

26. Cf. Fromm, "Psychoanalytic Characterology and Its Application to the Understanding of Culture" (1949c), pp. 81f.; *The Anatomy of Human Destructiveness* (1973a), pp. 79f.

27. Cf. E. Fromm, "Psychoanalytic Characterology" (1949c), p. 82. See also C.

Thompson, *Die Psychoanalyse,* pp. 76f: "According to Freud, three things can happen to the libido during the formation of the character. Part of the libido which persists in a pregenital phase may remain unchanged throughout the entire life of the adult. The result of such a process was referred to as a perversion and not considered a genuine character development. The other two possibilities are the development of reaction formations against the drive and the sublimation of the drive. These two latter are responsible for the character and it was assumed that this was the way human beings mature. Since man was considered to be primarily a creature of the libido, it was only by way of reaction formation and sublimation that he would become a social being."

28. E. Fromm, "Psychoanalytic Characterology and Its Application to the Understanding of Culture" (1949c), p. 82.

29. Cf. C. Thompson, *Die Psychoanalyse,* p. 78.

30. Cf. E. Fromm, "Sozialpsychologischer Teil" (1936a), pp. 113–115.

31. Cf. E. Fromm, *Escape from Freedom* (1941a), p. 291.

32. E. Fromm, *Man for Himself* (1947a), p. 58.

33. Ibid.

34. See p. 14f.

35. E. Fromm, *Escape from Freedom* (1941a), p. 290. The connection between character traits and erogenous zones during the development of the libido that Freud observed is not rejected by Fromm. Such a connection does, in fact, exist, but it is not causal: character traits are the expression of the character orientation that was acquired through assimilation and socialization. Cf. E. Fromm and R. I. Evans, *Dialogue with Erich Fromm* (1966f), pp. 3f; C. Thompson, *Die Psychoanalyse,* p. 84; more extensively in E. Fromm, "Sex and Character" (1948b), pp. 47–58.

36. Here Fromm deliberately avoids the concept "libidinal forces," which he used in his early writings and took over from Freud, because he wants to make it clear that his understanding of character has nothing to do with Freud's libido theory. The concept "human energy" becomes "psychic energy" shortly after this quotation, and thus comes close to what C. G. Jung meant by "psychic energy." In a note to the translation of his essay "Über Methode und Aufgabe einer analytischen Sozialpsychologie" in *The Crisis of Psychoanalysis* (1970a), Fromm uses the term "passionate forces" rather than "libidinal forces."

37. E. Fromm, *The Heart of Man* (1964a), p. 59; cf. *The Anatomy of Human Destructiveness* (1973a), p. 226: "Character is the relatively permanent system of all noninstinctual strivings through which man relates himself to the human and natural world."

38. Cf. E. Fromm, *Marx's Contribution to the Knowledge of Man* (1968h), p. 65.

39. Ibid.

40. The concept "structure of drives" here still has the same meaning it has in Freud's libido theory.

41. E. Fromm, "Die Entwicklung des Christusdogmas" (1930a), is quoted here from the reprint in (*The Dogma of Christ and Other Essays* [1963a]). In this, his first sociopsychological work, Fromm attempts to understand the "ideas and ideologies," by which he means belief in Christ up to the Nicene Creed, by looking at men and their social and economic conditions and not by interpreting men by their "ideas and ideologies." In contrast to all previous attempts (such as T. Reik's *Dogma und Zwangsidee*), the psychoanalytical interpretation of the development of the dogma of Christ becomes possible only on the basis of an analysis of the "socio-economic situation of those social groups that adopted and passed on the Christian

doctrine." And it is only through the knowledge of the common psychic characteristics of this group that were molded in this fashion that an adequate understanding of the "ideas and ideologies" becomes possible. Cf. Fromm, "The Dogma of Christ" (1963a), pp. viif.

42. E. Fromm, *The Dogma of Christ and Other Essays* (1963a), p. 9.

43. E. Fromm, "Über Methode und Aufgabe einer analytischen Sozialpsychologie" (1932a), p. 53; cf. Fromm, "Die psychoanalytische Characterologie und ihre Bedeutung für die Sozialpsychologie" (1932b), especially p. 267f; *To Have or to Be?* (1976a), p. 133.

44. On what follows, see especially E. Fromm, *Escape from Freedom* (1941a), pp. 277–299; "Sex and Character" (1948b); "Psychoanalytic Characterology and Its Application to the Understanding of Culture" (1949c); "The Human Implications of Instinctivistic 'Radicalism'" (1955b); *The Sane Society* (1955a), pp. 78–83; *Beyond the Chains of Illusion* (1962a), pp. 78–87; "The Application of Humanist Psychoanalysis to Marx's Theory" (1965c); E. Fromm and M. Maccoby, *Social Character in a Mexican Village* (1970b), pp. 16–19 and pp. 230–236; E. Fromm, *To Have or to Be?* (1976a), pp. 133–135; *The Anatomy of Human Destructiveness* (1973a), pp. 252f. The following are some of the titles in the secondary literature: G. B. Hammond, *Man in Estrangement*, pp. 25–31; M. Birnbach, *Neo-Freudian Social Philosophy*, pp. 81–83; D. Riesman, *The Lonely Crowd;* U. Essbach-Kreuzer, *Die Theorien des Sozialcharakters in den Arbeiten von Erich Fromm.* Negative criticism: J. H. Schaar, *Escape from Authority*, pp. 89–98; O. Fenichel, *Psychoanalyse und Gesellschaft bei Erich Fromm.* In her essay "Aufklärung und Radikalismus—Kritik der psychologischen Anthropologie Fromms," Agnes Heller suggests that her own judgment is flawless, but considering her inadequate nuances, certain imputations, and obtrusive labeling, her claim must be questioned.

45. E. Fromm, *The Anatomy of Human Destructiveness* (1973a), p. 253.

46. E. Fromm, "Sex and Character" (1948b), p. 309; "Psychoanalytic Characterology and Its Application to the Understanding of Culture" (1949c), p. 84; *Beyond the Chains of Illusion* (1962a), p. 78.

47. Cf. Fromm and Maccoby, *Social Character in a Mexican Village* (1970b).

48. *Escape from Freedom* (1941a), p. 278.

49. Cf. *Beyond the Chains of Illusion* (1962a), pp. 77f.

50. Ibid., p. 78.

51. Ibid., pp. 86f.

52. When Fromm assumes that the social character has a mediating function, he is also attempting to solve the problem of the mediation of base and superstructure, which is so vigorously argued in Marxism. He emphasizes that "in the concept of the social character, the connection between the economic basis and the superstructure is understood in their interaction" (Fromm and Maccoby, *Social Character in a Mexican Village* [1970b], p. 18n.); see also Fromm, "The Application of Humanist Psychoanalysis to Marx's Theory" (1965c), p. 212. For a reaction to this attempted solution, see A. Schaff, *Marxismus und das menschliche Individuum*, pp. 53–57 and 130f. Fromm used this model of the social character repeatedly: in the historical analyses of the link between Protestantism and early capitalism (in *Escape from Freedom*) and with reference to the 19th and 20th centuries (in *The Sane Society* [1955a]). "Die Entwicklung des Christusdogmas" (1930a) is basically done in the same way, even though its formulations are still those of Freud's libido theory.

53. Cf. Fromm, "The Application of Humanist Psychoanalysis to Marx's Theory" (1965c), p. 212; *Beyond the Chains of Illusion* (1962a), p. 87.

54. E. Fromm, "On Psychoanalytic Characterology and Its Application to the Understanding of Culture" (1949c), pp. 84f; *Beyond the Chains of Illusion* (1962a), pp. 78f; *The Sane Society* (1955a), p. 79.

55. Cf. Fromm, *Escape from Freedom* (1941a), pp. 282f. This element of satisfaction that is present because someone whose action is determined by the social character of his group wishes to do what he must do also explains why people can yet—and sometimes only—be happy under political arrangements that suppress them, even though ideology and brainwashing are needed. Conversely, where we find an intent to change social conditions, the function of the social character explains why consciousness of the class situation and the progress of socialism in the Communist states, for example, does not result quasi-automatically in the change Marxists hope for. Cf. Fromm, "The Application of Humanist Psychoanalysis to Marx's Theory" (1965c), pp. 211f.

56. Fromm, *Escape from Freedom* (1941a), p. 283.

57. There is a contradiction between the sociological insight that the character structure is shaped by the role the individual must play in his culture, and the psychoanalytic insight according to which an individual's character is essentially shaped during childhood, although the child hardly has any contact with culture and society during those years. This contradiction is resolved when the family is seen as the "psychic agency of society." The family fulfills this task in two ways: (1) by the influence the character of the parents has on that of the child; (2) by the pedagogic methods used in a given culture. Cf. Fromm, "On Psychoanalytic Characterology and Its Application to the Understanding of Culture" (1949c), pp. 86f; *The Sane Society* (1955a), p. 82.

58. Cf. Fromm, "On Psychoanalytic Characterology and Its Application to the Understanding of Culture (1949c), pp. 85f.

59. For a discussion and grounding of these needs, see p. 60–66. Cf. Fromm, *Beyond the Chains of Illusion* (1962a), pp. 81: "If a social order neglects or frustrates the basic human needs beyond a certain threshhold, the members of such a society will try to change the social order so as to make it more suitable to their human needs. If this change is not possible, the outcome will probably be that such a society will collapse, because of its lack of vitality and its destructiveness."

60. Fromm, "On Psychoanalytic Characterology and Its Application to the Understanding of Culture (1949c), p. 6. Cf. Fromm, "The Application of Humanist Psychoanalysis to Marx's Theory" (1965c), p. 213: "Social change and revolution are caused not only by new productive forces which conflict with older forms of social organization, but also by the conflict between inhuman social conditions and unalterable human needs." Cf. ibid., p. 219.

61. Fromm and Maccoby, *Social Character in a Mexican Village* (1970b), p. 17.

62. E. Fromm in the discussion on "Psychoanalytic Characterology and Its Application to the Understanding of Culture (1949c), p. 10.

63. An erroneous interpretation of Fromm's social psychology is almost pervasive in the German reception and critique of Fromm. In his *Gesellschaft und Charakter*, Ronald Wiegand proposes to demonstrate the sociological implications of the neo-psychoanalysis "that was practiced by Erich Fromm, Karen Horney and Harry Stack Sullivan" (!). But instead of tracing Fromm's independent development of the sociopsychological method, he observes that "Fromm is hampered in his analyses

of religious experiences" and interprets this "as the after effect of his strongly religious childhood which even in Fromm's psychoanalytic training was not wholly dispelled" (p. 34). This essentially unqualified claim that is proved nowhere—Wiegand calls it "an argument that is surely not improper"—becomes the hub for a further judgment of Fromm that deteriorates in part into pure imputation (as, for example on pp. 50 and 341). The repetition of allegations (on pp. 47, 49, 334f, 340f) does not do away with tendentious peculiarity of the book but at most permits one to infer that the author worked in a scientifically irresponsible fashion. A reading of Bruno W. Reimann's *Psychoanalyse und Gesellschaftstheorie* yields a similar result. The polemical attacks (e.g., pp. 111f) and obvious distortions of Fromm's insights follow the criticism of Herbert Marcuse (see Introduction, note 14) and are based on a fundamental misunderstanding and incomprehension of what Fromm means by "character" and "social character." It is therefore not surprising that Reimann should feel that Fromm's attempt "to reconstruct the deformation processes of capitalist society remains abstract because it rests on a distortion of psychoanalytic theory and, lacking stringent analytical categories, is incapable of showing the negative mediation of concrete human nature with restrictive social patterns and patterns of domination. . . . Fromm's approach makes it impossible to lay hold of the psychic deformations of the social subject under oppressive social conditions. This becomes possible only when the category of the unconscious is not surrendered and the unconscious is reconstructed as a socially mediated potential, the libidinal component being retained" (pp. 112f)! Helmut Dahmer's critique of Fromm is wholly the product of his commitment to Wilhelm Reich's theories. See, e.g., H. Dahmer, *Psychoanalyse als kritische Theorie; Libido und Gesellschaft, Studien über Freud und die Freudsche Linke.* In contrast to these interpretations of Fromm's social psychology in the German language, all of which misunderstand the concept of character and therefore perpetuate a caricature of Fromm's sociopsychological method, it is pleasing to note that Predrag Vranicki's study in Vol. 2 of his *Geschichte des Marxismus* (pp. 865–877) attempts to understand Fromm's statements without prejudice. In spite of the critical distance in his judgment, a similar effort was made by U. Essbach-Kreuzer in "Die Theorie des Sozialcharakters in den Arbeiten von Erich Fromm."

64. E. Fromm, "Freud's Model of Man and Its Social Determinants (1970d), p. 31. On what follows, see also *Escape from Freedom* (1941a), pp. 289–296; *Sigmund Freud's Mission* (1959a), pp. 95–104; "The Human Implications of Instinctivistic Radicalism'" (1955b); "A Counter-Rebuttal to Herbert Marcuse" (1956b); R. de la Fuente Muniz, "Fromm's Approach to the Study of Personality," pp. 7–14.

65. On the revision of this doctrine of drives by the introduction of the death instinct, see pp. 23–25 and 49f.

66. Fromm, "Freud's Model of Man and Its Social Determinants" (1970d), p.31.

67. Cf. ibid., p. 33; *Escape from Freedom* (1941a), pp. 294f.

68. Cf. Fromm, "Freud's Model of Man" (1970d), pp. 39f.

69. Ibid., p. 39.

70. Ibid., p. 45.

71. Ibid., p. 34.

72. Cf. Fromm and Evans, *Dialogue with Erich Fromm* (1966f), pp. 67f. It is principally in *Beyond the Pleasure Principle* that Freud develops his new view. In that book, he asserts that there is a phylogenetic principle whose principal task is to restore an earlier state and ultimately to take organic life back to its original form

of inorganic existence: "If it is true that—at some immeasurably remote time and in a manner we cannot conceive—life once proceeded out of inorganic matter, then, according to our presumption, an instinct must have arisen which sought to do away with life once more and to reestablish the inorganic state. If we recognize in this instinct the self-destructiveness of our hypothesis, we may regard the self-destructiveness as an expression of a 'death instinct' which cannot fail to be present in every vital process" (*New Introductory Lectures on Psycho-Analysis*, Vol. XXII, p. 107).

73. E. Fromm, "Freud's Model of Man and Its Social Determinants" (1970d), p. 34.

74. Cf. the appendix "Freud's Theory of Aggressiveness and Destructiveness" in *The Anatomy of Human Destructiveness* (1973a), pp. 439–478.

75. Verification is presumably difficult because while Freud wished to see the life and death instincts as biological entitites intrinsic to man's nature, he could show no physiological base for such an assumption. In the case of the earlier libido theory, on the other hand, it was precisely the fact that it was anchored in the chemical and physiological and that the development of the libido was tied to physical erogenous zones that could be cited in support of the correctness of the theory. Cf. Fromm, "The Present Crisis of Psychoanalysis" (1967d), pp. 72f.

76. Cf. Freud, *Civilization and Its Discontents*, Vol. XXI, p. 111.

77. E. Fromm, *Escape from Freedom* (1941a), p. 294.

78. E. Fromm, "Freud's Model of Man" (1970d), p. 45.

79. S. Freud, *Civilization and Its Discontents*, Vol. XXI, p. 112.

80. E. Fromm, "Freud's Model of Man" (1970d), p. 45.

81. Fromm and Maccoby, *Social Character in a Mexican Village* (1970b), p. 14.

82. R. de la Fuente-Muniz, "Fromm's Approach to the Study of Personality," p. 8.

83. Cf. Fromm, "Freud's Model of Man" (1970d); *Sigmund Freud's Mission* (1959a), pp. 95–104; *The Heart of Man* (1964a), pp. 48–51.

84. E. Fromm, "Freud's Model of Man" (1970d), p. 31.

85. Very extensively in *The Anatomy of Human Destructiveness* (1973a), pp. 439–478.

86. Ibid., p. 462.

87. Cf. E. Fromm, "Zur Theorie und Strategie des Friedens" (1970h), pp. 30, 24; *The Heart of Man* (1964a), pp. 48–51.

88. E. Fromm, *The Heart of Man* (1964a), pp. 50: "This duality . . . is one between the primary and most fundamental tendency of life—to persevere in life—and its contradiction, which comes into being when man fails in this goal."

89. R. de la Fuente-Muniz, "Fromm's Approach to the Study of Personality," p. 8.

90. See pp. 29–31 and 142–145.

CHAPTER 2. THE CHARACTER THEORY

1. E. Fromm, *Man for Himself* (1947a), p. 50.

2. See ibid., pp. 51–53; C. Thompson, *Die Psychoanalyse*, pp. 75f. See also E. Fromm, "Aggressivität wurzelt im Charakter." This article, which is based on a conversation between Erich Fromm and Adalbert Reif that was published as "Aggression und Charakter" (1975b), can be viewed as a brief and easily understandable presentation of Fromm's characterology. The first systematic presentation of

the characterology is to be found in *Man for Himself* (1947a). It coincides with the comments in *The Anatomy of Human Destructiveness* (1973a), pp. 219–230, 251–254.

3. E. Fromm, *Man for Himself* (1947a), p. 52.

4. Cf. P. Mullahy, *Oedipus Myth and Complex*, pp. 258–269.

5. Fromm and Maccoby, *Social Character in a Mexican Village* (1970b), p. 8. Cf. Fromm, *Man for Himself* (1947a), pp. 54f; *The Anatomy of Human Destructiveness* (1973a), pp. 43f.

6. D. Riesman, "Psychological Types and National Character," p. 332.

7. E. Fromm, *The Anatomy of Human Destructiveness* (1973a), p. 43.

8. Fromm and Maccoby, *Social Character in a Mexican Village* (1970b), p. 11.

9. This insight into the difference between form of behavior and the character trait that determines this form of behavior has significant consequences for an ethical judgment: It is, then, not a matter of judging (and eventually condemning) someone on the basis of his overt behavior and of educating him to observe certain forms of behavior. What is decisive for ethical judgment is the diagnosis of the character trait in back of the form of behavior, and it is not the forms of behavior but these determining character traits that are the object of pedagogy.

10. On the concepts "dynamic" and "syndrome," cf. Fromm, *Escape from Freedom* (1941a), pp. 162f; *Man for Himself* (1947a), p. 56; C. J. Sahlin, *An Analysis of the Writings of Erich Fromm and Their Implications for Adult Education*, pp. 122–125. On the concept "system," cf. Fromm, *The Anatomy of Human Destructiveness* (1973a), p. 79.

11. E. Fromm, *Man for Himself* (1947a), p. 57.

12. Ibid. On the historical development of this view of character that is an original contribution, see especially his essay "Selfishness and Self-Love" (1939b), in which he makes use of the example of love and hate to develop the "principle" that love and hate, e.g., "are actualizations of a constant readiness" (p. 250). He postulates "that character is a structure of numerous readinesses . . . which are constantly present and are actualized but not caused by an outside stimulus" (p. 521). In contrast to Freud, Fromm already felt at that time that while some of these "readinesses" are rooted in biological instinct, "many others have arisen as a reaction to individual and social experiences" (p. 521). The distinction between character traits and the character orientations that determine them is not sufficiently evident when Fromm calls character traits "passions." That is the reason the use of the concepts "rational" and "irrational passions" for character traits that correspond to a productive and a nonproductive character orientation, respectively—a use that Fromm borrowed from Spinoza—is not adopted here. Cf. Fromm, *The Anatomy of Human Destructiveness* (1973a), pp. 263–267. That talk about "passions" may cause a reader to forget the relation to characterology that is shown by Hans Peter Balmer's essay "Befreiung von Destruktivität? Erich Fromm in der Debatte um die menschliche Aggression." While this author does mention Fromm's characterology (see p. 494f), he does not appear to have understood its significance. For otherwise he could not have written: "At the center are questions that arise in connection with Fromm's doctrine of affects[!] Is it possible to sustain a division of passions into 'rational' and 'irrational' ones, using object relatedness[!] as a criterion?" (p. 497). In view of such misunderstandings of the sociopsychological approach of Fromm's characterology, it is not surprising that Balmer does not hesitate to argue for a necrophilous view of human life and go along with George Bataille in making a case for a "need for destruction and loss" (p. 500):

"Bataille's dialectic sees in death the 'ultimate meaning of eroticism,' i.e. the anticipation of the ultimate border crossing. . . . Passion, the 'exuberance of eroticism,' is never without violence. . . ." (p. 501).

13. Fromm, *Man for Himself* (1947a), p. 59; cf. also p. 18 and Chapter I, note 37.

14. Cf. Fromm and Maccoby, *Social Character in a Mexican Village* (1970b), p. 11.

15. E. Fromm, *Man for Himself* (1947a), p. 59.

16. Cf. Fromm, *The Anatomy of Human Destructiveness* (1973a), pp. 111, 227, e.g.

17. See pp. 142–145.

18. On what follows, cf. particularly *Man for Himself* (1947a), pp. 59–61; *Social Character in a Mexican Village* (1970b), p. 12f; *The Anatomy of Human Destructiveness* (1973a), pp. 251–253.

19. See pp. 18–22.

20. Precisely because of this insight, it was plausible that Freud should define his character doctrine in terms of instinctual drives.

21. On this, see especially Fromm, "The Psychological Problem of Aging" (1966g).

22. Cf. especially Fromm and Maccoby, *Social Character in a Mexican Village* (1970b), pp. 21–23. Every psychotherapeutic effort depends on this possibility for change. And every reform of the social structure would be ultimately meaningless if it could not have an impact on the character structure of the individuals involved.

23. *Man for Himself* (1947a), p. 61; see p. 47f.

24. While Fromm specifically notes in *Man for Himself* (1947a), p. 61, that the orientations are to be understood as ideal types that are not descriptions of the character of any particular individual, "ideal types" should not be understood here as utopian entities. Fromm's ideal types resemble diagnostic findings in medicine in the sense that they occur in reality when an orientation acquires an unambiguous dominance.

25. On this, cf. *Man for Himself* (1947a), pp. 62–82; *Dialogue with Erich Fromm* (1966f), pp. 2–12; *Social Character in a Mexican Village* (1970b), pp. 69–71; M. McGrath, *An Examination of Erich Fromm's Ethics with Implications for the Philosophy of Adult Education*, pp. 21–32; C. J. Sahlin, *An Analysis of the Writings of Erich Fromm*, pp. 129–140.

26. How Fromm arrived at these orientations is not an easy question to answer. He simply deduced them from all the conceivable possibilities of a nonproductive relation to the world: "I can get things by receiving them passively; I can get things by taking them by force; I can get things by hoarding them; I can get things by marketing" (*Dialogue with Erich Fromm* [1966f], p. 3). The first three orientations are clearly close to Freud's pregenital character types: the receptive orientation corresponds to Freud's oral-receptive character, the exploitative to his oral-sadistic, and the hoarding to his anal character. The marketing orientation has no equivalent in Freud's characterology, while the destructive-necrophilous orientation resembles the anal character. On this, see Fromm, *The Anatomy of Human Destructiveness* (1973a), pp. 348f.

27. *Man for Himself* (1947a), p. 62.

28. Fromm, "Die psychologischen und geistigen Probleme des Überflusses" (1970j).

29. *Dialogue with Erich Fromm* (1966f), p. 4.

30. *Man for Himself* (1947a), p. 64.

31. Ibid., p. 65.

32. *The Sane Society* (1955a), pp. 91f.

33. Cf. especially *The Sane Society* (1955a) where Fromm deals with this fact of

man's estrangement from himself, his work, and his nature in present-day Western industrial civilization. Similar but more developed arguments are in *The Revolution of Hope* (1968a).

34. *Man for Himself* (1947a), p. 77. In *The Lonely Crowd,* David Riesman rightly described man in contemporary Western industrial civilization as "other-directed."

35. Especially in *The Heart of Man* (1964a), pp. 37–61, 108–114; Fromm, "Creators and Destroyers" (1964f), pp. 22–25; Fromm, "Prophets and Priests" (1967b), esp. pp. 77f; *Dialogue with Erich Fromm* (1966f), pp. 11f; *The Anatomy of Human Destructiveness* (1973a), pp. 330–358. Most of Fromm's interpreters have overlooked the fact that this orientation, which he demonstrated in connection with a further systematization of the socialization process, is relevant also to the process of assimilation, even though it differs from the other nonproductive orientations. On the relation of this necrophilous-destructive orientation to Freud's anal character type (in its negative form) and to the theory of the death instinct, see *The Heart of Man* (1964a), pp. 39, 48–55; *Dialogue with Erich Fromm* (1966f), pp. 11f; C. J. Sahlin, *An Analysis of the Writings of Erich Fromm,* pp. 95–97.

36. *The Heart of Man* (1964a), p. 39. Cf. the definition in *The Anatomy of Human Destructiveness* (1973a), p. 332.

37. *The Heart of Man* (1964a), p. 41.

38. Ibid, p. 56; cf. Fromm, "The Case for Unilateral Disarmament" (1960c); Fromm and Maccoby, "A Debate on the Question of Civil Defense" (1962b); *The Anatomy of Human Destructiveness* (1973a), pp. 345–348.

39. *The Heart of Man* (1964a), pp. 57f.

40. Ibid., p. 45.

41. On this, see Fromm, *Man for Himself* (1947a), pp. 82–84; Fromm and Evans, *Dialogue with Erich Fromm* (1966f), pp. 13f; J. H. Schaar, *Escape from Authority,* pp. 102–104.

42. On the following, see *Escape from Freedom* (1941a), pp. 256–263; *Man for Himself* (1947a), pp. 84–88; *Marx's Concept of Man* (1961b), pp. 26–30; *The Heart of Man* (1964a), pp. 30–32; *Marx's Contribution to the Knowledge of Man* (1968h), esp. pp. 68–70; and *Dialogue with Erich Fromm* (1966f), pp. 24f; *Social Character in a Mexican Village* (1970b), pp. 71–73; M. McGrath, *An Examination of Erich Fromm's Ethics,* pp. 51–53; H. Marcuse, *Eros and Civilization,* pp. 236f.

43. *Escape from Freedom* (1941a), p. 258.

44. Cf. Fromm, *Marx's Concept of Man* (1961b), p. 29.

45. Cf. Fromm, "Marx's Contribution to the Knowledge of Man" (1968h) in (1970a), p. 68.

46. Marx, *MEGA* I, 3, 88.

47. On the concept of "alienation," see pp. 72–82.

48. M. Fritzhand, *Marx's Ideal of Man,* pp. 161f.

49. Cf. *Escape from Freedom* (1941a), pp. 256–263.

50. *Man for Himself* (1947a), pp. 85–90.

51. On the question of creativity, cf. Fromm, "The Creative Attitude" (1959c).

52. *Man for Himself* (1947a), p. 87.

53. See p. 49f.

54. *Man for Himself* (1947a), p. 88; *The Heart of Man* (1964a), p. 31.

55. *Man for Himself* (1947a), p. 88.

56. This differentiation between reproducing and generative capacities results in

an important differentiation between "intelligence" and "reason" in Fromm's work. Intelligence "is taking things for granted as they are, making combinations which have the purpose of facilitating their manipulation. . . . Reason, on the other hand, aims at understanding; it tries to find out what is behind the surface, to recognize the kernel, the essence of the reality which surrounds us. . . . Reason requires relatedness and a sense of self" (*The Sane Society* [1955a], p. 170). Cf. *Man for Himself* (1947a), pp. 102f; "Values, Psychology, and Human Existence" (1959b), esp. pp. 159–161; P. A. Bertocci and R. M. Millard, *Personality and the Good,* pp. 84–86.

57. *Man for Himself* (1947a), p. 90. Here Fromm sees himself as within the tradition of German Idealism, of Karl Marx, and of Zen Buddhism, all of which attempt to overcome the subject-object split. "The object is an object, yet it ceases to be an object, and in this new approach, man becomes one with the object, although he and it remain two" (Fromm, *Marx's Concept of Man* [1961b], p. 33, n. 22). "The eye has become a human eye, just as its object has become a social, human object, made by man for man. The senses have therefore become theoreticians in their immediate praxis. They relate to the thing for its own sake, but the thing itself is an objective human relation to itself and to man, and vice-versa" (Karl Marx, *Early Writings,* p. 352). In Zen Buddhism, as in Western mysticism, the same thing is expressed by the concept "experience": "I see the world as it is and experience it as my world, the world created and transformed by my creative grasp of it, so that the world ceases to be a strange world 'over there' and becomes my world" (Fromm, 'Psychoanalysis and Zen Buddhism" [1960a], p. 91). See also G. B. Hammond, *Man in Estrangement,* pp. 69–71.

58. *Man for Himself* (1947a), p. 91.

59. The concept of "individuation" as a positive self-realization, as coined by Jung, is not used by Fromm in that sense. While he does speak of "self-realization" in *Escape from Freedom* (1941a), p. 257, the development of the idea of a syndrome of growth and a syndrome of decay (*The Heart of Man* [1964a]) makes clear that individuation can also be negative. Cf. Fromm and Evans, *Dialogue with Erich Fromm* (1966f), pp. 24f.

60. The most important sources for more precise statements and elaborations of the substance of this matter are "Sozialpsychologischer Teil" (1936a), esp. pp. 110–128; *Escape from Freedom* (1941a), pp. 136–206; *Man for Himself* (1947a), pp. 107–112; *The Heart of Man* (1964a), pp. 37–94; *Dialogue with Erich Fromm* (1966f), pp. 16–24; *Social Character in a Mexican Village* (1970b), pp. 73–76; *The Anatomy of Human Destructiveness* (1973a), esp. pp. 268–299, 330–368.

61. *Escape from Freedom* (1941a), p. 158.

62. In line with Fromm's approach of taking man's relatedness to the world, to others, and to himself as his point of departure, masochism and sadism are not understood exclusively as sexual perversions. The opposite is true: sexual masochism and sadism may be the expressions of masochistic and sadistic relatedness. Fromm therefore also speaks of "moral masochism," e.g., or of the "masochistic character" (*Escape from Freedom* [1941a], p. 148).

63. Fromm, *The Art of Loving* (1956a), p. 16.

64. *Escape from Freedom* (1941a), p. 143. Cf. on what follows, *Escape,* pp. 142ff.

65. It is precisely these self-destructive forms of the masochistic orientation that show the common root and the closeness of masochism and sadism. This closeness consists in the ambivalence of every type of symbiotic relatedness. The hostility

that is found in both masochism and sadism is more conscious in the latter and is put into practice directly, while hostility in masochism is usually unconscious and expresses itself only indirectly. Cf. *Escape from Freedom* (1941a), p. 159.

66. In *Escape from Freedom* (1941a), the nonproductive orientations are therefore understood as escape mechanisms that become activated when human beings are incapable of realizing their "freedom from" as a "freedom to." The escape mechanism of symbiotic relatedness is called "authoritarianism" in that work.

67. Cf. *Escape from Freedom* (1941a), pp. 152f.

68. Ibid., pp. 154f.

69. Ibid., pp. 155f.

70. See also Fromm's studies at the Institute for Social Research: Sozialpsychologischer Teil" (1936a); "Geschichte und Methoden der Erhebungen" (1936b); *Arbeiter und Angestellte am Vorabend des Dritten Reiches. Eine sozialpsychologische Untersuchung* (1980a). A detailed "psychology of Nazism" is also part of *Escape from Freedom* (1941a), pp. 207–239, for which Fromm uses *Arbeiter und Angestellte* as source material. See also Fromm's comment in *Escape*, p. 212. n. 3.

71. "Sozialpsychologischer Teil," (1936a), p. 123.

72. *The Art of Loving* (1956a), p. 17.

73. Cf. ibid., pp. 16f; *Escape from Freedom* (1941a), pp. 158f. Thus Hitler's reaction to human beings was primarily sadistic, whereas his reaction to his fate, to history, and the "higher powers" of nature was masochistic. Cf. Fromm, *The Art of Loving* (1956a), p. 17; and his analysis of Hitler's character in *The Anatomy of Human Destructiveness* (1973a), pp. 369–433.

74. *Escape from Freedom* (1941a), p. 144. Cf. the less systematic presentation in *The Anatomy of Human Destructiveness* (1973a), pp. 288–292.

75. Cf. *Escape from Freedom* (1941a), pp. 144f.

76. *The Anatomy of Human Destructiveness* (1973a), pp. 288f.

77. *Escape from Freedom* (1941a), p. 157.

78. Cf. *Man for Himself* (1947a), p. 111. In a conversation, Fromm proposed this distinction between the oral- and anal-sadistic orientation.

79. The general term "withdrawal" is used by Fromm for this group of nonproductive orientations (*Man for Himself* [1947a], p. 111).

80. *Escape from Freedom* (1947a), pp. 185–186.

81. *Social Character in a Mexican Village* (1970b), p. 74.

82. See esp. *The Art of Loving* (1956a), pp. 14f, where conformist tendencies of earlier periods are also described (pp. 8–10).

83. *The Sane Society* (1955a), pp. 152f.; cf. *Dialogue with Erich Fromm* (1966f), pp. 21f.

84. Cf. Fromm, "Values, Psychology, and Human Existence" (1959b), p. 159: "instead of the pre-individualistic clan identity, a new herd identity develops in which the sense of identity rests on the sense of an unquestionable belonging to the crowd."

85. Cf. *Man for Himself* (1947a), p. 112.

86. On what follows, cf. especially *Escape from Freedom* (1947a), pp. 159, 179f.

87. Cf. Fromm, "Zur Theorie und Strategie des Friedens" (1970h). *The Anatomy of Human Destructiveness* (1973a) presents all three forms of destructive behavior at some length. Fromm distinguishes between two malignant forms of destructive behavior: the destructiveness that is marked by cruelty; and necrophilia, which is another kind of destructiveness. In the interest of greater clarity, the terms "Ne-

crophilous destructiveness" and "Necrophilous-destructive orientation" were used in the text.

88. On the dispute with Konrad Lorenz and other ethologists regarding an aggressive drive or aggressive behavior, see pp. 142–145.

89. On this, compare, e.g., the heated controversy regarding reform of the abortion law that sometimes tells us something about the destructive character structure of the fighters for a "right to life" or a "right to one's own belly," and which can hardly be called rational argumentation.

90. On this, cf. *Escape from Freedom* (1947a), pp. 181f.

91. Ibid., p. 184.

92. On what follows, cf. *The Sane Society* (1955a), pp. 34–36; *The Heart of Man* (1964a); pp. 62–94; *Dialogue with Erich Fromm* (1966f), pp. 68–70; *Social Character in a Mexican Village* (1970b), pp. 74–76; Fromm, "Einige post-marxsche und post-freudsche Gedanken über Religion and Religiosität" (1972b), p. 475; *The Anatomy of Human Destructiveness* (1973a), p. 200–205.

93. In *Escape from Freedom* (1941a), there is a brief reference to the possibility of a narcissistic orientation (p. 185), but in that passage, narcissism is dismissed as an escape mechanism from freedom which is of interest only to individual psychology. The first reflections on narcissism occur in *The Sane Society* (1955a), pp. 34–36; they are explicated subsequently in *The Heart of Man* (1964a).

94. Cf. Freud, *On Narcissism: An Introduction,* Vol. XIV; *Totem and Taboo,* Vol. XIII, in *The Standard Edition of the Complete Psychological Works* (1961).

95. Fromm, "Einige post-marxsche und post-freudsche Gedanken über Religion und Religiosität" (1972b), p. 475.

96. *The Anatomy of Destructiveness* (1973a), p. 201.

97. *The Sane Society* (1955a), p. 36.

98. On this, and on the consequences of criticizing a narcissistically oriented individual, see *The Heart of Man* (1964a), pp. 74–77.

99. Ibid., p. 77.

100. While this narcissism is solipsistic and xenophobic, it need not be identical with what is customarily called "egoism," for in contrast to narcissism, egoism is not normally blind to objective reality. Quite the contrary, it seeks its advantage by a correct assessment of the claims of others. Cf. *The Heart of Man* (1964a), p. 70, n.9. Similar considerations apply when narcissism is rationalized as a biological function of self-preservation. Cf. *Heart of Man,* pp. 72f.

101. Cf. the historical survey in ibid., pp. 78–85.

102. Cf. ibid., pp. 85–87.

103. On what follows, cf. especially *Man for Himself* (1947a), pp. 96–107; *The Sane Society* (1955a), pp. 31–34; *The Art of Loving* (1956a).

104. *Man for Himself* (1947a), pp. 96f.

105. Cf. what was said above on the concept "productivity," p. 000.

106. *The Sane Society* (1955a), p. 32.

107. See p. 36f.

108. *Man for Himself* (1947a), p. 98.

109. Cf. See ibid., p. 98. On the various objects of productive love, cf. Fromm, *The Art of Loving* (1956a): love between parents and child, pp. 32–38; between brothers, pp. 39–41; mother love, pp. 41–44; erotic love, pp. 44–48; love of self, pp. 48–53; love of God, pp. 53–69. These criteria for productive love reveal a fundamental difference from Freud's understanding of love. The libido theory postulates a fixed

quantity of energy that can only be used alternatively: "Accordingly, the alternative for a person is to love others and not to love himself, or to love himself and so be selfish and incapable of loving others" (De la Fuente-Muniz, *Fromm's Approach to the Study of Personality*, p. 11).

110. *Man for Himself* (1947a), p. 98.

111. Cf. *The Art of Loving* (1956a), pp. 27–28.

112. Cf. *Man for Himself* (1947a), p. 101; *The Art of Loving* (1956a), pp. 23–27.

113. *The Art of Loving* (1956a), p. 27. On the distinction between childish and mature love and the development of the capacity for love, cf. *Art of Loving* pp. 32–34.

114. *Man for Himself* (1947a), p. 97. On what follows, ibid., pp. 102–107, and the works listed in note 56.

115. Cf. note 56.

116. *Man for Himself* (1947a), p. 102.

117. Ibid., p. 103.

118. Here Fromm turns against both a subjectivity in which thinking is not controlled by the object, and an objectivity that proposes to exclude all engaged or committed interest. Cf. *Man for Himself* (1947a), p. 105.

119. Ibid.

120. On what follows, cf. especially *Man for Himself* (1947a), pp. 78–82, 112–117; and *Social Character in a Mexican Village* (1970b), pp. 77–80.

121. The modifications of *Man for Himself* (1947a), p. 111, are based on conversations with Fromm and are legitimated, in part, by his reflections in *The Anatomy of Human Destructiveness* (1973a), pp. 348f, 462f.

122. The affinity of orientations in the processes of assimilation and socialization is not to be understood here as a blend but as the obvious precondition for blends or mixtures, corresponding to the two different possibilities of relatedness to the world.

123. *Man for Himself* (1947a), p. 113.

124. Cf. the extensive tables in ibid., pp. 115f.

125. Ibid., p. 117.

126. Cf. especially *The Heart of Man* (1964a), p. 37–114.

127. Ibid., p. 45.

128. Ibid., p. 46.

129. Ibid., pp. 46f.

130. See pp. 33f and 41–43.

131. Cf. *The Heart of Man* (1964a), pp. 37–45.

132. On what follows, cf. ibid., pp. 48–55, and *The Anatomy of Human Destructiveness* (1973a), pp. 439–478, and pp. 23–26 of this text.

133. *The Heart of Man* (1964a), p. 50.

134. Ibid., p. 51. Cf. B. Landis, "Fromm's Theory of Biophilia-Necrophilia."

135. Cf. *The Heart of Man* (1964a), p. 51; *Foreword* (1960e); *Essay* (1970i).

136. *The Heart of Man* (1964a), pp. 52f. On the relation of the necrophilous and biophilous orientation to Freud's anal and genital character, see ibid., pp. 53–55. Concerning the social conditions for a necrophilous character development in our present industrial society, see ibid., pp. 55–61.

137. See p. 26.

138. See pp. 37–45.

139. Cf. pp. 43–45.

140. Cf. *The Heart of Man* (1964a), p. 77.

141. On the following, cf. ibid., pp. 95–108.

142. *Social Character in a Mexican Village* (1970b), p. 77.

143. Cf. *The Heart of Man* (1964a), pp. 107f. In *Social Character in a Mexican Village* (1970b), Fromm writes: "The patriarchal equivalent of fixation to mother, the obedient submission to father, has similar effects, although it seems that the depth and intensity of the fixation to or fear of the mother is greater. In fact, there are many clinical reasons for the assumption that submission to father is an attempt to escape the incestuous regression." Cf. *The Heart of Man* (1964a), p. 103.

144. Cf. ibid., pp. 100–102.

145. On what follows, cf. ibid., pp. 108–114.

146. In contrast to Freud's view that the most abnormal orientation exists where the individual regresses to the earliest phase of libidinal development, Fromm's clinical observations led him to believe that the degree of pathology does not depend on the evolutionary phase of libido development. Human beings can regress to the pathological on every level of development; the degree of pathology depends only on the degree of regression within a given orientation. On this, cf. ibid., pp. 111–113.

147. *Escape from Freedom* (1941a), pp. 183f.

148. *The Heart of Man* (1964a), p. 114. See the last part of this study for an elaboration of the biophilia-necrophilia alternative and of the growth and decay syndromes in the having and being modes.

CHAPTER 3. CONCEPTS OF THE NATURE AND HISTORY OF MAN

1. *Man for Himself* (1947a), p. 45.

2. On what follows, cf. ibid., pp. 20–40; *The Sane Society* (1955a), pp. 12–27; *The Heart of Man* (1964a), pp. 17–23, 115–117; "Introduction" (1968g), pp. 3–24; *The Anatomy of Human Destructiveness* (1973a), pp. 219–230. P. Vranicki, *Geschichte des Marxismus,* Vol. II, pp. 865–876, provides a brief but good overview of Fromm's anthropology.

3. The anthology *The Nature of Man* (1968b), which was edited jointly by Fromm and Ramon Xirau, represents a sort of peak. The book contains an Introduction by Fromm and assembles seventy-two essays on man's nature, ranging from the Upanishads to such authors as Edith Stein, Adam Schaff, and David Riesman.

4. Cf. *The Sane Society* (1955a), p. 13: "What has often been called 'human nature' is but one of its many manifestations—and often a pathological one—and the function of such mistaken definition usually has been to defend a particular type of society as being the necessary outcome of man's mental constitution."

5. Cf. "Introduction" (1968g), pp. 3f; *The Anatomy of Human Destructiveness* (1973a), pp. 219f.

6. *The Sane Society* (1955a), p. 13.

7. Cf. "Introduction" (1968g), pp. 5f.

8. Ibid., p. 6. On Fromm's total view of man and the concept "totality," cf. R. Funk, "Zu Erich Fromm—Leben und Werk."

9. "Introduction" (1968g), p. 7. Fromm specifically notes (note 2) that progress does not mean a having more but a constant growth of the consciousness of ourselves.

10. *Marx's Concept of Man* (1961b), p. 25. On Fromm's interpretation of such concepts as "being," and "nature of man in general," but also "true" in contrast to

"real human being," as Marx used them, see *Marx's Contribution to the Knowledge of Man* (1968h), pp. 62–76; *Beyond the Chains of Illusion* (1962a), pp. 27–32; "The Application of Humanist Psychoanalysis to Marx's Theory" (1965c), pp. 219–221; A. Schaff, *Marxismus und das menschliche Individuum,* pp. 111–120.

11. Marx, *Early Writings,* p. 328; cf. Fromm, *Marx's Contribution to the Knowledge of Man* (1968h), p. 64.

12. Cf. *The Heart of Man* (1964a), p. 116.

13. Cf. ibid.; also "The Application of Humanist Psychoanalysis to Marx's Theory" (1965c), p. 220.

14. *The Anatomy of Human Destructiveness* (1973a), p. 223.

15. Cf. ibid., p. 224.

16. This refers to a capacity for thought that is common to both man and animal, namely, "the use of thought as an instrument for the manipulation of objects in order to satisfy one's needs" (ibid., p. 224). Cf. also concepts such as "instrumental reason" and "technical reason" that are current today.

17. *The Anatomy of Human Destructiveness* (1973a), p. 225.

18. *Man for Himself* (1947a), p. 39.

19. "Introduction" (1968g), p. 8.

20. "The Application of Humanist Psychoanalysis to Marx's Theory" (1965c), p. 220.

21. *The Anatomy of Human Destructiveness* (1973a), p. 225. J. J. Forsyth and J. M. Beniskos, "Biblical Faith and Erich Fromm's Theory of Personality," therefore interpret incorrectly when they write: "Man's true nature . . . is . . . the dichotomy between body and soul, between his animal and his spiritual nature."

22. "Introduction (1968g), p. 9.

23. Ibid. The question-and-answer game of human life should not be seen as a unique event but as a continuing process. For the moment an inner imbalance is resolved, new contradictions emerge and require that a new balance be searched for. This is the reason why it is unnecessary to postulate an innate drive for progress. Actually, this striving is a result of the fact that man is a contradictory being who must always renew his attempt to find a new, and possibly better, balance. Cf. *The Anatomy of Destructiveness* (1973a), p. 226.

24. "Introduction" (1968g), p. 9.

25. In this book, the attempt is made to distinguish between consciousness of self, endowment of reason, and imagination on the one side, and reason and love on the other, by referring to the former as "specifically human qualities" and to the latter as "human capacities" or "human powers." On the origin of the definition of the capacity for reason and love as human characteristics, see pp. 183–188 and Chap. 6, note 22, passages in which the doctrine of God's negative attributes and characteristics in the Jewish tradition is discussed.

26. It is important to remember this although Fromm sometimes uses the concept "nature" or "being" when he means "characteristics" or when—and this is especially true of his early writings—he wants to have the concept "nature of man" include the productive answer to man's contradictions. On this, cf. pp. 134–136.

27. On what follows, cf. *Man for Himself* (1947a), pp. 38–45; *The Sane Society* (1955a), pp. 22–27; "Values, Psychology, and Human Existence (1959b), pp. 152f; *The Heart of Man* (1964a), pp. 115–121; "Introduction" (1968g), pp. 8f; *The Anatomy of Human Destructiveness* (1973a), pp. 225f.

28. *Man for Himself* (1947a), p. 40.

29. The designation "existential" was chosen by Fromm without conscious refer-

ence to a philosophical school such as the philosophy of existence or existentialist philosophy. Cf. *Man for Himself* (1947a), p. 41, n.1.

30. Ibid., p. 41. In *The Sane Society* (1955a), he writes: "The necessity to find ever new solutions for the contradictions in his existence, to find ever-higher forms of unity with nature, his fellowmen and himself, is the source of all psychic forces which motivate man, of all his passions, affects and anxieties."

31. The argument as it is advanced here and elsewhere is correct as long as the presupposition is accepted and it is not disputed philosophically that man is in fact his own master. Only doubt about the ultimate validity of this assumption—be it nihilistic or the expression of the faith of a redemptive religion—will affect the understanding of dichotomy and, in the case of a nihilistic position, the forms of reaction to the dichotomies.

32. *The Heart of Man* (1964a), p. 117.

33. *Man for Himself* (1947a), p. 45. This identification of the development of specific human qualities as the answer to the dichotomies, and the substantive definition of productive living, is discussed further on pp. 134–136.

34. Cf. ibid., p. 43.

35. Although the distinction between existential and historical dichotomies appears perfectly plausible at first, there is a problem where man's historicalness is being taken seriously as belonging to his existence in the sense that historical dichotomies are invariably part and parcel of man's existence and therefore themselves existential dichotomies—that is, an intrinsic part of that existence. On this, see Fromm's account of the concept of alienation on pp. 72–82, esp. 79–82.

36. On what follows, cf. *Man for Himself* (1947a), pp. 45–50; *The Sane Society* (1955a), pp. 25–66; "Values, Psychology, and Human Existence" (1959b), pp. 152–162; *The Heart of Man* (1964a), pp. 118f; "Introduction" (1968g), pp. 9, 17–24; *The Anatomy of Human Destructiveness* (1973a), pp. 230–242; See also Schaar, *Escape from Authority*, pp. 42–54; McGrath, *An Examination of Erich Fromm's Ethics*, pp. 14–19; C. J. Sahlin, *An Analysis of the Writings of Erich Fromm*, pp. 154–180; J. J. Forsyth and J. M. Beniskos, "Biblical Faith and Erich Fromm's Theory of Personality," pp. 69–91.

37. *The Anatomy of Human Destructiveness* (1973a), p. 226.

38. Cf. ibid., p. 226. On the definition of the function of character and of character traits and character orientations as productive (rational) and nonproductive (irrational), see pp. 29–31 and 34–36.

39. Cf. *The Sane Society* (1955a), p. 25. C. J. Sahlin, *An Analysis of the Writings of Erich Fromm*, p. 71. Fromm's anthropological approach, so fundamentally different from Freud's, expresses itself here once again. While Freud's point of departure is a concept of sexuality that emphasizes instinct, and a sexuality that "needs" others as love objects, sexuality in Fromm functions as a means, as, e.g., for man's specific need for interpersonal relatedness in the form of productive love.

40. On this, cf. *Marx's Contribution to the Knowledge of Man* (1968h), pp. 70–72.

41. Fromm himself sees no change here but merely "an expansion of the discussion on the same subject." Cf. *The Anatomy of Human Destructiveness* (1973a), p. 230, n. 8.

42. *The Sane Society* (1955a), pp. 25–66.

43. *The Anatomy of Human Destructiveness* (1973a), pp. 230–242.

44. It is not just Fromm's lack of interest in systematization that should be blamed for his lack of precision in the definition and number of human needs. The various needs are interpretations of man's fundamental conflict and are nuanced

differently, depending on the perspective from which they are interpreted. (In this regard, the needs can be compared to the fundamental conditions postulated in existential philosophy, although Fromm does not derive the needs from reflection by way of a phenomenological analysis of existence.) Fromm does not reflect "being with" and "being there" (Dasein) as a being toward death, like Heidegger, to then arrive at needs. His thought is based on the experiences of his psychoanalytic practice—i.e., faulty reactions to the problem of human existence. This experiential approach allows the formulation of fundamental conflicts and problems (isolation, impotence, being different, separateness, etc.), which are not themselves negative answers to other problems and conflicts underlying them but fundamental problems (in the sense of fundamental givens) to which man must react and which can be called needs for that reason. The demonstration of these fundamental problems (dichotomies) and needs through reflection on man's phylogenetic birth and the break with nature entailed in that process is actually merely a way of verifying the discoveries that resulted from reflection on psychotherapeutic experiences.

45. *The Sane Society* (1955a), p. 30.

46. Ibid., p. 36.

47. *Dialogue with Erich Fromm* (1966f), p. 19.

48. *The Anatomy of Human Destructiveness* (1973a), p. 231, n. 9. Cf. the explication of this concept in "Introduction" (1968g), pp. 18f.

49. In Fromm's thought, the striving for independence and freedom almost have the place value of a human need and are the very essence of his understanding of humanism, for "Man can be free inasmuch as he is aware, inasmuch as he can become awake to reality" ("Introduction" [1968g], p. 15). For that reason, the need for rootedness initially means the renunciation of natural symbiotic ties and entails criticism and striving for independence.

50. *The Anatomy of Human Destructiveness* (1973a), pp. 232f.

51. *The Sane Society* (1955a), pp. 60–61.

52. *The Anatomy of Human Destructiveness* (1973a), p. 234.

53. Cf. *Man for Himself* (1947a), pp. 47–50.

54. *The Anatomy of Human Destructiveness* (1973a), p. 231.

55. Ibid., p. 232.

56. Ibid., p. 235.

57. Ibid., p. 236f.

58. See pp. 34–37.

59. Fromm, *You Shall Be as Gods* (1966a), pp. 88f.

60. On the following, cf. Fromm, "Der Sabbath" (1927a), esp. pp. 228f; *Psychoanalysis and Religion* (1950a), pp. 42–44; *The Sane Society* (1955a), pp. 234–236; "Psychoanalysis and Zen Buddhism" (1960a); "The Prophetic Concept of Peace" (1960d), pp. 19–25; "Afterword" (1961c), pp. 257f; *You Shall Be as Gods* (1966a), pp. 87–157.

61. *The Sane Society* (1955a), p. 234.

62. The following comments are limited to the presentation of the history of the messianic idea as Fromm sees it. For a critical discussion of the conceptual model behind such a view of history, see pp. 106–112.

63. *The Sane Society* (1955a), p. 235.

64. "The Prophetic Concept of Peace" (1960d), p. 22.

65. Ibid., p. 19.

66. Ibid., p. 21.

67. Cf. *You Shall Be as Gods* (1966a), p. 89.

68. In his text, Fromm uses the word *"Leitmotiv."* Cf. ibid., p. 89.

69. Ibid., pp. 91–108. Fromm attempts to interpret the texts about the exodus and the revelation to Moses in such a way that they show man to be the sole originator and shaper of history: "Man is left to himself and makes his own history" (ibid., p. 92).

70. Cf. ibid., pp. 108–114.

71. Ibid., p. 114. In his humanistic approach, failure is seen positively. God does not change men by changing their hearts. Instead, God wants man to assume all responsibility for his history and become its maker. Cf. ibid., pp. 115–121.

72. *You Shall Be as Gods* (1966a), p. 115.

73. Ibid., p. 117. Cf. Fromm, "Die Aktualität der prophetischen Schriften" (1975d): "The prophet is concerned "about the goal of . . . a complete knowledge of God or, in non-theological language, the goal that man fully develop his psychic powers, his life and his reason, that he have his center within himself and be free to become what, as human being, he is capable of becoming."

74. *You Shall Be as Gods* (1966a), pp. 117f.

75. A comparison with the characterization of the prophets in L. Baeck, *Das Wesen des Judentums*, pp. 26–30, and in M. Friedländer, *Die jüdische Religion*, pp. 41–43, shows that Fromm's view of the prophets is not representative of Jewish orthodoxy but is a humanistic interpretation of the rationalist understanding of the prophets to be found in Moses Maimonides. But see the comments on p. 000.

76. *You Shall Be as Gods* (1966a), p. 123.

77. Cf. Fromm, "Afterword" (1961c), p. 257.

78. Fromm, *You Shall Be as Gods* (1966a), pp. 123f. It is obvious that in characterizing these conditions that he sees as standing in a "dialectical relationship" with each other, Fromm is transferring the image of the birth of the individual to the history of mankind: what applies to the child as it leaves the state of unconscious harmony and enters into a new and autonomous relatedness to the world as his reason and capacity for love develop applies to human history generally. In analogy to the humanistic conscience, we have the prophets, who represent the conscience of mankind. In *Beyond the Chains of Illusion* (1962a), p. 35, Fromm sees this parallel realized in Karl Marx's understanding of history, and compares child and adult to the history of mankind.

79. *You Shall Be as Gods* (1966a), p. 124.

80. Ibid., p. 133. Since Fromm does not explicitly reflect on the fact that messianic time as he understands it is seen in terms of the process of individuation (cf. note 78), this development of messianic time can only strike him as a decadent form of the original, prophetic messianism. When the history of individual man and of mankind become parallel developments, the further elaboration of the messianic idea into a metahistorical messiah takes account only of the matter of man's meaning. Since there is illness, sin, and death, the individual realization of the powers of reason and love can no longer provide the experiential substrate for the hope that the perfection of man through man will occur in history. The messianic idea therefore necessarily transcends the self-redemption of man and of his history. Fromm's term, "apocalyptic orientation," by which he refers to this breakthrough to the "vertical" (*You Shall Be as Gods* [1966a], p. 133), does not correspond to the normal use of the term "apocalypticism." Gershom Scholem, for example, turns rather vigorously against the kind of interpretation Fromm subscribes to: "The bible and the apocalyptists know nothing of any progress toward redemption within history. Redemption is not the result of inner-worldly developments, as for

example in the modern, western re-interpretation of messianism since the Enlightenment. . . . Rather, it is an irruption of transcendence into history . . ." (Scholem, *Über einige Begriffe des Judentums,* p. 133). This criticism does not only refer to the apocalyptic version of the messianic idea: ". . . precisely in those texts that helped crystallize the messianic idea, it is nowhere made dependent on human activity. Neither the Day of the Lord in Amos nor Isaiah's vision of the future are causally related to such activity" (ibid., p. 138). That Gershom Scholem's criticism is not representative of all interpretors of Jewish messianism is shown by the work of Jews such as Hermann Cohen, who emphasizes the Noachian as Messianic (*Religion of Reason Out of the Sources of Judaism*), and Leo Baeck, who speaks of the "moral concept of world history": "The true world history is the history of the good; it will have realized itself when the good has been recognized by all" (*Das Wesen des Judentums,* pp. 260f). Fromm's distinction derives from Joseph Klausner's differentiation between the messianic idea and Jewish eschatology, as Klausner puts it. While both have the same origin, he writes, eschatology differs from messianism in expecting "a kingdom that is not of this world" (J. Klausner, *The Messianic Idea in Israel,* pp. 418f; cf. pp. 237–243, 516–523; and Klausner, *Die messianischen Vorstellungen des jüdischen Volkes im Zeitalter der Tannaiten*).

81. Cf. *You Shall Be as Gods* (1966a), pp. 134f.

82. Cf. ibid., p. 137.

83. Ibid., pp. 139f. In Fromm's thought, we find both versions in a more evolutionary and dialectical view of the development of man and his history. See pp. 100–101 and pp. 239–243.

84. Cf. *You Shall Be as Gods* (1966a), pp. 143–147. On the history of the calculation of time in Jewish messianism, see A. H. Silver, *A History of Messianic Speculation in Israel: From the First Through the Seventeenth Centuries.*

85. Thus "the Hasidic conception of the Torah is an elaboration of the traditional belief that God wants to win through man the world created by Him. He wants to make it truly His world, His kingdom, but through human deed" (Martin Buber, *The Origin and Meaning of Hasidism,* p. 50). For an extensive presentation of Hasidism, see pp. 195–205.

86. Cf. *Marx's Concept of Man* (1961b), pp. 63–69.

87. This humanistic approach is described by Fromm as follows: "Marx's socialism is the realization of the deepest religious impulses common to the great humanistic religions of the past . . . provided we understand that Marx, like Hegel and like many others, expresses his concern for man's soul, not in theistic, but in philosophical language" (ibid., p. 63). That this is not just a question of language is shown on pp. 205–218, esp. pp. 214–215.

88. Ibid., p. 68.

89. The verification of messianism in Hermann Cohen's Neo-Kantianism will not be discussed here. But see pp. 188–195. While it is true that the political element of the prophetic marks the reactivation of a prophetic-political messianism in the "Reform Judaism" of the nineteenth and twentieth centuries, and especially in "Zionism," it lacks the universalist component of Jewish messianism. For this reason, Fromm was no friend of Zionism. On this matter, see L. Jacobs, *Principles of the Jewish Faith,* pp. 369–389; H. Graupe, *Die Entstehung des modernen Judentums,* pp. 343–353. On the development of "Reform Judaism" in the United States, cf. especially D. Philipson, "Reform Judaism" in *Universal Jewish Encyclopedia,* Vol. VI, pp. 240f; and the "Pittsburgh Platform" of 1855, in which the Reformed Jews decided, among other things: "We consider ourselves no longer a nation but a

religious community and therefore expect neither a return to Palestine nor a sacrificial worship under the sons of Aaron, nor the restoration of any of the laws concerning the Jewish state."

90. For a critique of Fromm's Marx reception, see pp. 205–218. The distinctive quality of Fromm's view of history is primarily the effort to show that the historical-philosophical positions are legitimate interpretations of the theology of history of the Old Testament, especially of messianism.

91. *Marx's Concept of Man* (1961b), p. 13. The quotation in the quotation cannot be found in Marx, *MEGA* I, 6, 179, as indicated, however.

92. K. Marx, *MEGA* I, 5, 10.

93. Marx's *Concept of Man* (1961b), p. 15; cf. esp. *Beyond the Chains of Illusion* (1962a), pp. 34f.

94. Although not in direct connection with Marx's theory of labor, Fromm referred to the meaning of work in the Jewish Sabbath ritual—a meaning that may well have influenced Marx. If Marx initially spoke of "the 'abolition of labor' as the aim of socialism" (*Marx's Concept of Man* [1961b], p. 40), and did not as yet distinguish between free and alienated labor, he saw labor as it is understood in the Sabbath ritual: if the Sabbath is the anticipation of messianic time, it makes sense to ban every type of work. The Sabbath is "a symbol of redemption and freedom" (Fromm, *The Forgotten Language* [1951a], p. 248). "Work is a symbol of struggle and discord; rest a symbol of dignity, peace and freedom" (ibid., p. 247; cf. Fromm, "The Sabbath" [1927a], esp. pp. 233f; *You Shall Be as Gods* [1966a], pp. 194–199).

95. Marx, *Capital,* Vol. I, p. 192.

96. *Marx's Concept of Man* (1961b), p. 42.

97. On the alienation of man by the alienation of work, see pp. 72—82.

98. *Marx's Concept of Man* (1961b), p. 198. (and cf. Marx, *German Ideology*): "Life is not determined by consciousness, but consciousness by life. In the first method of approach, the starting-point is consciousness taken as the living individual; in the second it is the real living individuals themselves, as they are in actual life, and consciousness is considered solely as their consciousness." According to Fromm, Marx does not assert in this sentence that ideas and ideals are not real and effective: "Even as far as the influence of ideas on human evolution is concerned, Marx was by no means as oblivious to their power as the popular interpretation of his work makes it appear" (*Marx's Concept of Man* [1961b], p. 22).

99. *Marx's Concept of Man* (1961b), p. 22.

100. Ibid., p. 19.

101. *Beyond the Chains of Illusion* (1962a), p. 35.

102. Ibid., pp. 36f.

103. Independence and freedom are central concepts in Fromm's critique of religion. Cf. pp. 93–95.

104. *Marx's Concept of Man* (1961b), p. 38.

105. This critique of an identification is not only aimed at what are currently socialist states. What is involved here is the goal of history, which is not to be seen in a social system but only in free—i.e., wholly productive—man.

106. *Marx's Concept of Man* (1961b), p. 61.

107. Ibid., p. 60.

108. *Capital,* Vol. III, p. 828.

109. *Marx's Concept of Man* (1961b), pp. 64f, 68f.

110. Marx, *MEGA* I, 3, p. 125.

111. Cf. *Marx's Concept of Man* (1961b), p. 19.

112. On what follows, cf. Fromm, *Psychoanalysis and Religion* (1950a), pp. 117–119; *The Sane Society* (1955a), pp. 120–124; *Marx's Concept of Man* (1961b), pp. 44–46; *Beyond the Chains of Illusion* (1962a), pp. 57–59; *You Shall Be as Gods* (1966a), pp. 42–51; *Dialogue with Erich Fromm* (1966f), pp. 87–90.

113. *Marx's Concept of Man* (1961b), p. 47.

114. *Beyond the Chains of Illusion* (1962a), p. 44.

115. *Marx's Concept of Man* (1961b), p. 47.

116. G. B. Hammond, *Man in Estrangement*, p. 8; cf. *Beyond the Chains of Illusion* (1962a), p. 44.

117. See pp. 70–72.

118. *Beyond the Chains of Illusion* (1962a), p. 44. On the problem of this definition, especially in the context of the theory of history, see p. 79–82.

119. Marx, *Early Writings*, p. 324; cf. Marx, *Grundrisse*, pp. 23–26, 168–170; F. Tomberg, *Der Begriff der Entfremdung in den 'Grundrissen' von Karl Marx;* R. Wiegand, *Gesellschaft und Charakter*, pp. 11–27.

120. Marx, *Early Writings*, pp. 229–230.

121. Cf. *Marx's Concept of Man* (1961b), p. 50.

122. Cf. *Beyond the Chains of Illusion* (1962a), p. 46.

123. *Dialogue with Erich Fromm* (1966f), pp. 88f. On the problematics of this identification of the concept of alienation, cf., e.g., J. H. Schaar, *Escape from Authority*, pp. 192–197; J. S. Glen, *Erich Fromm: A Protestant Critique*, pp. 126–137; G. B. Hammond, *Man in Estrangement*, pp. 33–35, 65–69; P. Tillich, *Der Mensch im Marxismus und Christentum*, pp. 194–209; R. Schacht, *Alienation*.

124. *Psychoanalysis and Religion* (1950a), p. 118.

125. *Marx's Concept of Man* (1961b), p. 44; cf. *The Sane Society* (1955a), pp. 121f.

126. *You Shall Be as Gods* (1966a), pp. 47f. Fromm actually calls for an "ideology" whose task it would be not only to ferret out earlier and present idols but also to unmask the idolatrous attitude of submissiveness (for which he reproaches Calvinism, e.g.). This view is so radical that it ultimately leads to a substitution of an "ideology" for theology as the attempt to make statements about God (ibid., pp. 47–49). Cf. the discussion below pp. 183–188.

127. *The Sane Society* (1955a), p. 124; cf. *Marx's Contribution to the Knowledge of Man*, (1968h), pp. 68f.

128. *The Sane Society* (1955a), p. 124. That is the reason a number of languages used to employ the term "alienation" in their medical nomenclature to refer to psychotic phenomena. Even today, an "alienist" is a physician who treats diseases of the mind. Cf. ibid., p. 121.

129. Ibid., p. 124.

130. *Beyond the Chains of Illusion* (1962a), p. 59; on this matter, see especially Fromm's central work on this problem, *The Sane Society* (1955a).

131. Cf. *Marx's Concept of Man* (1961b), pp. 56f.

132. E. Fromm, *May Man Prevail?* (1961a), p. 79. Cf. *Escape from Freedom* (1941a), pp. 118–135, and the comments on the "marketing orientation" on p. 000 above.

133. *May Man Prevail?* (1961a), pp. 68–85; A. Schaff, *Marxismus und das menschliche Individuum*, pp. 168–182, 254–259.

134. This is a question raised by A. Gewirth, *Review*, pp. 291f.

135. *Beyond the Chains of Illusion* (1962a), p. 59. On the problem of raising the consciousness of the dependent masses, cf. F. Tomberg, *Der Begriff der Entfremdung in den "Grundrissen" von Karl Marx*.

136. *The Sane Society* (1955a), pp. 262f. The critique of Marx does not aim at taking reality and real man as the point of departure for its method, but it does

object to a foreshortened view of man and his intellectual and spiritual needs and qualities. Cf. *Marx's Concept of Man* (1961b), pp. 21f, on this problem.

137. Cf. *The Sane Society* (1955a), p. 265; F. Tomberg, *Der Begriff der Entfremdung in den "Grundrissen" von Karl Marx*, p. 156.

138. Cf. *The Sane Society* (1955a), pp. 264ff; G. B. Hammond, *Man in Estrangement*, pp. 33–35.

139. *Dialogue with Erich Fromm* (1966f), pp. 89f.

140. G. B. Hammond, *Man in Estrangement*, p. 35, interprets Fromm's position in this way: "Fromm returns to the non-Marxian view that alienation is primarily a form of awareness or unawareness." But see below, pp. 81–82.

141. *Dialogue with Erich Fromm* (1966f), p. 90.

142. *The Sane Society* (1955a): "The analysis of society and of the historical process must begin with man, not with an abstraction, but with the real, concrete man, in his physiological and psychological qualities. It must begin with a concept of the essence of man, and the study of economics and of society serves only the purpose of understanding how circumstances have crippled man, how he has become alienated from himself and his powers."

143. Ibid., pp. 22–66, 270–352.

144. Ibid., p. 275.

145. Ibid.

146. Ibid., p. 276.

147. See ibid., pp. 306–321, for an extensive presentation.

148. The question remains whether the monastic traditions such as the Benedictine did not realize the same sort of thing at an earlier period, so one can hardly talk about a fundamentally new kind of life with others.

149. *The Sane Society* (1955a), p. 321.

150. A. Gewirth, *Review*, p. 292; A. Briggs, *Review*, p. 739; M. Birnbach, *Neo-Freudian Social Philosophy*, pp. 197–203, all raise doubts concerning the exemplariness of the work communities for a new economic and social order.

151. G. B. Hammond, *Man in Estrangement*, p. 65.

152. Fromm, "Psychoanalysis and Zen Buddhism" (1960a), p. 65.

153. This is not the place to determine whether such a vision of the future is "realistic." As for Fromm, it can be said that the analysis of the history of the struggle against idolatry in Judaeo-Christian culture, e.g., suggests the possibility of such a development of man, although it is also true that he judges the present situation as almost hopelessly alienated. What we can do here is to show the stringency of the argument: under the conditions stipulated, does man in fact have the power to redeem himself?

154. In his later work, Fromm took account of the differences in meaning of the concept of alienation by developing the concepts syndrome of growth and syndrome of decay.

155. See pp. 58–60.

156. From this perspective, the two meanings of Fromm's concept of alienation, necessity and pathological phenomenon, become clearer. Negative alienation as (pathological) regression is an expression of the necessary positive alienation of man, who is determined by existential dichotomies. However, it is also a negative answer to this situation insofar as the possibility of a positive reaction that is implicit in the alienated situation is being neglected. But because nonproductive reactions are possible as an expression of the necessary situation of alienation, historical dichotomies come into play. These can be overcome to the extent that productive forces gain the upper hand in reactions to the existential dichotomies.

PART TWO: The Humanism of Erich Fromm and its Critique

1. Fromm, "Humanism and Psychoanalysis" (1963f), p. 69; cf. "Introduction" (1965b), p. vii.
2. Fromm, "Afterword" (1966d), p. 262.
3. Cf. "Humanism and Psychoanalysis" (1963f), p. 70; *Beyond the Chains of Illusion* (1962a), pp. 17, 27–29.
4. "Humanism and Psychoanalysis" (1963f), pp. 70–72.
5. Cf. Fromm, "Der Traum ist die Sprache des universalen Menschen" (1972a), pp. 8–14.
6. Psychoanalysis has significance for humanism primarily because, once the anthropological inadequacies of Freud have been removed, it constitutes the basis for such a "belief." Cf. Fromm, "Humanism and Psychoanalysis" (1963f), pp. 74–78; Fromm, "The Application of Humanist Psychoanalysis to Marx's Theory" (1965c), pp. 207–222.
7. "Humanism and Psychoanalysis," (1963f), p. 77.
8. Ibid., p. 72.
9. Cf. *Beyond the Chains of Illusion* (1962a), p. 27; *The Sane Society* (1955a), pp. 12–14.
10. Cf. "Humanism and Psychoanalysis," (1963f), pp. 72–74.
11. *You Shall Be as Gods* (1966a), p. 13.
12. *Beyond the Chains of Illusion* (1962a), p. 142.
13. "Introduction" (1970k), p. 8. Cf. *The Heart of Man* (1964a), p. 15. Humanism is "the paradoxical blend of relentless criticism, uncompromising realism, and rational faith."
14. "Introduction" (1970k), p. 8. Cf. Fromm, *The Forgotten Language* (1951a), pp. 74f.
15. Cf., e.g., *Beyond the Chains of Illusion* (1962a), p. 142; "Introduction" (1965b), pp. viif; "The Application of Humanist Psychoanalysis to Marx's Theory" (1965c), pp. 207–209; "Afterword" (1966d); M. Markovic, "The Possibilities of Radical Humanism," pp. 280–283; A. Schaff, *Marxismus und das menschliche Individuum* pp. 220–222, 322, 324. Also, see below, pp. 205–218.

CHAPTER 4. HUMANIST RELIGION

1. *Psychoanalysis and Religion*, (1950a), p. 34.
2. *Die Entwicklung des Christusdogmas. Eine psychoanalytische Studie zur sozialpsychologischen Funktion der Religion* (1930a).
3. "Sozialpsychologischer Teil" (1936a), exp. pp. 79f.
4. Ibid., p. 79.
5. Cf. *Escape from Freedom* (1941a), pp. 166f.
6. Ibid., p. 167.
7. Cf. ibid., p. 168.
8. On conformism, the mechanisms of anonymous authority, and on anonymous authority generally, cf. *Escape From Freedom* (1941a), pp. 185–206; *The Sane Society* (1955a), pp. 152–163; "Foreword," (1960e), p. 12f.
9. In *The Sane Society* (1955a), p. 152, Fromm defines irrational authority as overt authority. It is clear from the context that not only every external but also internal authority (such as that of conscience) belongs in the category of overt authority. But

as one examines the use of the word "irrational" in Fromm's entire *oeuvre*, it becomes clear that the definition of irrational authority as overt authority must not be taken too narrowly.

10. Cf. the following: *Escape from Freedom* (1941a), pp. 164–166; "Faith as a Character Trait" (1942c); *Man for Himself* (1947a), pp. 9–14; *The Sane Society* (1955a), pp. 95–98; *To Have or to Be?* (1976a), pp. 36–39; C. Thompson, *Psychoanalysis: Its Evolution and Development*, p. 114.

11. Cf. *Escape from Freedom* (1941a), p. 164; *The Sane Society* (1955a), p. 95.

12. *Man for Himself* (1947a), p. 9.

13. Cf. *Escape from Freedom* (1941a), pp. 165f; *The Sane Society* (1955a), pp. 95f.

14. Cf., e.g., Fromm's use of "irrational" in *The Anatomy of Human Destructiveness* (1973a), pp. 230f. On the problem of the identification of the irrational, with the unconscious and the rational with consciousness and their attributions by Freud, as opposed to Jung and Adler, cf. Fromm, "Freud's Model of Man and Its Social Determinants" (1970d), pp. 35–37.

15. *Man for Himself* (1947a), pp. 201, 204, cf. also *The Art of Loving* (1956a), pp. 102f; "Faith as a Character Trait" (1942b), p. 313: "Irrational faith . . . is based on one's emotional submission to irrational authority. . . . Rational faith . . . on productive intellectual and emotional activity."

16. *The Anatomy of Human Destructiveness* (1973a), p. 263.

17. *To Have or to Be?* (1976a), pp. 90, 92–97, where Fromm gives an overview of the history of the "activity : passivity" antithesis.

18. See p. 88f.

19. The concept "rational authority" thus implies that its goal is its dissolution (cf. *Escape from Freedom* [1941a], p. 165). But it is probably an adequate interpretation of Fromm when one says that the self-dissolution of rational authority is, in the majority of cases, an intent rather than an actual goal, and that this depends on the degree of competence subordinates can attain. This postulate of the self-dissolution of authority is the hub of Schaar's comprehensive critique, which accuses Fromm of misunderstanding both the nature of freedom and authority, and the functions they have in the lives of individuals and communities. See Schaar, *Escape from Authority*, p. 284.

20. On what follows, cf. *Psychoanalysis and Religion*, (1950a), pp. 53f; Fromm, *The Revolution of Hope* (1968a), pp. 62–67.

21. See pp. 60–62.

22. Cf. *Psychoanalysis and Religion* (1950a), p. 53.

23. The various concepts being used here are intended to make clear that alienation, ideology, idolatry, and irrationality all refer to the same process: man renounces his powers of reason and love, his capacity to think and devise theories, his dignity and freedom, his independence and productivity, and makes himself the slave of irrational forces.

24. Schaar, *Escape from Authority*, p. 288. When Schaar observes that men long to be governed, he means to criticize Fromm's concept of authority. He does not consider the possibility, however, that such a desire is already the result of an irrational relation of dependency.

25. Cf. the comments on the "revolutionary character," below, pp. 93–97.

26. Cf. Fromm, "The Revolutionary Character" (1963b) in (1963a), pp. 103–105.

27. Cf. "Sozialpsychologischer Teil" (1936a); *Arbeiter und Angestellte am Vorabend des Dritten Reiches* (1980a).

28. See pp. 37–40. A distinction must be made between this type of authoritar-

ian character and another attitude that is especially characteristic of rural or peasant societies and which acknowledges traditional authorities. Such "traditionally authoritarian" individuals do not depend sado-masochistically or symbiotically on the power of an irrational authority. Cf. E. Fromm and M. Maccoby, *Social Character in a Mexican Village* (1970b), pp. 81f.

29. "The Revolutionary Character" (1963b), p. 104. Cf. *Social Character in a Mexican Village* (1970b), p. 80. For a detailed analysis of the authoritarian character, cf. "Sozialpsychologischer Teil" (1936a); *Escape from Freedom* (1941a), pp. 141–179.

30. *Escape from Freedom* (1941a), p. 168.

31. The experience of one's impotence need not be conscious: "Bourgeois man, in contrast to certain types of religious individual is usually not conscious of the feeling of impotence" (Fromm, "Zum Gefühl der Ohnmacht" [1937a], p. 96). The comments on the feeling of impotence were later modified by Fromm: certain characteristics are not to be attributed to the authoritarian character that is marked by symbiosis, but to narcissism.

32. *Escape from Freedom* (1941a), p. 172.

33. Ibid, p. 171.

34. Ibid., p. 162.

35. Cf. "Sozialpsychologischer Teil" (1936a), pp. 115–117; and more recent corrections in *Social Character in a Mexican Village* (1970b), esp. pp. 80f.

36. That is the reason all political and socially relevant power systems attempt to establish and stabilize a state religion, party ideology, etc., and that all significant ideological and religious revolutions also result in changes in the power structure.

37. On the problem of obedience: disobedience, cf. "Sozialpsychologischer Teil" (1936a), pp. 115–117; *Escape from Freedom* (1941a), pp. 168–170; "The Revolutionary Character" (1963b); pp. 113–116; "Disobedience as a Psychological and Moral Problem" (1963d); "Prophets and Priests" (1967b), pp. 70–72; *You Shall Be as Gods* (1966a), pp. 72–74; *To Have or to Be?* (1976a), esp. pp. 120–125.

38. "Sozialpsychologischer Teil" (1936a), pp. 115f. Schaar's criticism, according to which the greatest mistake Fromm makes is that he is blind to the fact that where authority is absent, fashion rules, is based very precisely on this circular thinking of the authoritarian character who must always think in categories of submission and command to be able to live (*Escape from Authority*, p. 295).

39. Fromm draws a rigorous distinction between rebel and revolutionary because there is a difference in the dominance in the character structure: "The authoritarian character is never a 'revolutionary'; I should like to call him a 'rebel.' There are many individuals and political movements that are puzzling to the superficial observer because of what seems to be an inexplicable change from 'radicalism' to extreme authoritarianism. Psychologically, those people are typical 'rebels' (*Escape from Freedom* [1941a], pp. 169–170). Cf. "The Revolutionary Character" (1963b), pp. 105f.

40. Cf. the bibliographical indications in note 37. See also *Social Character in a Mexican Village* (1970b), p. 82, n. 15.

41. This is emphasized by Fromm in "The Revolutionary Character" (1963b), p. 103.

42. Ibid., p. 108.

43. Ibid., p. 110.

44. Ibid., p. 117.

45. Ibid., p. 117.

46. Cf. *Social Character in a Mexican Village* (1970b), p. 82, n. 15.

47. Ibid.
48. "The Revolutionary Character" (1963b), p. 117.
49. Ibid., p. 113.
50. "Prophets and Priests" (1967b), p. 70.
51. Ibid.
52. "Disobedience as a Psychological and Moral Problem" (1963d), p. 97.
53. Ibid., p. 99. Cf. *You Shall Be as Gods* (1966a), p. 72.
54. "Disobedience as a Psychological and Moral Problem" (1963d), p. 100. One notes that he wants to eliminate this misunderstanding as regards obedience to a person but not to an institution.
55. Ibid., p. 101.
56. *To Have or to Be?* (1976a), pp. 120–125.
57. Ibid., p. 121. The equation of an act of disobedience and an act of liberation goes along with Fromm's refusal to discuss a necessary and positive obedience to a rational authority. In a section of the manuscript of *To Have or to Be?*, which was removed during the last revision in order to tighten up the presentation, Fromm wrote: ". . . I decided to use the term 'disobedience' only with reference to irrational authority, and this for the following reason: in the history of civilization, religious and secular authority was principally irrational authority. . . . Rational authority was comparatively rare, as was disobedience to it for that same reason. . . . That there is no specific term for disobedience to rational authority merely reflects the historical tendency to confuse the two types of disobedience. But perhaps it is preferable to do without a good word and not to use a 'correct' one that has been used ideologically and is confusing for that reason" (manuscript of May 1975, p. 114). This is not to say, of course, that Fromm does not acknowledge such a thing as obedience to rational authority; he simply refuses to call it by that name. J. S. Glen, *Erich Fromm: A Protestant Critique*, who criticizes both Fromm and Nietzsche for their rejection in principle of any heteronomous authority, is probably correct when he notes that neither of them understood the intention of the Gospel. In his view, they considered everything a law that, either as positive or negative legalism, demanded obedience, and believes they were influenced by what they saw in the life of the Church and their experiences with Christians of their acquaintance (p. 88). In this connection, it is interesting to note the significance that obedience to the law and to paternal authority have in the education of children in religious Jewish families. Cf. the dissertation by Johannes Barta, *Jüdische Familienerziehung. Das jüdische Erziehungswesen im 19. and 20. Jahrhundert*, esp. pp. 80–83.
58. Cf. "The Revolutionary Character" (1963b): "Disobedience is a dialectical concept because actually every act of disobedience is an act of obedience. . . . Every act of disobedience is obedience to another principle." But see the comments on Fromm's use of dialectics, pp. 228–243.
59. *You Shall be as Gods* (1966a), p. 70.
60. Ibid.
61. Cf. ibid., pp. 71f.
62. On the following, see ibid., pp. 72f.
63. See p. 51f.
64. Cf. ibid., p. 73.
65. Ibid.
66. Ibid. It is striking that Fromm's formulation "perhaps" is somewhat vague, as is his restriction of this development to the phylogenetic aspect.

67. Ibid.

68. Ibid., p. 73. Cf. also p. 75: "The idea of serfdom to God was, in the Jewish tradition, transformed into the basis for the freedom of man from man. God's authority thus guarantees man's independence from human authority." Although the argument is presented in a less developed form, we already find this concession of an obedience toward a rational authority that is simultaneously disobedience toward an irrational one in Fromm, "The Revolutionary Character" (1963b) in (1963a), p. 114f.

69. Ibid., p. 73.

70. Cf. ibid., pp. 76f. This "final stage" resembles the description of the revolutionary character, although it reaches universal humanism through the total negation of all authority. Cf. "The Revolutionary Character" (1963b), p. 116.

71. "The Revolutionary Character" (1963b), pp. 116f.

72. This applies especially where his psychoanalytic experience and knowledge become an object of interest for Fromm, and where the gap between historical-philosophical theory and dialectical thought on the one hand, and empirical findings on the other, must not become too large. In this connection, one should recall that the revolutionary character is absent from the investigation into the social character of Mexican peasants (*Social Character in a Mexican Village* [1970b], p. 82). And one should call attention to the presence of a "traditional authoritarian," a patriarchal orientation that lacks the distinguishing characteristic of the authoritarian character, i.e., sadomasochistic submissiveness (cf. ibid., pp. 260–262).

73. Cf. the comments on obedience above.

74. Cf. Fromm's critique of the definition in the Oxford Dictionary: Fromm, *Psychoanalysis and Religion* (1950a), p. 34.

75. Ibid., p. 21; cf. "Psychoanalysis and Zen Buddhism" (1960a) pp. 92f. On the basis of this concept of religion, Fromm can call Marxism the most significant religious movement of the nineteenth century (*Vorwort* [1967c], p. 11). In *Psychoanalysis and Religion,* even Fascism and National Socialism are called "secular religions."

76. Cf. *Psychoanalysis and Religion* (1950a), p. 26. It is true that this statement does not apply to the concept of religion according to Freud, since Fromm believed that religion in Freud is an illusion that must be overcome. Cf. Fromm, "Die Entwicklung des Christusdogmas" (1930a) in (1963a), p. 25; and T. Pröpper, *Der Jesus der Philosophen and der Jesus des Glaubens*, esp. p. 68.

77. Fromm, "Die Entwicklung des Christusdogmas" (1930a), p. 22.

78. Cf. ibid., p. 22f. On the theological criticism of this early work of Fromm's, cf. T. Pröpper, *Der Jesus der Philosophen und der Jesus des Glaubens*, pp. 58–69.

79. Cf. "Die Entwicklung des Christusdogmas" (1930a), p. 25.

80. Ibid., p. 25.

81. Ibid., p. 27.

82. "External situation" refers to economic and social conditions.

83. Ibid., p. 27.

84. Ibid., p. 27.

85. Ibid., p. 67.

86. Ibid., p. 90. The element of newness introduced by the Nicene Council was, according to Fromm, "to have changed the tension between God and his Son into harmony since it avoided the concept that a man could become God [and thus] eliminated from the formula the revolutionary character of the older doctrine, namely, hostility to the father."

87. Ibid., p. 62; cf. pp. 90f.

88. Ibid., p. 91.

89. Anchoring religion in a need for a frame of orientation and an object of devotion does not mean that the socioeconomic conditions are not essential shaping factors. The abandonment of the Freudian theory of drives and the formulation of inherent existential needs have no effect on the mechanism by which they make their effects felt. The only exception would be if socioeconomic forces were such as to negate the need for a frame of orientation and an object of devotion. Cf. Fromm's analysis of reformers and the period of the Reformation in *Escape from Freedom* (1941a), pp. 63–102, for a statement on the dependence of religion on socioeconomic conditions; see also the brief summary in *Psychoanalysis and Religion* (1950a), pp. 52f.

90. "Die Entwicklung des Christusdogmas" (1930a), p. 25.

91. See below, pp. 106–112.

92. This is the reason a critique of Fromm's concept of religion cannot confine itself to the functionalization of religion. This reproach also applies to Paul Tillich who, in his review of *Psychoanalysis and Religion* (1950a), writes that Fromm sympathizes with Freud's theory of projection and claims that he fights against a heteronomous, supranaturalistic theism. Conversely, it should be said that for a theistic religion, the need for a frame of orientation and an object of devotion represents a significant anthropological fact.

93. The comments on authority (see pp. 88–101) permit a briefer presentation of authoritarian and humanistic religion. On what follows, cf. *Psychoanalysis and Religion* (1950a), pp. 34–55.

94. See p. 91.

95. See p. 100f.

96. *Psychoanalysis and Religion* (1950a), p. 35.

97. Ibid., p. 37.

98. Cf. J. S. Glen, *Erich Fromm: A Protestant Critique*, pp. 101f.

99. *Psychoanalysis and Religion* (1950a), p. 37.

100. Ibid., p. 49.

101. Ibid., p. 49f. The assumption that man was originally in full possession of his powers of reason and love corresponds to dialectical thought. The opposite view, according to which man must first detach himself phylo- and ontogenetically from fixations and irrational relations of authority if he is to come into his own, has its origin in the recognition of the data of evolution and empirical science. In this connection, one is struck by the formulation that God is a symbol of what man is potentially, or of what he can become.

102. W. Keilbach, "Theismus," p. 16. Cf. J. Möller, *Die Chance des Menschen—Gott gennant*, pp. 311–313.

103. See pp. 106–112. The failure of the attempt to bring humanism and theism together as regards the concept of God does not mean that theistic systems fail to meet the demands of a humanistic religion. But when the attempt is made to demonstrate humanistic religion in theistic systems, two perspectives become possible: one of them adopts the interpretation of the concept of God that Fromm advances; the other starts off from his distinction between rational and irrational authority, applies it to theistic systems, and then tries to discover in theistic religions concepts of God that are based on rational authority—which is counter to Fromm's approach. But the first perspective should not speak of humanistic religion in theistic systems because the theistic systems have been interpreted human-

istically to begin with. The second perspective cannot claim to find in theistic systems either what Fromm means by humanism or what humanism is generally understood to be, for a necessary part of such a humanism is the interpretation of God as nothing more than a symbol of man's own powers.

104. *Psychoanalysis and Religion* (1950a), p. 37. Fromm spent a good deal of time thinking about certain forms of humanistic religion, but his thought did not always find literary expression. Among the examples mentioned, the following have special importance: Buddhism (cf. *Psychoanalysis and Religion*); Zen-Buddhism (cf. "Psychoanalysis and Zen Buddhism" [1960a]); Judaism (cf. *You Shall Be as Gods* [1966a]); and Meister Eckhart (cf. *To Have or To Be?* [1976a], pp. 59–65). Fromm's studies of the Upanishads, Sufism, Plotinus, the Pseudo-Dionysius, the "cloud of unknowing," and various forms of Eastern meditation did not find literary expression. In *Psychoanalysis and Religion*, the following are mentioned as humanistic religions: early Buddhism (pp. 38–40); Zen Buddhism (pp. 40f); Spinoza's religious thought (p. 41); the Old Testament (pp. 42–47); Hasidism (pp. 47f); and early Christianity (pp. 48f). Cf. the listing in "Afterword" (1966d) in (1961b).

105. According to Fromm, Martin Luther is no revolutionary and the theology of the Reformation no humanistic religion for that reason: "While Luther freed people from the authority of the Church, he made them submit to a much more tyrannical authority, that of a God who insisted on complete submission of man and annihilation of the individual self as the essential condition to his salvation" (*Escape from Freedom* [1941a], p. 81).

106. On what follows, cf. especially *The Art of Loving* (1956a), pp. 53–60; *Beyond the Chains of Illusion* (1962a), pp. 157–159; *You Shall Be as Gods* (1966a), pp. 17–62; J. J. Petuchowski, "Erich Fromm's Midrash of Love," pp. 547–549.

107. *The Art of Loving* (1956a), p. 71; *You Shall Be as Gods* (1966a), pp. 18f: " 'God' is one of many different poetic expressions of the highest value in humanism, not a reality in itself." In spite of this *a priori* assertion, Fromm wants this position to be viewed as the result of his analysis of the history of the concept of God.

108. Cf. *You Shall Be as Gods* (1966a), p. 18.

109. Some of what appears in the following comments was already mentioned above, in connection with the rational authority concept. For the sake of the completeness of the theory, it is repeated here.

110. *The Art of Loving* (1956a), p. 54.

111. *You Shall Be as Gods* (1966a), p. 22.

112. On the occasionally rather arbitrary interpretations of biblical texts, cf. ibid., pp. 13–15, and notes on pp. 24 and 26.

113. Ibid., p. 24.

114. Ibid., p. 25.

115. *The Art of Loving* (1956a), p. 58.

116. Cf. *You Shall Be as Gods* (1966a), pp. 29–32.

117. Ibid., p. 31.

118. *The Art of Loving* (1956a), p. 59. On the function of the prophets in the realization of this idea of God, cf. *You Shall Be as Gods* (1966a), pp. 117–121; "The Prophetic concept of Peace" (1960d) in (1963a), pp. 141–148; "Die Aktualität der prophetischen Schriften" (1975d).

119. Fromm provides a brief sketch in *You Shall Be as Gods* (1966a), pp. 61f.

120. *The Art of Loving* (1956a), p. 81.

121. In a theism that is characterized by the presence of a revealed God, the history of man is a history of God "for" man and there is the eschatological hope for union of God and man. The humanist predisposition as regards the concept of God

becomes relevant in the interpretation of certain stages in the history of the concept of God. Examples would be the "fall" and the "revelation of the name." The various criticisms are summarily alluded to in the title of the book that represents the most extensive treatment of the history of the concept of God. Its title is the promise of the serpent in Paradise: "You Shall Be as Gods." But Fromm interprets this as: "You shall be gods!"

122. Cf. the critique of religion in Ludwig Feuerbach and Karl Marx, which can be summarized in the thesis that what man takes to be the highest being is in fact his (i.e., man's) true being.

123. Using the *theologia negativa* as the expression, in theological language, of man's coming into his own has primarily a religio-critical meaning that goes counter to the view held in the history of theology. For a *theologia negativa* "must not be confused, even conceptually, with some negative aspect of the religious-mystical experience (ever greater absence of God, etc.) and its negative expression" (H. Vorgrimmler, "Negative Theologie," pp. 864f). It does not satisfy Fromm that the *theologia negativa* should be a corrective for an excessive emphasis on dogma and thus an aid to the act of faith. That is the reason he does not believe that *theologia negativa* pleads for "God's word" as against "talk about God." For his understanding of *theologia negativa* is in line with his humanistic approach and his understanding of mysticism, as will become apparent in Part Four.

124. What is meant is the person for whom religion does not involve a transcendent God.

125. I.e., provided he accepts Fromm's interpretation of the history of the concept of God.

126. *The Art of Loving* (1956a), pp. 59f.

127. *You Shall Be as Gods* (1966a), p. 53; cf. *The Art of Loving* (1956a), pp. 60f.

128. *You Shall Be as Gods* (1966a), p. 226. The "finger that points to the moon" is a popular expression in Buddhist teaching. See, e.g., S. Ohasama, *Zen*, p. 4.

129. *You Shall Be as Gods* (1966a), p. 57. In contrast to his other writings, Fromm here deliberately avoids concepts such as "religion" and "religious," and uses "X experience" instead in order to make it clear that religious experience can occur outside of theistic systems. But this concept means several things. Sometimes it is the expression of an experiential substrate that is not defined closely; at other times, it means the same thing as "humanistic religion," and is thus a term for an experience that is being understood humanistically—as, e.g., when Fromm refers to the person "who has experienced the value X as the supreme value and tries to realize it in his life" (ibid., p. 228). In a note (on p. 57), Fromm establishes a connection between the X experience and Paul Tillich's "ground of being," or "depth" (as a substitute for "God"), and with Altizer's "atheistic Christianity." Fromm's understanding of what the X experience is comes very close to Günter Dux's sociological view of the function of religion: "It is the function of religion to thematize the depth structure of man's view of reality. For it is only through this act of conscious reflection that it becomes possible for man to become aware of his position in the world and to arrive at an interpretation of his life that will make sense and be relevant to his actions" (G. Dux, *Ursprung, Funktion und Gehalt der Religion*, p. 60).

130. This path via the interpretation of the history of the concept of God is indicated where a Western concept of religion is the point of departure, because here—in contrast to Eastern mysticism—the X experience is presented inside a theistic framework. Cf. *You Shall Be as Gods* (1966a), p. 57 and note.

131. Ibid., pp. 58–60. In the paraphrase following that passage, the use of the

term "X experience," which has already been interpreted humanistically is adopted by Fromm.

132. In his study of Buddhism, the books by Georg Grimm were of special import. Most significant among these was *Die Lehre des Buddha. Die Religion der Vernunft.*

133. Cf. *Psychoanalysis and Religion* (1950a), p. 40: "Zen proposes that no knowledge is of any value unless it grows out of ourselves; no authority, no teacher can really teach us anything except to arouse doubts in us; words and thought systems are dangerous because they easily turn into authorities whom we worship. Life itself must be grasped and experienced as it flows, and in this lies virtue." Or, p. 38: "The concept of Nirvana as the state of mind the fully awakened one can achieve is not one of man's helplessness and submission but on the contrary one of the development of the highest powers man possesses."

134. *You Shall Be as Gods* (1966a), p. 61.

135. *The Art of Loving* (1956a), pp. 61–69, ties the development of the requirements for a humanistic X experience to the postulate of a paradoxical logic. Because Fromm's understanding of Aristotelian and paradoxical logic is problematical (cf. below, notes 152 and 205), the sketch is presented as a consequence of his humanistic approach so that there is no need for a paradoxical logic.

136. This is especially true for the problem of God. Fromm asserts, e.g., that the concept "God" (not the experience of a highest value underlying the concept) is really "dead": "In the contemporary world which is no longer guided by Aristotle's systematic thought and by the idea of kingship, the God-concept has lost its philosophical and its social basis" (*You Shall Be as Gods* [1966a], p. 228). That is also the reason why a quarrel over atheism is pointless, a nineteenth-century relic. The only question Fromm considers decisive today is whether man as highest value is dead (ibid., pp. 228f). Cf. his talk about the "City of God" as thesis, the "Earthly City" as antithesis, and the "City of Being" as synthesis, in *To Have or to Be?* (1976a), p. 202.

137. *The Art of Loving* (1956a), p. 65. On the opposites identified above, see *ibid.*, pp. 62–69, where Fromm deduces them from a paradoxical logic.

138. *To Have or to Be?* (1976a), p. 202.

139. Ibid.

140. Ibid., p. 202.

141. *You Shall Be as Gods* (1966a), p. 229.

142. *Escape from Freedom* (1941a), p. 174.

143. Ibid., pp. 174f. In contrast to irrational authority, which can be personified in idols, the "magic helper" is the expression of a milder form of dependence, though the term emphasizes the forms of relations of dependency more strongly. Fromm's distinctions are quite clear, however. The magic helper is to be seen not only in God and other magical or transcendent persons, but also in parents, wife, husband, lover, superior, etc. The emergence of a new magic helper (as when someone "falls in love") brings about the collapse of the religious forms of relatedness to the magic helper that had been in force up to that moment. The psychology of the magic helper is the psychology of the authoritarian character, and explains both changes in spirituality and spiritual forms and in the mechanisms of falling in love, and of the failure of such love.

144. *Escape from Freedom* (1941a), p. 176.

145. See the following section.

146. Cf. *The Heart of Man* (1964a), pp. 132f.

147. In conversations with the author and in unpublished manuscripts, Fromm,

who did such exercises daily, referred to the publications of Nyanaponika Thera, specifically his *Der einzige Weg* and *Geistestraining durch Achtsamkeit. Die buddhistische Satipatthana-Methode.* See also Fromm's contribution to the *Festschrift* honoring the seventy-five-year-old Nyanaponika Mahathera, "Die Bedeutung des Ehrwürdigen Nyanaponika Mahathera für die westliche Welt" (1976b).

148. Cf. "Die Bedeutung des Ehrwürdigen Nyaponika Mahathera für die westliche Welt" (1976b) and A. A. Häsler, "Das Undenkbare denken und das Mögliche tun" (1977b), p. 19.

149. Fromm's reflections on self-analysis have not been published so far. The comments in P. Nischk, *Kursbuch für die Seele,* are a result of misunderstandings rather than knowledge of the subject matter.

150. Ideologies are to be understood as social rationalizations. On the meaning of psychoanalysis for "becoming conscious," cf. Fromm, "Psychoanalysis and Zen Buddhism" (1960a), esp. pp. 121–127.

151. "Description" is heteronomous definition in the sense that it must use objective language and therefore cannot avoid the subject-object dichotomy. On this, see the antiphilosophical position of Daisetz T. Suzuki as drawn in H. Rzepkowski, *Das Menschenbild bei D. T. Suzuki,* pp. 28f.

152. The difficult question of the extent to which paradoxical statements of the simultaneity of opposites are expressions of a paradoxical logic which contrasts with Aristotelian logic cannot be pursued here. But the following forms must be distinguished from a paradoxical logic such as Fromm presents in *The Art of Loving* (1956a), pp. 61–69: (1) the antilogic of the *mondo* or *koan* in Zen Buddhism according to Suzuki, which eliminates logic altogether (cf. Suzuki's essay in *Zen Buddhism and Psychoanalysis* [1960a], pp. 43ff); (2) the paradoxical formulations of theistic mystics. Especially in a nontheistic interpretation, one has the impression that their statements about God can be made "understandable" only by a paradoxical logic. This objection does not mean that paradoxical logic might not most aptly verbalize mystical experiences of identity. But such logic need not be understood as the antithesis of Aristotelian logic but as going beyond discursive thought, and therefore as a negation of such thought in favor of mystical experience. Cf. W. Johnston, *Der ruhende Punkt,* pp. 100–105.

153. Martin Buber, *Hasidism,* p. 146. This is the reason all mysticisms are open to the reproach of pantheism, though such reproach misses its target.

154. G. Simmel, *Hauptprobleme der Philosophie,* p. 15. In this book, Simmel discusses two fundamental attempts "to grasp the totality of Being in a more real way. . . . One of them is the way of mysticism, the other that of Kant" (p. 13).

155. *The Art of Loving* (1956a), p. 65.

156. Cf. W. Johnston, *Der ruhende Punkt. Zen und christliche Mystik,* pp. 145f: "It is that mysticism in which one descends to the motionless point or the depth of the soul and thereby acquires a kind of knowledge that is more than conceptual and therefore inexpressible, a kind of meta-thought through which one grasps the unity of all things—a unity that reveals itself increasingly as one progressively rids oneself of all concepts, images and essences and remains wholly calm and receptive."

157. *The Art of Loving* (1956a), p. 27. This definition of mysticism also reveals Fromm's nontheistic position in contrast to the understanding of mysticism as *cognitio dei experimentalis* in Thomas Aquinas. It is a definition Gershom Scholem paraphrases as an experimental knowledge of God that is acquired through living experience (cf. *Major Trends in Jewish Mysticism,* p. 4).

158. Since part of what follows comes from hitherto unpublished writings by Fromm, the comments are primarily based on a taped reply Fromm made to a lecture by Alfons Auer. It was given during the symposium celebrating Fromm's seventy-fifth birthday. In what follows, this document will be referred to as "Fromm *contra* Auer."

159. Fromm, "Fromm *contra* Auer" (1975e), p. 5.

160. Where the ONE can be determined, it becomes an idol: "The ONE is a nameless principle an effigy of which cannot be made. Idols are things man himself creates. They are the work of his hands to which he submits" (ibid.)

161. Within philosophical thought also, the vision of the ONE on the basis of the multiplicity of phenomena has found a variety of expressions. As, in mysticism, the experience of the ONE is grasped as the experience of NOTHINGNESS, so does ontology grasp being as the abstraction and negation of every existent. Cf. J. Möller, *Glauben und Denken im Widerspruch?;* and *Die Chance des Menschen—Gott genannt,* especially the historical survey of the problem of God, pp. 11–17.

162. It is doubtful that one can go along with Fromm and simply speak of the "religions of the East" (as in *The Art of Loving* [1956a], p. 67). For here also, we are dealing with certain trends both within and outside of the major religions that are viewed as heretical, and all of which are rightly called mysticism.

163. The Upanishads are part of the Vedas, the oldest religious writings of the Hindus in Sanskrit, "that pass on deeper insights on the nature of sacrifice but especially on God, world and soul which are destined only for the initiates" (H. von Glasenapp, "Preface" p. 6). H. Zimmer gives a good survey, including bibliographical information, in *Philosophie und Religion Indiens;* the German paperback contains a detailed general index and an extensive bibliography. P. Deussen provides a comprehensive orientation in *Allgemeine Geschichte der Philosophie mit besonderer Berücksichtigung der Religionen,* Vol. I, sections 1 and 2.

164. *Brihad-Aranyaka Upanishad,* quoted from H. Zimmer, *Philosophie und Religion Indiens,* p. 326. The literal meaning of "Atman" is breath, wind. Cf. the theological concept "spirit" in Christianity.

165. Ibid., quoted from A. Hillebrandt, *Upanishaden,* p. 88.

166. H. Zimmer, *Philosophie und Religion Indiens,* p. 301. On the identification of Atman and Brahman, cf. H. Oldenberg, *Die Lehre der Upanishaden und die Anfänge des Buddhismus,* pp. 47ff.

167. *Brihad-Aranyaka-Upanishad* (IV,4), quoted from A. Hillebrandt, *Upanishaden,* p. 84.

168. Ibid., p. 87.

169. Ibid., p. 77.

170. Cf. H. Oldenberg, *Die Lehre der Upanishaden,* p. 55, and the discussion on the interpretation of this statement in P. Deussen, *Allgemeine Geschichte der Philosophie mit besonderer Berücksichtigung der Religionen,* Vol. I, section 2, pp. 136f.

171. S. Ohasama, *Zen,* pp. 39f.

172. "Fromm *contra* Auer," (1975e), p. 3.

173. There is thus a reason why Fromm's first interest in Buddhism should have coincided with his turning away from orthodox Judaism. His reading of G. Grimm's *Die Lehre des Buddha* played a decisive role in this event, for in this book, as in Hermann Cohen's writings on the philosophy of religion, Fromm found a "religion of reason" which makes Buddhism appear as a science (cf. the title of another work by Georg Grimm, *Die Wissenschaft des Buddhismus*). "For the first time, he [Fromm] saw a spiritual system, a way of life, based on pure rationality and

without any irrational mystification or appeal to revelation or authority" (B. Landis and E. Tauber, "Erich Fromm: Some Biographical Notes," p. xii).

174. For some definitions of the relationships between Zen Buddhism and Buddha, see D. T. Suzuki, *Die grosse Befreiung,* pp. 41–45; but also W. Johnston, *Der ruhende Punkt,* pp. 29–31; and S. Ohasama, *Zen,* pp. 5–7.

175. The meaning Zen Buddhism has for an understanding of Buddha's teaching is not affected by this.

176. Suzuki, *Die grosse Befreiung,* p. 43.

177. S. Ohasama, *Zen,* p. 6.

178. "Psychoanalysis and Zen Buddhism" (1960a), p. 115.

179. Suzuki, *Living by Zen,* p. 101.

180. Ibid., p. 118–119.

181. Ibid., p. 68.

182. Suzuki, *Die grosse Befreiung,* p. 123. Suzuki emphasizes time and again that Satori is not a "higher unity in which two contradictory terms are synthesized" (*Living by Zen,* p. 87). That is why paradoxical statements in Zen differ from paradoxical-sounding statements in dialectical thought.

183. Suzuki, *Die grosse Befreiung,* p. 55.

184. Ibid., p. 60. If they propose to convey the direct intuitive grasp, common sense and reason are part of such external authority. Zen as mysticism wishes to be hampered by nothing in its direct intercourse with itself (ibid., p. 60).

185. Cf. H. Rzepkowski, *Das Menschenbild bei D. T. Suzuki,* p. 43, and the sources listed there.

186. D. T. Suzuki, *Mysticism: Christian and Buddhist,* p. 30.

187. "The bifurcation of reality is the work of the intellect; indeed it is the way in which we try to understand it in order to make use of it in our practical life. . . . The bifurcation helps us to handle reality, to make it work for our physical and intellectual needs, but in truth it never appeals to our inmost needs. For the latter purpose reality must be taken hold of as we immediately experience it" (Suzuki, *Living by Zen,* p. 55). In line with this distinction, it is possible to differentiate consistently between two kinds of insight, knowledge, experience, unity, vision, consciousness, etc., in Zen.

188. Suzuki, *Living by Zen,* pp. 80–81.

189. Suzuki, preface to Eugen Herrigel, *Zen in the Art of Archery,* p. 8.

190. Ibid., p. 9; cf. *Die grosse Befreiung,* pp. 123ff.

191. *Die grosse Befreiung,* pp. 47ff.

192. Ibid., pp. 52–54. Westerners who reproach Zen with being nihilistic and pantheistic usually do not take into account the distinctive quality of the mystical experience. On this, see Suzuki's answers in *Die grosse Befreiung,* pp. 66ff, 109f; and Suzuki, *Mysticism: Christian and Buddhist,* pp. 48–51; see also H. Rzepkowski, *Das Menschenbild bei D. T. Suzuki,* pp. 47–50.

193. "When the Buddha was born, he is said to have extended one hand toward heaven, the other toward earth, and to have exclaimed: 'Beyond the heavens and beneath the heavens, I am the only Venerable One' " (Suzuki, *Die grosse Befreiung,* p. 54). On the question of grounding humanism in the mystical experience of the ONE, see pp. 274–278.

194. Suzuki writes similarly: "Satori is God's coming to self-consciousness in man—the consciousness all the time underlining human consciousness, which may be called super-consciousness." (*Living by Zen,* p. 87) Cf. Suzuki, *Die grosse Befreiung,* p. 135: "Zen does not require the help of a Creator; when it grasps the basis

for life's being lived as it is lived, it is satisfied. . . . Whoever has God excludes that which is Not-God. This means self-limitation. Zen needs absolute freedom, even from God."

195. Suzuki, *Die grosse Befreiung,* p. 50, quoted from H. Rzepkowski, *Das Menschenbild bei D. T. Suzuki,* p. 48. The encompassing concept of negation that makes the Zen monk renounce all cognitive reason over a period of years because Satori can be experienced only when man denies himself as a creature of reason means that there are hardly any individuals who attain Satori, even in Japan. Fromm therefore believed that Zen Buddhism had few chances of becoming widely effective. There is, an addition, a significantly different assessment of the function of reason and love in Zen. Although Fromm makes very positive statements about Zen, he becomes skeptical when the question concerning the role reason and love play in self-redemption is raised.

196. "Fromm *contra* Auer" (1975e), p. 5.

197. Ibid., p. 6.

198. Ibid.

199. Others that could be mentioned here are not as unambiguous, according to Fromm. Examples would be gnostic trends, the Pseudo-Dionysius, and some representatives of a prominent *theologia negativa* associated with the Kabbala.

200. M. Nambara, *Die Idee des absoluten Nichts in der deutschen Mystik und ihre Entsprechungen im Buddhismus,* p. 276. This concept of the ONE as NOTHINGNESS goes beyond what the Christian *theologia negativa* means. Since following Christ in word and deed is always part of "Christian" *theologia negativa, theologia negativa* in the Christian sense has largely a corrective function; it does not serve the self-dissolution of theology. For Fromm, however, a nontheistic mysticism is the quintessence of a *theologia negativa* (cf. *The Art of Loving* [1956a], p. 60). But Minoru Nambara, *Die Idee des absoluten Nichts in der deutschen Mystik und ihre Entsprechungen im Buddhismus,* p. 276, points out that it is precisely Meister Eckhart who understands the Neoplatonic method of the *via negationis* in a way that leads to a NOTHING that corresponds to the Buddhist NOTHING—which means that Fromm would assent to Eckhart's understanding of this matter.

201. Cf. Nambara, *Die Idee des absoluten Nichts,* p. 276.

202. Ibid.

203. "Fromm *contra* Auer" (1975e), p. 6.

204. Fromm, *Psychoanalysis and Religion* (1950a), p. 125.

205. This inconsistency forms the background for the curious identification of paradoxical logic and dialectic (in Marx's and Hegel's meaning of the term), and the contrast between it and Aristotelian logic as developed in *The Art of Loving* (1956a), p. 62.

206. In the context of this problem, J. H. Schaar's critique that the striving for such experience entails the destruction of the reason that redeems man must be taken seriously. (Schaar, *Escape from Authority,* pp. 314–316).

207. This is developed on pp. 274–293.

CHAPTER 5. THE HUMANISTIC ETHIC

1. *Man for Himself* (1947a), pp. 6–7; cf. ibid., pp. vii–xi.

2. "Medicine and the Ethical Problem of Modern Man" (1963c) in (1963a), p. 118; on the following, cf. ibid., pp. 118f.

3. *Man for Himself* (1947a), pp. 16–20; M. McGrath, "An Examination of Erich Fromm's Ethics with Implications for Philosophy of Education," pp. 38–42.

4. The term "art" here does not coincide with the Aristotelian *technē*; cf. *Man for Himself* (1947a), p. 17, n. 2.

5. On this concept, see pp. 133–135.

6. *Man for Himself* (1947a), pp. 17f.

7. On what follows, cf. (*ibid.* pp. 8–14; 237–244; Fromm, "Die gesellschaftliche Bedingtheit der psychoanalytischen Therapie" (1935a), p. 395; *The Revolution of Hope* (1968a), pp. 86–92.

8. The criticism of an authoritarian ethic is largely identical with the rejection of an "idealist morality" (cf. Fromm, "Die gesellschaftliche Bedingtheit der psychoanalytischen Therapie" [1935a]) and an "absolute ethic" (cf. *Man for Himself* [1947a], pp. 237–244).

9. *Man for Himself* (1947a) p. 10.

10. See pp. 88–91.

11. Cf. *Man for Himself* (1947a), pp. 237–239.

12. *Ibid.*, p. 5.

13. Cf. *The Revolution of Hope* (1968a), pp. 87f.

14. *Man for Himself* (1947a), p. 241; cf. *The Revolution of Hope* (1968a), p. 88.

15. Cf. *The Revolution of Hope* (1968a), p. 88.

16. *Man for Himself* (1947a), p. 13.

17. Ibid.

18. Ibid., p. 7.

19. Fromm, "Values, Psychology, and Human Existence" (1959b), p. 151.

20. See pp. 152–180.

21. Cf. especially *Man for Himself* (1947a), pp. 20–24.

22. See p. 129f.

23. Cf. Paul Tillich, "Ist eine Wissenschaft von Werten möglich?" esp. p. 173.

24. Fromm, "Man Is Not a Thing" (1957a), p. 10.

25. Cf. *Man for Himself* (1947a), p. 20, n. 4. The term is Karl Marx's (cf. *Early Writings*).

26. *Man for Himself* (1947a), p. 23. See Fromm's personal statement about the way he links theory and clinical observation, in *Beyond the Chains of Illusion* (1962a), pp. 9f.

27. *Man for Himself* (1947a), p. 24.

28. Cf. G. B. Hammond, *Man in Estrangement*, p. 39, and pp. 60–66.

29. "Man Is Not a Thing" (1957a), p. 10.

30. Cf. Fromm, *Beyond the Chains of Illusion* (1962a), pp. 149–151.

31. *Man for Himself* (1947a), p. 20; cf. pp. 55–58.

32. *Man for Himself* (1947a), p. 19. On what follows, cf. *The Heart of Man* (1964a), pp. 115–117.

33. See pp. 55–66.

34. Fromm and Marx disagree on this point.

35. Cf. *The Heart of Man* (1964a), p. 117.

36. *Man for Himself* (1947a), p. 18.

37. Ibid., pp. 19f.

38. Cf. the critique by A. Gewirth, *Review*, 290f.

39. "The Application of Humanist Psychoanalysis to Marx's Theory" (1965c), p. 220.

40. Cf. pp. 60–66.

41. The term "construct" is intended to convey what Fromm calls "model of human nature" (cf. p. 133). Cf. also Fromm's concept of "rational vision" in *Man for Himself* (1947a), p. 205.

42. Cf. *The Revolution of Hope* (1968a), pp. 89–92.

43. Cf. p.133f.

44. *Man for Himself* (1947a), p. 7.

45. Ibid., p. 16.

46. Cf. also Fromm's statement in *Beyond the Chains of Illusion* (1962a): ". . . believing in the superior value of blending empirical observation with speculation . . . I have always tried to let my thinking be guided by the observation of facts, and have striven to revise my theories when the observation seemed to warrant it" (p. 9) Cf. *Man for Himself* (1947a), pp. 204–206.

47. *The Revolution of Hope* (1968a), p. 89.

48. Ibid., p. 91.

49. Ibid., p. 89. See the very similar formulation in *Man for Himself* (1947a), p. 20: "Good in humanistic ethics is the affirmation of life, the unfolding of man's powers."

50. "Values, Psychology, and Human Existence" (1959b), p. 162.

51. "Humanistic Planning" (1970e), in (1971a), p. 85.

52. *The Revolution of Hope* (1968a), p. 89.

53. *Man for Himself* (1947a), pp. 25–30.

54. "Humanistic Planning" (1970e), p. 80; cf. "Zur Theorie and Strategie des Friedens" (1970h), pp. 242f.

55. In a similar way, Fromm also criticizes the current "fairness ethics" according to which fairness, as ethical principle, governs the life of the marketing-oriented personality (see *The Sane Society* [1955a], pp. 172–174).

56. Cf. Part One of this study, and "Values, Psychology, and Human Existence" (1959b), pp. 162–164; *The Revolution of Hope* (1968a), pp. 89–92; "Humanistic Planning" (1970e), pp. 85f.

57. "Humanistic Planning" (1970e), p. 86.

58. *The Heart of Man* (1964a), p. 47.

59. The concepts "progression" and "regression," which Fromm used especially in his later works, imply the same thing as the terms "productive/nonproductive," "biophilic/necrophilic," "syndrome of growth and syndrome of decay."

60. *Beyond the Chains of Illusion* (1962a), pp. 174f.

61. Ibid.

62. *The Heart of Man* (1964a), p. 149.

63. Ibid., pp. 19–21.

64. Ibid., p. 121.

65. *Beyond the Chains of Illusion* (1962a), p. 177.

66. Cf. *Man for Himself* (1947a), p. 50.

67. See p. 27f.

68. *Beyond the Chains of Illusion* (1962a), p. 177. Cf. also the comments on the social character pp. 18–22.

69. On both points of view, cf. pp. 29–31.

70. *Man for Himself* (1947a), p. 59.

71. *The Revolution of Hope* (1968a), p. 91.

72. As early as 1941, Fromm wrote as follows on destructiveness (*Escape from Freedom* [1941a], p. 184): "It seems that if this tendency [to unfold life] is thwarted the energy directed toward life undergoes a process of decomposition and changes

into energies directed toward destruction. In other words: the drive for life and the drive for destruction are not mutually independent factors but are in a reversed interdependence. The more the drive toward life is thwarted, the stronger is the drive toward destruction; the more life is realized, the less is the strength of destructiveness. Destructiveness is the outcome of unlived life."

73. *The Heart of Man* (1964a), p. 148.

74. Cf. ibid., p. 150.

75. Cf. the schematic presentation of the syndrome of growth and the syndrome of decay, p. 54.

76. See pp. 29–31.

77. See pp. 18–26 and 49f.

78. On what follows, cf. Fromm, "Epilogue" (1970g); "Zur Theorie und Strategie des Friedens (1970h), pp. 19–22; *The Anatomy of Human Destructiveness* (1973a), esp. pp. 16–32. For the extensive secondary literature on Konrad Lorenz, see J. Rattner, *Aggression und menschliche Natur* (with extensive bibliography), esp. pp. 26–55.

79. *The Anatomy of Human Destructiveness* (1973a), pp. 16f.

80. "Zur Theorie und Strategie des Friedens" (1970h), p. 23.

81. On this point, Konrad Lorenz' approach differs fundamentally from Freud's death instinct. Cf. *The Anatomy of Human Destructiveness* (1973a), pp. 19f.

82. Cf. K. Lorenz, *On Aggression*.

83. *The Anatomy of Human Destructiveness* (1973a), p. 19.

84. Ibid., p. 20.

85. "Zur Theorie und Strategie des Friedens" (1970h), p. 24.

86. See pp. 41–43. The reasoning by analogy from animal to man, the incorrectness of which Fromm demonstrates repeatedly (cf. *The Anatomy of Human Destructiveness* [1973a], pp. 20–26), is part of this critique of Konrad Lorenz. The danger of such reasoning was exemplified by Lorenz himself when, in a newspaper article in 1940, he sought to legitimize the Nuremberg racial laws.

87. Cf. "Zur Theorie und Strategie des Friedens" (1970h), pp. 24f; *The Anatomy of Human Destructiveness* (1973a), pp. 89–101.

88. "Zur Theorie und Strategie des Friedens" (1970h), p. 25.

89. For what follows, see ibid., pp. 25–28.

90. Cf. *The Anatomy of Human Destructiveness* (1973a), pp. 188–209.

91. "Zur Theorie und Strategie des Friedens" (1970h), pp. 27f.

92. Ibid., pp. 28f; *The Anatomy of Human Destructiveness* (1973a), pp. 268–299.

93. Cf. ibid., pp. 325–368.

94. As early as 1939, in the article "Selfishness and Self-Love" (1939b), Fromm distinguished between a reactive hatred, where it is the situation that creates the hatred, and a character-conditioned hatred, where an "idling" but ever-ready hostility is "actualized" by the situation. Cf. p. 514.

95. On what follows, cf. *Man for Himself* (1947a), pp. 231–237; *The Heart of Man* (1964a), pp. 123–143; *Dialogue with Erich Fromm* (1966f), pp. 93–96. On the parallel between the "alternativism" of Fromm and of Spinoza, Marx, and Freud, cf. *The Heart of Man* (1964a), pp. 126f, 143–148; "The Application of Humanist Psychoanalysis to Marx's Theory" (1965c), pp. 220f.; *Marx's Concept of Man* (1961b), p. 61; and *Dialogue with Erich Fromm* (1966f), pp. 96–98: "Freud's Model of Man and Its Social Determinants" (1970d), pp. 93f. On the connection between freedom and neurosis, cf. Fromm, "Psychoanalysis and Zen Buddhism" (1959e), pp. 89f.

96. *Man for Himself* (1947d), p. 233.

97. Ibid., p. 232.

98. *The Heart of Man* (1964a), pp. 128; cf. 131f.

99. Ibid., p. 132.

100. Ibid.

101. Ibid. Freedom is thus the behavior that is appropriate to his specifically human powers: "freedom is nothing other than the capacity to follow the voice of reason, of health, of well-being, of conscience, against the voices of irrational passions" (pp. 130–131). Cf. also "Psychoanalysis and Zen Buddhism" (1959e), p. 90; "Introduction" (1968g), pp. 14f.

102. *Man for Himself* (1947a), p. 233.

103. Fromm uses the word "awareness" but makes clear that this does not refer to pure theoretical knowledge or opinion but rather to experience, experimenting, observing, gaining a conviction.

104. The capacity of "awareness" that enables man to do the good does not exist independently of the character structure. Like any part of that structure, it is determined by the whole and conversely helps determine that whole. The efficacy of "awareness" will be the greater the less it is held captive by irrational passions. But if, as in serious neuroses, irrational passions have an excessive strength, the capacity of "awareness" will remain inoperative because it is determined by those irrational passions. Cf. *Man for Himself* (1947a), pp. 233f.

105. Cf. *The Heart of Man* (1964a), p. 139. The use of this concept goes back to Hegel; cf. *Dialogue with Erich Fromm* (1966f), p. 94.

106. *The Heart of Man* (1964a), p. 140.

107. Ibid., p. 142.

108. Ibid., pp. 142f.

109. Cf. *Man for Himself* (1947a), pp. 141–143.

110. "Freud's Model of Man and Its Social Determinants" (1970d), p. 38.

111. *The Sane Society* (1955a), p. 47.

112. *The Art of Loving* (1956a), p. 37.

113. "Freud's Model of Man" (1970d), p. 39.

114. Cf. *Man for Himself* (1947a), pp. 143–158.

115. Ibid., pp. 144f.

116. Ibid., p. 146.

117. Ibid., p. 148.

118. This characteristic of the internalized authoritarian conscience results in a double role, i.e., to submit to authority and to be compelled to exercise it. "Man thus becomes not only the obedient slave but also the strict taskmaster who treats himself as his own slave" (p. 151). This means that an authoritarian character must always develop a measure of sadism and destructiveness if he is to play the role of taskmaster. Cf. Freud, *Civilization and Its Discontents.*

119. On this, see *Man for Himself* (1947a), pp. 158–172; "Medicine and the Ethical Problem of Modern Man" (1963c) in (1963a), pp. 119–121; *You Shall Be as Gods* (1966a), pp. 54–56; P. A. Bertocci and R. M. Millard, *Personality and the Good,* pp. 81–84.

120. "Medicine and the Ethical Problem of Modern Man" (1963c), p. 119.

121. *You Shall Be as Gods* (1966a), p. 55.

122. *Man for Himself* (1947a), p. 160.

123. The title of a radio talk by Fromm (1971a).

124. "Der Traum ist die Sprache des universalen Menschen" (1972a), p. 12. In this connection, cf. the probably incorrect critique of Fromm's view of dreams and his interpretations of them by Medard Boss, *Der Traum und seine Auslegung,* pp. 67–71.

125. Cf. *Man for Himself* (1947a), pp. 165f.

126. Ibid., p. 170.

127. ibid., p. 250.

128. On this, see A. Auer, "Ein Modell theologisch-ethischer Argumentation: 'Autonome Moral,' " pp. 28–41; W. Korff, *Norm und Sittlichkeit*, pp. 26–28; Korff, *Theologische Ethik*, pp. 9–11.

129. Auer, "Ein Modell . . .", p. 31.

130. Ibid., p. 30.

131. Cf. W. Korff, *Norm und Sittlichkeit*, pp. 18f.

132. As regards the distinction between the process of discovering norms and the grounding of the meaning of norms, see also the distinction between grounding and ultimate grounding of norms and between the "natural and the theological grounding of the normative": in W. Korff, *Norm und Sittlichkeit*, p. 42. The pair of concepts being used here, "the discovery of norms" and the "grounding of norms," was adopted from A. Auer, "Tendenzen heutiger theologischer Ethik."

133. W. Korff, *Norm und Sittlichkeit*, p. 27.

134. Ibid.

135. Ibid., p. 41; cf. A. Auer, "Ein Modell . . .", p. 32.

136. Ibid., pp. 32f.

137. Cf. W. Korff, *Norm und Sittlichkeit*, p. 41; and A. Auer, *Autonome Moral und christlicher Glaube*, p. 22. "It is thus the task of ethics to translate into the language of bindingness the insights into reality, into its significant forms and structures of order, and to transform indicatives about reality into imperatives for action."

138. Cf. Korff, *Norm und Sittlichkeit*, p. 41.

139. Ibid.

140. Ibid., pp. 41, 27; Cf. Korff, *Theologische Ethik*, pp. 70–79; and Auer, *Autonome Moral und christlicher Glaube*, p. 27.

141. W. Korff, *Theologische Ethik*, p. 73.

142. Ibid., p. 70.

143. A general overview of the development of Catholic moral theology in our time is in F. Furger, *Zur Begründung eines christlichen Ethos—Forschungstendenzen in der katholischen Moraltheologie*, and A. Auer, "Tendenzen heutiger theologischer Ethik."

144. Other positions that see the bindingness of the moral grounded in revelation, in tradition, in "nature," in the teaching of the church or other "authorities" need not be considered here because they must refer to the positions of the *Glaubensethik* or to that of "autonomous morality" if they are going to define the grounding nexus more closely; or they must define the moral apodictically or positivistically, which would mean that they would fail to fulfill their task of grounding the moral in its claim to be binding. A presentation of such "authoritarian" views of the moral is in A. K. Ruf. *Grundkurs Moraltheologie*, Vol. I, *Gesetz und Norm*.

145. Cf. A. Auer, "Die Autonomie des Sittlichen nach Thomas von Acquin."

146. F. Böckle, "Glaube und Handeln," p. 32. Discussions about the moral in Christianity are as old as the history of the Christian mission: the discussion centers around what is specifically Christian. But during the last few decades, it has been especially historical findings and the discoveries of the modern human sciences that have called into question the understanding of the moral. As "autonomous morality," it again became a topic of discussion. Franz Böckle (p. 30, n. 37) has the debate about the specific characteristics of a Christian ethic within theological ethics begin with a scientific meeting of the *Societas Ethica* in Lund in 1966. (But cf.

the comments and bibliographical material in F. Furger, *Zur Begründung eines christlichen Ethos—Forschungstendenzen in der katholischen Moraltheologie,* esp. p. 15, n. 13, and p. 85, n. 174; and A. Auer, *Autonome Moral und christlicher Glaube,* pp. 160–184). The following contributions can be considered especially productive of further discussion (additional literature in F. Böckle, "Glaube und Handeln," p. 30, n. 37; p. 32, n. 40, where an [incomplete] listing of representatives of an "autonomous morality" can be found): F. Böckle, "Was ist das Proprium einer christlichen Ethik?"; W. van der Marck, *Grundzüge einer christlichen Ethik;* J. Fuchs, "Gibt es eine spezifisch christliche Moral?" J. Gründel, "Ethik ohne Normen? Zur Begründung und Struktur christlicher Ethik"; A. Auer, *Autonome Moral und christlicher Glaube;* "Ein Modell theologisch ethischer Argumentation: 'Autonome Moral' "; "Die ethische Relevanz der Botschaft Jesu"; W. Korff, *Norm und Sittlichkeit;* B. Schüller, *Die Begründung sittlicher Urteile;* "Zur Diskussion um das Proprium einer christlichen Ethik," esp. pp. 322–334; D. Mieth, "Autonome Moral im christlichen Kontext." In addition, see the contributions in J. Gründel, F. Rauh, V. Eid, eds., *Humanum* (*Festschrift Egenter*); and K. Demmer and B. Schüller, eds., *Christlich glauben und handeln* (*Festschrift Fuchs*). Because Alfons Auer's views on "autonomous morality" provoked the most intense discussion, the comments below are primarily statements of his opinions. They have recently been presented in A. Auer, "Die Bedeutung des Christlichen bei der Normfindung," and in *Autonome Moral und christlicher Glaube* (1977). In the latter essay, all contributions that are relevant to the subject are listed. Auer also enumerates all those others who, in his opinion, represent an "autonomous morality in the Christian context." He names J. Fuchs, F. Böckle, B. Schüller, D. Mieth, R. Hofmann, St. Pfürtner, B. Fraling, H. Juros, Th. Styczen, P. Hofmann, V. Eid, H. Rotter, E. McDonagh, and W. Korff.

147. Cf. Auer, *Autonome Moral und christlicher Glaube,* pp. 16f.

148. Ibid., p. 35.

149. Cf. ibid., pp. 17–21.

150. A. Auer, "Ein Modell . . .", p. 35.

151. Cf. ibid.; *Autonome Moral und christlicher Glaube,* p. 29; "The rationality of the moral results from man's rational nature."

152. Auer, "Ein Modell . . .", p. 29.

153. Auer, *Autonome Moral und christlicher Glaube,* p. 29.

154. Ibid., pp. 132f, 32f.

155. Cf. ibid., pp. 39–48.

156. Cf. F. Böckle, "Unfehlbare Normen?" pp. 287, 289: "Norms which are meant to directly govern our responsible behavior toward man and world must be open to rational human insight as a matter of principle. . . . There are mysteries of the faith but there can be no mysterious moral norms of action whose rightness in interpersonal action would not be clearly understandable and unambiguously determinable."

157. Auer, *Autonome Moral und christlicher Glaube,* p. 173.

158. Cf. A. Auer, "Ein Modell . . .", p. 173.

159. Cf. especially A. Auer, "Die ethische Relevanz der Botschaft Jesu."

160. Ibid., p. 59.

161. Cf. ibid., pp. 60–67.

162. A. Auer, "Ein Modell . . .", p. 42.

163. W. Korff, *Theologische Ethik,* pp. 34f.

164. Cf. ibid., pp. 31–33; and A. Auer, *Autonome Moral und christlicher Glaube,* p. 172: "The transcendental causal efficacy of the creator and the dependence this

entails do not in any way jeopardize the autonomy of the world. On the contrary, they ground its possibility."

165. Cf. W. Korff, *Theologische Ethik*, pp. 37–39, here p. 37.

166. Ibid., p. 39.

167. Cf. the essay of the same title by Dietmar Mieth.

168. On what follows, cf. A. Auer, *Autonome Moral und christlicher Glaube*, pp. 127–131; "Die Autonomie des Sittlichen nach Thomas von Aquin;" W. Korff, *Norm und Sittlichkeit*, pp. 42–61; *Theologische Ethik*, pp. 79–86. In their reception of Thomas Aquinas, both Auer and Korff rely principally on W. Kluxen, *Philosophische Ethik bei Thomas von Aquin*, esp. pp. 230–241; and L. Oeing-Hanhoff, "Der Mensch: Natur oder Geschichte?" Cf. also Oeing-Hanhoff, "Thomas von Aquin und die gegenwärtige katholische Theologie," esp. pp. 281–290.

169. W. Korff, *Theologische Ethik*, p. 79.

170. Cf. Auer, *Autonome Moral und christlicher Glaube*, pp. 128f.

171. Ibid., p. 130. Auer explicates this autonomy of the moral as autonomy vis-à-vis physiological and biological laws, metaphysics, and the faith.

172. W. Korff, *Theologische Ethik*, p. 80; cf. *Norm und Sittlichkeit*, p. 49.

173. W. Korff, *Norm und Sittlichkeit*, p. 49.

174. Cf. ibid., p. 61.

175. The following publications advocate this position, which in the meantime has also come to be the one Germany's Catholic bishops prefer: R. Stoeckle, *Grenzen der autonomen Moral; Handeln aus dem Glauben*, esp. pp. 9–32; "Christlicher Glaube and Ethos der Zukunft"; A. Laun, "Zur Frage einer spezifisch christlichen Ethik"; G. Ermecke, "Katholische Moraltheologie am Scheideweg," esp. pp. 52f; J. Ratzinger, "Kirchliches Lehramt-Glaube-Moral"; J. Rief, "Normen und Normenfindung." The discussion of *glaubensethische* positions being carried on among Protestant theologians cannot be considered here.

176. Especially Bernhard Stoeckle's writings give evidence of a number of misunderstandings that obviously cannot be cleared up here. Although Auer, "Ein Modell . . .," discusses these misunderstandings in Stoeckle's *Grenzen der autonomen Moral* and clarifies both the autonomy concept and what is meant by the autonomy of the moral, and also explicates the effect the Christian horizon of meaning has on the discovery and grounding of norms (cf. Auer, "Die ethische Relevanz der Botschaft Jesu"), Stoeckle wants "the title 'Handeln aus dem Glauben' to express more than is inferred by those who limit the moral function of belief to the opening up of a particular horizon of meaning and the discovery of new motives" (B. Stoeckle, *Handeln aus dem Glauben*, p. 11). But it cannot be determined what this "more" really is.

177. B. Stoeckle, *Handeln aus dem Glauben*, p. 9.

178. B. Stoeckle, *Grenzen der autonomen Moral*, p. 130. It must be asked, however, whether Stoeckle's own position actually realizes this paradox or whether he merely postulates this contrast because it alleges a necessary difference of the Christian. Such contrasts, which are always accompanied by a suggestive "must," are quite popular with Stoeckle. He also constructs a threat: "It must finally be understood how decisively the Christian faith is being challenged by the growing propagation of 'autonomous morality.' " Josef Rief's expression of unease regarding "autonomous morality" is not much more persuasive: "The approach of autonomous morality misses the essence of the moral and represents no innerworldly possibility" ("Normen und Normenfindung," p. 31).

179. B. Stoeckle, *Grenzen der autonomen Moral*, p. 133, speaks of a "theonomous

ethic that is to be preferred to an autonomous conception of morality." This is another instance in which he documents his misunderstanding of the autonomy of the moral. The same applies to Rief, "Normen und Normenfindung," p. 17.

180. A. Auer, "Die Autonomie des Sittlichen nach Thomas von Aquin," p. 31, which deals with Thomas Aquinas' *Summa Theologiae*, I–II, 90, 1c: "*Regula autem et mensura humanorum actuum est ratio, quae est primum principium actuum humanorum. . . .*"

181. B. Stoeckle, *Grenzen der autonomen Moral*, p. 139.

182. Cf. Böckle, "Glaube und Handeln," p. 32.

183. J. Rief, "Normen und Normenfindung," p. 21.

184. Ibid., p. 27. Against his own better knowledge, and counter to the insights of an "autonomous morality" oriented around the human sciences, Rief simply asserts this although Wilhelm Korff, *Norm und Sittlichkeit*, e.g., has shown that in his intercourse with others, man always plays the triple role creature of need, aggressor, and keeper (pp. 76–112).

185. Cf. J. Rief, "Normen und Normenfindung," p. 20.

186. J. Ratzinger, "Kirchliches Lehramt-Glaube-Moral, p. 59.

187. Ibid., p. 56.

188. Ibid., p. 65. For a critique of these statements, cf. Schüller's review of J. Ratzinger's book. For a critique of the *glaubensethische* position on the basis of a humanistic ethos, see p. 285f.

189. See pp. 83–128, esp. 112–117, 119–121, 124–128.

190. See especially pp. 205–218 and 239–244.

191. This shared characteristic may be noted independently of the criticism that Fromm's concept of authority neglects the possibility of rational authority in a number of respects.

192. Cf. p. 131f.

193. Cf. p. 132. This last variant has been given a new boost by research in comparative behavior. The kind of contribution ethology can make in the discovery of moral norms is discussed extensively by W. Korff, *Norm und Sittlichkeit*, esp. pp. 76–101, 113–128. Also in F. Rauh, "Die Funktion der vergleichenden Verhaltensforschung für das Humanum," esp. pp. 143–145, 156f. Cf. also B. Schüller, *Die Begründung sittlicher Urteile*, esp. pp. 102–107; and W. Lepenies, "Schwierigkeiten einer anthropologischen Begründung der Ethik," esp. pp. 321–324.

194. Cf. W. Korff, *Norm und Sittlichkeit*, pp. 68, p. 65: ". . . because his nature is a rational nature, man is a rational, moral and normative being."

195. Ibid., p. 71.

196. Ibid., p. 72.

197. Cf. A. Auer, *Autonome Moral und christlicher Glaube*, pp. 39–43.

198. The terms "*naturale Unbeliebigkeit*" and "*naturale Unbeliebigkeitslogik*" were formulated by Wilhelm Korff and are based on the concept "*Unbeliebigkeit*," which was introduced by Max Müller (cf. Korff, *Norm und Sittlichkeit*, pp. 10, 76). With the concept "*Unbeliebigkeit*," Korff characterizes the self-acting, naturally dispositive reason of human action. Because he uses the terms "*naturale Unbeliebigkeit*" and "*naturale Unbeliebigkeitslogik*," he avoids the misunderstandings and misinterpretations that the concepts "natural law" and "nature" give rise to. The natural dispositive reason of human action that is referred to by the term "*Unbeliebigkeit*" does not imply an ethical statement. For what is naturally given is not normative (ibid., p. 70).

199. *Ibid.*, p. 76.

200. The peculiarity of ultimate natural constraints to be predisposing only is the

reason terms such as "dispose" and "dispositive" were used in preference to "determine" and "determinative."

201. Cf. W. Korff, *Norm und Sittlichkeit*, p. 78. In the field of theological ethics, Wilhelm Korff was the first to attempt to work out such a logic of natural non-optionality (*naturale Unbeliebigkeitslogik*). He views all social interaction as configurations of ultimate, coordinate laws of motivation whose internal referential nexus first assures the humane rationality of such interaction. This interdependence of the satisfaction of needs, self-assertion, and the readiness to care for others that Korff characterized as "social perichoresis" (cf. ibid., p. 97) is the structural law of everything social and a result of the phenotypicalness of man's intercourse with man. In contrast to Alfred Vierkandt and Hans Georg Gadamer, who had worked out this phenotypicality before him, Korff does not stop here but develops the insight that the differing forms of man's intercourse with man are structural laws without which the social would not exist. Research in the physiology of behavior and its analysis finally confirmed Korff in the view that in their relations with each other, men play the triple role of creature of need, aggressor, and keeper (ibid., p. 91). The "social perichoresis" as natural-social fundamental law is the *norma normarum* and an ultimate motivational law; it is no norm but a metanorm. For it is the "true standard and criterion for the evaluation and classification of concrete styles of social action. It permits no extrapolation because only a form of action that unfolds within the perichoresis defines itself as humanly rational on this, its natural basis" (ibid.).

202. On the meaning of these insights for a theological ethic, see below, p. 000.

203. Examples would be Martin Heidegger's analysis of *Dasein* and the philosophical anthropologies that predate the emergence of the human and social sciences.

204. The possibility of arriving at (philosophical)-anthropological statements by way of a summation of the diverse data of diverse disciplines need not be considered since it is immediately apparent that man is a unity that permits at most a perspectivist view but never a division.

205. On "virtue" as a key concept in ethics, cf. W. Korff, *Theologische Ethik*, pp. 50–53; and, as a representative example, V. Eid, "Tugend als Werthaltung." Cf. also the bibliography in Eid.

206. With certain qualifications, this also applies to Bruno Schüller's approach, although he tried to overcome the narrowness that lies in restricting himself to the characteristics of an act by viewing and judging human behavior in terms of the consequences of acts so that he can say that "the moral character of an act is wholly determined by its good or evil results" (B. Schüller, "Neuere Beiträge zum Thema 'Begründung sittlicher Normen,' " p. 117; also, Schüller, *Die Begründung sittlicher Urteile*, esp. pp. 22f). But one wonders if such a "teleological" theory of ethical normativeness can really overcome the reductionist quality of traditional casuistic morality. For the rejection of a "deontological" theory of ethical normativeness in favor of a "teleological" one implies the exclusive orientation around man's behavior that also characterizes casuistry and will therefore continue to be subject to the criticism of wanting to reduce man to his behavior and of making what is moral conform to optimal adaptation. But this criticism is not intended to deprecate the merits of a "teleological" ethic as compared to a kind of casuistry that is exclusively interested in the so-called *casus conscientiae* and wants to know above all "when, where and how a particular fact should be judged sinful or tolerable" (F. Furger, "Katholische Moraltheologie in der Schweiz," p. 222).

207. It would certainly be of interest if this case were to be decided according to

all the rules of casuistic art, including a "teleologically" understood casuistry. Is the child's behavior to be interpreted as thrift or as avarice? To what extent does a morally negative evaluation of the fact that the child decides on a different use for the money and thereby opposes the parents' purpose compete with a possibly morally positive evaluation of thrift? What criteria can decide whether something is a good or a virtue or set up an order of rank for virtues ("nonmoral" and "moral" value in Schüller's sense) and have this ranking be binding? Isn't the child actually very well behaved when he is thrifty and thus obediently reproduces the character trait of his parents, as he does his share to meet their economic needs?

208. Cf. Part Three of this study.

209. Although discoveries in the physiology of behavior have significance for Wilhelm Korff's "social perichoresis" of the satisfaction of needs, self-assertion, and the readiness to care for others because such findings confirm that the varying forms of man's intercourse with man are laws that structure the social, which would not exist without such laws, this criticism does not apply to him since for him the analysis of discoveries in the physiology of behavior is merely empirical confirmation of the fact that the phenotypicalness of man's dealings with man actually represents those structural laws. Fromm's and Korff's approaches can therefore be constructively mediated with each other. In Fromm's account of the nonproductive character orientation, it can be shown that the nonproductivity results from the destruction of the stable configuration of satisfaction of need, self-assertion, and readiness to care for others that obtains in a given instance. In the description of the productive character orientation, on the other hand, Fromm himself recurs to criteria that show that the configuration of the three components remains intact.

210. The depression of entire civilizations has recently been even more marked in capitalist than in communist states. The so-called oil crisis and the collapse of the international monetary system have resulted in the destruction of the frame of orientation according to which happiness lies in maximizing the standard of living, and this disintegration has affected large parts of the population of the Western world. Consumption-oriented capitalism cannot maintain its function as a substitute religion. It brings on not only a depression in finance and enterprise but also among the masses that spreads like an epidemic that can be dealt with only over time, and usually by new, mostly irrational substitute religions. The necessity to find a substitute for the frame of orientation and the objects of devotion and to rebuild when natural causes or socioeconomic and political changes have destroyed its validity also explains in part why periods of change and optimism are followed with an almost lawlike regularity by periods of reaction and authoritarianism. In such phenomena, we see the desperate effort to react at least regressively and nonproductively to an existential need when no other kind of reaction is possible, for the failure to satisfy existential needs would threaten life itself.

211. Fromm's "alternativism" theory is grounded in this distinctive quality of moral action. See pp. 145–148.

212. See note 167.

213. Cf. A. Auer's contribution in the *Festschrift* for Josef Fuchs, "Die Autonomie des Sittlichen nach Thomas von Aquin." More extensively than in his *Autonome Moral und christlicher Glaube,* Auer shows here that Thomas Aquinas asserted the autonomy of the moral vis-à-vis the natural order, metaphysics, and the faith. The postulate of an autonomous morality can be demonstrated in the tradition of Thomistic thought.

214. It is only when the meaning of moral norms is grounded that the distinguishing characteristics of the two ethics articulate themselves.

215. Thomas Aquinas, *Summa Theologiae,* I–II, 18, 5c, quoted according to A. Auer, "Die Autonomie des Sittlichen nach Thomas von Aquin," p. 33.

216. Auer, "Die Autonomie . . . ," with reference to Aquinas, *Summa Theologiae,* I–II, 100, 1c.

217. See p. 159f, and Auer, "Die Autonomie . . . , p. 34f.

218. Ibid., p. 35, with reference to *Summa Theologiae,* I–II, 1,3 ad 3.

219. The concept "instinct substitution" serves to indicate the difference between Fromm's and Arnold Gehlen's anthropological views. While Gehlen considers that in the case of man, we are dealing merely with a reduction of instinct for which reason institutions become equivalents that compensate for his lost instinctual sureness, Fromm's concern is clearly the substitution of character for instinct. Of course, the actual difference between Gehlen's and Fromm's anthropologies is not the subtle distinction between instinct reduction and instinct substitution, but the fact that for Gehlen, it is institutions that are the equivalent. In Fromm's case, the equivalent is character, i.e., a psychic or psychosocial entity that replaces instinct and gives human thought, feeling, and action a specific orientation. The concept "(character)-orientation" therefore implies an openness and a lack of fixity that are not present in the concept "institution" and that are present even where man is a part of institutional entities. On the concept of instinct reduction in the context of the theory of institutions, cf. A. Gehlen, *Der Mensch,* p. 79; or Gehlen, *Anthropologische Forschung,* pp. 69–77.

220. In theological ethics, Thomas Aquinas is probably the only one who pursues a similar goal with the *"inclinationes naturales"* (self-preservation, preservation of the species, the search for truth, communal life, rational and virtuous action). There is, however, "a methodical insufficiency in his work where he inquires into the *ratio* of the natural inclinations for this *ratio* does not derive from scientific analysis but is prereflective, and based on experience . . ." (W. Korff, *Norm und Sittlichkeit,* p. 52). With the concept of character, Fromm attempts to do justice to the methodical demand. But that concept also leads him to exclude all instinctive or quasi-instinctive components from the concept "human needs" and to see those needs as a result of instinct substitution.

221. The fact that Fromm was able to limit the nonproductive character orientations to a certain number of ideal types has particular practical value in the matter of establishing concrete ethical norms. And the various nonproductive character orientations in the process of assimilation and socialization also have the heuristic function of defining *e contrario* what productive character orientation means.

PART THREE: Sources and Forms of the Thought of Erich Fromm

CHAPTER 6: SOURCES OF FROMM'S THOUGHT

1. Fromm, *You Shall Be as Gods* (1966a), p. 29; on what follows, cf. ibid., pp. 28–38.

2. Ibid., p. 31.

3. Cf. P. van Imschoot, "Name," 1215.

4. *You Shall Be as Gods* (1966a), pp. 40f, attempts to limit the meaning of these

articles of faith as if they played no role whatever. But cf. M. Friedländer, *Die jüdische Religion,* a presentation of the Jewish religion that quite consciously orients itself around the thirteen articles of Maimonides.

5. The following comments are more than a discussion of Fromm's understanding of Maimonides. On Maimonides' doctrine of attributes, see Moses ben Maimon, *Guide of the Perplexed,* esp. Vol. I, chaps. 51–61; D. Kaufmann, *Geschichte der Attributenlehre in der jüdischen Religionsphilosophie des Mittealters von Saadja bis Maimuni,* esp. pp. 428–468; H. Cohen, *Religion und Sittlichkeit,* pp. 40–43; *Charakteristik der Ethik Maimunis; Rēligion der Vernunft aus den Quellen des Judentums* (*Religion of reason out of the sources of Judaism*); *Jüdische Schriften,* Vol. 3, pp. 44f; J. Guttmann, *Die Philosophie des Judentums,* pp. 180–205; L. Baeck, *Maimonides. Der Mann, sein Werk und seine Wirkung;* E. Fromm, *You Shall Be as Gods* (1966a), pp. 32–37.

6. On the history of this doctrine of God's negative attributes in the Middle Ages, see D. Kaufmann, *Geschichte der Attributenlehre in der jüdischen Religionsphilosophie des Mittelalters von Saadja bis Maimuni.*

7. Ibid., p. 442.

8. H. Cohen, *Charakteristik der Ethik Maimunis,* p. 94; Cf. Kaufman, *Geschichte der Attributenlehre,* pp. 431f.

9. Maimonides, *Guide of the Perplexed,* p. 201.

10. H. Cohen, *Religion of Reason,* p. 63. Cf. Cohen, *Charakteristik der Ethik Maimunis,* pp. 95f. In this connection of negation and privation, Cohen sees the decisive step by which the Jewish religion became a religion of reason. Maimonides elaborates on this notion in chap. 58 of *Guide of the Perplexed.*

11. D. Kaufmann, *Geschichte der Attributenlehre,* p. 435.

12. Ibid.

13. J. Guttmann, *Die Philosophie des Judentums,* p. 183; cf. *Guide of the Perplexed,* Vol. I, chap. 59.

14. Cf. Guttmann, *Die Philosophie des Judentums,* p. 184.

15. Fromm opts for this position, *You Shall Be as Gods* (1966a), pp. 37ff.

16. Guttmann, *Die Philosophie des Judentums,* pp. 185: Cf. H. Cohen, *Charakteristik der Ethik Maimunis,* p. 94. In the negative form of the knowledge of God in Maimonides, Guttmann sees the way "Maimonides and similarly earlier Jewish and Islamic thinkers could see in the concept of God of Neo-platonism the scientific expression of their belief in God" (p. 186). For Maimonides, however, this reshaping of the idea of God does not represent a concession to science. For him, "the philosophical sublimation of the idea of God is a religious demand" (p. 181). In the most radical fashion possible, the concept of God is freed of every sensuous admixture here and the meaning of the religious idea of the one God is being grasped. If one disregards the admittedly decisive difference that Maimonides is concerned with preserving the purity of the idea of God, one notices that Fromm's concern is very close indeed to this form of negative theology.

17. *Guide of the Perplexed,* p. 213.

18. J. Guttmann, *Die Philosophie des Judentums,* p. 182; cf. Maimonides, *Guide of the Perplexed,* chap. 58.

19. Cf. Guttmann, *Die Philosophie des Judentums,* p. 182.

20. Cf. Maimonides, *Guide of the Perplexed,* p. 192.

21. Ibid., p. 194.

22. Cf. Cohen, *Religion of Reason,* pp. 99f. "Love and justice" parallel Fromm's

topos "reason and love." The affinity of ideas becomes apparent when Fromm adds "justice" to "reason and love."

23. *Guide of the Perplexed,* p. 198.

24. Ibid., p. 198.

25. Ibid., p. 211.

26. Ibid., p. 216.

27. Cf. ibid., chap. 60, p. 225.

28. Ibid., p. 225.

29. "Not by such methods as would prove the necessity of ascribing to Him anything extraneous to His essence or asserting that He has a certain perfection, when we find it to be a perfection in relation to us" (p. 215).

30. Hermann Cohen, whom Fromm repeatedly quotes in support of his humanistic interpretation of Jewish tradition, cannot be quoted in support of this view because—albeit from the perspective of Neo-Kantianism—he holds fast to the postulate of an unmistakable Jewish God (as "idea"). Cf. Cohen's concept of "correlation." The temptation to interpret negative theology humanistically as positive anthropology in order to be able to negate God in favor of man results from a merely apparent parallel: while it is true that the *theologia negativa* negates all statements about God, it does not do so in order to negate God in favor of man but in order to affirm both God and man in their distinctiveness.

31. H. Cohen, *Religion und Sittlichkeit,* p. 41.

32. Ibid. J. Guttmann, *Die Philosophie des Judentums,* pp. 186f, calls attention to the fact that Maimonides ultimately "subordinates the moral concept of the God of the bible to the neoplatonic one" (p. 186), which means that the former goes further because, at least in prophetic monotheism, the Bible makes the ethical concept of God primary and engages in a negative theology on its basis. The ideas being elaborated here are therefore more strongly governed by Hermann Cohen's interpretation of Maimonides, which also influenced Erich Fromm.

33. Cf. H. Cohen, *Religion und Sittlichkeit,* p. 42: "God's essence lies wholly in morality."

34. Ibid., p. 43.

35. Cf. Cohen, *Charakteristik der Ethik Maimunis,* p. 90.

36. Here also, it must be remembered that while the negation of a "dogmatic" concept of God in favor of an "ethical" one creates a conception of religion that differs fundamentally from the Christian concept of God, this does not involve a dissolution or substitution of the concept of God, Fromm's different interpretation notwithstanding. The "ethical" concept of God can only be interpreted as a humanistic concept of religion if the *theologia negativa* of Maimonides is dissolved. But that theology establishes the "ethical" concept of God.

37. Cf. *Guide of the Perplexed,* p. 198.

38. Fromm's question as to what it means in the tradition of negative theology that man affirms God's existence (*You Shall Be as Gods* [1966a], p. 37) must be answered by Maimonides and other representatives of the Jewish faith in a way that disappoints Fromm's expectations: it is precisely not a sign of unenlightened thinking to hold fast to God's existence but an inner necessity of a *"theologia,"* particularly if it wants to be a *theologia negativa.*

39. L. Baeck, *Das Wesen des Judentums,* p. 31. Fromm advanced a similar formulation in a radio talk: "The goal is what the prophets called the full knowledge of God or, in non-theological language, that man fully develop his psychic powers, his

life and his reason, have his center within himself and be free to become what, as a human being, he is capable of becoming" (Fromm, "Die Aktualität der prophetischen Schriften" [1975d], p. 71). Fromm understands these sentences humanistically, although they could also form part of a doctrine of negative attributes and be understood (mono-)theistically.

40. Many statements by Jewish thinkers suggest a dissolution of religion in ethics. But in most instances, such a judgment can only be made when the concept of God is dissolved pantheistically, idealistically, materialistically, or naturalistically-humanistically, and this occurs *expressis verbis.* More often than not, it will become apparent that there only seems to be a dissolution of religion in ethics. Actually, identifying statements will turn out to be indissolubly linked to a negative theology of the One God that derives from the ban on images or at least to the postulate of an "idea of God." Concerning the relation between religion and ethics in Judaism, the following holds: the Jewish religion "values moral action most highly, it predicates only moral attributes of God, God is the God of the moral law. But an ethics without the belief in God does not exist for it . . . only in God does morality have its ground and its guarantee" (L. Baeck, *Das Wesen des Judentums,* p. 162).

41. On what follows, see H. Cohen, *Religion und Sittlichkeit; Der Begriff der Religion im System der Philosophie;* "Gesinnung" (1910) in *Der Nächste; Religion of Reason Out of the Sources of Judaism; Jüdische Schriften,* Vols. I, III, and introduction to Vol. I by Franz Rosenzweig; J. Guttmann, *Die Philosophie des Judentums,* pp. 345–362; *Religion und Wissenschaft im mittel alterlichen und modernen Denken;* H. van Oyen, *Hermann Cohen,* pp. 345–352; H. M. Graupe, *Die Entstehung des modernen Judentums,* pp. 295–305, and the bibliography on p. 295. The Kant interpretation in M. Lazarus, *Die Ethik des Judentums,* will not be discussed here; cf. the critique by H. Cohen, *Jüdische Schriften,* Vol. III, pp. 19f.

42. H. Cohen, *Jüdische Schriften,* Vol. III, p. 36.

43. H. Cohen, *Religion und Sittlichkeit,* p. 47.

44. H. Cohen, *Jüdische Schriften,* Vol. I, p. 294.

45. H. Cohen, *Religion und Sittlichkeit,* p. 34.

46. Hermann Cohen defines as myth a religion in which knowledge of God is more than morality. This also applies to Christianity (cf. *Religion und Sittlichkeit,* pp. 43ff).

47. Guttmann, *Die Philosophie des Judentums,* p. 350.

48. H. Cohen, *Religion of Reason,* p. 160.

49. Guttmann, *Die Philosophie des Judentums,* p. 349.

50. F. Rosenzweig, Einleitung XXXIII. Franz Rosenzweig emphatically rejects an understanding of the concept of idea in Cohen that sees in God "only an idea" and where God himself is viewed as no more than "a 'poetic expression' for the idea of God."

51. H. Cohen, *Jüdische Schriften,* Vol. I, p. 296; cf. "Gesinnung" in *Der Nächste,* pp. 8f.

52. H. Cohen, *Jüdische Schriften,* pp. 20f. Also in *Reason and Hope: Selections from the Jewish Writings of Hermann Cohen,* p. 221.

53. "Functional" here in contrast to "metaphysical." Cf. H. M. Graupe, *Die Entstehung des modernen Judentums,* pp. 300f.

54. H. Cohen, *Religion und Sittlichkeit,* p. 33.

55. That is the reason Hermann Cohen views Jewish monotheism as the most

persuasive example of a religion of reason and why the complete title of his posthumous work is *Religion of Reason Out of the Sources of Judaism.*

56. Cohen, *Religion of Reason,* p. 7.

57. Ibid., p. 12.

58. H. M. Graupe, *Die Entstehung des Modernen Judentums,* p. 301.

59. J. Guttmann, *Philosophie des Judentums,* p. 352.—In this phase of thought, the idea of God passed from religion to ethics, religion was perfected in ethics and Judaism found its philosophical justification in the eyes of H. Cohen (cf. ibid., p. 353).

60. For the first time in the essay "Der Begriff der Religion im System der Philosophie," published in 1915, and explicitly in *Religion of Reason.*

61. If this distinctive quality of religion has such weight that one would have to acknowledge religion's independence from ethical reason, it could no longer be a religion of reason (and Hermann Cohen's life work to show that the Jewish religion is a religion of reason would have failed), or one would have to postulate two autonomous kinds of reason (and Hermann Cohen would have to renounce his claim to be a philosopher) Cf. Cohen, *Religion of Reason,* pp. 12f.

62. J. Guttmann, *Philosophie des Judentums,* p. 354.

63. Cf. the demonstration of the distinctiveness of religion through the phenomenon of suffering and sin in Cohen, *Religion of Reason,* pp. 16–20.

64. H. Cohen, *Religion und Sittlichkeit,* p. 35; *Religion of Reason,* p. 20: "As man in ethics is merely an example of humanity, so God is only the guarantor of humanity."

65. H. Cohen, *Der Begriff der Religion im System der Philosophie,* p. 61.

66. H. Cohen, *Religion of Reason,* p. 86.

67. Ibid., p. 88.

68. "Revelation establishes the correlation of man and God" (ibid., p. 82). Revelation is implicit in creation because creation involves the creation of man as a rational being. That is the reason Cohen can write: "Revelation is the creation of reason" (ibid., p. 72).

69. Ibid., p. 82. Cohen specifically refers to the tradition of Jewish medieval philosophy: "The attempt of the Jewish philosophers of the Middle Ages to establish an accord between reason and revelation and therefore . . . the origin of revelation in reason, may be justifiably considered the legitimate continuation of monotheism."

70. Ibid., p. 105. Cf. also: "God and man have to remain separated, insofar as they are to be united" (ibid). It is by this idea of correlation that it can be most clearly shown that Fromm's concept of religion as a "mysticism of the ONE" differs fundamentally from Cohen's. Where Cohen looks for a philosophical solution, Fromm is a mystic, yet he does not have to renounce the fascination of a "religion of reason."

71. H. Cohen, *Der Begriff der Religion im System der Philosophie,* p. 66.

72. Ibid.

73. Ibid.

74. H. Cohen, *Religion of Reason,* p. 114.

75. Cf. Guttmann, *Philosophie des Judentums,* p. 356.

76. H. Cohen, *Der Begriff der Religion . . . ,* pp. 66f; cf. the criticism of Cohen's conception of reconciliation in J. Guttmann, *Philosophie des Judentums,* pp. 361f.

77. This attempt of a religion of reason is to be understood in the Kantian sense

"according to which philosophy not merely has to assign religion its place in the system of reason but also to derive it from reason" (Guttmann, *Philosophie des Judentums*, p. 360).

78. Cohen, *Religion of Reason*, p. 109.

79. Guttmann, *Philosophie des Judentums*, p. 361. Man's sufficiency to maintain his humanness for which the transcendence of God as "idea" is the necessary condition is based on "man's autonomous morality . . . which is achieved and not limited by the goal toward which, like any other human activity, it must aim" (Cohen, *Der Begriff der Religion im System der Philosophie*, p. 66).

80. Ibid.

81. Cf. Guttmann, *Religion und Wissenschaft im mittealterlichen und im modernen Denken*, p. 162.

82. Ibid.

83. It is in the relation between reason and revelation that one must see the essential difference between Jewish and Christian rationalism, for the Christian concept of revelation comprehends more than revelation and a natural religion that is accessible to reason. Traditionally speaking, the supernatural is posited along with the Christian concept of revelation so that "a distinction is to be made between the natural morality of reason and a higher level of the morality of grace" (Guttmann, *Religion und Wissenschaft*, p. 162; cf. pp. 155f, 174f, 185f).

84. Cf. ibid., p. 163.

85. Cf. H. J. Schoeps, *Geschichte der jüdischen Religionsphilosophie in der Neuzeit*, pp. 3–21.

86. Guttmann, *Die Philosophie des Judentums*, p. 360.

87. This is the subtitle of Fromm's *You Shall Be as Gods.*

88. *You Shall Be as Gods* (1966a), p. 13.

89. Cf. ibid., p. 5.

90. Cf. ibid., p. 13.

91. It is precisely the rationalistic interpretation of religion as morality that can ground ethos and ethics with the concept of God. But in Fromm's humanism where the critique of religion must ground man as moral being, another solution is required, and that is mysticism.

92. By this he means all attempts to mediate God and man. In this sense, he views Christianity as a relapse into myth that cultivates idolatry. Cf. H. Cohen, *Religion und Sittlichkeit*, pp. 32f; L. Baeck, *Das Wesen der Judentums*, pp. 92–95.

93. H. Cohen, *Der Begriff der Religion im System der Philosophie*, p. 66.

94. L. Baeck, *Das Wesen der Judentums*, p. 87. This is probably the correct characterization of the Jewish concept of religion and of the relation to God, which indicates that "moral optimism" has its base in this ethical monotheism.

95. G. Scholem, *Major Trends in Jewish Mysticism*, p. 7.

96. Ibid.

97. To what extent it is truly a new unity and not a regression to a unity prior to all disunity depends significantly on the degree to which myth plays a role as an uncritical monism of God, nature, and man.

98. On this, see *Major Trends*, p. 6f, where Scholem opposes a religio-philosophical view that argues for a "chemically pure mysticism."

99. R. Otto, "Geleitwort," IX.

100. Scholem, *Major Trends in Jewish Mysticism*, p. 10.

101. Charles Benett, *A Philosophical Study of Mysticism*, quoted by Scholem, *Major Trends*, p. 20. Scholem considers this an element of Jewish mysticism,

although *mutatis mutandis* it is also true of Buddhism, even though that religion is not tied to a theory of history.

102. On the question whether the philosophical presentation of Jewish monotheism gave rise to the Kabbala or not, see Scholem, *Major Trends in Jewish Mysticism*, p. 23f.

103. Cf. ibid., pp. 37–39.

104. Ibid., p. 13.

105. Ibid.

106. In contrast to the German Hasidism of the Middle Ages.

107. On what follows, cf. especially M. Buber, *Der grosse Maggid und seine Nachfolger; Hasidism; Der Chassidismus und die Krise des abendländischen Menschen*, pp. 83–94; *Der Weg des Menschen nach der chassidischen Lehre;* S. Dubnow, *Geschichte des Chassidismus*, 2 vols.; *Weltgeschichte des jüdischen Volkes;* L. Gulkowitsch, *Der Hasidismus, religionswissenschaftlich untersucht;* S. A. Horodezky, *Religiöse Strömungen im Judentum. Mit besonderer Berücksichtigung des Chassidismus;* S. Hurwitz, *Archetypische Motive in der chassidischen Mystik*, pp. 121–212; P. Levertoff, *Die religiöse Denkweise der Chassidim nach den Quellen;* W. Rabinowitsch, *Der Karliner Chassidismus. Seine Geschichte und seine Lehre;* G. Scholem, *Major Trends in Jewish Mysticism.*

108. S. Dubnow, *Weltgeschichte des jüdischen Volkes*, Vol. II, p. 466, views Habad Hasidism as a system of thought "that strove for a synthesis of Bescht and Maimonides, as it were" ("Bescht" stands for Israel Baal Shem Tov, the founder of Hasidism). In contrast to Simon Dubnow, Martin Buber sees Habad Hasidism as a "synthesis of Hasidism and rabbinism."

109. On the historical data, cf. G. Scholem, *Major Trends in Jewish Mysticism*, pp. 324f; on messianism, cf. Scholem, *The Messianic Idea in Judaism and Other Essays in Jewish Spirituality;* on the link between Sabbatianism and Hasidism, *Major Trends*, pp. 330f.

110. Scholem, *Major Trends*, p. 329. Fromm's criticism of Scholem on the question of the significance of messianism in Hasidism (*You Shall Be as Gods* [1966a], p. 148) is really superfluous when one considers the context of Scholem's remark. He does not propose to dispute the messianic element in Hasidism but merely observes that Hasidism eliminated a personified messianism and differs in that respect from Sabbatianism.

111. Already with the death of the Baal Shem Tov (1760), but especially after the death of his successor, Rabbi Baer in 1772, so-called Zaddikism developed in which the successors as the only true Zaddikim were elevated to the position of mediators of the experience of God. Mystical immediacy was increasingly personified, and by virtue of their mediating role, the Zaddikim became the objects of a despotic cult. See Dubnow, *Weltgeschichte des jüdischen Volkes*, Vol. II, pp. 462–466; and his *Geschichte des Chassidismus*, Vol. II, pp. 278f. Habad Hasidism, which was founded by Shneur Zalman, was the only countermovement.

112. Scholem, *Major Trends in Jewish Mysticism*, p. 336.

113. L. Gulkowitsch, *Der Hasidismus*, p. 48. The story of the divine sparks originated in late kabbalistic cosmogony and doctrine of creation (cf. Scholem, *Major Trends*). The Lurianic Kabbala (so called after Isaac Luria, the most prominent representative of the so-called Safed Kabbala who settled in Palestine around 1570) teaches in the doctrine of the "breaking of the vessels" that "we have to assume that the divine light which flowed into primordial space—of which three dimensional space is a late development—unfolded in various stages and appeared under a

variety of aspects. . . . Since however the divine scheme of things involved the creation of finite beings and forms, each with its own allotted place in the ideal hierarchy, it was necessary that these isolated lights should be caught and preserved in special 'bowls' created—or rather emanated—for this particular purpose" (*Major Trends,* p. 265). Where the divine light manifests itself, it becomes visible under ten aspects that are called "Sefirot." They are visible only to the human eye, but in them, undifferentiated God makes himself accessible to man (cf. S. Hurwitz, *Archetypische Motive in der chassidischen Mystik,* pp. 141f). While those bowls that corresponded to the three highest Sefirot could "give shelter to" the light, the other vessels broke: "The impact proved too much for the vessels which were broken and shattered" (*Major Trends,* p. 265). "The breaking of the bowls . . . is the cause of that inner deficiency which is inherent in everything that exists and which persists as long as the damage is not mended. For when the bowls were broken . . . the fiendish nether worlds of evil, the influence of which crept into all stages of the cosmological process, emerged from the fragments. . . . In this way, the good elements of the divine order came to be mixed with the vicious ones. Conversely, the restoration of the ideal order, which forms the original aim of creation, is also the secret purpose of existence" (*Major Trends,* p. 268).

114. M. Buber, *The Origin and Meaning of Hasidism,* pp. 238–239.

115. On the kabbalistic interpretation of the *Shekhina,* cf. especially Scholem, *Major Trends,* pp. 229–233.

116. Cf. Gulkowitsch, *Der Hasidismus,* p. 35.

117. *Major Trends,* p. 275.

118. Cf. Scholem, *The Messianic Idea in Judaism,* p. 43: Isaac Luria, who died in 1572, at the age of thirty-eight, in Palestine, "did not have the gift of the pen" and is known to posterity primarily by the presentation of his system by his disciple Hayim Vital. Cf. *Major Trends,* p. 253.

119. B'eer mayim chayim, quoted from S. A. Horodezky, *Religiöse Strömungen im Judentum,* p. 61.

120. M. Buber, *Hasidism,* p. 27. This interpretation also gives the breaking of the vessels a positive meaning, as is shown in the following comparison, which is mentioned by Rabbi Salomo von Luzk (a disciple of the Bescht disciple Rabbi Baer) in his *Magid debarav le-Jakob,* and conveys an idea of the simplicity of the metaphorical language of Hasidism. "When a tailor, for example, cuts up a large piece of cloth into delicate smaller pieces, the ignorant can view that as harmful but those who know that these pieces are needed to make a sleeve or such-like will understand that there was no other way except to cut up the whole. Thus, in the beginning, there was only He, the Blessed, but later he created worlds. . . . A breaking must occur so that the light may be known" (quoted from S. A. Horodezky, *Religiöse Strömungen im Judentum,* p. 80).

121. M. Buber, *Hasidism,* p. 55.

122. Ibid., p. 57.

123. On the history of this concept, cf. Scholem, *Major Trends* and *Die Lehre vom 'Gerechten' in der jüdischen Mystik,* pp. 239f; Nissan Mindel, *Rabbi Shneur Zalman,* p. 271, adopts the definition of Habad Hasidism that the Zohar gives. Accordingly, that individual is a Zaddik "who deals benevolently with his creator."

124. Cf. P. Levertoff, *Die religiöse Denkweise der Chassidim,* p. 34.

125. Cf. M. Buber, *Der Hassidismus und die Krise des abendländischen Menschen,* p. 87. In this contribution, which also describes his changed position on Hasidism, Buber rejects the misunderstanding that this view of sanctification is the same as self-redemption (pp. 87f).

126. M. Buber, *Hasidism,* p. 63.

127. L. Gulkowitsch, *Der Hasidismus,* p. 50. Simon Dubnow vigorously attacks this view. As an antipode of Buber's, he considers Hasidism a perversion. After six hundred pages on the topic, he comes to the following conclusion: "There is thus justification for the observation that Hasidism shifted the focus of religion from morality to faith. . . . The new Hasidim understood the principle of unity with God to be no more than a mystical marriage of the human soul with its creator which could be accomplished through prayer, ecstasis, and by taking one's thoughts back to their original source" (S. Dubnow, *Weltgeschichte des judischen Volkes,* Vol. II, p. 277). With this view, Dubnow stands at the end of an interpretation of Hasidism that was widespread in the nineteenth century and which judged it primarily by its flawed development in Zaddikism and the Zaddikim cult. But see Scholem, *Major Trends,* pp. 342ff.

128. M. Buber, *Hasidism,* p. 56.

129. Ibid., p. 57.

130. Ibid., p. 158.

131. Scholem who, in connection with a phrase in Buber's first book on Hasidism speaks of Hasidism as "the Kabbala become ethos," also feels that this formulation captures the specifically Hasidic.

132. By and large, the literature on Habad Hasidism is either unsatisfactory or exists only in Hebrew. Simon Dubnow's presentation (*Geschichte des Chassidismus,* Vol. II, esp. pp. 100–115) is ignorant of the Kabbala and the concerns of mysticism generally; S. A. Horodezky, *Religiöse Strömungen im Judentum,* pp. 174–178, does not provide much more than some general information. W. Rabinowitsch, *Der Karliner Chassidismus,* deals with Habad Hasidism only secondarily but furnishes much historical material on the life of Shneur Zalman, among other things. This life is also treated in Dubnow, *Geschichte des Chassidismus,* pp. 92–99. There is a very extensive, although uncritical, discussion of the life in N. Mindel, *Rabbi Shneur Zalman of Ladi.* The following comments rely primarily on Rabbi Shneur Zalman, *Liqqutei Amarim* (*Tanya*), Vol. I, and the introduction by Nissan Mindel; M. Buber, *Der grosse Maggid und seine Nachfolger,* pp. lxxiv–lxxvii; and *Hasidism;* Scholem, *Major Trends;* Hurwitz, *Archetypische Motive in der chassidischen Mystik.*

133. M. Buber, *Der grosse Maggid und seine Nachfolger LXXV.* This is the basis for the much quoted rationalism of the Habad school. Actually, Shneur Zalman seeks a balance between kabbalistic mysticism and rabbinical scholarship.

134. *Major Trends,* p. 340.

135. Ibid., p. 341.

136. Ibid. Cf. N. Mindel, introduction, *Liqqutei Amarim* (*Tanya*), Vol. I, p. xviii: "Such basic beliefs as the Existence of G-d, *creatio ex nihilo,* Revelation, and others, are taken for granted by the author. Others, such as the Divine attributes, Providence, Unity, Messianism, etc., are treated as integral parts of his ethical system, and illuminated by the light of Qabbalah."

137. Ibid., p. xiv.

138. Shneur Zalman, *Liqqutei Amarim,* pp. 22f.

139. Ibid., p. 24.

140. Ibid., p. 30, n. 1.

141. Ibid., pp. 30f.

142. S. Dubnow, *Geschichte des Chassidismus,* p. 106.

143. This is Shneur's etymological explanation of the concept *hokhmah;* cf. *Liqqutei Amarim,* pp. 31, 110, and the variant pp. 274f.

144. *Liqqutei Amarim,* p. 111. S. Hurwitz, *Archetypische Motive in der chassidis-*

chen Mystik, interprets *hokhma* according to texts by the Maggid of Mezritsh as unconsciousness in the human realm whereas *bina* is consciousness. In the divine realm, as *sophia,* it is a kind of elemental spiritual substance.

145. *Liqqutei Amarim,* p. 32.

146. Cf. S. Hurwitz, *Archetypische Motive in der chassidischen Mystik,* p. 143f.

147. Ibid., p. 143.

148. *Liqqutei Amarim,* p. 33.

149. See p. 118f.

150. *Liqqutei Amarim,* p. 267.

151. Ibid., p. 33.

152. The *middot* are the seven action attributes of God, which the Kabbala understands as aspects (Sefirot) of the En Sof. In man, the *middot* are the seven emotional attributes of the soul. Cf. N. Mindel, *Liqqutei Amarim* (*Tanya*), Glossary and Notes, pp. 343f.

153. *Liqqutei Amarim,* p. 33.

154. S. Hurwitz, *Archetypische Motive in der chassidischen Mystik,* p. 143.

155. Cf. Hurwitz' attempt to show a parallel between kabbalistic speculation and psychological insight. "One might say that from our perspective, the development of man's consciousness from the unconscious appears as a kind of refraction or reflection of the development of divine reason (*bina*) from divine wisdom (*hokhma*). In this way, the human soul is made worthy of becoming a mirror image of a drama within the divinity, just as conversely a differentiation of the divine image corresponds to man's becoming conscious" (ibid., p. 201).

156. *Liqqutei Amarim,* p. 34.

157. Ibid., p. 35.

158. Ibid., p. 40; cf. p. 325.

159. Cf. ibid., pp. 45f.

160. Cf. ibid., pp. 47f, 29, 126.

161. On this, cf. especially Shneur Zalman's doctrine of Tsimtsum (*Liqqutei Amarim,* chaps. 48, 49, and chap. 6, p. 48), and Luria's doctrine of Tsimtsum (Scholem, *Major Trends,* pp. 260–265). On Luria's *qelipot* doctrine, cf. *Major Trends,* p. 268; on the Hasidic *qelipot* doctrine, *Liqqutei,* pp. 136–143.

162. Cf. Shneur Zalman, *Liqqutei,* p. 312, where the overcoming of evil is declared to be the purpose of creation: "The purpose of all the 'contractions' is the creation of the material human body and the subjugation of the *sitra ahra,* to bring about the pre-eminence of light supplanting darkness. . . ."

163. Ibid., p. 49.

164. Ibid., p. 52.

165. Ibid., pp. 22–24.

166. On this and what follows, cf. ibid., pp. 62f.

167. Dubnow, *Geschichte des Chassidismus,* vol. II, p. 107.

168. Shneur Zalman, *Liqqutei Amarim,* pp. 63f.

169. Ibid., p. 66.

170. Cf. the comments on Habad reason, pp. 200–201.

171. Shneur Zalman, *Liqqutei Amarim,* p. 325.

172. Ibid., p. 68.

173. Cf. ibid., pp. 68–70.

174. Cf. ibid., pp. 73–76.

175. Ibid., p. 77. The meaning of the last part of the quotation becomes clear when the divine soul in the body is assigned specific "loci" where it manifests itself,

such as the brain (thought), mouth (speech), and the other 248 members (action) that correspond to the 248 commandments of the Torah.

176. The heart is primarily the seat of the affects, and the left ventricle of the heart the locus of the animal soul.

177. Shneur Zalman, *Liqqutei Amarim,* p. 99.

178. Ibid.

179. Ibid., p. 343, as the quotation of a formulation by Buber.

180. Scholem, *Major Trends,* p. 341.

181. Fromm mentions Hasidism only in his discussion of the messianic idea (cf. *You Shall Be as Gods* [1966a], pp. 148–152), but hardly elsewhere. Since Habad Hasidism probably had a considerable influence through the socialist and Habadnik Schneur Salman Rabinkov when Fromm was a student and still a practicing Orthodox Jew—an influence Fromm confirmed in conversations with the author—it is probably for personal reasons connected with his turn away from Orthodox Judaism that Jewish mysticism, and Hasidism in particular, found so little resonance in his literary output. Up to a point, the interest in Hasidic psychology expressed itself in Fromm's study of Spinoza's *Ethics.* The mere fact that over a period of years, Fromm held seminars on Spinoza's *Ethics* in the United States, in which he did not deal with the ontology in Books I and II but rather with the psychological material in Books III to V suggests a survival of his interest in Hasidic psychology, considering that there is an extensive kinship between Shneur Zalman's psychology, which is written in the language of the Kabbala, and Spinoza's psychology, which is written in the language of Scholasticism. Since the focus of these comments is ideas and their reception insofar as they had a direct influence on Fromm's thought, a discussion of connections to Spinoza's thought was considered unnecessary.

182. This applies only on the basis of a humanistic interpretation, however, since for Shneur Zalman, the secular sciences sully the divine soul (cf. *Liqqutei Amarim,* pp. 57–61).

183. Cf. Fromm, *You Shall Be as Gods* (1966a), p. 115, where these words introduce a section.

184. Fromm understood his *Beyond the Chains of Illusion* (1962a) as an intellectual autobiography in which, in addition to Sigmund Freud, Karl Marx is assigned a dominant place.

185. *Beyond the Chains of Illusion* (1962a), p. 12; cf. pp. 17 and 25f.

186. Fromm, "Introduction" (1965b), VII.

187. Fromm, *Marx's Concept of Man* (1961b), p. 63. Cf. *To Have or to Be?* (1976a), p. 202.

188. *Marx's Concept of Man* (1961b), p. 6. The tragedy of this misunderstanding also lies in the fact that in some political circles in the West this false interpretation is considered to be Marxist in its very essence, a misunderstanding that contributes to the falsification of Marx's theories. This reproach must also be leveled at Western social democracies insofar as their program of an increase in the "quality of life" simply aims at a maximization of consumption and misinterprets "materialism" as greater material well-being (cf. ibid., pp. 2–5). See also Fromm, "Problems of Interpreting Marx" (1965d); *To Have or to Be?* (1976a), pp. 158–160.

189. H. Steiner gives a critical and informative discussion of these schools of Marx interpretation; see *Marxisten-Leninisten über den Sinn des Lebens. Eine Studie zum kommunistischen Menschenbild.*

190. P. Vranicki, *Geschichte des Marxismus,* provides a comprehensive overview

of the history of Marxism. Cf. in Vol. 2, pp. 865–877, the only correct presentation of Fromm's philosophical anthropology to have appeared in German. W. Post, *Kritik der Religion bei Karl Marx,* reports on the present state of Marx research, pp. 16–70. There are also suggestions for further reading on p. 16. The volume *Neomarxismus,* however, which was published in the series *Kolleg Philosophie* by A. von Weiss, contains little that is of help, even though the book shows a good knowledge of Marxist movements in the United States (pp. 92–95) and is aware of Fromm's importance to the reception of Marx in the United States.

191. But there are also significant differences within this group of Marx interpreters. W. Post, *Kritik der Religion bei Karl Marx,* p. 90, n. 52, and pp. 90ff, tries to divide the various types of interpretation of the earliest Marx texts and early writings into six groups. This list of types of interpretation could be supplemented by the attempts that discover Marx the Jew in the early writings. A. Massiczek, *Der menschliche Mensch. Karl Marx' jüdischer Humanismus,* esp. p. 476, is exemplary here. The interpreters are judged by whether they respect Marx's affinity with the Jewish prophets.

192. Fromm, *Marx's Concept of Man* (1961b), pp. 69–79. R. Wiegand, *Gesellschaft und Charakter,* p. 345, believes that *Grundrisse,* first published in Moscow in 1939, is the connecting link between the young and the "mature" Marx.

193. Alfred Schmidt, who was director of the Frankfurt Institute for Social Research for a while, is representative of this group. In what follows, *Der Begriff der Natur in der Lehre von Marx* will represent that type of Marx interpretation that contrasts with Fromm's.

194. *Beyond the Chains of Illusion* (1962a), p. 142. Cf. "The Application of Humanist Psychoanalysis to Marx's Theory," (1965e), pp. 207f. A Gebö, *Der entfremdete Marx. Zur existentialistisch-'humanistischen' Marximus-Deutung,* opposes this view of Fromm's.

195. Sv́etozar Stojanović, Gajo Petrović, and Mihailo Marković are especially noteworthy. The latter two contributed one article each to the *Festschrift* honoring Fromm's seventieth birthday: G. Petrović, "Humanism and Revolution," pp. 288–298; and M. Marković, "The Possibilities for Radical Humanism," pp. 275–287.

196. Cf. Adam Schaff's contribution to the Fromm *Festschrift,* "What Does It Mean to 'Be a Marxist' "?; and Schaff, *Marxismus und das menschliche Individuum,* esp. pp. 220ff, 322ff; Schaff, "Marxism and the Philosophy of Man" in Fromm, *Socialist Humanism* (1965a).

197. *Das Prinzip Hoffnung,* Bloch *Gesamtausgabe,* Vol. 5. See also the very extensive Marx interpretation by A. Massiczek, *Der menschliche Mensch. Karl Marx' jüdischer Humanismus,* p. 25.

198. Especially *La Pensée de Karl Marx.* Calvez' study continues a tradition of "religious socialism" whose most prominent representative was Paul Tillich. Cf. the essays by Theodor Steinbüchel on Marx interpretation, which have been published in Alfons Auer's *Sozialismus,* a collection of essays.

199. Cf. H. Rolfes, *Der Sinn des Lebens im marxistischen Denken,* p. 29.

200. K. Marx, preface to the second edition of *Capital,* p. 25.

201. Cf. Marx, "Die deutsche Ideologie," *MEGA* I, 5, 29.

202. K. Marx, "Die heilige Familie," *MEGA* I, 3, 370.

203. W. Post, *Kritik der Religion bei Karl Marx,* p. 301.

204. Th. Steinbüchel, "Karl Marx. Gestalt-Werk-Ethos," p. 13; also "Zur philosophischen Grundlegung des marxistischen Sozialismus," pp. 63–65.

205. H. Rolfes, *Der Sinn des Lebens im marxistischen Denken,* pp. 35f. Rolfes calls this view of Marx "anthropological attitude to reality" (p. 36).

206. P. Tillich, *Christentum und Marxismus,* p. 175. On the differentiation of this concept of materialism from others, cf. Marx, *Die heilige Familie;* and Calvez, *La Pensée de Karl Marx,* pp. 325–330.

207. K. Marx, "On the Jewish Question" in *Early Writings,* p. 234; cf. *Early Writings,* p. 356: "A being sees himself as independent only when he stands on his own feet, and he only stands on his own feet when he owes his existence to himself."

208. Cf. W. Post, *Kritik der Religion bei Karl Marx,* p. 301.

209. Ibid, a formulation of Jürgen Habermas.

210. Ibid.

211. "Private property here means what is based on exploitation and increases man's alienation more and more by reducing to the one meaning of having the multiform relations man has to objects" (Rolfes, *Der Sinn des Lebens im marxistischen Denken,* p. 63).

212. W. Post, *Kritik der Religion bei Karl Marx,* p. 302.

213. Marx, *Early Writings,* p. 348. This quotation from the Paris Manuscripts of 1844 may be considered the confession of faith of the "humanistic" Marx interpreters.

214. W. Post, *Kritik der Religion bei Karl Marx,* p. 302.

215. On the concept of "history," see pp. 70–72; on alienation, see pp. 73–74; on "nature and man," pp. 55–58.

216. On what follows, cf. especially A. Schmidt, *Der Begriff der Natur in der Lehre von Marx.*

217. W. Post, *Kritik der Religion bei Karl Marx,* p. 180.

218. A. Schmidt, *Der Begriff der Natur in der Lehre von Karl Marx,* p. 26f. Fromm also believes that the goal and meaning of history must be posited by man. But because man is defined as contradictory being, the goal of history becomes a new unity with nature. On this matter and on what follows, cf. W. Post, *Kritik der Religion bei Marx,* pp. 240–248, and J.-Y. Calvez, *La Pensée de Karl Marx,* pp. 446–454.

219. Cf. A. Schmidt, *Der Begriff der Natur in der Lehre von Karl Marx,* pp. 109–110.

220. K. Marx, *MEGA* I, 3, p. 114.

221. A. Schmidt, *Der Begriff der Natur in der Lehre von Karl Marx,* p. 117.

222. Ibid., p. 137.

223. Ibid., p. 120.

224. Cf. especially Calvez, *La Pensée de Karl Marx,* pp. 78–82; Rolfes, *Der Sinn des Lebens im marxistischen Denken,* pp. 47–66; W. Post, *Kritik der Religion bei Marx,* pp. 91–103.

225. W. Post, *Kritik,* p. 110.

226. H. Rolfes, *Der Sinn des Lebens im marxistischen Denken,* p. 42.

227. See above, p. 000, and the comments on alienation as idolatry.

228. L. Feuerbach, *Das Wesen des Christentums,* p. 33.

229. Cf. H. Rolfes, *Der Sinn des Lebens im marxistischen Denken,* p. 42f.

230. K. Marx, "Anekdota zur neuesten deutschen Philosophie und Publizistik" (1942), quoted in Post, *Kritik,* p. 89. On the authenticity of this article, see p. 88, n. 48. More recently the essay containing the quotation, "Luther als Schiedsrichter zwischen Strauss und Feuerbach," has also been ascribed to Feuerbach himself.

231. K. Marx, "Critique of Hegel's 'Philosophy of Right,'" in *Early Writings,* p. 244.

232. Ibid.

233. Ibid. Cf. Marx, *Early Writings*, p. 349: "Religious estrangement as such takes place only in the sphere of consciousness, of man's inner life, but economic estrangement is that of real life—its supersession therefore embraces both aspects."

234. This is the reason Marx is not interested in atheism as a criticism of religion. For atheism always addresses itself to the religious individual. "Precisely because of its peculiar humanism," Jean-Yves Calvez sees Marxism as atheistic (*Karl Marx*, p. 455). But he also feels that Marxism is a practical atheism, for "Marx's humanism is the overcoming of abstract humanism and of theoretical atheism" (p. 461). Cf. also Rolfes, *Der Sinn des Lebens*, pp. 39f, 77–97.

235. Calvez, *Karl Marx*, p. 53.

236. Marx, "Critique of Hegel's Philosophy of Right, Introduction," in *Early Writings*, p. 244. Cf. W. Post, *Kritik der Religion bei Karl Marx*, pp. 170–172.

237. Cf. Post, *Kritik*, p. 112. Cf. Calvez, *Karl Marx*, on the further development of the criticism of religion into a criticism of philosophy and of politics on the basis of an insight into man's philosophical and political alienation. Cf. W. Post, *Kritik*, pp. 73–183; Rolfes, *Der Sinn des Lebens im marxistischen Denken*, pp. 45–50.

238. Cf. Marx, *Early Writings*, p. 328: ". . . free conscious activity constitutes the species-character of man."

239. On this dispute in the "Anti-Dühring," see A. Schmidt, *Der Begriff der Natur in der Lehre von Karl Marx*, p. 115f.

240. K. Marx, *Das Kapital*, Vol. III, p. 828.

241. Ibid.

242. Marx, *Early Writings*, p. 348.

243. This is the way the characterizations "humanistic" and "anthropological" Marx are to be understood.

244. The scientific tool for the empirical investigation of psychic peculiarities is not discovered until Freud develops his psychoanalytical method.

245. On this, see especially Fromm, "Marx's Contribution to the Knowledge of Man" (1968h).

246. Cf. Marx, *Early Writings*, pp. 358ff, e.g.

247. Cf. Marx, "Die deutsche Ideologie," pp. 344–349.

248. See p. 56f.

249. Cf. Marx, *Early Writings*, p. 328: "But productive life is species-life. It is life-producing life. The whole character of a species, its species-character, resides in the nature of its life activity, and free conscious activity constitutes the species-character of man."

250. Cf. Marx, *Early Writings*, pp. 345f.

251. Cf. above, Fromm's character theory, pp. 27–54.

252. See pp. 18–22, the comments on the "social character," and especially Fromm, "The Application of Humanist Psychoanalysis to Marx's Theory" (1965c), pp. 210–214.

253. Cf. W. Post, *Kritik*, pp. 304f.

254. Cf. A. Massiczek, *Der menschliche Mensch*, pp. 566–570.; and Marx's statements themselves in *Early Writings*, pp. 357f.

255. Marx, *Early Writings*, p. 244. On the expression "opium of the people," cf. H. Gollwitzer, "Die marxistische Religionskritik und der christliche Glaube," pp. 23–28.

256. W. Post, *Kritik*, p. 304.

257. Cf. e.g., "alienation" instead of the theological concept "sin," or "true man" instead of "saved man," etc.

258. In his talk, "Gibt es eine Ethik ohne Religiosität," given on the occasion of the symposium honoring Fromm's seventy-fifth birthday in May 1975 in Locarno, A. Auer therefore rightly asks if this use of language was not designed to take advantage of the "surplus value" of traditional ideas.

259. Cf. Schmidt, *Der Begriff der Natur in der Lehre von Karl Marx,* p. 29: "In the concept of God, Marx sees the abstract expression of domination, always connected with a dogmatic, antecedent, unitary meaning of the world as a whole" (the concept "abstract" is to be understood negatively). Cf. W. Post, *Kritik,* p. 198f.

260. Marx, *Early Writings,* p. 356.

261. Here we have much of the reason for Fromm's aversion to all dogmatic belief. A criticism of statements concerning religious belief would mean that religion is being taken seriously in more than in its function to deceive man about his true situation. At a deeper level, the reason for Marx's and Fromm's aversion must be looked for in their rootedness in specifically Jewish traditions in which a disinclination against making any kind of theological statement was cultivated. Cf. the comments on the doctrine of negative attributes, pp. 181–188, and A. Massiczek, *Der Menschliche Mensch,* pp. 570–574.

262. H. Gollwitzer, "Die Marxistische Religionskritik und der christliche Glaube," p. 37; in line with Fromm's terminology, religion here is always to be understood as authoritarian religion.

263. W. Post, *Kritik der Religion bei Marx,* p. 305; cf. Werner Post's criticism (pp. 304–309) of this indifference of Karl Marx toward the contents of religion.

264. K. Marx, *Early Writings,* p. 357.

265. Ibid.

266. Cf. Fromm, *The Sane Society* (1955a), p. 235f.

267. This does not mean that Fromm came to a definitive conclusion regarding the problem of religion. The comments below will show that Fromm's understanding differs from Marx's in the sense that with the religio-critical grounding of humanism, the problem of religion arises again as a question concerning a humanistic religion. Both are concerned with the grounding of humanism in a critique of theistic = authoritarian = heteronomous religions whose end in history both believed to have occurred with the Enlightenment.

268. It is in this way that Fromm's efforts to interpret humanistically the religious traditions of the Old Testament, Buddhism, the Vedas, and the mysticism especially of Meister Eckhart must be legitimated. *To Have or to Be?* (1976a) represents a culmination of these efforts. Cf. the concluding part of this study.

269. Marx, *Early Writings,* p. 357.

270. Ibid., p. 356. Fromm believes that Buddhism realizes the same insight. Both the Buddha and Karl Marx are concerned with a "radical knowledge" that, as an encompassing "science of man," studies human existence. On this, cf. Fromm, "Fromm contra Auer," p. 3, and the present work, p. 133f.

271. See for detail pp. 119–128.

272. Fromm, *Marx's Concept of Man* (1961b), p. 64. Those who classify "Marx statements about religion . . . as (conscious) criticism and (unconscious) adoption of religious, especially Jewish and Christian elements," arrive at a similar result when they infer from this distinction "that Marx's teaching is a 'religion without God.' " (W. Post, *Kritik,* p. 279). Examples would be Th. Steinbüchel, "Karl Marx: Gestalt—Werk—Ethos," pp. 28–34; and A. Massiczek, *Der menschliche Mensch,* pp. 466–508.

273. This view cannot remain altogether uncontradicted. Karl Marx does not wish to make man into God but: "The criticism of religion ends with the doctrine

that for man, the supreme being is man, and thus with the categorical imperative to overthrow all conditions in which man is a debased, enslaved, neglected and contemptible being—conditions that are best described in the exclamation of a Frenchman on the occasion of a proposed tax on dogs: Poor dogs! They want to treat you like human beings" (*Early Writings*, p. 251); cf. also W. Post, *Kritik*, pp. 171f.

274. K. Marx, *Early Writings*, p. 244; cf. Gollwitzer, "Die marxistische Religionskritik," p. 66–71.

275. Cf. W. Post, *Kritik*, pp. 257–259; 304.

276. K. Marx, *Early Writings*, p. 243.

277. J.-Y. Calvez also criticizes Marx on this point and sees the root for the idea that every division in man must be abolished in the "postulate of identity and immanence" that German Idealism adopted. But this criticism does not apply to Fromm because with the postulate of a humanistic religion, he understands man's perfect form and man's history as a "presentist eschatology."

278. Fromm (*Marx's Concept of Man* [1961b], p. 64; cf. *To Have or To Be?* [1976a], p. 165) feels that because of how he views socialism, one can speak of a "religious" Marx who can be discovered behind all the criticism of religion. This would mean that what Fromm calls "humanistic religion" is contained in a manner of speaking in Marx's concept of "socialism," and that Marx's concept of religion would be equated with Fromm's concept of authoritarian religion. To judge the legitimacy of such an interpretation, a distinction would have to be made between an interpretation of Marx's ideas as reflecting a specific historical horizon, and an interpretation of his thought from a historical distance in which Marx's approaches are developed. Fromm's contribution to the interpretation of Marx lies along the latter line. But in the first type of interpretation, one would have to inquire why Marx showed scant interest in the development of a "religious" socialism, and why this interest decreased with advancing age.

279. A critical judgment of theology and religion can therefore call their role "ideology." For "ideology is . . . theory that bears no relation to how things really are, is camouflage of actual conditions, pseudo-autonomy of consciousness, the faithful reflection of untrue praxis, in short, ideology simulates rational insights where, because social processes are opaque, alienated and wrong, practical and theoretical irrationality predominates" (W. Post, *Kritik*, p. 233). Socialism strives to overcome ideology and idolatry because it is antiauthoritarian as regards both the state and the Church (cf. Fromm, *Marx's Concept of Man* [1961b], p. 68).

280. The fact that it has become necessary once again to think about religion does not mean that there is a need to regress to Feuerbach's critique of religion, as R. Xirau intimates in his contribution to the Fromm *Festschrift* (see "What Is Man's Struggle?").

281. In this context, we will merely allude to the controversial Marx interpretation that is associated with this observation. It seems plausible that those interpreters whose concern is the "economic" Marx will tend to feel that the stringency of Marx's materialist approach is better and more easily preserved when one confines oneself to the economic discoveries and changes. It is equally plausible that there is a danger in codifying certain insights into a Marxist orthodoxy.

Fromm's interpretation of the "humanistic" Marx, on the other hand, derives its legitimation from the serious consideration of man's psyche and the postulate of a humanistic religion. With this postulate, Fromm enlarges the understanding of Marx and can rightfully refer to the Marx of the *Early Writings* in so doing.

282. K. Marx, *Early Writings*, p. 357.

CHAPTER 7. FORMS OF FROMM'S THOUGHT

1. See the following studies by E. Topitsch: *Vom Ursprung und Ende der Metaphysik*, esp. pp. 280–313; *Seelenglaube und Selbstinterpretation*, esp. pp. 193–199; *Marxismus und Gnosis*, esp. pp. 258–268; *Über Leerformeln; Atheismus und Naturrecht*. Cf. the dissertation by Michael Schmid, *Leerformeln und Ideologiekritik*, which does not advance our knowledge of the matter, especially since the author distanced himself from a number of his statements when the study was published.

2. E. Topitsch, *Über Leerformeln*, pp. 233f.

3. Cf. ibid., p. 237; and *Vom Ursprung und Ende der Metaphysik*, pp. 282f.

4. E. Topitsch, *Atheismus und Naturrecht*, p. 126.

5. E. Topitsch, *Über Leerformeln*, p. 234.

6. On the sociomorphous and technomorphous conceptual model, cf. especially E. Topitsch, *Vom Ursprung und Ende der Metaphysik*.

7. Topitsch, *Über Leerformeln*, p. 235.

8. Ibid. Cf. *Seelenglaube und Selbstinterpretation*, p. 193: "Accordingly, mythical cosmology already has principally three functions: an empirical-pragmatic one, an ethical-political one, and an aesthetic-contemplative one."

9. *Über Leerformeln*, p. 233.

10. Cf. ibid., p. 236.

11. E. Topitsch, *Marxismus und Gnosis*, p. 266.

12. Cf. *Über Leerformeln*, pp. 237f.

13. Cf. ibid., pp. 263f.

14. Cf. ibid., p. 233.

15. Cf. T. Adorno, "Der Positivismusstreit in der deutschen Soziologie," for a critique of Neopositivism from a philosophical, theological-ethical perspective; cf. W. Korff, *Norm und Sittlichkeit*, pp. 25f, 34.

16. Cf. Topitsch, *Marxismus und Gnosis*, p. 266.

17. On the concept "reality," as used by Topitsch, cf., e.g., the use of "immediate reality" (*unmittelbare Wirklichkeit*) and "original reality" (*ursprüngliche Wirklichkeit*) in *Seelenglaube und Selbstinterpretation*, pp. 198f. In contrast to a concept of reality that is reductionist and limited to facticity or cognizable reality, see the understanding of reality as "being that presses toward unfolding and perfection," in A. Auer, *Autonome Moral und christlicher Glaube*, p. 35.

18. Cf. pp. 55–66 and 133–136.

19. Topitsch, *Seelenglaube und Selbstinterpretation*, p. 172. On the historical development of shamanism and its influence on Indian and Western thought, see ibid., pp. 172–175, 181–187.

20. Topitsch, *Marxismus und Gnosis*, p. 240.

21. Ibid., p. 240, where he speaks of a "philosophical process of rationalization."

22. Ibid., p. 242, and *Seelenglaube und Selbstinterpretation*, p. 187.

23. *Seelenglaube und Selbstinterpretation*, pp. 187f.

24. Ibid., p. 288, and *Marxismus und Gnosis*, pp. 242f.

25. *Marxismus und Gnosis*, p. 243. Following H.-Ch. Puech, Topitsch therefore calls this gnostic doctrine "transforming mysticism" (p. 243, n. 24).

26. *Seelenglaube und Selbstinterpretation*, p. 187.

27. Ibid., p. 288.

28. *Marxismus und Gnosis*, p. 245. Here Topitsch reports reflections that are to be found in Jakob Taubes, *Abendländische Eschatologie*, pp. 31–40. They are based on ideas in Hans Leisegang, *Denkformen*, and represent Taubes' effort to delimit

Leisegang's theory of a circular dialectic. Taubes also refers to Hans Jonas, *Gnosis und spätantiker Geist.*

29. Cf. *Marxismus und Gnosis*, pp. 248–252.

30. Cf. E. Benz, *Die christliche Kabbala*. Ernst Benz shows in some detail that there were links between Christoph Oetinger and the Zohar, the Kabbala readers Johann Jakob Schütz and Knorr von Rosenroth, and the Kabbalists Isaac Luria and Koppel Hecht.

31. For Johann Albrecht Bengel, "the story ends . . . as a dialectical drama, with the abrupt transformation of the realm of evil into the Kingdom of God" (Topitsch, *Marxismus und Gnosis*, p. 253). This abrupt transformation is indicated by an increase of evil and is predicted for the year 1836 by Johann Albrecht Bengel.

32. Cf. *Marxismus und Gnosis*, pp. 256–258, and Topitsch, *Die Sozialphilosophie Hegels als Heilslehre und Herrschaftsideologie; Über Leerformeln*, pp. 247–251.

33. *Marxismus und Gnosis*, p. 258.

34. Cf. the contributions of various authors to the article "Dialektik" in *Historisches Wörterbuch der Philosophie*, ed. by J. Ritter, Vol. II, cols. 164–226.

35. Cf. *Marxismus und Gnosis*, p. 247, where Topitsch sees an early form of Hegel's concept of dialectics in the understanding of dialectics of the Pseudo-Dionysius translator Scotus Erigena.

36. H. H. Kohlenberger, "Dialektik," col. 189.

37. Cf. G. F. Hegel, *Sämtliche Werke* (Glockner), Vol. I, p. 49.

38. *Über Leerformeln*, p. 247.

39. Ibid., p. 248; cf. Kohlenberger, "Dialektik," col. 190 and the bibliography in cols. 192f.

40. Kohlenberger, "Dialektik," col. 190.

41. K. R. Popper, "Was ist Dialektik?" p. 263.

42. *Marxismus und Gnosis*, p. 258. The question of the extent to which this criticism can be maintained if the argument does not proceed from an anti-Idealist point of view but respects Hegel's concept of the Absolute cannot be pursued here.

43. Cf. *Marxismus und Gnosis*, p. 258, and *Über Leerformeln*, pp. 248–250. More extensively in Popper, "Was ist Dialektik?", pp. 267–272, 278–283.

44. Cf. Popper, "Was ist Dialektik?", pp. 273f.

45. Cf. *Über Leerformeln*, p. 251, and *Marxismus und Gnosis*, pp. 258f. Topitsch sees an important reason for the illegitimate expansion of dialectics in the fact that "the origin of the dialectical forms of thought in gnostic myths of salvation has perhaps been even more thoroughly forgotten than the origin of natural law doctrines in the socio-cosmic myth of archaic high cultures."

46. This is true even when there is no agreement with Topitsch's reductionist concept of science, and therefore not just falsifiable scientific facts are the object of science.

47. This aspect of Topitsch's critique of dialectics is decisive for the criticism of Fromm. See pp. 239–243.

48. *Über Leerformeln*, p. 254.

49. Ibid., pp. 251f.

50. Cf. the critique on p. 221f.

51. *Seelenglaube und Selbstinterpretation*, pp. 188f; *Über Leerformeln*, p. 254; and J.-Y. Calvez, *Karl Marx: Darstellung und Kritik seines Denkens*, p. 298.

52. K. Popper, "Was ist Dialektik?", p. 283.

53. Ibid., p. 285.

54. Cf. J. Frese, "Dialektik," cols. 198f. This delimitation does not imply that

dialectics was not in fact understood in this way, or that it does not continue to be so understood, with Karl Marx being quoted in support.

55. Ibid., col. 200.

56. Cf. ibid., cols. 198f.

57. Cf. especially J. Taubes, *Abendländische Eschatologie,* esp. pp. 184–188; A. Rich, "Die kryptoreligiösen Motive in den Frühschriften von Karl Marx"; E. Topitsch, *Marxismus und Gnosis,* pp. 259–265.

58. *Marxismus und Gnosis,* pp. 261f.

59. Karl Marx, *Early Writings,* p. 324; also, see p. 73f.

60. Cf. *Marxismus und Gnosis,* pp. 262f.

61. J. Taubes, *Abendländische Eschatologie,* pp. 36, 37.

62. In view of the fact that Marx's thought has its origin in the ecstatic-cathartic conceptual construct, one should choose an interpretation whose point of departure is the Marx of the early writings.

63. On the nexus between theory of history and (dialectical) critique, cf. R. Schaeffler, *Religion und kritisches Bewusstsein,* esp. pp. 71–81.

64. Cf. *Marxismus und Gnosis,* pp. 264f.

65. Ibid., p. 265.

66. Cf. Fromm, *The Art of Loving* (1956a), pp. 61–65; and the present work, p. 231f.

67. See p. 197f.

68. See pp. 195–197.

69. G. Scholem, *Major Trends in Jewish Mysticism,* p. 35.

70. Cf. ibid., pp. 41ff.

71. Ibid., p. 36.

72. Ibid., pp. 177ff.

73. See p. 197f and Chap. 6, notes 113 and 120.

74. Scholem, *Major Trends in Jewish Mysticism,* p. 341.

75. See the reference to the "Kabbala become ethos" and presented as "mystic psychology."

76. See p. 204f, for further details.

77. Quoted from Fromm, "Psychoanalysis and Zen Buddhism" (1959e), p. 81.

78. See pp. 215–218.

79. See pp. 66–72.

80. See pp. 121–124.

81. See the comments on "awareness" p. 118f and 146f.

82. Cf. the comments on "satori," pp. 122–124.

83. Cf. the comments on the humanism concept of Fromm, pp. 85–87.

84. The hostility to myth is shared by Fromm and Cohen (see Chap. 6, n. 46), who goes back to the history of the Jewish philosophy of religion and its rationalism that was influenced by the doctrine of negative attributes.

85. Fromm's struggle against all irrationality will probably not be seen correctly unless it is understood in the context of his attempt to ground a humanism that will be faithful to the ecstatic-cathartic conceptual model, yet also fully satisfy the demands of *ratio.*

86. Cf. the critical observations in notes 135, 152, and 205 to Chap. 4. According to these critical observations, it is hardly possible to reconcile Hegel's dialectic and the paradoxical logic of the East, for the former is not paradoxical. And it is also only with qualifications that the antilogic of Zen Buddhism can be subsumed under the concept of a paradoxical logic.

87. On what follows, cf. Fromm, *The Art of Loving* (1956a), pp. 61–68.

88. Ibid., p. 62.
89. Ibid., p. 64.
90. Ibid., pp. 64f.
91. Ibid., p. 65.
92. Cf. ibid., pp. 65f.
93. Ibid., p. 67.
94. See p. 56.
95. Examples would be Max Scheler's definition of man as "spiritual being," Helmut Plessner's definition of man as "excentric" being (a definition that comes closest to an ecstatic-cathartic construct), and Arnold Gehlen's view of man as a "creature of lack."
96. On this and what follows, see p. 228f.
97. Cf. the Kabbalistic doctrine of the "breaking of the vessels!"
98. Topitsch, *Seelenglaube und Selbstinterpretation*, p. 187.
99. See p. 69f.
100. Cf. the statements on the eschatological nature of mystical knowledge, pp. 119–128.
101. Demonstrating the condition for the possibility of a humanistic ethos is not tantamount to grounding a humanistic ethic.
102. The origin of the concept "totality" as used by thinkers associated with an ecstatic-cathartic conceptual construct lies in this need for an encompassing experience of meaning.
103. Topitsch, *Marxismus und Gnosis*, p. 258.
104. See p. 226.
105. See p. 227f.
106. See the comments on the attitude of the revolutionary character toward obedience and disobedience, pp. 95–97.
107. See p. 97f.
108. See pp. 89–91, 198, 104f.
109. Cf. pp. 106–112.
110. Cf. Fromm's formulation in *The Art of Loving* (1956a), p. 59: "God is I, inasmuch as I am human."
111. See pp. 183–188.
112. See p. 109f.
113. Such critical questions would, on the one hand, have to address the understanding of *theologia negativa* generally and its specific function within the religion in which it develops. On the other, they would have to analyze whether certain contents and phenomena can justifiably be interpreted in terms of a *theologia negativa*. See the beginnings of such a critique, pp. 109–112 and notes 121 and 123 to Chap. 4.
114. Especially in *You Shall Be as Gods* (1966a), pp. 17–62; see pp. 106–109.
115. The term "biomorphous" should be understood in analogy to "technomorphous" and "sociomorphous," and refers to a conception of man and his history that is oriented around the empirically discoverable biological data of the individual, and of mankind.
116. This does not mean that Fromm does not also think in line with the ecstatic-cathartic model when it comes to the *urgeschichtliche* development (in his theory of history, he does so exclusively). On this, see n. 101 to Chap. 4.
117. On this, cf. p. 104f.
118. See pp. 102–104.
119. See pp. 106–112.

120. The dialectical interpretation of the process of negation of authoritarian relations of dependency means that there is no room for the everyday experience of rational authority. The dialectical interpretation of the history of the concept of God results in a specific (i.e., dialectical) understanding of *theologia negativa*, religion, theonomy, and autonomy.

PART FOUR: Humanism as Science and as Religious Ethos in Fromm's Work

CHAPTER 8. THE ART OF LIVING: TO HAVE OR TO BE?

1. Cf. p. 18. The statements apply to both the individual and to social entities. Cf. the comments on the social character on pp. 18–22.
2. Cf. pp. 49–54.
3. Cf. the schematic illustration, p. 53.
4. The term "discovery" is justified because Fromm discovers the characterological concepts "having" and "being" as keys to the understanding of philosophical and religious statements, indeed as keys to the interpretation of human reality past and present. The thing itself to which the alternative refers is, of course, no discovery of Fromm's. On the contrary, Fromm tries to show that what the alternative refers to is present in the teachings of all the great teachers of mankind. The diaries by Gabriel Marcel that were published under the title *Etre et Avoir* are abstract philosophical reflections that differ, in part, in their intent. (But see G. G. Abril, *Erich Fromm y Gabriel Marcel. La esperanza frustrada y la esperanza absoluta*.) While this book has little to do with the psychosocial concept of having and being, Balthasar Staehelin's *Haben und Sein* confines itself to statements that result from the examination of psychoanalytic and psychotherapeutic discoveries and insights.
5. K. Marx, *Early Writings*, pp. 360–361. Cf. p. 351, where Marx makes the following comments on having: "All his human relations to the world—seeing, hearing, smelling, tasting, feeling, thinking, contemplating, sensing, wanting, acting, loving—in short, all the organs of his individuality, like the organs which are directly communal in form, are in their objective approach or in their approach to the object the appropriation of that object. This appropriation of human reality, their approach to the object, is the confirmation of human reality. It is human effectiveness and human suffering, for suffering humanly conceived, is an enjoyment of the self for man."
6. Fromm, *To Have or to Be?* (1976a), p. 16. That the impulse toward making this distinction and its verification through characterology come from Fromm's reading of Marx is also shown by the comments in *Marx's Concept of Man* (1961b), p. 35–37; and "The Application of Humanist Psychoanalysis to Marx's Theory," (1965c) p. 215f. Without specific reference to Marx, the alternative is mentioned in *The Revolution of Hope* (1968a) , p. 82–84. The strength of the influence Marx's discussion of the problem had on Fromm is shown by the many conceptual borrowings. When Fromm speaks of the "expression of one's essential human faculties," for example (in *To Have or to Be?*, p. 117), he is adopting Marx's "expression of human powers" which we find especially in the *Paris Manuscripts of 1844*.
7. Contrary to what the Marx quotations might suggest, Fromm is not concerned with universalizing the hoarding orientation. Nor do the distinctive qualities of having coincide with Freud's anal character.

8. Cf. *To Have or to Be?* (1976a), p. 105.

9. Ibid., p. 87.

10. Ibid., pp. 76–77.

11. Cf. ibid., pp. 26f.

12. Ibid., p. 77.

13. Ibid.

14. Cf. ibid., p. 81. This definition of having must be distinguished from the having that is required if life is to be possible. It is not such "functional having" that is meant when the mode of having is mentioned; the latter is a concept that refers to character and man's attitude toward life.

15. Cf. ibid., p. 81.

16. On what follows, cf. ibid., pp. 88–92, and the comments on the "productive orientation," pp. 34–37.

17. *To Have or to Be?* (1976a), p. 88.

18. Fromm clarifies the distinctiveness of the being mode by a comparison from optics: a blue glass is blue because it absorbs all other colors. It is called blue precisely because it does not keep back the blue wavelengths: "It is named not for what it possesses but for what it gives out" (ibid., p. 89).

19. Ibid., p. 91. Fromm calls this nonalienated activity "productive activity" but emphasizes that "productive" is not the same thing as "producing"; rather, it characterizes activity as the free activity of a subject.

20. It is only in the final version of *To Have or to Be?* that Fromm called these characteristics "aspects" (p. 108). In the earlier versions, he used "qualities."

21. Cf. ibid., pp. 91f, and the comments on the historical development of the understanding of "activity" and "passivity" in Aristotle, Thomas Aquinas, Meister Eckhart, Spinoza, and Marx, ibid., pp. 92–97.

22. Ibid., p. 109.

23. Ibid.

24. Cf. ibid., pp. 109f.

25. Ibid., p. 110.

26. Ibid., Cf. the biblical *logion* Luke 17:33: "Whoever seeks to gain his life will lose it, but whoever loses his life will preserve it." Also Matthew 13:12: "For to him who has will more be given, and he will have abundance; but from him who has not, even what he has shall be taken away."

27. On what follows, cf. Fromm, *To Have or to Be?* (1976a), pp. 111–116.

28. Ibid., p. 112.

29. Ibid., p. 113.

30. Ibid. This insight is important if one wishes to understand Fromm's criticism of a capitalist economic order, for this order needs man's greed if it is to function. Cf. the comments in ibid., Part III, esp. pp. 154–167.

31. Cf. ibid., pp. 113f.

32. Ibid., p. 115.

33. Ibid.

34. It is this alternative that defines Fromm's concept of humanist socialism and the criticism of existing socialist states that it implies. Among democratic socialist states, Sweden probably shows more clearly than any other how little a socialist social and, in part, economic policy can achieve as long as it follows the dictate of having.

35. On what follows, cf. *To Have or to Be?* (1976a), pp. 120–125.

36. That Fromm should use the religious concept of sin and forgiveness to illus-

trate the having mode while he limits sin and forgiveness in the being mode to the interpersonal sphere is probably connected with the religio-critical perspective of the authority concept, but does not affect the presentation of the different ways of understanding sin and forgiveness. The result, i.e., the characteristics of the relation sin/forgiveness in the having mode, would be the same if a purely anthropological concept of guilt in the interpersonal sphere had been chosen. The choice of a religious concept of guilt to illustrate the having mode only becomes problematical when it implies that the religious concept of sin and forgiveness is typical for the having mode, while the one that refers to the interpersonal level only is a characteristic of the being mode. Cf. pp. 96–98.

37. This is the reason why, from Fromm's perspective, the concept of justification that the Reformation introduced merely shifts the accent but actually does not overcome the mode of having that is typical of justification by works. For to human existence that knows that it owes itself to *sola gratia*, the following applies: "We have security . . . as long as we are—nobody" (ibid., p. 121).

38. Fromm finds this view of sin also in the biblical story of the fall, namely in the talk about nakedness and shame before and after the fall. The fall itself is no act of disobedience but the becoming aware of his reason that enables man to distinguish between good and evil, but that also makes him realize that the original unity of the two human beings is gone, that they have become strangers to each other. Cf. ibid., pp. 122–124.

39. Ibid., pp. 123, 124.

40. Ibid., pp. 124f.

41. Ibid., pp. 116–119.

42. Ibid., p. 116.

43. Ibid.

44. Cf. Fromm's reflections on the expression *post coitum animal triste*, ibid., p. 117.

45. Cf. ibid., p. 116.

46. Ibid., p. 117.

47. Ibid., p. 119.

48. This statement also applies when one goes along with many psychologists, analysts of *Dasein*, and existential philosophers and assumes that the fear of dying and of death is repressed in most cases, and that it is not just a problem for the aging person. The desire for immortality in all its guises (mummification, funerary gifts, belief in a beyond, legacies, literary legacy, children, monuments, last will and testament, etc.) and the tabooing of death (here American funeral institutes seem to have attained the highest degree of perfection) suggest that fear of dying is felt by all men (cf. ibid., p. 126). The question is whether the preponderance of the fear of death over the affirmation of life does, in fact, justify one in postulating an Existential. It is true that the fear of death defines the condition of the individual whose dominant interest is having, and to the extent that the having dominance is statistically preponderant, the condition of fear of dying can create the impression of ubiquity. But this does not prove an Existential. To speak of a proof nonetheless suggests merely that such philosophizing corresponds to an existence in the philosopher of a having orientation.

49. Ibid., p. 126.

50. It is at this point that we see the decisive difference from existential philosophy. Fromm follows Spinoza, whom he quotes: "The sages reflect about life, not about death."

51. *To Have or to Be?* (1976a), p. 127.

52. Ibid.

53. Ibid.

54. Ibid., p. 129.

55. A glance at leisure-time behavior shows that leisure time is anything but a sphere of timelessness. It is merely another kind of rule of time over man. Depending on their dominance, the having or being modes stamp the individual's use of both working time and leisure time. Cf. ibid., p. 129.

56. Ibid., p. 128.

57. Ibid. The quarrel of dogmatists over the controversial questions of the real presence and transsubstantiation, and also more fundamental questions as to how religious acts are initiated and mediated in religions that refer to a historically manifest revelation, can be explained by the differing understanding of time in the two modes.

58. *To Have or to Be?* (1976a), p. 128.

59. Ibid. It goes without saying that Fromm's humanistic religious experience as a mysticism of the ONE can only be grasped against the background of the understanding of time in the being mode.

60. Fromm demonstrates the alternative of having and being with reference to the following forms of action: learning, remembering, conversing, reading, exercising authority, knowing, believing, loving. See ibid., pp. 28–47. In this connection, one should point out the revelatory linguistic peculiarities and idiomatic changes in the use of the verbs "having" and "being." Of special importance is the observation that in cultures and societies where the tendency to react in the having mode is growing, verbs of activity are increasingly replaced by terms that denote having. See ibid., pp. 20–24, esp. p. 20f.

61. Ibid., p. 24.

62. Ibid., p. 33.

63. Ibid., p. 34.

64. Ibid., pp. 41–44.

65. Ibid., p. 42.

66. From this approach, there result a number of critical reflections that apply to an ecclesiastically and theologically mediated faith: The conflict between scientific theology and the teachings of the Church with its papal, episcopal, and presbyterial representation is due to the concern of the public administrators of the faith that this very functionality of a faith oriented around having be preserved. Whether this concern is called "office" or "service" is merely a matter of terminology. Of course, the interpretation of the conflict between theology and the teachings of the Church cannot ignore the fact that this quarrel within scientific theology bears all the marks of a struggle for possessions—i.e., that the scholarly or scientific articulation of the meaning of faith is concerned only with the preservation of the possession of truth. Competing with the teaching of the Church, theology then attempts to administer a faith that is understood in the mode of (scientific) having. A reorientation of the self-understanding of theology and the teaching of the Church would have to begin with the understanding of the faith itself. And it would have to define the functionality of theology and Church teaching in terms of the task of furthering the act of faith in the being mode and renounce all administration of a possession of the faith. Cf. R. Funk, *Frömmigkeit zwischen Haben und Sein*, pp. 41–46.

67. *To Have or to Be?* (1976a), p. 42.

68. Cf. ibid., p. 43.

69. Ibid.
70. Cf. ibid., p. 43f.
71. Cf. ibid., pp. 44–47.
72. Ibid., p. 44.
73. Ibid., p. 46.
74. Ibid.
75. Cf. ibid., p. 46f.
76. Ibid., pp. 105–106.
77. Ibid., p. 106f.
78. See the comments on social character in ibid., pp. 133f.
79. Fromm concretizes this demand in some detail in the concluding section of *To Have or to Be?* He emphasizes the possibility, but also the urgency, of a fundamental change because the current development of the international economy and the increase in political, social, and personal conflicts bear all the marks of a syndrome-like convergence of the fundamental having orientation which threatens that present-day human civilizations will totally collapse.
80. Ibid., p. 133.
81. Ibid., p. 24.
82. Along with the having/being alternative, it is postulated that every scientific or artistic product, every historical development, every theoretical conception in the sciences, every religious confession, every dream and every fantasy, every custom and every fad, every cultural development, every ethos and ethic, philosophy and so on, can be evaluated and criticized by the having/being alternative, provided the phenomena in question can be comprehensively described. Fromm made such evaluations and criticism in some areas that go beyond the investigation of character. There are his studies on the capitalist and socialist social order and on (especially American) politics, particularly the politics of rearmament; his research on the Reformation; his writings on religion and the critique of religion and his comments on humanistic ethics. Although the having/being alternative is not named in any of these publications, Fromm's discovery of the sociopsychological method during the early thirties involved both the specific understanding of character and the productive or nonproductive character orientation as a yardstick of evaluation and criticism.
84. Cf. *To Have or to Be?* (1976a), p. 15.
85. Cf. the comparison of poems by Basho and Tennyson in ibid., p. 16.
86. Cf. the comments on Spinoza's differentiation between "activity" and "passivity" in ibid., pp. 93–96.
87. Cf. the interpretation of the poems "Gefunden" and "Eigentum" in ibid., p. 18f.
88. Cf. the comments in ibid., pp. 156–160.
89. Cf. Fromm, "Die Zwiespältigkeit des Fortschritts" (1975c) and *To Have or to Be?* (1976a), pp. 161–164.
90. *To Have or to Be?* (1976a), p. 157.
91. Fromm's comments on the New Testament (ibid., pp. 53–59) are based on studies the author of this work made for him. The following presentation of the having/being alternative in the New Testament therefore goes beyond the material in *To Have or to Be?* Cf. also R. Funk, *Frömmigkeit zwischen Haben und Sein*, pp. 21–31.
92. *To Have or to Be?* (1976a), p. 48; cf. Genesis 12:1.
93. Ibid., p. 48f.

94. Ibid., pp. 52f; cf. Fromm, "Die Aktualität der prophetische Schriften" (1975d).

95. *To Have or to Be?* (1976a), p. 53. The question as to what is specifically Jewish interested Fromm from the very beginning. His dissertation *Das jüdische Gesetz* (1922a) already tries to answer it. As he investigated the function of the law in Karaism, Reformed Judaism, and Hasidism, he encountered what is specific to Hasidism in contrast to Reform Judaism and Karaism. Hasidism "does not seek to change religion for the sake of the economy but to overcome need through the power of religion. . . . Karaism and Reform lack new religious ideas, they dogmatize religion. Hasidism, in contrast, integrates its specific religious life in the sociological structure of Judaism, avoids dogma, and retains the objective validity of the law. Reform Judaism is the non-creative, ideological way out that takes the place of mass baptism. Hasidism is the creative, religious way out that overcomes pseudo-messianism" (*Das jüdische Gesetz* [1922a], p. 237). In these concluding lines of Fromm's dissertation, in the characterization "creative/non-creative" we have the first alternative; alternatives persist in the antithetical concepts "productive/non-productive" and in the "having/being" alternative.

96. Siegfried Schulz' *Q. Die Spruchquelle der Evangelisten* can be considered the standard work on the transmission of the *logia* source. An extensive discussion of this work by New Testament scholars has not yet taken place, and this is especially true of his distinction between the oldest *Q* texts that are marked by a Judaeo-Christian eschatological enthusiasm and other *Q* texts that came into existence later and which also contain stories, apothegmata, apocalyptic sayings, and parables (cf. pp. 53, 165–168, 482–486). In spite of these reservations, the following comments are based on Schulz' work. Recently, that author radicalized his position in the essay "Der historische Jesus. Bilanz der Fragen und Lösungen" and now counts most of the texts of the oldest layer of *Q* among the *ipsissima* of Jesus (cf. pp. 10, n. 35). Much less use was made of Dieter Lührmann's *Die Redaktion der Logienquelle*, and Paul Hoffmann's *Studien zur Theologie der Logienquelle*. See E. Käsemann, "Das Problem des historischen Jesus." R. Bultmann, "Das Verhältnis der urchristlichen Christusbotschaft zum historischen Jesus"; K. Kertelge, ed., *Rückfrage nach Jesus*; W. Kasper, *Jesus der Christus*, pp. 38–44, for a discussion of the questions concerning the historical Jesus in our time.

97. This could only be accomplished by a thorough discussion of Christologies. Of course, the theological dogmatists and systematists would have to be willing to entertain the question whether the cognitive concern of a Christology does not bypass the historical Jesus *a priori*. For it could be that every (Christological) statement and conceptualization abets the temptation to paralyze the radicalism of the religious ethos. Why is it that the historical Jesus does not teach a particular confession of faith but a religious ethos in word and deed? It is probably true that "the content of a faith can only be recognized in the act of faith," but is it really true that the act of faith is necessarily "meaningless unless it is directed toward a content?" (W. Kasper, *Jesus der Christus*, p. 25). On the problems raised by contemporary Christology, see Kasper, pp. 13–26. On Christological statements generally, cf. n. 98.

98. Although it is not being carried out here, such a procedure certainly does not obviate the need for a careful exegesis according to all the rules of historical and critical research. The having/being alternative might be of use in theological and systematic work on the New Testament because every systematic study approaches the exegetical data with certain conscious, unavowed, or unreflected conceptions. It is precisely in this task that the having/being alternative might serve as a key and

grid, for it not only assures a comprehensive plausibility of textual statements but also accords with the assumption that Christ, as a Jew who was close to Essene circles, represents an eschatology that is wholly marked by a radicalized and decisive ethos. The question as to the legitimacy of understanding and using the having/being alternative as a common denominator and therefore as an interpretive key to Jesus' message and life receives an affirmative answer in discoveries that Herbert Braun conveys in his essay "Der Sinn der neutestamentlichen Theologie." He observes a constant that persists through all the gospels and the epistles of Paul, a paradox that is typical in the life of the historical Jesus: "alongside the radicalized Torah, we find a radicalized grace that is equally repugnant to official and heretical Judaism," (p. 248). Jesus represented "the paradoxical unity of a radicalized demand and limitless acceptance" (p. 249). "It is in this way that God makes demands on, and acts toward, man in concrete individuation . . . and this acting of his is an eschatological acting" (pp. 250f). The paradoxical unity is "the defining characteristic of what is Christian, the New Testament constant of believing self-understanding" (p. 276) that expresses itself in the Christological statements. ("Anthropology is the constant; Christology is the variable," p. 272.) Historically, the believing self-understanding is passed on neither by formulae nor as an "idea." The believing self-understanding of the paradoxical unity of radicalized demand and limitless acceptance "belongs to that third category of phenomena . . . that occur and become valid and binding only in the act of their occurrence. . . . It is an event that occurs from time to time" (p. 277).

Even though Herbert Braun interprets his findings in terms of reformed theology and therefore cannot translate the constant of the paradoxical unity of Torah demand and grace into the having/being alternative, the parallels must not be overlooked: there is a constant that is seen as the paradoxical unity of ethos and plenitude of being—which is bestowed through grace (the paradox here refers to both the alternative character and the unexpectedness in the demand/acceptance relation). The peculiarity of the paradox that it can only be realized by engaging oneself in it is emphasized. The decisive difference between the two constants, the paradoxical unity and the having/being alternative, becomes apparent when the new experience is verbalized. For Fromm, the religious experience of the being mode as the mystical experience of the ONE is the experience of the totality of man's humanness and its potentialities. For the reform theologian Herbert Braun, the event makes possible an acknowledgment of both forlornness and salvation in such a way "that this self-understanding comes to him from outside himself" (p. 282).

99. This applies not only to the Lucan tradition. Regarding the Matthean community toward the end of the first century, E. Schweizer, *Matthäus und seine Gemeinde*, p. 163, writes that "there must still have been individuals who literally followed Christ. They gave up their possessions and proclaimed the Kingdom of God as wandering prophets and charismatic individuals." Cf. the entire section "Von Jesus zur Mönchsbewegung der katholischen Kirche." (pp. 163–170, and P. Hoffmann and V. Eid, *Jesus von Nazareth und eine christliche Moral*, pp. 214–230, and the bibliography given there.

100. Cf. H. Conzelmann, *Der erste Brief an die Korinther*, p. 257, and the excursus on the parallels in Tyrtaeus, Plato, and Maximus of Tyre (pp. 258–260).

101. On the following, cf. Meister Eckhart, *Die deutschen Werke*, Vol. II, pp. 478–517, 727–731.

102. Ibid., p. 727; cf. pp. 488 and 507f, n. 10.

103. *To Have or to Be?* (1976a), p. 61. Cf. the references to Eckhart texts in Meister Eckhart, *Die deutschen Predigten*, Vol. II p. 528, n. 3, where "detachment" is mentioned as the principal virtue and most important presupposition for the experience of *unio mystica*.

104. Meister Eckhart, *Die deutschen Werke*, Vol. II, p. 729.

105. Fromm, *To Have or to Be?* (1976a), p. 62.

106. Meister Eckhart, *Die deutschen Werke*, Vol. II, p. 730.

107. Ibid., p. 730.

108. D. Mieth, *Christus—das Soziale im Menschen*, pp. 117f.

109. Meister Eckhart, *Die deutschen Werke*, Vol. II, p. 731.

110. Whether it must also be asserted that the question regarding the philosophical truth of the concept of God is irrelevant cannot be decided here since metaphysics and philosophy occasionally understand themselves as negative theology. On this problem, see J. Möller, *Die Chance des Menschen—Gott genannt; Glauben und Denken im Widerspruch*. There is a bibliography on more recent formulations of the problem on the part of philosophy and theology in H. Küng, *On Being a Christian*.

111. On the question of the self-understanding of humanistic religion, see the comments on the "X experience as the mysticism of the ONE," pp. 119–128.

112. Cf. p. 118f.

113. Most aptly formulated in the *"Cogito ergo sum"* of Descartes. What is meant is every philosophy that seeks to ground being in man's "having" certainty of thought, of consciousness, of cognition, of knowledge, etc.

114. Cf. the comments of the *lex* model in Thomas Aquinas, p. 156f.

115. On the concept "interpretive key," see the interpretation of the *lex* model by W. Korff in *Norm und Sittlichkeit*, p. 49.

CHAPTER 9. FROMM'S HUMANISM AS A CHALLENGE TO A CHRISTIAN THEOLOGY

1. Fromm himself attributed a growing importance to the dialogue between humanists and Christians. Concerning the significance of humanism within the Roman Catholic Church, one need only mention men such as Pope John XXIII and Teilhard de Chardin or, among theologians, Karl Rahner and Hans Küng, according to Fromm (cf. "Afterword" [1961b], p. 261). It must be admitted, however, that so far this dialogue has taken place primarily in the English-speaking world. See R. Banks, "A Neo-Freudian Critique of Religion: Erich Fromm on the Judaeo-Christian Tradition"; P. A. Bertocci and R. M. Millard, *Personality and the Good. Psychological and Ethical Perspectives*; R. B. Betz, *An Analysis of the Prophetic Character of the Dialectical Rhetoric of Erich Fromm*; A. M. Caligiuri, *The Concept of Freedom in the Writings of Erich Fromm*; O. B. Curtis, *The Role of Religion in Selfhood: An Examination of Humanist Psychoanalysis in Erich Fromm and Christian Selfhood in Wayne Oates*; M. C. Ebersole, *Christian Faith and Man's Religion*; J. J. Forsyth and J. M. Beniskos, "Biblical Faith and Erich Fromm's Theory of Personality"; J. S. Glen, *Erich Fromm: A Protestant Critique*; G. B. Hammond, *Man in Estrangement: A Comparison of the Thought of Paul Tillich and Erich Fromm*; S. Hiltner, *Psychotherapy and Christian Ethics: An Evaluation of the Ethical Thought of A. E. Taylor and Paul Tillich in the Light of Psychotherapeutic Contributions to Ethics by J. C. Fluegel and Erich Fromm*; V. A. Jensen, *Failure and Capability in Love: An*

Integrative Study of the Psychology of Erich Fromm and the Theology of Erich Brunner; J. J. Petuchowski, "Erich Fromm's Midrash of Love: The Sacred and the Secular Forms"; Y. Suzuki, *An Examination of Doctrine of Man of Erich Fromm and Reinhold Niebuhr*; W. C. Tilley, *The Relationship of Self-Love for the Other with Special Reference to the Thought of R. Niebuhr and Erich Fromm.*

2. H. Küng, *On Being a Christian*, p. 37.

3. See p. 195f and 273f.

4. On the philosophical problem of this "demand that the divine and the human coexist," see J. Möller, *Die Chance des Menschen*, pp. 286–324. On the (unresolved) question of the relation between philosophy and mysticism, n. 23, p. 321, is especially informative.

5. On the theological problematic generally, see H. Küng, *On Being a Christian*; on the specifically theological-ethical question, see pp. 155–159.

6. The "human reality which paradoxically in its fullness is itself inexpressible . . . can be expressed to a limited degree in different and even contradictory concepts" (Fromm, "Afterword" [1961b], p. 263).

7. See the distinction drawn between theology and mysticism, p. 120f.

8. Cf. pp. 157–159.

9. By emphasizing the paraenetic quality of the exemplifications, B. Schüller shows convincingly ("Zur Diskussion über das Proprium einer christlichen Ethik," esp. pp. 332–334), that such critical clarification did not have to await the having/being alternative as a key to the understanding of Jesus' demands.

10. While the understanding of Jesus' demands as concretions of a demand that an attitude be adopted touches on some of the concerns of *Gesinnungsethik* and *Situationsethik*, it differs from them in essential points.

11. A. Auer, "Ein Modell theologisch-ethischer Argumentation: 'Autonome Moral,' " p. 42.

Bibliography of Works by Erich Fromm

This bibliography attempts to be as complete as possible. It therefore contains titles to which no reference is made in the text.

All titles are chronologically ordered and numbered according to the date and language of their first publication. The numbers preceding the titles correspond to the numbers in parentheses in the notes.

1922a "Das jüdische Gesetz. Ein Beitrag zur Soziologie des Diasporajudentums." Ph.D. dissertation. Heidelberg: 1922.

1926b "Dauernde Nachwirkung eines Erziehungsfehlers," *Zeitschrift für Psychoanalytische Pädagogik.* Vienna: 1926/27.

1927a "Der Sabbath." In *Imago. Zeitschrift für Anwendung der Psychoanalyse auf die Natur- und Geisteswissenschaften.* Vienna: Internationaler Psychoanalytischer Verlag, 1927.

1929a "Psychoanalyse und Soziologie." *Zeitschrift für Psychoanalytische Pädagogik.* Vienna: 1928/29.

1930a "Die Entwicklung des Christusdogmas. Eine psychoanalytische Studie zur sozialpsychologischen Funktion der Religion." *Imago.* Vienna: 1930. English version 1963a, pp. 1–70.

1930b "Der Staat als Erzieher. Zur Psychologie der Strafjustiz." *Zeitschrift für Psychoanalytische Pädagogik.* Vienna: 1930.

1930c Review of S. Bernfeld, *Die Schulgemeinde und ihre Funktion im Klassenkampf. Zeitschrift für Psychoanalytische Pädagogik.* Vienna: 1930.

1930d "Ödipus in Innsbruck. Zum Halsmann-Prozess." *Psychoanalytische Bewegung.* Vienna: 1930.

1931a "Zur Psychologie des Verbrechers und der strafenden Gesellschaft." *Imago.* Vienna: 1931. Quoted according to the reprint of the German version, 1970a.

1931b "Politik und Psychoanalyse." In *Psychoanalytische Bewegung.* Vienna: Internationaler Psychoanalytischer Verlag, 1931.

1932a "Über Methode und Aufgabe einer Analytischen Sozialpsychologie: Bemerkungen über Psychoanalyse und historischen Materialismus." In *Zeitschrift für Sozialforschung.* Leipzig: Hirschfeld Verlag, 1932. English version in 1970a.

1932b "Die psychoanalytische Charakterologie und ihre Bedeutung für die Sozialpsychologie." In *Zeitschrift für Sozialforschung*. Leipzig: Hirschfeld Verlag, 1932. English version in 1970, pp. 163–189.

1932c Review of Fedor Vergin, *Das unbewusste Europa. Psychoanalyse der europäischen Politik*. In *Zeitschrift für Sozialforschung*. Leipzig: Hirschfeld Verlag, 1932.

1932d Review of Sir Galahad, *Mütter und Amazonen. Umriss weiblicher Reiche*. In *Zeitschrift für Sozialforschung*. Leipzig: Hirschfeld Verlag, 1932.

1932e Review of Otto Heller, *Der Untergang des Judentums*. In *Zeitschrift für Sozialforschung*. Leipzig: Hirschfeld Verlag, 1932.

1933a "Robert Briffaults Werk über das Mutterrecht." In *Zeitschrift für Sozialforschung*. Paris: Librairie Felix Alcan, 1933.

1933b Review of Wilhelm Reich, *Der Einbruch der Sexualmoral. Zur Geschichte der sexuellen Ökonomie*. In *Zeitschrift für Sozialforschung*. Paris: Librairie Felix Alcan, 1933.

1933c Review of Fedor Vergin, *Das unbewusste Europa. Psychoanalyse der europäischen Politik*. *Imago*. Vienna: 1933.

1933d Review of Lord Raglan, *Jocasta's Crime. An Anthropological Study*. In *Zeitschrift für Sozialforschung*. Paris: Librairie Felix Alcan, 1933.

1934a "Die sozialpsychologische Bedeutung der Mutterrechtstheorie." In *Zeitschrift für Sozialforschung*. Paris: Librairie Felix Alcan, 1934.

1934b Review of Willy Hellpach, *Elementares Lehrbuch der Sozialpsychologie*. In *Zeitschrift für Sozialforschung*. Paris: Librairie Felix Alcan, 1934.

1934c Review of Sandford Fleming, *Children and Puritanism*. In *Zeitschrift für Sozialforschung*. Paris: 1934.

1934d Review of S. M. and B. C. Grünberg, *Parents, Children and Money*. In *Zeitschrift für Sozialforschung*. Paris: 1934.

1934e Review of E. Heidbreder, *Seven Psychologies*. In *Zeitschrift für Sozialforschung*. Paris: 1934.

1934f Review of Jeoffrey Gorer, *The Revolutionary Ideas of the Marquis de Sade*. In *Zeitschrift für Sozialforschung*. Paris: 1934.

1934g Review of Louis Berg, *The Human Personality*. In *Zeitschrift für Sozialforschung*. Paris: 1934.

1934h Review of E. J. H. Buytendyik, *Wesen und Sinn des Spiels*. In *Zeitschrift für Sozialforschung*. Paris: 1934.

1934i Review of Alexander Kerensky, *The Crucified Liberty*. In *Zeitschrift für Sozialforschung*. Paris: 1934.

1935a "Die gesellschaftliche Bedingtheit der psychoanalytischen Therapie." In *Zeitschrift für Sozialforschung*. Paris: 1935.

1935b Review of A. Forel, *Rückblick auf mein Leben*; V. P. Snowden, *An Autobiography*, R. H. B. Lockhart, *Retreat from Glory*. In *Zeitschrift für Sozialforschung*. Paris: 1935.

1935c Review of I. S. Wile, *The Sex Life of the Unmarried Adult: An Inquiry into and an Interpretation of Current Sex Practice*. In *Zeitschrift für Sozialforschung*. Paris: 1935.

1935d Review of Gerhard Adler, *Entdeckung der Seele*. In *Zeitschrift für Sozialforschung*. Paris: 1935.

1935e Review of C. G. Jung, *Wirklichkeit der Seele*. In *Zeitschrift für Sozialforschung*. Paris: 1935.

1935f Review of Heinrich Meng, *Strafen und Erziehen*. In *Zeitschrift für Sozialforschung*. Paris: 1935.

1935g Review of Peter Browe, *Beiträge zur Sexualethik des Mittelalters.* In *Zeitschrift für Sozialforschung.* Paris: 1935.

1936a "Sozialpsychologischer Teil." In M. Horkheimer, ed., *Schriften des Instituts für Sozialforschung.* Vol. V. *Studien über Autorität und Familie. Forschungsberichte aus dem Institut für Sozialforschung.* Paris: 1936.

1936b "Geschichte und Methoden der Erhebung." In M. Horkheimer, ed., *Schriften des Instituts für Sozialforschung.* Vol. V. *Studien über Autorität und Familie. Forschungsberichte aus dem Institut für Sozialforschung.* Paris: 1936.

1936c Review of John Dollard, *Criteria for the Life History.* In *Zeitschrift für Sozialforschung.* Paris: 1936.

1936d Review of Margaret Mead, *Sex and Temperament in Three Primitive Societies.* In *Zeitschrift für Sozialforschung.* Paris: 1936.

1936e Review of George Britt, *Forty Years—Forty Millions.* In *Zeitschrift für Sozialforschung.* Paris: 1936.

1936f Review of Conrad Aiken, *King Coffin.* In *Zeitschrift für Sozialforschung.* Paris: 1936.

1936g "Die Arbeiter- und Angestellten-Erhebung." In M. Horkheimer, ed., *Schriften des Instituts für Sozialforschung.* Vol. V. *Studien über Autorität und Familie. Forschungsberichte aus dem Institut für Sozialforschung.* Paris: 1936.

1937a "Zum Gefühl der Ohnmacht." In *Zeitschrift für Sozialforschung.* Paris: 1937.

1937b Review of Margaret Mead, *Cooperation and Competition among Primitive Peoples.* In *Zeitschrift für Sozialforschung.* Paris: 1937.

1937c Review of Harold D. Lasswell, *Politics: Who Gets What, When, How.* In *Zeitschrift für Sozialforschung.* Paris: 1937.

1937d Review of R. Osborn, *Freud and Marx.* In *Zeitschrift für Sozialforschung.* Paris: 1937.

1937e Review of J. F. Brown, *Psychology and the Social Order.* In *Zeitschrift für Sozialforschung.* Paris: 1937.

1937f Review of Carl J. Warden, *The Emergence of Human Culture.* In *Zeitschrift für Sozialforschung.* Paris: 1937.

1937g Review of Paul Thomas Young, *Motivation of Behavior. The Fundamental Determinants of Human and Animal Activity.* In *Zeitschrift für Sozialforschung.* Paris: 1937.

1938a Review of Roger W. Babson, *Actions and Reactions. An Autobiography.* In *Zeitschrift für Sozialforschung.* Paris: 1938.

1939a "The Social Philosophy of 'Will Therapy.'" *Psychiatry.* Washington: The William Alanson White Psychiatric Foundation, 1939.

1939b "Selfishness and Self-Love." *Psychiatry.* Washington: The William Alanson White Psychiatric Foundation, 1939.

1939c Review of Wilhelm Stekel, *Die Technik der analytischen Psychotherapie.* In *Studies in Philosophy and Social Science* (formerly *Zeitschrift für Sozialforschung*). New York: Social Studies Association, 1939.

1939d Review of D. D. Bromley and F. Britten, *You and Sex.* In *Studies in Philosophy and Social Science.* New York: Social Studies Association, 1939.

1941a *Escape from Freedom.* New York: Farrar & Rinehart, 1941.

1942a "Should We Hate Hitler?" *Journal of Home Economics.* Washington, Apr. 1942.

1942b "Faith as a Character Trait." *Psychiatry*. Washington: The William Alanson White Psychiatric Foundation, 1942.

1943a "On the Problems of German Characterology." *Transactions of the New York Academy of Science* 4 (1943): 79–83.

1943b "Sex and Character." *Psychiatry* (1943): 21–31. Quoted from the reprint in R. N. Anshen, ed., *The Family: Its Functions and Destiny*. New York: Harper, 1949.

1943c "What Shall We Do with Germany?" *Saturday Review of Literature*, May 29, 1943.

1944a "Individual and Social Origins of Neurosis." *American Sociological Review* (1944): 380–384.

1947a *Man for Himself: An Inquiry into the Psychology of Ethics*. New York: Rinehart & Co., 1947.

1948a "Introduction." In P. Mullahy, ed., *Oedipus: Myth and Complex: A Review of Psychoanalytic Theory*. New York: Hermitage Press, 1948.

1948b "Sex and Character: The Kinsey Report Viewed from the Standpoint of Psychoanalysis." In D. P. Geddes and E. Curie, eds., *About the Kinsey Report*. New York: The American Library, 1948. Quotations are from the reprint in Himmelhoch and Fava, eds., *Sexual Behavior in American Society*. New York: Norton, 1955.

1949a "The Nature of Dreams." *Scientific American* (1949): 44–47.

1949b "The Oedipus Complex and the Oedipus Myth." In R. N. Anshen, ed., *The Family: Its Functions and Destiny*. New York: Harper & Bros., 1949.

1949c "Psychoanalytic Characterology and Its Application to the Understanding of Culture." In S. S. Sargent and M. W. Smith, eds., *Culture and Personality*. New York: Viking Press, 1949.

1950a *Psychoanalysis and Religion*. New Haven: Yale University Press, 1950.

1951a *The Forgotten Language: An Introduction to the Understanding of Dreams, Fairy Tales and Myths*. New York: Rinehart & Co., 1951.

1951b "Man-Woman." In M. M. Hughes, ed., *The People in Your Life: Psychiatry and Personal Relations*. New York: Alfred A. Knopf, 1951.

1952a "The Contribution of the Social Sciences to Mental Hygiene." *Proceedings of the Fourth Congress of Mental Health* (Mexico City, 1951), ed. by A. Millan. Mexico City: La Prensa Medica Mexicana, 1952.

1954a "The Psychology of Normalcy." *Dissent* (Spring 1954): 139–143.

1955a *The Sane Society*. New York: Rinehart and Winston, 1955.

1955b "The Human Implications of Instinctivistic 'Radicalism': A Reply to Herbert Marcuse." *Dissent* (1955): 342–349.

1955c "The Present Human Condition." *The American Scholar* 25 (1955/56): p. 29–35.

1955d "Remarks on the Problem of Free Association." *Psychiatric Research Reports* 2 (1955): 1–6.

1955e "Psychoanalysis." In J. R. Newman, ed., *What Is Science? Twelve Eminent Scientists and Philosophers Explain Their Various Fields to the Laymen*. New York: Simon & Schuster, 1955.

1956a *The Art of Loving*. New York and Evanston: World Perspectives Vol. 9, Harper & Row, 1956.

1956b "A Counter-Rebuttal to Herbert Marcuse." *Dissent* (1956): 81–83.

1956c "Bases Filosoficas del Psicoanalisis." *Revista Psicologia* 2 (1956): 59–66.

1956d "Palabras a la edicion espanola." In E. Fromm, 1955a, Spanish edition.

1957a "Man Is Not a Thing." *Saturday Review* (March 16, 1957): 9–11.

1957b "Socialismo o Robotismo?" *El Sol.* Uruguay: Nov. 1957.

1958a Psychoanalysis—Scientism or Fanaticism?" *Saturday Review* (June 14, 1958): 11–13, 55f.

1958b "Interview" (with Mike Wallace). In *Survival and Freedom,* No. 5. New York: The Fund for the Republic, 1958.

1958c "Los factores sociales y su influencia en la desarrollo del nino." *La Prensa Medica Mexicana* 23 (1958): 227–228.

1958d "The Moral Responsibility of Modern Man." *Merril-Palmer Quarterly of Behavior and Development* 5 (1958): 3–14.

1959a *Sigmund Freud's Mission: An Analysis of His Personality and Influence.* New York: World Perspectives Vol. 21, Harper and Brothers, 1959.

1959b "Values, Psychology, and Human Existence." In A. H. Maslow, ed., *New Knowledge in Human Values.* New York: Harper & Bros., 1959.

1959c "The Creative Attitude." In H. A. Anderson, ed., *Creativity and Its Cultivation.* New York: Harper & Bros., 1959.

1959d "Love in America." In H. Smith, ed., *The Search for America.* Englewood Cliffs, N.J.: Prentice-Hall, 1959.

1959e "Psychoanalysis and Zen Buddhism." *Psychologia* 2 (1959): 79–99.

1959f "Freedom in the Work Situation." In M. Harrington and P. Jacobs, eds., *Labor in a Free Society.* Berkeley and Los Angeles: University of California Press, 1959.

1960a "Psychoanalysis and Zen Buddhism." In D. T. Suzuki, E. Fromm, and R. de Martino, *Zen Buddhism and Psychoanalysis.* New York: Harper, 1960.

1960b *Let Man Prevail—A Socialist Manifesto and Program.* New York: The Call Association, 1960.

1960c "The Case for Unilateral Disarmament." *Daedalus: Journal of the American Academy of Arts and Sciences.* Cambridge, Mass.: Wesleyan University Press, 1960.

1960d "The Prophetic Concept of Peace." In S. Yamaguchi, ed., *Buddhism and Culture: A Festschrift in Honor of D. T. Suzuki.* Kyoto: Narkana Press, 1960. Quotations are from 1963a.

1960e "Foreword." In A. S. Neill, *Summerhill—A Radical Approach to Childrearing.* New York, 1960.

1960f "Foreword." In E. Bellamy, *Looking Backward (2000–1887).* New York: New American Library, 1960.

1961a *May Man Prevail? An Inquiry into the Facts and Fictions of Foreign Policy.* New York: Doubleday, 1961.

1961b *Marx's Concept of Man.* With a translation from Marx's Economic and Philosophical Manuscripts, by T. B. Bottomore. New York: F. Ungar Publishing Co., 1961.

1961c "Afterword." In George Orwell, *1984.* New York: The New American Library, Signet Classics, 1961.

1961d "Vorwort." In E. Fromm and H. Herzfeld, eds., *Der Friede. Idee und Verwirklichung. Festausgabe für Adolf Leschnitzer.* Heidelberg: L. Schneider Verlag, 1961.

1961e "Sane Thinking in Foreign Policy." In E. Fromm et al., eds., *Sane Comment.* New York: National Committee for a Sane Nuclear Policy, 1961.

1961f "Das neue kommunistische Programm." In *Blätter für deutsche und internationale Politik.* Köln: Pahl-Rugenstein Verlag, 1961.

1961g "Communism and Co-Existence: The Nature of the Totalitarian Threat Today: An Analysis of the 81st Party Manifesto." *Socialist Call* 4 (1961): 3–11.

1962a *Beyond the Chains of Illusion: My Encounter with Marx and Freud.* New York: Simon and Schuster, Credo Series, 1962.

1962b "A Debate on the Question of Civil Defense" (with Michael Maccoby). *Commentary: A Jewish Review* 33 (1962): 11–23.

1962c "The Philosophy Basic to Freud's Psychoanalysis." *Pastoral Psychology* 13 (1962): 26–32.

1963a *The Dogma of Christ and Other Essays on Religion, Psychology and Culture.* New York: Holt, Rinehart & Winston, 1963.

1963b "The Revolutionary Character." In 1963a.

1963c "Medicine and the Ethical Problem of Modern Man." In 1963a.

1963d "Disobedience as a Psychological and Moral Problem." In C. Urquhart, ed., *A Matter of Life.* London: Jonathan Cape, 1963.

1963e "C. G. Jung: Prophet of the Unconscious: A Discussion of 'Memories, Dreams, Reflections' by C. G. Jung; Recorded and Edited by Aniell Jaffe." *Scientific American* 209 (1963): 283–290.

1963f "Humanismo y Psicoanalisis." *La Prensa Medica Mexicana* 28 (1963): 120–126.

1963g *War Within Man: A Psychological Inquiry into the Roots of Destructiveness. A Study and Commentary.* Comments by J. Frank and others. Philadelphia: American Friends' Service Committee, 1963.

1964a *The Heart of Man: Its Genius for Good and Evil.* New York and London: Religious Perspectives Vol. 12, Harper & Row, 1964.

1964b "Second Preface." In *May Man Prevail? An Inquiry into the Facts and Fictions of Foreign Policy.* 2nd ed. New York: Doubleday, 1964.

1964c "Our Way of Life Makes Us Miserable." *The Saturday Evening Post*, July 25, 1964, pp. 8–10.

1964d "Foreword." In *Karl Marx, Selected Writings in Sociology and Social Philosophy*, trans. by T. B. Bottomore. Edited with an introduction and notes by T. B. Bottomore and M. Rubol. New York: McGraw-Hill, 1964.

1964e "Foreword." In M. R. Green, ed., *Interpersonal Psychoanalysis: The Selected Papers of Clara M. Thompson.* New York/London: Basic Books, 1964.

1964f "Creators and Destroyers." *The Saturday Review*, January 4, 1964, pp. 22–25.

1964g "The Assassin (Kennedy's Murderer)." *The Correspondent* 30, Jan./Feb., 1964.

1964h "Foreign Policy After the Test Ban." *The Correspondent* 30 (Jan./Feb. 1964): 58–62.

1964i "Détente Through Firmness." *The Correspondent* 31 (Mar./Apr. 1964): 6–9.

1964k "Legitimate Discontents." *The Correspondent* 32 (Fall 1964), 16.

1965a *Socialist Humanism: An International Symposium*, edited by Erich Fromm. New York: Doubleday, 1965.

1965b "Introduction." In 1965a.

1965c "The Application of Humanist Psychoanalysis to Marx's Theory." In 1965a.

1965d "Problems of Interpreting Marx." In I. L. Horowitz, ed., *The New Sociology: Essays in Social Science and Social Theory in Honor of C. Wright Mills.* New York: Oxford University Press, 1965.

1965e "Preface." In A. Reza Arasteh, *Rumio the Persian: Rebirth in Creativity and Love.* Lahore: Ashraf Press, 1965.

1965f "Interview" (with Richard Heffner). *McCall's* 92 (Oct. 1965): 132–133, 213f.

1965g *Different Forms of Violence* 4 pages. New York: Fellowship Publications of New York, 1965.

1965h "Foreword II." In *Escape from Freedom.* New York: Avon Books, 1965.

1965i "Editorial." *Revista de Psicoanalisis, Psiquiatria y Psicologia* 1 (1965).

1965k "Summary for the Opposition." *The Correspondent* 34, Spring-Summer 1965.

1965l "Los fundamentos y el disarrollo del psicoanalisis." *Revista de Psicoanalisis, Psiquiatria y Psicologia* 1 (1965): 10–19.

1966a *You Shall Be as Gods: A Radical Interpretation of the Old Testament and Its Tradition.* New York: Holt, Rinehart & Winston, 1966.

1966b "The Grundpositionen der Psychoanalyse." In *Fortschritte der Psychoanalyse. Internationales Jahrbuch zur Weiterentwicklung de Psychoanalyse.* Vol. II. Göttingen: Verlag für Psychologie C. J. Hogrefe. Originally given as lecture in 1961.

1966c "The Psychological Aspects of the Guaranteed Income." In R. Theobald, ed., *The Guaranteed Income, Next Step in Economic Evolution?* New York: Doubleday & Co., 1966.

1966d "Afterword." In 1961b. New ed. 1966.

1966e "A Clinical View of the Problem of Human Rights." *American Journal of Orthopsychiatry* 36 (1966): 195–197.

1966f *Dialogue with Erich Fromm* (with Richard Evans). New York: Harper & Row, 1966.

1966g "The Psychological Problem of Aging." *Journal of Rehabilitation* (Sept./Oct. 1966): 10–13, 51–57.

1966h "Is Germany on the March Again?" *War/Peace Report,* Mar. 1966, pp. 3f.

1966i "A Global Philosophy for Man." *The Humanist* 26 (1966): 117–122.

1966j "Marxismus, Psychoanalyse und 'wirkliche Wirklichkeit.'" *Tagebuch. Monatshefte für Kultur, Politik, Wirtschaft* 21 (1966): 5–6.

1966k "El complejo de Edipo: Comentarios al 'Análisis de la fabia de un niño de cinco años." *Revista de Psicoanalisis, Psiquiatria y Psicologia* 4 (1966): 26–33. Quotations from the English translation in *Contemporary Psychoanalysis* 4 (1968): 178–188.

1966l "Scientific Research in Psychoanalysis: An Editorial." *Contemporary Psychoanalysis* 2 (1966): 168–170.

1966m Review of K. M. y S. Grossman, *The Wild Analyst. Revista de Psicoanalisis, Psiquiatria y Psicologia* 2 (1966): 89f.

1966n "La investigacion cientifica en el Psicoanalisis." *Revista de Psicoanalisis, Psiquiatria y Psicologia* 3 (1966): 3–6.

1967a "Memories of Dr. D. T. Suzuki." *The Eastern Buddhist,* New Ser. 2 (Aug. 1967): 86–89.

1967b "Prophets and Priests." In R. Schoenman, ed., *Bertrand Russell: Philosopher of the Century: Essays in His Honor.* London: George Allen & Unwin, 1967.

1967c "Vorwort." In Heinz Brandt, *Ein Traum, der nicht ausführbar ist. Mein Weg zwischen Ost und West.* Munich: Paul List Verlag, 1967.

1967d "The Present Crisis in Psychoanalysis." *Praxis. Philosophische Zeitschrift.* (Zagreb) 3 (1967): 70–80.

1967e "Do We Still Love Life?" *McCall's* 94 (Aug. 1967): 57, 108–110.

1967f "Foreword II." In E. Fromm, 1950a, pp. vi–viii.
1967g "Observaciones sobre el problema de la destructividad." *Revista de Psicoanalisis, Psiquiatria y Psicologia* 5 (1967): 3–5.
1968a *The Revolution of Hope: Toward a Humanized Technology.* New York: Harper & Row, World Perspectives Vol. 38, 1968.
1968b *The Nature of Man.* Readings selected, edited, and furnished with an introductory essay by Erich Fromm and Ramon Xirau. New York: Macmillan, 1968.
1968c "In the Name of Life." *Psychiatry and Social Science Review,* July 1968.
1968d "Why Is America Violent?" *National Catholic Reporter,* June 12, 1968.
1968d "On the Sources of Human Destructiveness." In *Alternatives to Violence: A Stimulus to Dialogue.* New York: Time-Life Books, 1968.
1968f "The Condition of the American Spirit: Are We Fully Alive?" *Newsday,* Jan. 13, 1968.
1968g "Introduction." In 1968b.
1968h "Marx's Contribution to the Knowledge of Man." In *Social Science Information* 3. Den Haag, 1968, pp. 7–17.
1968i "Hacia el año 2000." *El Nacional* (Mexico), Mar. 4, 1968.
1968j "Editorial." *Revista de Psicoanalisis, Psiquiatria y Psicologia* 9 (1968): 3f.
1969a "In the Name of Life." In Alexander Klein, ed., *Natural Enemies? Youth and the Clash of Generations.* New York: J. B. Lippincott, 1969.
1969b "Letter to Lord Bertrand Russell." In *Bertrand Russell: The Autobiography of Bertrand Russell 1944–1967.* Vol. 3. London: George Allen & Unwin, 1969.
1970a *The Crisis of Psychoanalysis: Essays on Freud, Marx and Social Psychology.* New York: Holt, Rinehart & Winston, 1970.
1970b *Social Character in a Mexican Village: A Sociopsychoanalytic Study* (with Michael Maccoby). Englewood Cliffs, N.J.: Prentice-Hall, 1970.
1970c "The Crisis of Psychoanalysis." In 1970a.
1970d "Freud's Model of Man and Its Social Determinants." In 1970a.
1970e "Humanistic Planning." In 1970a.
1970f "The Significance of the Theory of Mother Right for Today." In 1970a.
1970g "Epilogue." In 1970a.
1970h "Zur Theorie und Strategie des Friedens." In O. Schatz, ed., *Der Friede im nuklearen Zeitalter. Eine Kontroverse zwischen Realisten und Utopisten.* Munich: 4. Salzburger Humanismusgespräch, 1970.
1970i "Essay." In *Summerhill, For and Against.* New York: Hart Publishing Co., 1970.
1970j "Die psychologischen und geistigen Probleme des Überflusses." In O. Schatz, ed., *Die erschreckende Zivilisation.* Vienna: Europa Verlag, 1970.
1970k "Introduction." In Ivan Illich, *Celebration of Awareness: A Call for Institutional Revolution.* New York: Doubleday & Co., 1970.
1970i "Introduction." In A. Schaff, *Marxism and the Human Individual.* New York: McGraw-Hill, 1970.
1971a "Vorwort" to the German edition of 1968a.
1971b Letter to Martin Jay, May 14, 1971. Unpublished.
1972a "Der Traum ist die Sprache des universalen Menschen." In H. J. Schultz, ed., *Was weiss man von den Träumen.* Stuttgart/Berlin: Kreuz Verlag, 1972.
1972b "Einige post-marxsche und post-freudsche Gedanken über Religion und

Religiosität." *Concilium. Internationale Zeitschrift für Theologie* 8. Einsiedeln/Mainz (1972): 472–476.

1972c "The Erich Fromm Theory of Aggression." *The New York Times Magazine*, Feb. 27, 1972.

1973a *The Anatomy of Human Destructiveness.* New York: Holt, Rinehart & Winston, 1973.

1974a "Einführung." In H. J. Schultz, ed., *Psychologie für Nichtpsychologen.* Stuttgart: Kreuz Verlag, 1974.

1974b *Im Namen des Lebens. Ein Gespräch mit Hans Jürgen Schultz.* Stuttgart: Deutsche Verlags-Anstalt, 1974.

1974c "Hitler, wer war er und was heisst Widerstand gegen diesen Menschen? Erich Fromm im freien Gespräch mit Hans Jürgen Schultz." In H. J. Schultz, ed., *Der zwanzigste Juli—Alternative zu Hitler?* Stuttgart: Kreuz Verlag, 1974.

1974d "Ein Gespräch mit Erich Fromm" (with Robert Jungk). *Bild der Wissenschaft*, Oct. 1974, pp. 59–62.

1974e "Vorwort." In Boris Luban-Plazza, ed., *Praxis der Balint-Gruppen. Beziehungsdiagnostik und Therapie.* Munich: J. F. Lehmann, 1974.

1974f "L'erede di Freud guidica il referendum. UN colloquio con Erich Fromm," (with Giulio Nascimbeni). *Corriere della Sera*, May 23, 1974.

1974g "Foreword." In Miahilo Markovic, *From Affluence to Praxis Philosophy and Social Criticism.* Ann Arbor: University of Michigan Press, 1974.

1975a "Remarks on the Policy of Détente." In *Détente: Hearings before the Committee on Foreign Relations, United States Senate, 93rd Congress, Second Session, On United States Relations with Communist Countries*, Aug./Oct. 1974. Washington: U.S. Government Printing Office, 1975.

1975b *Aggression und Charakter. Ein Gespräch mit Adalbert Reif.* Zurich: Verlag die Arche, 1975.

1975c "Die Zwiespältigkeit des Fortschritts. Zum 100. Geburtstag von Albert Schweitzer." *Evangelische Kommentare* 8. Stuttgart (1975): 757f.

1975d "Die Aktualität der prophetischen Schriften." In H. J. Schultz, ed., *Sie werden lachen—die Bibel. Überraschungen mit dem Buch.* Stuttgart/Berlin: Kreuz Verlag, 1975.

1975e "Anmerkungen zur psychoanalytischen Theorie und Therapie." Lecture at a Symposium on the occasion of his 75th birthday in late May 1975 in Locarno. Audiothek des Buchclubs "ex libris." Zurich, 1975. Tonband-Cassette CWO 7034.

1975f "Introduction." In U. Bernath and E. Day Campbell, eds., *You Are My Brother: Father Wassons's Story of Hope for Children.* Huntington, Ind.: Our Sunday Visitor, 1975.

1975g "Rache des ungelebten Lebens. Erich Fromm über Katastrophen-Filme." *Der Spiegel* 9 (Feb. 24, 1975).

1975h "Prigionieri delcaos. Intervista con Erich Fromm" (by Maria Luigia Pace e Gian Luigi Rosa). *Panorama*, Milan, Dec. 16, 1975, pp. 124–134.

1975i "In fondo, l'uomo e un buon uomo. Colloquio con Erich Fromm (with Luciano Aleotti). *L'Espresso*, Feb. 16, 1975, pp. 56–59, 94.

1975k "La paura dell'anno 2000. Intervista von Erich Fromm," (with Guiliano Ferrieri). *L'Europeo* (Milan), June 27, 1975, pp. 30f.

1976a *To Have or to Be?* New York: Harper & Row, World Perspectives, Vol. 30, 1976.

1976b "Die Bedeutung des Ehrwürdigen Nyanaponika Mathera für die westliche Welt." In K. Onken, ed., *Des Geistes Gleichmass. Festschrift zum 75. Geburtstag des Ehrwürdigen Nyanaponika Mahathera.* Konstanz: Christiani Verlag, 1976.

1976c "The Will to Live." *Preventive Medicine: An International Journal Devoted to Practice and Theory* 5 (1976): 518–521.

1976d "The Secret Diaries by Albert Speer." Book jacket text of Albert Speer, *The Secret Diaries.* New York: Macmillan, 1976.

1976e "Über biologische und soziale Wurzeln der menschlichen Destruktivität." Lecture at the 1st Biennial for Psychiatry at Basle, Mar. 12–13, 1975. Basel: Sandoz Produkte, 1976.

1976f "How Will We Live? America's Future—A Discussion with Americans." *The Philadelphia Inquirer,* July 4, 1976.

1977a "Vita activa." In M. J. Schultz, ed., *Was der Mensch braucht. Anregungen für eine neue Kunst zu leben.* Stuttgart/Berlin: Kreuz Verlag, 1977.

1977b "Das Undenkbare denken und das Mögliche tun." A conversation with Erich Fromm (with Alfred A. Häsler) *ex libris,* May 1977.

1977c "Interview über 'Haben oder Sein' mit Adalbert Reif." *Arbeiter-Zeitung* 16, Vienna, April 23, 1977.

1978a "Religion und Gesellschaft." In Rainer Funk, *Mut zum Menschen. Erich Fromms Denken und Werk, seine humanistische Religion und Ethik.* Mit einem Nachwort von Erich Fromm. Stuttgart: Deutsche Verlags-Anstalt, 1978.

1978b "Das Undenkbare, das Unsagbare, das Unaussprechliche." *Psychologie heute* 5. Weinheim (1978): pt. 11.

1978c "Brief an Karola Bloch." In K. Bloch and A. Reif eds., *Denken heisst Überschreiten. In memoriam Ernst Bloch 1885–1977.* Köln/Frankfurt: Europäische Verlagsanstalt, 1978.

1979a *Greatness and Limitations of Freud's Thought.* New York: Harper & Row, 1980.

1979b "Konsumreligion." *Neues Forum,* Vienna (1979): 301/302.

1979c "Wir sitzen alle in einem Irrenhaus. Heinrich Jaenecke im Gespräch mit Erich Fromm." *Der Stern,* Hamburg, Apr. 19, 1979.

1979d "Erich Fromm: du Talmud à Freud. Interview avec Gerard Khoury." *Le Monde Dimanche,* Oct. 21, 1979.

1980a *Arbeiter und Angestellte am Vorabend des Dritten Reiches. Eine sozialpsychologische Untersuchung,* edited by Wolfgang Bonss, transl. into German by Wolfgang Bonss, with the collaboration of Cornelia Rülke and Rosemarie Thrul. Stuttgart: Deutsche Verlags-Anstalt, 1980.

1980b "Wer hat Interesse an der Wahrheit. Interview with Robert Neun." *Für uns* 4, Solothurn 1980.

1980c "Ich habe die Hoffnung, dass die Menschen ihr Leiden erkennen: den Mangel an Liebe." Ein Gespräch mit Heinrich Jaenecke. *Der Stern* (Mar. 27, 1980), p. 14.

1980d "Die Kranken sind die Gesündesten/Ein Interview, geführt kurz vor seinem Tode" (with Micaela Lämmle and Jürgen Lodemann). *Die Zeit,* Hamburg, Mar. 21, 1980.

1980e *Erich Fromm, il coraggio di essere. Intervista di Guido Ferrari.* Bellinzona: Edizioni Casagrande, 1980.

1981a *On Disobedience and Other Essays.* New York: The Seabury Press, 1981.

Secondary Literature

1. Works about Erich Fromm are indicated as follows:
   M = Monographs and Dissertations
   A = Articles, essays, excerpts
   R = Reviews
2. Encyclopedia articles are listed by author.

A Abril, G. G. "Erich Fromm y Gabriel Marcel. La esperanza frustrada y la esperanza absoluta." *Estudio Agustiniano* 9 (Valladolid 1974): 215–246.

Adorno, Theodor W. "Die revidierte Psychoanalyse." In *Reden und Vorträge: Sociologica II,* edited by Max Horkheimer and Theodor W. Adorno, pp. 94–112. Frankfurt: 1962.

——— et al. *Der Positivismusstreit in der deutschen Soziologie.* Neuwied: 1972.

Agus, Jacob B. *The Evolution of Jewish Thought from Biblical Times to the Opening of the Modern Era.* London/New York: 1959.

M Alsofrom, Ann. "A Factor Analysis of Erich Fromm's Nonproductive Orientations." Ph.D. dissertation, Columbia University, 1972.

M Amis, William Daughety. "Social Structure and Personality: The Contribution of Erich Fromm to Sociological Theory." Ph.D. dissertation, University of North Carolina. Ann Arbor: 1960.

A Anshen, Ruth Nanda. "Authority and Power: Erich Fromm and Herbert Marcuse." *Journal of Social Philosophy* 5 (Sept. 1974): 1–8.

A Arlow, Jacob A. "Truth or Motivations? Toward a Definition of Psychoanalysis." *The Saturday Review* 41 (June 14, 1958): 14, 54.

Auer, Alfons. *Autonome Moral und christlicher Glaube.* Düsseldorf: 1971.

A ———. *"Gibt es eine Ethik ohne Religiosität?"* Report at symposium on the occasion of Erich Fromm's 75th birthday, May 25, 1975, Locarno. Private manuscript.

R ———. Review of "Anatomie der menschlichen Destruktivität." *Herder Korrespondenz* 1 (Freiburg, 1975), 32–35.

———. "Ein Modell theologisch-ethischer Argumentation: 'Autonome Moral.' " In *Moralerziehung im Religionsunterricht,* edited by A. Auer, A. Biesinger and H. Gutschera, pp. 27–57. Freiburg/Basel/Wien: 1975.

———. "Die ethische Relevanz der Botschaft Jesu." In *Moralerziehung im Religionsunterricht,* edited by A. Auer, A. Biesinger and H. Gutschera, pp. 58–90. Freiburg/Basel/Wien: 1975.

———. "Tendenzen heutiger theologischer Ethik." In *Konturen heutiger Theologie,* workshop summaries, edited by G. Bitter and G. Miller, pp. 308–325. Munich: 1976.

———. "Autonome Moral und christlicher Glaube." *Katechetische Blätter 102* (1977): 60–76.

———. "Die Bedeutung des Christlichen bei der Normfindung." In *Normen im Konflikt. Grundfragen einer erneuerten Ethik,* edited by Joseph Sauer, pp. 29–54. Freiburg/Basel/Wien: 1977.

———. "Die Autonomie des Sittlichen nach Thomas von Aquin." In *Christlich glauben und handeln. Fragen einer fundamentalen Moraltheologie in der Diskussion,* Festschrift for Josef Fuchs, edited by K. Demmer and B. Schüller, pp. 31–54. Düsseldorf: 1977.

Bachofen, Johann Jacob. *Das Mutterrecht.* Basel: 1861.

Baeck, Leo. *Das Wesen des Judentums.* 6th ed. Frankfurt: 1932.

———. *Der Sinn der Geschichte.* Berlin: 1946.

———. *Maimonides: Der Mann, sein Werk und seine Wirkung.* Düsseldorf: 1954.

———. *Dieses Volk. Jüdische Existenz.* Vols. I and II. 1955, 1957.

Leo Baeck Institute. *Zur Geschichte der Juden in Deutschland im 19. und 20. Jahrhundert.* Jerusalem: 1971.

Baerwald, H. and Adler, S. *Geschichte der Realschule der israelitischen Gemeinde (Philanthropin) zu Frankfurt am Main 1804–1904.* Frankfurt: 1904.

A Baker, John F. "Erich Fromm." *Publishers Weekly* 210 (Sept. 9, 1976): 38 fn.42.

A Balmer, Hans Peter. "Befreiung von der Destruktivität? Erich Fromm in der Debatte um die menschliche Aggression." *Politische Studien* 29 (1976): 493–502.

Balthasar, Hans Urs von. "Zur Ortsbestimmung christlicher Mystik." In *Grundfragen der Mystik,* edited by W. Beierwaltes et al., pp. 37–71. Einsiedeln: 1974.

A Banks, Robert. "A Neo-Freudian Critique of Religion: Erich Fromm on Judeo-Christian Tradition." *Religion* 5 (1975): 117–135.

Barta, Johannes. "Jüdische Familienerziehung. Das jüdische Erziehungswesen im 19. und 20. Jahrhundert." Ph.D. dissertation, Zurich/Einsiedeln/Köln, 1974.

M Basabe Baracalá, José. *Síntesis del pensamiento de Fromm: individuacion, libertad y neurósis.* Barcelona: 1974.

Behari, Banke. *Mysticism in the Upanishads.* Gorakhpur, India: 1940.

Beierwaltes, Werner, et al. *Grundfragen der Mystik.* Einsiedeln: 1974.

R Benedict, Ruth. Review of "Escape from Freedom." *Psychiatry* 5 (1942): 111–113.

R ———. Review of "Man for Himself." *New York Herald Tribune Weekly Book Review* 24 (May 30, 1948): 6.

A Bertocci, Peter Anthony and Millard, Richard Marion. *Personality and the Good: Psychological and Ethical Perspectives,* esp. 69–93. New York: 1963.

M Betz, Richard Brian. "An Analysis of the Prophetic Character of the Dialectical Rhetoric of Erich Fromm." Ph.D. dissertation, Northwestern University, 1974.

R Bircher, Ralph. "Wesenszüge der neuen Gesellschaft." Review of "Haben oder Sein." *Der Wendepunkt* 55 (Erlenbach/Switzerland, 1978): 189–293.

A Birnbach, Martin. *Neo-Freudian Social Philosophy*. Stanford: 1961.

R Bittorf, Wilhelm. Review of "Anatomie der menschlichen Destruktivität." *Der Spiegel* 28 (Oct. 10, 1974): 190–193.

Bloch, Ernst. *Das Prinzip Hoffnung*. Vol. 5. Complete Works. Frankfurt: 1959.

R Block, Irving. "Radical Humanism and the Bible." Review of "You Shall Be as Gods." *Tradition: A Journal of Orthodox Jewish Thought* (Winter 1968): 131–137.

Böckle, Franz. "Was ist das Proprium einer christlichen Ethik?" *Zeitschrift für Evangelische Ethik* 11 (1967): 148–159.

———. "Theonome Autonomie. Zur Aufgabenstellung einer fundamentalen Moraltheologie." In *Humanum. Moraltheologie im Dienste des Menschen*, Festschrift Egenter, edited by J. Gründel et al., pp. 17–46. Düsseldorf: 1972.

———. "Unfehlbare Normen?" In *Fehlbar?*, edited by H. Küng, pp. 180–304. Zurich/Einsiedeln/Köln: 1973.

———. "Glaube und Handeln." In *Zwischenzeit und Vollendung der Heilsgeschichte*, pp. 21–115. Vol. 5. Mysterium Salutis. Grundriss heilsgeschichtlicher Dogmatik, edited by J. Feiner and M. Löhrer. Zurich/Einsiedeln/Köln: 1976.

R Boisen, Anton T. Review of "Escape from Freedom." *Psychiatry* 5 (1942): 113–117.

M Boivin, Rene. "Erich Fromm's Concept of Man." Ph.D. dissertation, privately published, Canada, 1973.

A Bonss, Wolfgang. "Kritische Theorie und empirische Sozialforschung. Anmerkungen zu einem Fallbeispiel." In E. Fromm, 1980a, S. 7–46.

R Borkenau, Franz. Review of "Die Entwicklung des Christusdogmas." *Zeitschrift für Sozialforschung* 1 (Leipzig, 1932): 174f.

A Boss, Medard. *Der Traum und seine Auslegung*, esp. pp. 67–70. Bern/Stuttgart: 1953 and 1974.

A Brams, Jerome. "From Freud to Fromm." *Psychology Today*, No. 1 (1968): 32–35, 64f.

A Brandl, Gerhard. "Das gemeinsame Anliegen. Eine Betrachtung zum Tode von Erich Fromm." *Zeitschrift für Individualpsychologie* 5 (Munich/Basel, 1980): 135–148.

Braun, Herbert. "Der Sinn der neutestamentlichen Theologie." In *Gesammelte Studien zum Neuen Testament und seiner Umwelt*, 3rd ed., pp. 243–282. Tübingen: 1971.

Briffault, Robert. *The Mothers*. New York: 1927.

R Briggs, Asa. Review of "The Sane Society." *The New Statesman and Nation: The Week-end Review* 51 (London, June 23, 1956): 739.

A Brossard, Chandler. "Erich Fromm—Influential and Controversial Psychoanalyst." *Look* (May 5, 1964): 50–52.

A Brown, J. A. C. *Freud and the Post-Freudians*. pp. 145–160. Baltimore: 1961.

A Browning, Don S. "Erich Fromm: The Productive Personality and the Coming of the Messianic Time." In *Generative Man: Psychoanalytic Perspectives*, edited by D. S. Browning, pp. 105–144. Philadelphia: 1973.

A Brumlik, Micha. "Radikaler Humanismus und Ideologie. Erich Fromm und das Haben." *Links* 123 (Hamburg, 1980): 15–19.

R Bryan, George. Review of "The Anatomy of Human Destructiveness." *Library Journal* 98 (1973): 3567.

R Brynes, Asher. Review of "Man for Himself." *The Saturday Review of Literature* 31 (Feb. 7, 1948): 25f.

Buber, Martin. "Der Chassidismus und die Krise des abendländlischen Menschen." *Juden, Christen, Deutsche,* edited by Hans Jürgen Schultz, pp. 83–94. Stuttgart/Olten/Freiburg: 1961.

———. *Der grosse Maggid und seine Nachfolger.* Frankfurt: 1922.

———. *Hasidism.* New York: Philosophical Library, 1948.

———. *The Origin and Meaning of Hasidism,* translated by Maurice Friedman. New York: Harper Torchbooks, 1966.

———. *Der Weg des Menschen nach der chassidischen Lehre.* 6th ed. Heidelberg: 1972.

Bultman, Rudolf. "Das Verhältnis der urchristlichen Christusbotschaft zum historischen Jesus." In *Exegetica,* edited by E. Dinkler, pp. 445–469. Tübingen: 1967.

A Buri, Fritz. "Religion-Haben und Religiös-Sein." *Theologia Practica* 13 (1978): 83–88.

M Caliguiri, Angelo M. "The Concept of Freedom in the Writings of Erich Fromm. An Exposition and Evaluation." Ph.D. Dissertation, Universitas Gregoriana Roma, 1966.

Calvez, Jean-Yves, S. J. *Karl Marx: Darstellung und Kritik seines Denkens.* Olten/Freiburg: 1964.

A Calzavara, Elisa. "Introduzione." In *Erich Fromm, Psicoanalisi dell' amore,* pp. 7–17. Rome: 1971.

R Camon, Ferdinando. "Perchè Fromm piace tanto?" *Il Giorno* (Feb. 19, 1978): 10.

A Campbell, James Alexander. *Freud and the Post-Freudians.* Baltimore: 1961; London: 1963.

A Caparrós Benedicto, Antonio. "El carácter social según Erich Fromm." *Convivium* 42 (1974): 3–27.

———. *El carácter social según Erich Fromm. Estudio crítico de su obra.* Salamanca: 1975.

M Catemario, Armando. *La società malata; saggio sulla filosofia di Fromm.* Naples: 1962.

A Chrzanowski, Gerard. "Das psychoanalytische Werk von Karen Horney, Harry Stack Sullivan und Erich Fromm." In *Die Psychologie des 20. Jahrhunderts.* Vol. III, pp. 497–507. Zurich: 1977.

R Clayre, Alasdair. "A Deadly Civilization." Review of "The Anatomy of Human Destructiveness." *The Guardian Weekly* 110 (Jan. 5, 1974): 26.

Cohen, Hermann. *Der Begriff der Religion im System der Philosophie.* Giessen: 1915.

———. "Charakteristik der Ethik Maimunis." In *Moses ben Maimon. Sein Leben, seine Werke und sein Einfluss.* Vol. I. Leipzig: 1908.

———. *Ethik des reinen Willens.* 2nd ed. Berlin: 1907.

———. Jüdische Schriften. Vol. 1. *Ethische und religiöse Grundfragen, mit einer Einleitung von Franz Rosenzweig.* Berlin: 1924.

———. *Jüdische Schriften.* Vol. 2. *Zur jüdischen Zeitgeschichte.* Berlin: 1924.

———. *Jüdische Schriften.* Vol. 3. *Zur jüdischen Religionsphilosophie und ihrer Geschichte.* Berlin: 1924.

———. *Der Nächste. Vier Abhandlungen über das Verhalten von Mensch zu Mensch nach der Lehre des Judentums. Mit einer Vorbemerkung von Martin Buber.* Berlin: 1935.

———. *Reason and Hope. Selections from the Jewish Writings of Hermann Cohen.* Translated by Eva Jospe. New York: W. W. Norton & Co., 1971.

———. *Religion of Reason out of the Sources of Judaism.* Translated by Simon Kaplan. New York: Frederick Ungar, 1972.

———. *Religion und Sittlichkeit. Eine Betrachtung zur Grundlegung der Religionsphilosophie.* Berlin: 1907.

Conzelmann, Hans. *Der erste Brief an die Korinther* (Meyers Kommentar V). Göttingen: 1969.

R Cox, Harvey. Review of "You Shall be as Gods." *The New York Times Book Review,* Nov. 27, 1966.

A Crass, E. "Der Apostel eines radikalen Humanismus. Erich Fromm zum 80. Geburtstag." *Integral* 5, Vienna (1980): 27–33.

M Curtis, Oliver B. "The Role of Religion in Selfhood: An Examination of Humanistic Psychoanalysis in Erich Fromm and Christian Selfhood in Wayne Oates." Ph.D. dissertation, Baylor University, 1972.

R Cvekl, Jiři. Review of "The Heart of Man." In *Erich Fromm, Lidské srdce,* pp. 125–132. Prague: 1969.

R Czapiewski, Winfried. Review of "Anatomie der menschlichen Destruktivität." *Theologischer Literaturdienst* No. 4 (Würzburg, 1975): 63f.

R ———. Review of "Haben oder Sein." *Theologischer Literaturdienst,* No. 3, Würzburg (1977): 47f.

Dahmer, Helmut. "Psychoanalyse als kritische Theorie." In *Politische Orientierungen,* pp. 252–259. Frankfurt: 1973.

A ———. *Libido und Gesellschaft. Studien über Freud und die Freudsche Linke.* Frankfurt: 1973.

M Daly, Charles E. "The Epistemological and Ethical Theory of Erich Fromm as the Basis for a Theory of Moral Education." Ph.D. dissertation, New York University, 1977.

Demmer, Klaus and Schüller, Bruno, eds. *Christlich glauben und handeln. Fragen einer fundamentalen Moraltheorie in der Diskussion.* Festschrift for Josef Fuchs. Düsseldorf: 1977.

M Denbo, Sheryl J. "Synthesis of Liberation: Marx–Freud and the New Left: An Examination of the Work of Wilhelm Reich, Erich Fromm and Herbert Marcuse." Ph.D. dissertation, Rutgers University, 1975.

R Denker, Rolf. "Ein Weg, den man nicht gehen wird." Review of "Haben oder Sein." *Frankfurter Allgemeine Zeitung,* Feb. 23, 1977.

Deussen, Paul. *Allgemeine Geschichte der Philosophie unter besonderer Berücksichtigung der Religionen.* Vol. 1, Pts. 1 and 2. Leipzig: 1906/1907.

M Devitis, Joseph Liberatore. "The Concept of Repression in the Social and Educational Thought of Erich Fromm and Herbert Marcuse." Ph.D. dissertation, University of Illinois, 1972.

R Dinnage, Rosemary. "The Necrophilous Type." Review of "The Anatomy of Human Destructiveness." *Times Literary Supplement* (Dec. 27, 1974): 1458.

R Review of "The Sane Society." *Dissent,* New York (1956): 84–89.

M Dobren'kov, Vladimir Ivanovich. *Soziologitscheskaja Konzepzija Erika Fromma* (*Das soziologische Konzept Erich Fromms*). Moscow: 1969.

M ———. *Kritika neofreidistskoi konseptsii Erika Fromma* (*Kritik der neofreudianischen Konzeption von Erich Fromm*). Moscow: 1972.

M ———. *Neofreidizim w poiskakh istiny; illiusu i sabluschdenia Erika Fromma* (*Neofreudianismus und die Suche nach der Wahrheit. Die Illusionen und Irrtümer von Erich Fromm.*). Moscow: 1974.

A Donzelli, M. "Una interpretatione del Vecchio Testamento e della sua tradizione." *Nuova rivista storica* (1971): 675–687.

A Dreitzel, Hans Peter. "Die gesellschaftlichen Leiden und das Leiden an der Gesellschaft." In *Vorstudien zu einer Pathologie des Rollenverhaltens*, pp. 10–17. Stuttgart: 1968.

Dubnow, Simon. *Weltgeschichte des jüdischen Volkes*. 2nd, abridged ed. in 3 vols. Vol. II. *Die europäische Periode in der Geschichte des jüdischen Volkes. Von den Anfängen der abendländischen Diaspora bis zum Ausgang des 18. Jahrhunderts.* Revised in collaboration with Dr. A. Steinberg. Jerusalem: 1971.

———. *Weltgeschichte des jüdischen Volkes*. 2nd, abridged ed. in 3 vols. Vol. III. *Neueste Geschichte* (*1789–1914*). *With an Epilogue 1914–1928*. Revised in collaboration with Dr. A. Steinberg. Jerusalem: 1971.

A Dunayevskaya, Ray. "Erich Fromm: Socialist Humanist." *News and Letters* 25 (Detroit, 1980): 10.

Dux, Günter. "Ursprung, Funktion und Gehalt der Religion." In *Internationales Jahrbuch für Religionssoziologie*, edited by Günter Dux, Thomas Luckmann, and Joachim Matthes. Vol. VIII. *Zur Theorie der Religion und Sprache*, pp. 7–67. Opladen: 1973.

A Dvorak, Josef. "Schizophren ist normal. Zum Tode Erich Fromms." *Forum*, Vienna (July/Aug. 1980): 44–47.

A Ebersole, Mark C. *Christian's Faith and Man's Religion*. New York: 1961.

Meister Eckhart. *Die deutschen Werke*. Edited by Josef Quint. Vol. II. In *Die deutschen und lateinischen Werke*, edited by Josef Quint and Josef Koch. Stuttgart: 1971.

Eid, Volker. "Tugend als Werthaltung." In *Humanum. Moraltheologie im Dienst des Menschen* (*Festschrift Egenter*), edited by J. Gründel et al., pp. 66–83. Düsseldorf: 1972.

Enomiya-Lasalle, Hugo M. Zen unter Christen. *Östliche Meditation und christliche Spiritualität*. Graz/Vienna/Köln: 1973.

Ermecke, Gustav. "Katholische Moraltheorie am Scheideweg." *Münchner Theologische Zeitschrift* 28 (1977): 47–54.

A Essbach-Kreuzer, Uschi. "Die Theorie des Sozialcharakters in den Arbeiten von Erich Fromm." *Zeitschrift für psychosomatische Medizin* 18 (1972): 171-191.

R Eysenck, H. J. "Utopia in Dreamland." Review of "The Anatomy of Human Destructiveness." *The Spectator* 233 (Oct. 26, 1974): 535.

M Fairbairn, James Ronald. "The Achievement of Human Existence: A Critique of Erich Fromm's Philosophical Anthropology." Ph.D. dissertation, Duke University, 1973.

R Fenichel, Otto. Review of "Escape from Freedom." *Psychoanalytic Review* 31 (1944): 133–152. Also in *Collected Papers of Otto Fenichel* 2nd ser. pp. 260–277. Edited by Hanna Fenichel and David Rapaport. London: 1955.

A Ferraris, Luigi. "Possibilità della psicoanalisis: sguardo al passato e al futuro. Erich Fromm." *Pubblicazioni Mediche Ticinesi* 6 (May 1976): 25–27.

Feuerbach, Ludwig. *Das Wesen des Christentums. Sämtliche Werke*. Vol. 6, Pt. 2. Edited by Wilhelm Bolin and Friedrich Jodl. Stuttgart/Bad Cannstatt: 1960.

Fischer, Heribert. *Meister Eckhart. Einführung in sein philosophisches Denken.* Freiburg/Munich: 1974.

R Flad-Schnorrenberg, Beatrice. Review of "Anatomie der menschlichen Destruktivität." *Frankfurter Allgemeine Zeitung,* No. 233 (Oct. 8, 1974); 13 L.

A Flego, Gvozden. "Frommovo shvácanje ĉovjeka." In *E. Fromm, Imati ili Biti?* pp. 9–44. Zagreb: 1979.

A Forsyth, James J. and Beniskos, J. M. "Biblical Faith and Erich Fromm's Theory of Personality." *Revue de l'Université d'Ottawa* 40 (1970): 69–91.

M Franck, Isaac. "The Concept of Human Nature: A Philosophical Analysis of the Concept of Human Nature in the Writings of G. W. Allport, S. E. Asch, Erich Fromm, A. H. Maslow, and C. R. Rogers." Ph.D. dissertation, University of Maryland, 1966.

R Frenzel, Ivo. "Der humanistische Protest. Erich Fromms Ausblick auf eine neue Gesellschaft." Review of "Haben oder Sein." *Süddeutsche Zeitung,* Munich (Feb. 19, 1977): 82.

Freud, Sigmund. *The Standard Edition of the Complete Psychological Works.* Vols. XIII, XIV, XXI. London: The Hogarth Press.

A Friedenberg, Edgar Z. "Neo-Freudianism & Erich Fromm." *Commentary: A Jewish Review* 34 (1962): 305–313.

Friedländer, Michael. *Die jüdische Religion.* Basel: 1936/1971.

Fritzhand, Marek. "Marx's Ideal of Man." In *Socialist Humanism,* edited by Erich Fromm, pp. 157–165. New York: 1965.

Fromm-Reichmann, Frieda. "Psychoanalytische Trieblehre." *Zeitschrift für Psychoanalytische Pädagogik* 3 (1929): 266–268.

Fuchs, Josef. "Gibt es eine spezifisch christliche Moral?" *Stimmen der Zeit* 95 (1970): 99–112.

A Fuente-Muniz, Ramón de la. "Fromm's Approach to the Study of Personality." *Psychiatric Research Report,* Washington (1956): 7–14.

A Funk, Rainer. "Zu Erich Fromm—Leben und Werk." *Wissenschaft und Weltbild* 28 (1975): 154–156.

A ———. "Der Fluch, kein Mann zu sein. Psychoanalyse im Widerstreit." *Academia* 28 (Mar./Apr. 1977): 20–22.

A ———. *Frömmigkeit zwischen Haben und Sein. Religionspsychologische Anfragen an die "Bewegung Lefèbvre."* Zurich/Einsiedeln/Köln: 1977.

A ———. "Hat die Liebe in unserer Gesellschaft noch eine Chance? Reflexionen in Anschluss an Erich Fromm." *Meditation* 4, Säckingen (1978): 83–85.

A ———. "Mut zum Menschen. Erich Fromm." *Magazin R. Kultur an Rhein und Ruhr,* No. 7 (Dortmund, 1979): 14–16.

A ———. "Laudatio. Zur Verleihung des Nelly-Sachs-Preises der Stadt Dortmund an Erich Fromm." *Mitteilungen aus dem Literaturarchiv der Stadt Dortmund,* No. 7, Dortmund (1980): 13–22.

A ———. "Einleitung des Herausgebers." In *Erich Fromm, Gesamtausgabe.* Vol. 1, pp. ix–xlviii, edited by Rainer Funk. Stuttgart: 1980.

———. "Liebe—was ist das eigentlich?" *Bunte* (Offenburg, Mar. 20, 1980): 135–140.

———. "Das Wagnis, aus sich selbst zu leben." *Psychologie Heute* 7, Weinheim (1980): 12–18.

Furger, Franz. "Zur Begründung eines christlichen Ethos—Forschungstendenzen in der katholischen Moraltheologie." In *Theologische Berichte* IV, pp. 11–87, edited by Josef Pfammatter and Franz Furger. Zurich/Einsiedeln/Köln: 1974.

———. "Katholische Moraltheologie in der Schweiz. Diskussion und Schwerpunkte." *Zeitschrift für Evangelische Ethik* 20 (1976): 219–231.

R Gassert, Siegmar. "Individuum und Gesellschaft im Reflexionsbezug." *Basler Nationalzeitung, Wochenendbeilage,* Pt. III, Basel, Dec. 21, 1974.

A Gedö, Andraś. *Der entfremdete Marx. Zur existentialistisch- "humanistischen" Marxismus-Deutung.* Berlin: 1971.

Gehlen, Arnold. *Der Mensch. Seine Natur und seine Stellung in der Welt.* 10th ed. Frankfurt: 1974.

———. *Anthropologische Forschung. rowohlts deutsche enzyklopädie 138.* Reinbeck bei Hamburg: 1974.

R Gewirth, Alan. Review of "The Sane Society." *Ethics: An International Journal of Social, Political and Legal Philosophy,* 66 (1955/56): 289–292.

R Gill, Thomas Harvey. Review of "Escape from Freedom." *Psychiatry* 5, Washington (1942): 109–111.

Glasenapp, Helmuth von. "Vorwort." In *Upanishaden. Altindische Weisheit aus Brahmanas und Upanishaden,* translated and introduced by Alfred Hillebrandt. Zurich: 1973.

M Glen, J. Stanley. "Erich Fromm: A Protestant Critique." Philadelphia, Ph.D. dissertation, 1966.

Gollwitzer, Helmut. *Die marxistische Religionskritik und der christliche Glaube Siebenstern Taschenbuch 33.* 5th ed. Hamburg: 1974.

A Görlich, Bernard. "Die Kulturismus-Revisionismus-Debatte. Anmerkungen zur Problemgeschichte der Kontroverse um Freud." In *Der Stachel Freud. Beiträge und Dokumente zur Kulturismus-Kritik.* Edited by Bernard Görlich, pp. 13–89. Frankfurt: 1980.

A Gotesky, R. *Personality: The Need for Liberty and Rights.* New York: 1967.

R Gradwohl, Roland. "Ist der Mensch böse?" *Israelitisches Wochenblatt* No. 47, Zurich, Nov. 21, 1975.

Graupe, Heinz Mosche. *Die Entstehung des modernen Judentums. Geistesgeschichte der deutschen Juden 1650–1942.* Hamburg: 1969.

A Green, Arnold W. "Sociological Analysis of Horney and Fromm." *The American Journal of Sociology* 51 (1945/46): 533–540.

Green, Maurice R. "Her Life." In *Interpersonal Psychoanalysis, Selected Papers,* edited by Clara M. Thompson, pp. 347–377. New York/London: 1964.

R Gregor, A. James. "Erich Fromm and the Young Karl Marx." Review of "Marx's Concept of Man." *Studies on the Left* 3 (1962): 85–92.

A Greinacher, Norbert. "Erich Fromm." In *Die Religion der Religionskritik,* edited by Wilhelm Schmidt, pp. 28–37. Munich: 1972.

Grimm, Georg. *Die Lehre des Buddha. Die Religion der Vernunft.* 6th to 8th ed. Munich: 1920.

———. *Die Wissenschaft des Buddhismus.* Leipzig: 1923.

Gründel, Johannes. "Ethik ohne Normen? Zur Begründung und Struktur christlicher Ethik." In *Ethik ohne Normen? Zu den Weisungen des Evangeliums,* edited by Johannes Gründel and Hendryk van Oyen, pp. 9–88. Freiburg: 1970.

———. Rauh, Fritz, and Eid, Volker, (eds.) *Humanum. Moraltheorie im Dienste des Menschen* (*Festschrift Egenter*). Düsseldorf: 1972.

Gulkowitsch, Lazar. *Der Hasidismus, religionswissenschaftlich untersucht.* Leipzig: 1927.

M Gutiérrez, José. *El método psicoanalítico de Erich Fromm.* Bogotá: 1961.

Guttmann, Julius. "Religion und Wissenschaft im mittelalterlichen und modernen Denken." In *Festschrift zum 50-jährigen Bestehen der Hochschule für die Wissenschaft des Judentums in Berlin,* pp. 145–216. Berlin: 1922.

———. *Die Philosophie des Judentums. Geschichte der Philosophie in Einzeldarstellungen.* Pt. 1. *Das Weltbild der Primitiven und die Philosophie des Morgenlandes.* Vol. 3. Munich: 1933.

R Hadley, Ernest E. Review of "Escape from Freedom." *Psychiatry* 5, Washington (1942): 131–134.

M Hammond, Guyton Bowers. *Man in Estrangement. A Comparison of the Thought of Paul Tillich and Erich Fromm.* 2nd ed. Charlotte, N.C.: 1967.

R Häsler, Alfred A. "Zwischen Lebenstrieb und Todestrieb." Review of "Anatomie der menschlichen Destruktivität." *Die Tat,* Zurich (Aug. 13, 1976): 34.

R Hasler, Ludwig. "Die sogenannte Aggression." Review of "Anatomie der menschlichen Destruktivität." *Der Bund. Beilage "Der kleine Bund"* 126, Bern (Feb. 2, 1975): 1.

R Hathaway, Richard O. "Analyzing Aggression." Review of "The Anatomy of Human Destructiveness." *The Christian Century* (Mar. 13, 1974): 297.

M Hausdorff, Don. *Erich Fromm.* New York: 1972.

R Heer, Friedrich. Review of "Anatomie der menschlichen Destruktivität." *Salzburger Nachrichten,* Dec. 6, 1974.

R ———. "Die Lust an der Gewalt." Review of "Anatomie der menschlichen Destruktivität." *Die Welt,* Hamburg, Nov. 7, 1974.

Hegel, Georg Wilhelm Friedrich. *Sämtliche Werke, herausgegeben von Hermann Glockner (Jubiläumsausgabe).* 20 vols. Stuttgart: 1927.

A Heigl, Franz. "Die humanistische Psychoanalyse Erich Fromms." *Zeitschrift für psychosomatische Medizin* 7 (1961): 77–84, 153–161, 235–249.

Heinrichs, Hans-Jürgen (ed.). *Materialien zu Bachofens "Das Mutterrecht." suhrkamp taschenbuch wissenschaft 136.* Frankfurt: 1975.

Heller, Agnes. "Aufklärung und Radikalismus-Kritik der psychologischen Anthropologie Fromms." In *Instinkt, Aggression, Charakter. Einleitung zu einer marxistischen Sozialanthropologie,* pp. 7–53. Hamburg: 1977.

A Herberg, Will. "Freud, the Revisionists, and Social Reality." In *Freud and the 20th Century,* edited by Benjamin Nelson, pp. 141–160. London: 1958; New York: 1957.

R Herichon, E. Review of "The Sane Society." *L'homme et la société. Revue internationale de recherche et de synthèse sociologique* No. 11, Paris (1969): 230–233.

Herrigel, Eugen. *Zen in the Art of Archery.* Translated by R. F. C. Hull. New York: Pantheon, 1953.

R Hill, Lewis B. Review of "Escape from Freedom." *Psychiatry* 5, Washington (1942): 117–118.

Hillebrandt, Alfred. *Upanishaden. Altindische Weisheit aus Brahmanas und Upanishaden. Übertragen und eingeleitet von Alfred Hillebrandt.* Diederichs Taschenausgabe 13. Düsseldorf/Köln: 1958.

M Hiltner, Seward. "Psychotherapy and Christian Ethics: An Evaluation of the Ethical Thought of A. E. Taylor and Paul Tillich in the Light of Psychotherapeutic Contributions to Ethics by J. C. Fluegel and Erich Fromm." Ph.D. dissertation, University of Chicago, 1953.

A ———. "Erich Fromm and Pastoral Psychology." *Pastoral Psychology* 6 (1955): 11–12.

R Hingst, Wolfgang. "Ungelebtes Leben—Ursprung der Destruktivität." Review of "Anatomie der menschlichen Destruktivität." *Frankfurter Hefte*, Frankfurt, June 1977.

Hoffmann, Paul. *Studien zur Theologie der Logienquelle* Neutestamentliche Abhandlungen, edited by Joachim Gnilka, NF Vol. 8. Münster: 1972.

——— and Eid, Volker. *Jesus von Nazareth und eine christliche Moral. Sittliche Perspektiven der Verkündigung Jesu.* Quaestiones Disputatae 66. Freiburg/Basel/Vienna: 1975.

Horkheimer, Max. *Verwaltete Welt. Gespräch zwischen Max Horkheimer und Oskar Hersche.* Zurich: 1970.

R Horney Eckhart, Marianne. "L' Chaim." Review of Bernhard Landis and Edward S. Tauber, "In the Name of Life. Essays in Honor of Erich Fromm." *Contemporary Psychoanalysis* 9 (1972): 106–111. Also *Contemporary Psychoanalysis* 11 (1975): 465–470.

Horodezky, S. A. *Religiöse Strömungen im Judentum. Mit besonderer Berücksichtigung des Chassidismus.* Bern/Leipzig: 1920.

Howard, A. R., and James, Walter T. *A Study of Karen Horney and Erich Fromm in Relation to Alfred Adler.* Carlish: 1947.

M Hurwitz, Siegmund. "Archetypische Motive in der chassidischen Mystik." In *Zeitlose Dokumente der Seele. Studien aus dem C. G. Jung-Institut Zürich*, Vol. II, edited by C. A. Meier. Zurich: 1952.

A Hyman, Stanley Edgar. "Psychoanalysis and the Climate of Tragedy." In *Freud and the 20th Century*, edited by B. Nelson, pp. 163–181. London: 1958.

A Illich, Ivan. "The Dawn of Epimethean Man." Paper prepared for a symposium in honor of Erich Fromm. Centro Intercultural de Documentacion, No. 75, 227/1–16. Cuernavaca: 1972.

Imschoot, Paul von. "Name." In Bibel-Lexikon, edited by Herbert Haag, pp. 1215f. Einsiedeln/Zurich/Köln: 1968.

A Israel, Joachim. *Der Begriff Entfremdung. Makrosoziologische Untersuchung von Marx bis zur Soziologie der Gegenwart.* rowohlts deutsche enzyklopädie 359. Hamburg: 1972.

Jacobs, Louis. *Principles of the Jewish Faith: An Analytic Study.* London: 1964.

A Jacoby, Russell. *Social Amnesia: A Critique of Conformist Psychology from Adler to Laing.* New York: 1975.

A Jaenecke, Heinrich. "Der Prophet des Untergangs." *Stern* (Apr. 19, 1979): 76–82.

A James, Walter T. "Karen Horney and Erich Fromm in Relation to Alfred Adler." *Individual Psychology Bulletin* 6 (1947): 105–116.

A Jay, Martin. *The Dialectical Imagination: A History of the Frankfurt School and the Institute of Social Research 1923–1950.* London: 1973.

A ———. "The Frankfurt School's Critique of Marxist Humanism." *Social Research* 39 (1972): 285–305.

M Jensen, Vern Arthur. "Failure and Capability in Love: An Integrative Study of the Psychology of Erich Fromm and the Theology of Erich Brunner." Ph.D. dissertation, 1966.

Jodl, Friedrich. *Geschichte der Ethik in der neueren Philosophie.* Vol. I. *Bis zum Ende des 18. Jahrhunderts, mit einer Einleitung über die antike und christliche Ethik.* Stuttgart: 1882.

———. *Ethik und Moralpädagogik gegen Ende des 19. Jahrhunderts.* Sonderdruck aus *Geschichte der Ethik als philosophischer Wissenschaft.* Vol. II. 2nd ed. Stuttgart/Berlin: 1913.

Johnston, William. *Der ruhende Punkt. Zen und christliche Mystik.* Freiburg/Basel/Vienna: 1974.

Jonas, Hans. *Gnosis und spätantiker Geist.* Vol. I. Göttingen: 1934.

A Jungk, Robert. "Ein Gespräch mit Erich Fromm." *Bild der Wissenschaft* 11 (Oct. 1974): 59–62.

A Kalivoda, Robert. "Marx und Freud." In *Weiterentwicklungen des Marxismus,* edited by W. Gelmüller, pp. 140–148. Darmstadt: 1977.

Käsemann, Ernst. "Das Problem des historischen Jesus." In *Exegetische Versuche und Besinnungen,* Vol. 1, pp. 187–214. Göttingen: 1964.

Kasper, Walter. *Jesus der Christus.* Mainz: 1974.

Kaufmann, David. *Geschichte der Attributenlehre in der jüdischen Religionsphilosophie des Mittelalters von Saadja bis Maimuni.* Gotha: 1877.

R Kecskemeti, Paul. Review of "The Sane Society." *Commentary* 21 (1956): 176–179.

Keilbach, Wilhelm. "Theismus." In *Lexikon für Theologie und Kirche.* Vol. X, cols. 16–18. Freiburg: 1965.

M Kennedy, William Martin. "Implications for Counseling from Erich Fromm's View of Man's Ethical Responsibility." Ph.D. dissertation, East Texas State University, 1973.

Kertelge, Karl, ed. *Rückfrage nach Jesus.* Quaestiones Disputatae 63. Freiburg/Basel/Vienna: 1974.

Klausner, Joseph. *The Messianic Idea in Israel: From Its Beginning to the Completion of the Mishnah.* New York: 1955.

———. *Die messianischen Vorstellungen des jüdischen Volkes im Zeitalter der Tannaiten, kritisch untersucht und im Rahmen der Zeitgeschichte dargestellt.* Berlin: 1904.

Kluxen, Wolfgang. *Philosophische Ethik bei Thomas von Aquin.* Mainz: 1964.

R Knight, Frank H. Review of "Escape from Freedom." *The American Journal of Sociology* 48 (1942/43): 299.

A Kodalle, Klaus-M. "Erich Fromm." In *Das Unbehagen an Jesus,* pp. 43–51. Olten/Freiburg: 1978.

Köhler, Hans. *Die Wirkung des Judentums auf das abendländische Geistesleben.* Berlin: 1952.

Kohlenberger, H. K. "Dialektik bei Hegel." In *Historisches Wörterbuch der Philosophie,* edited by Joachim Ritter, Vol. 2, cols. 189–193. Basel/Darmstadt: 1972.

Korff, Wilhelm. *Norm und Sittlichkeit. Untersuchungen zur Logik der normativen Vernunft.* Tübinger Theologische Studien 1. Mainz: 1973.

———. *Theologische Ethik. Eine Einführung. Unter Mitarbeit von Walter Fürst und Josef Torggler.* Freiburg/Basel/Vienna: 1975.

Kranzler, Gershon. *Rabbi Shneur Zalman of Ladi: A Brief Presentation of His Life, the Work and the Basic Teachings of the Founder of Chabad Chassidism.* New York: 1948.

Krieger, Hans. Review of "Anatomie der menschlichen Destruktivität." *Die Zeit,* Hamburg, Jan. 2, 1975.

R ———. "Krank am Besitz." Review of "Haben oder Sein." *Die Zeit,* Hamburg, Jan. 21, 1977.

Küng, Hans. *On Being a Christian.* Translated by Edward Quinn. Garden City, N.Y.: Doubleday, 1976.

A Kwaver, Jay S. "A Case Seminar with Erich Fromm." *Contemporary Psychoanalysis* 11 (1975): 453–455.

A Landis, Bernhard. "Fromm's Theory of Biophilia—Necrophilia. Its Implications for Psychoanalytic Practice." *Contemporary Psychoanalysis* 11 (1975): 418–434.

—— and Tauber, Edward S., eds. *In the Name of Life. Essays in Honor of Erich Fromm.* New York: 1971.

A —— and Tauber, Edward S. "On Erich Fromm." In *In the Name of Life. Essays in Honor of Erich Fromm*, pp. 1–11. New York: 1971. Also in *Contemporary Psychoanalysis* 11 (1975): 407–417.

M Lang, Virgil Robert. "A Comparison of Aspects of the Riesman, Fromm and Morris Typologies Relevant to Self-Concept." Ph.D. dissertation, St. John's University, 1968.

Langer, Georg M. *Neun Tore. Das Geheimnis der Chassidim.* Introduction by Gershom Scholem. Munich/Planegg: 1959.

Lazarus, Moritz. *Die Ethik des Judentums.* Vol. 1. Frankfurt: 1898. Vol. 2, edited from the author's papers by J. Winter and August Wünsche, Frankfurt: 1911.

Laun, A. "Zur Frage einer spezifisch christlichen Ethik." *Spiritualität in Moral* (*Festschrift Hörmann*), edited by G. Virth, pp. 33–58. Vienna: 1975.

M Lee, Lester C. "An Investigation of Erich Fromm's Theory of Authoritarianism." Ph.D. dissertation, Claremont Graduate School, 1963.

Leisegang, Hans. *Denkformen.* 2nd ed. Berlin: 1951.

Lepenies, Wolf. "Schwierigkeiten einer anthropologischen Begründung der Ethik." *Concilium. Internationale Zeitschrift für Theologie* 8 (1972): 318–327.

Leschnitzer, Adolf. *Saul und David. Die Problematik der deutsch-jüdischen Lebensgemeinschaft.* Heidelberg: 1954.

M Lessin, Edward John. "Aspects of Structure in Fromm's Marketing Orientation." Ph.D. dissertation, Michigan State University, 1968.

Levertoff, Paul. *Die religiöse Denkweise der Chassidim nach den Quellen dargestellt.* Leipzig: 1918.

A Lindzey, G., et al. "Erich Fromm." In *Psychology*, edited by G. Lindzey et al., pp. 540f. New York: 1975.

A Lipset, Seymour M. "World Peace and Russian Realities: Some Questions raised by Dr. Fromm's Analysis." *Socialist Call* 28 (Summer 1961): 11–13.

Lorenz, Konrad. *On Aggression.* Translated by Marjorie Kerr Wilson. New York: Harcourt Brace & World, 1966.

A Lorenzer, Alfred and Görlich, Bernard. "Die Sozialität der Natur und die Natürlichkeit. Zur Interpretation der psychoanalytischen Erfahrung jenseits vom Biologismus und Soziologismus." In *Der Stachel Freud*, edited by B. Görlich et al., pp. 297–349. Frankfurt: 1980.

A Luban-Plozza, Boris. "Aggressivität gegen die Kunst. Über Gedanken zur Aggression von Erich Fromm." *Hospitalis* 46 (1976).

A ——. "Erich Fromm: Alcuni Appunti Introduttivi." In Psicoterapia e Psicologia Umanistico-Esistenziale, pp. 3–21. Padua: 1977.

A ——. "Er suchte das innerste Wesen des Menschen. *Südschweiz*, Locarno, Mar. 20, 1980.

Lührmann, Dieter. *Die Redaktion der Logienquelle, mit einem Anhang: Zur weiteren Überlieferung der Logienquelle.* Neukirchen-Vluyn: 1970.

R Lütkehaus, Ludger. "Anatomie der Erwerbsgesellschaft." Review of "Haben oder Sein." *Frankfurter Hefte*, Frankfurt, 1977.

A Maccoby, Michael. "Bibliophilia-Necrophilia and Television." In *Television Today*, edited by R. Stavins, pp. 333–336. Washington: 1969.

A ———. "Emotional Attitudes and Political Choices." *Politics and Society* 2 (Winter 1972): 209–239.

A ———. *The Gamesman: The New Corporate Leaders.* New York: 1976.

Maimonides, M. *Guide of the Perplexed.* Translated by M. Friedländer. New York: Hebrew Publishing Company, n.d.

R Mainberger, Gonsalv K. "Mahnmal in verwüsteter Landschaft." Review of "Haben oder Sein." *Neue Zürcher Zeitung,* Zurich (May 7, 1977): 66.

A Mandolini Guardo, Ricardo C. *De Freud a Fromm. Historia general del psicoanálisis,* esp. pp. 418–466. Buenos Aires: 1965.

Marcel, Gabriel. *Sein und Haben* (*Être et avoir*). *Übersetzung und Nachwort von Ernst Behler.* Paderborn: 1954.

Marck, W. van der. *Grundzüge einer christlichen Ethik.* Düsseldorf: 1967.

Marcuse, Herbert. *Eros and Civilization.* Boston: 1955.

A ———. "Epilog. Kritik des Neo-Freudianischen Revisionismus." In *Triebstruktur und Gesellschaft. Ein philosophischer Beitrag zu Sigmund Freud,* pp. 234–269. Frankfurt: 1970.

A ———. "A Reply to Erich Fromm." *Dissent* 3 (1956): 79–81.

A Marković, Mihailo. "The Possibilities for Radical Humanism." In *In the Name of Life: Essays in Honor of Erich Fromm,* edited by B. Landis and E. S. Tauber, pp. 275–287. New York: 1971.

R Marschalek, Manfred. "Von Natur aus böse?" Review of "Anatomie der menschlichen Destruktivität." *Arbeiter-Zeitung,* Vienna (Nov. 23, 1974): 8–10.

Marx, Karl. *Early Writings.* New York: Vintage, 1975.

———. *Das Kapital. Kritik der politischen Ökonomie.* According to the 4th ed., revised and edited by Friedrich Engels, Hamburg, 1890. Vols. I–III. Berlin: Institut für Marxismus-Lenismus beim ZK der SED, 1972.

———. *Grundrisse der Kritik der politischen Ökonomie* (Rohentwurf 1857–1858). Berlin: 1974.

———, and Engels, Friedrich. *Historisch-kritische Gesamtausgabe* [MEGA]. *Works, Writings, and Letters.*

Part I. *Collected Works and Writings Other than Capital.* 6 vols. (Cited as I, 1–6.)

Part II. *Capital with its Drafts.*

Part III. *Correspondence.*

Part IV. *General Index.*

Edited at the behest of the Marx-Engels-Lenin Institute, Moscow, by V. Adoratsky. Berlin: 1932.

———. *Zur Kritik der politischen Ökonomie.* In *Works,* vol. 13. Berlin: Institut für Marxismus-Leninismus beim ZK der SED, 1961.

Massiczek, Albert. *Der menschliche Mensch. Karl Marx' jüdischer Humanismus.* Vienna/Frankfurt/Zurich: 1968.

M Mattingly, Garrett. Review of "Escape from Freedom." *The Saturday Review of Literature* 24 (Aug. 30, 1941): 6.

M McGrath, Michael. "An Examination of Erich Fromm's Ethics with Implications for Philosophy of Education." Ph.D. dissertation, University of Kentucky, 1968.

M ———. *Fromm: Ethics and Education.* Lexington, Ky.: 1969.

Mead, George Herbert. *Mind, Self and Society.* Chicago: 1934.

R Mead, Margaret. Review of "Escape from Freedom." *The New York Herald Tribune Book Review* 18 (Sept. 21, 1941): 18.

R Meier-Seethaler, Carola. "Vom Mut zur Veränderung des Herzens." Review of "Haben oder Sein?" *Basler Nationalzeitung Wochenendbeilage* (Jan. 29, 1977): 1 and 5.

R Menninger, Karl. "Loneliness in the Modern World." Review of "Escape from Freedom." *The Nation* 154 (Mar. 14, 1942): 317.

A Mickleson, Donna. "Bob Dylan, Erich Fromm and Beyond: A Look at the New Politics." In *To Make a Difference,* edited by O. Butz, pp. 155–174. New York: 1967.

Mieth, Dietmar. *Christus—das Soziale im Menschen. Texterschliessungen zu Meister Eckhart.* Topos Taschenbücher 4. Düsseldorf: 1972.

———. "Autonome Moral im christlichen Kontext. Zu einem Grundlagenstreit der theologischen Ethik." *Orientierung* 40, Zurich (Feb. 15, 1976): 31–34.

Mindel, Nissan. *Rabbi Shneur Zalman of Liadi.* Vol. I. *Biography.* New York: 1969.

———. "Introduction." In *Rabbi Shneur Zalman of Liadi, Liqqutei Amarim* (*Tanya*), 5th rev. ed. Vol. I, pp. xiii–xxxii. New York: 1975.

———. "Glossary and Notes." In *Rabbi Shneur Zalman of Liadi. Liqqutei Amarim* (*Tanya*), 5th rev. ed. Vol. I, pp. 337–350. New York: 1975.

Möller, Joseph. *Glauben und Denken im Widerspruch? Philosophische Fragen an die Theologie der Gegenwart.* Munich/Freiburg: 1969.

———. *Die Chance des Menschen—Gott genannt. Was Vernunft und Erfahrung heute von Gott sagen können.* Zurich: 1975.

R Montagu, M. F. Ashley. Review of "Escape from Freedom." *Psychiatry* 5, Washington (1942): 122–129.

Morgan, L. H. *Systems of Sanguinity and Affinity of the Human Family.* Washington: 1870.

———. *Ancient Society.* Chicago: 1877.

A Moritz, Charles, ed. "Erich Fromm." In *Current Biography 1967,* pp. 129–131. New York: 1967.

R Mosse, Hilde L. "Bypaths on the Road to Vienna." Review of "Sigmund Freud's Mission." *Saturday Review,* March 11, 1959, pp. 39f.

A Mueller, Ferdinand-Lucien. *Histoire de la Psychologie.* Paris: 1976. Pp. 473–483.

R Mullahey, Patrick. Review of "Escape from Freedom." *Psychiatry* 5 (Washington, 1942): 118–122.

A ———. *Oedipus Myth and Complex: A Review of Psychoanalytic Theory.* Introduction by Erich Fromm. New York: 1948.

R ———. Review of "The Sane Society." *Psychiatry* 18, Washington (1955): 399–409.

A Munzinger Archive. "Erich Fromm." International Biographical Archive: 1975/3 and 1976/3.

A Nagler, Simon H. "Erich Fromm." In *Interpreting Personality. A Survey of Twentieth-Century Views,* edited by A. M. Freedman and H. I. Kaplan, pp. 193–200. New York: 1972.

Nambara, Minoru. "Die Idee des absoluten Nichts in der deutschen Mystik und ihre Entsprechungen im Buddhismus." In *Archiv für Begriffsgeschichte. Bausteine zu einem historischen Wörterbuch der Philosophie,* edited by Erich Rothacker, Vol. 6, pp. 143–277. Bonn: 1960.

A Neel, Ann F. "Erich Fromm." In *Theories of Psychoanalysis: A Handbook,* pp. 303–309. Cambridge, Mass.: 1969.

M Neill, R. B. "Character, Society, and the Politics of Hope: A Comparative Look at the Theories of Wilhelm Reich, Erich Fromm, and Herbert Marcuse." Ph.D. dissertation, Simon Fraser University, British Columbia, 1975.

A Nesavas, Antanas. "Zmogaus koncepcija E. Froma filosofijoje." In *Filosofijos Istorijos Chrestomatija,* edited by J. Barzdaitis et al., pp. 451–458. Vilnius: 1974.

M Neufeld, Elmer. "Psychoanalysis, Science and Morality. A Critique of the Ethical Theory of Erich Fromm in Comparison to Lewis Feuer and Karen Horney." Ph.D. dissertation, University of Chicago, 1973.

R Niebuhr, Reinhold. Review of "Man for Himself." *Christianity and Society* 13 (1948): 26–28.

A Niel, Mathilde. "Presentation de la psychoanalyse humaniste d'Erich Fromm. In E. Fromm, *Société aliénée et société saine,* pp. 5–14. Paris: 1956.

A Nischk, Peter. *Kursbuch für die Seele. Nutzen und Elend der Psychotherapie.* Munich: 1976.

Nobel, Nehemia A. *Kriegspredigten gehalten in der Gemeinde-Synagoge am Börneplatz.* Frankfurt: 1914.

A Norell, Margit et al. "Reminiscences of Supervision with Erich Fromm." *Contemporary Psychoanalysis* 11 (1975): 456–464.

M Neurmberger, Robert Mansfield. "The Nature of Man and Guilt. Implications for Counseling Derived from an Analysis of the Philosophies of Cornelius van Til and Erich Fromm." Ph.D. dissertation, Michigan State University, 1967.

Nyanaponika Thera. *Der einzige Weg. Buddhistische Texte zur Geistesschulung in rechter Achtsamkeit.* Konstanz: 1956.

———. *Geistestraining durch Achtsamkeit. Die buddhistische Satipatthana-Methode.* Konstanz: 1975.

Oberndorf, C. P. *A History of Psychoanalysis in America.* New York: 1953.

M O'Brien, Kenneth. "The Humanist Perspective in Social Science: The Case of Erich Fromm." Ph.D. dissertation, Simon Fraser University, Canada, 1972.

A ———. "Death and Revolution: A reappraisal of Identity Theory." In *On Critical Theory,* edited by J. O'Neill, pp. 104–128. New York: 1976.

Oeing-Hanhoff, Ludger. "Der Mensch: Natur oder Geschichte? Die Grundlagen und Kriterien sittlicher Normen im Lichte der philosophischen Tradition." In *Naturgesetz und christliche Ethik,* edited by Franz Henrich, Münchner Akademie-Schriften 55, pp. 11–47. Munich: 1970.

———. "Thomas von Aquin und die gegenwärtige katholische Theologie." In *Thomas von Aquino. Interpretation und Rezeption,* edited by Willehad Paul Eckert, pp. 245–306. Mainz: 1974.

———. "Mensch und Recht nach Thomas von Aquin. Historischer Überblick und geschichtliche Perspektiven." *Philosophisches Jahrbuch* 82 (1975): 10–30.

Ohasama, Schuej. *Zen. Der lebendige Buddhismus in Japan. Ausgewählte Stücke des Zen-Textes, übersetzt und eingeleitet von Schuej Ohasama, herausgegeben von August Faust, mit einem Geleitwort von Rudolf Otto.* Gotha/Stuttgart: 1925/1967.

Oldenberg, Hermann. *Die Lehre der Upanishaden und die Anfänge des Buddhismus.* 2nd ed. Göttingen: 1923.

Otto, Rudolf. "Geleitwort." In Schuej Ohasama, *Zen. Der lebendige Buddhismus in Japan.* Gotha/Stuttgart: 1925/1967.

Oyen, Hendrik van. "Hermann Cohen." In *Juden, Christen, Deutsche,* edited by Hans Jürgen Schultz, pp. 345–352. Stuttgart/Olten/Freiburg: 1961.

A Pawlov, Dejan. "Erich Fromm und die Marxistische Philosophie des Menschen." In *Die philosophische Lehre von Karl Marx und ihre aktuelle Bedeutung. Philosophischer Kongress der DDR 1968,* edited by Dieter Berger et al., pp. 170–178. Berlin: 1968.

A Petrović, Gajo. "Humanism and Revolution." In *In the Name of Life: Essays in Honor of Erich Fromm,* edited by B. Landis and E. S. Tauber, pp. 288–298. New York: 1971.

A ———. "Frommovo shvácanje ĉovjeka." In E. Fromm, *Ĉovjek za Sebe,* pp. 179–191. Zagreb: 1965.

A Petuchowski, Jakob J. "Erich Fromm's Midrash of Love: The Sacred and the Secular Forms." *Commentary* 22 (1956): 543–549.

Philipson, David. "Reform Judaism." In *Universal Jewish Encyclopedia,* edited by Isaac Landman, Vol. VI, pp. 240–243. New York: 1942.

A Picard, Winfried. "George Herbert Mead und Erich Fromm." In *Die Grossen der Weltgeschichte,* edited by K. Fassman, Vol. X, pp. 592–607. Zurich: 1978.

R Piel, Edgar. "Im Teufelskreis von Haben und Sein." Review of "Haben oder Sein." *Merkur,* Stuttgart (1958): 1–4.

Popitz, Heinrich. *Der entfremdete Mensch. Zeitkritik und Geschichtsphilosophie des jungen Marx.* Basel: 1953.

Popper, Karl R. "Was ist Dialektik?" In *Logik der Sozialwissenschaften,* edited by Ernst Topitsch. Neue wissenschaftliche Bibliothek 6. Pp. 262–290. Köln/Berlin: 1965.

———. *Logik der Forschung.* 4th ed. Tübingen: 1971.

Post, Werner. *Kritik der Religion bei Karl Marx.* Munich: 1969.

A Prokopiuk, Jerzy S. "Sylwetki religioznawców." In *Przeglad Religioznawczy,* Warsaw (1962): 20–41.

A Pröpper, Thomas. *Der Jesus der Philosophen und der Jesus des Glaubens. Ein theologisches Gespräch mit Jaspers, Bloch, Kolakowski, Gardavsky, Machoveć, Fromm, Ben-Chorin.* Mainz: 1976.

R Pruyser, Paul W. Review of "The Anatomy of Human Destructiveness." *Theology Today* 31 (1974/1975): 256–260.

Rabinowitsch, Wolf. *Der Karliner Chassidismus: Seine Geschichte und Lehre. Mit einem Geleitwort von Simon Dubnow.* Tel Aviv: 1935.

Rattner, Josef. *Psychologie der zwischenmenschlichen Beziehungen. Eine Einführung in die neopsychoanalytische Sozialpsychologie von H. S. Sullivan.* Zurich: 1969.

———. *Aggression und menschliche Natur. Individual- und Sozialpsychologie der Feindseligkeiten und Destruktivität des Menschen.* Olten/Freiburg: 1970.

Ratzinger, Joseph. "Kirchliches Lehramt—Glaube—Moral." In *Prinzipien christlicher Moral,* Einsiedeln (1975): 43–66.

Rauh, Fritz. "Die Funktion der vergleichenden Verhaltungsforschung für das Humanum." In *Humanum. Moraltheologie im Dienste des Menschen* (*Festschrift Egenter*), edited by J. Gründel et al., pp. 142–157. Düsseldorf: 1972.

A Reich, Wilhelm. "Dialectical Materialism and Psychoanalysis." In W. Reich, *Sex-Pol. Essays 1929–1934,* edited by L. Baxandall, pp. 65–69. New York: 1972.

A Reif, Adelbert, ed. *Erich Fromm. Materialien zu seinem Werk.* Vienna: 1978.

A Reimann, Bruno W. *Psychoanalyse und Gesellschaftstheorie.* Darmstadt/Neuwied: 1973. Esp. pp. 93–113f.

Rich, A. "Die kryptoreligiösen Motive in den Frühschriften von Karl Marx." *Theologische Zeitschrift* 7/3, Basel (1951): 192–209.

Rief, Josef. "Normen und Normenfindung." In *Mitteilungen*, published by Hauptabteilung Schule/Hochschule im Erzbischöflichen Generalvikariat, No. 2, pp. 2–35. Köln: 1976.

A Riesman, David. "Psychological Types and National Character: An Informal Commentary." *American Quarterly* 5 (1953): 325–343.

———. *Individualism Reconsidered and Other Essays*. London: 1954.

———. *Die einsame Masse*. Eine Untersuchung der Wandlungen des amerikanischen Characters. Mit einer Einführung in die deutsche Ausgabe von Helmut Schelsky. Neuwied: 1956. (Translation of *The Lonely Crowd*.)

A Ripa, Ornella. "Quando un prete parla d'amore." *Gente Settimanale*, Milan, (Apr. 16, 1980): 41f., 44, 46, 48.

Ritter, Joachim, ed. *Historisches Wörterbuch der Philosophie*. Vol. 2, D–F. Basel/ Darmstadt: 1972.

Roberts, David E. "Theological and Psychiatric Interpretation of Human Nature." *Christianity and Crisis: A Bi-Weekly Journal of Christian Opinion* 7 (Feb. 3, 1947): 3–7.

R Röhl, Wolfgang. "Die Kultur des Todes." Review of "Anatomie der menschlichen Destruktivität." *das da. Monatsmagazin für Kultur und Politik*, Hamburg (Feb. 1975): 10f.

Rolfes, Helmuth. "Der Sinn des Lebens im marxistischen Denken. Eine kritische Darstellung. Mit einem Vorwort von J. B. Metz." Ph.D. dissertation, Düsseldorf, 1971.

Rosenzweig, Franz. "Introduction" in Hermann Cohen, *Jüdische Schriften*. Vol. 1. *Ethische und religiöse Grundfragen*, pp. i–lxiv. Berlin: 1924.

Rotenstreich, Nathan. *Humanism in the Contemporary Era*. Den Haag: 1963.

Ruben, Walter. *Die Philosophie der Upanishaden*. Bern: 1947.

Ruf, Ambrosius Karl. *Grundkurs Moraltheologie*. Vol. 1. *Gesetz und Norm*. Freiburg/Basel/Vienna: 1975.

R Rump, Gerhard Charles. Review of "Anatomie der menschlichen Destruktivität." *Psychologische Beiträge* 18, Meisenheim (1976): 122–125.

R Russell, Alfred. "Religion and American Society Today." Review of "You Shall Be as Gods." *Issues* 71 (1967): 54–62.

A Russo, Udo L. "Fromm, rivoluzionario della sperenza." *La Provincia*, Como, July 18, 1980.

A Ryszka, Franciszek. "Przedmowa." In E. Fromm, *Ucieczka od Wolności*, pp. 5–13. Warsaw: 1978.

Rzepkowski, Horst SVD. *Das Menschenbild bei Daisetz Teitaro Suzuki. Gedanken zur Anthropologie des Zen Buddhismus*. Studia Instituti Missiologici Societas Verbi Divini 12. St. Augustin: 1971.

A Saavedra, Victor. "La síntesis Fromiana." *Excelsior. Diorama de la Cultura*, Mexico (Mar. 23, 1980): 4f.

R Sablik, Karl. Review of "Anatomie der menschlichen Destruktivität." *Mitteilungen des Instituts für Wissenschaft und Kunst* 4, Vienna (1975): 101–103.

Sacharek, Joseph. *Faith and Reason: The Conflict over the Rationalism of Maimonides*. New York: 1935/1970.

Sadler, William A. "On the Verge of a Lonely Life." *Humanitas* 10 (Nov. 1974): 255–276.

M Sahlin, Clarence Joseph. "An Analysis of the Writings of Erich Fromm and Their Implications for Adult Education." Ph.D. dissertation, Indiana University, 1970.

A Salzman, Leon. "Erich Fromm." In *Developments in Psychoanalysis*, pp. 68–91. New York: 1962.

A Sánchez, J. Review of "Haben oder Sein." *Katechetische Blätter* 102, Munich (1977): 501–505.

M Santos, Maria Pires dos. *Libertade, amor, responsibilidade; a propósito de Erich Fromm*. Belo Horizonte: 1972.

A Sarlos, Beatrice. "Alienation as Symptom: Diagnostic Perspectives on a Concept." *Proceedings of Philosophy of Education* 30 (1974): 88–100.

R Savić, Obrad. "From i revolucija nade." In E. Fromm, *Revolucija Nade*, pp. 185–189. Belgrade: 1978.

M Schaar, John Homer. *Escape from Authority: The Perspectives of Erich Fromm*. New York: 1961.

A Schacht, Richard. *Alienation*. With an Introductory Essay by Walter Kaufmann. London: 1971.

R Schachtel, Ernest G. Review of "Escape from Freedom." *Zeitschrift für Sozialforschung* 9 (1941): 491–495.

R Schad, Wolfgang. "Anatomie der Zerstörung." Review of "Anatomie der menschlichen Destruktivität." *Die Drei* 3, Stuttgart (1975): 124–127.

R Schaefer, Alfred. Review of "Haben oder Sein," *Philosophischer Literaturanzeiger* 31, Meisenheim (1978): 105–107.

Schaeffler, Richard. *Die Religionskritik sucht ihren Partner. Thesen zu einer erneuerten Apologetik* Reihe Theol. Seminar. Freiburg: 1974.

———. *Religion und kritisches Bewusstsein*. Freiburg/Munich: 1973.

Schaff, Adam. "Marxism and the Philosophy of Man." In *Socialist Humanism*, edited by Erich Fromm, pp. 129–137. New York: 1965.

A ———. *Marxismus und das menschliche Individuum*. Vienna: 1965.

———. "What does it Mean to 'Be a Marxist'?" In *In the Name of Life: Essays in Honor of Erich Fromm*, edited by B. Landis and E. S. Tauber, pp. 299–312. New York: 1971.

A ———. *Entfremdung als soziales Phänomen*. Vienna: 1977. Pp. 211–225.

Schecter, David E. "Of Human Bonds and Bondage." In *In the Name of Life: Essays in Honor of Erich Fromm*, edited by B. Landis and E. S. Tauber, pp. 84–89. New York: 1971. Also in *Contemporary Psychoanalysis* 11 (1975): 435–452.

Scheffczyk, Leo. "Die Theologie und das Ethos der Wissenschaften." *Münchener Theologische Zeitschrift* 25 (1974): 336–358.

A Schirnding, Albert von. "Analytiker und Prophet. Zum Tode von Erich Fromm." *Süddeutsche Zeitung*, Munich (Mar. 19, 1980): 33.

Schmid, Michael. "Leerformeln und Ideologiekritik. Heidelberger Sociologica 11. Ph.D. dissertation, Tübingen, 1972.

R Schmidhäuser, Ulrich. "Haben oder Sein." *Theologie der Gegenwart* 21 (1978): 52–55.

Schmidt, Alfred. "Der Begriff der Natur in der Lehre von Marx." Ph.D. dissertation, Frankfurt, 1962.

A ———. "Die 'Zeitschrift für Sozialforschung.' Geschichte und gegenwärtige Bedeutung." In *Nachdruck "Zeitschrift für Sozialforschung."* Vol. 1, pp. 5–63. Munich: 1970.

A Schneider-Flume, Gunda. "Leben dürfen oder leben müssen. Die Bedeutung der humanistischen Psychoanalyse Erich Fromms für die theologische Anthropologie." In *Der Wirklichkeitsanspruch von Theologie und Religion. Die sozialethische Herausforderung. Ernst Steinbach zum 70. Geburtstag,* edited by Dieter Henke et al., pp. 207–229. Tübingen: 1976.

———. "Fromm." In *Religionskritik von der Aufklärung bis zur Gegenwart,* edited by K.-H. Weger, pp. 117–122. Freiburg: 1979.

A Schoenfeld, C. G. "Erich Fromm's Attack Upon the Oedipus Complex—A Brief Critique." *The Journal of Nervous and Mental Disease. An Educational Journal of Neuropsychiatry* 141/5 (1965): 580–585.

Schoeps, Hans Joachim. *Geschichte der jüdischen Religionsphilosophie in der Neuzeit.* Vol. 1. Berlin: 1935.

Scholem, Gershom. "Kabbala und Mythos." In *Der Mensch und die mythische Welt,* edited by Olga Fröbe-Kapteyn. Eranos Jahrbuch 1949, Vol. XVII, pp. 287–334. Zurich: 1950.

———. "Zur Entwicklungsgeschichte der kabbalistischen Konzeption der Schechinah." In *Mensch und Energie,* edited by Olga Fröbe-Kapteyn. Eranos Jahrbuch 1952, Vol. XXI, pp. 45–107. Zurich: 1953.

———. "Die Lehre vom 'Gerechten' in der jüdischen Mystik." In *Mensch und Frieden,* edited by Olga Fröbe-Kapteyn. Eranos Jahrbuch 1958, Vol. XXVII, pp. 237–297. Zurich: 1959.

———. "Gut und Böse in der Kabbala." In *Der Mensch im Spannungsfeld der Ordnungen,* edited by Olga Fröbe-Kapteyn. Eranos Jahrbuch 1961, Vol. XXX, pp. 29–67. Zurich: 1962.

———. *Ursprünge und Anfänge der Kabbala.* Vol. III. Studia Judaica. Forschungen zur Wissenschaft des Judentums, edited by E. L. Ehrlich. Berlin: 1962.

———. *Major Trends in Jewish Mysticism.* New York: Schocken Books, 1954/1961.

———. *"Uber einige Grundbegriffe des Judentums.* Edition Suhrkamp 414. Frankfurt: 1970.

———. "Die Krise der Tradition im jüdischen Messianismus." In *Tradition und Gegenwart,* edited by Adolf Portmann and Rudolf Ritsema. Eranos Jahrbuch 1968, Vol. XXXVII, pp. 9–44. Zurich: 1970.

———. *The Messianic Idea in Judaism and Other Essays on Jewish Spirituality.* New York: 1971.

Schüller, Bruno. *Die Begründung sittlicher Urteile. Typen ethischer Argumentation in der katholischen Moraltheologie.* Düsseldorf: 1973.

———. "Neuere Beiträge zum Thema 'Begründung sittlicher Normen.' " In *Theologische Berichte IV,* edited by Josef Pfammatter and Franz Furger, pp. 109–181. Einsiedeln/Zurich/Köln: 1974.

———. "Zur Diskussion über das Proprium einer christlichen Ethik." *Theologie und Philosophie* 51 (1976): 321–343.

———. Review of J. Ratzinger, "Prinzipien christlicher Moral." *Theologische Revue* 73 (1977): 143f.

A Schultz, Duane. "Erich Fromm." In *Theories of Personality,* Monterey (1976): pp. 86–101.

A Schultz, Hans Jürgen. "Humanist ohne Illusionen. Zu Werk und Person von Erich Fromm." *Evangelische Kommentare* 9 (1976): 36–38.

R ———. "Radikaler Humanismus." Review of "Revolution der Hoffnung." *Evangelische Kommentare* 5 (1972): 178f.

Schulz, Siegfried. *Q. Die Spruchquelle der Evangelien.* Zurich: 1972.

———. "Der historische Jesus. Bilanz der Fragen und Lösungen." In *Jesus Christus in Historie und Theologie. Neutestamentliche Festschrift für Hans Concelmann zum 60. Geburtstag,* edited by Georg Strecker, pp. 3–25. Tübingen: 1975.

A Schwarzman, K. A. "Gymanistitscheskaja etika E. Fromma." *Woprose Philosophii* 6 (1971): 100ff.

Schweizer, Eduard. *Matthäus und seine Gemeinde.* Stuttgarter Bibelstudien 71. Stuttgart: 1974.

R Seeber, David. Review of "Haben oder Sein." *Herder-Korrespondenz* 31 (1977): 214f.

Sekiguchi, Shindai. *Zen. A Manual for Westerners.* San Francisco: 1970.

Seligmann, Caesar. *Geschichte der jüdischen Reformbewegung von Mendelssohn bis zur Gegenwart.* Frankfurt: 1922.

M Shell, Kurt Leo. *Erich Fromm's "Escape from Freedom." A Critical Commentary.* New York: 1967.

Shneur Zalman. *Rabbi of Liadi, Liqqutei Amarim* (*Tanya*). 5th ed. Vol. I, trans. from the Hebrew with an introduction by Nissan Mindel. New York: 1975.

M Simmons, Henry C. *Valuing Suffering as a Christian: Some Psychological Perspectives.* Chicago: 1976.

R Singer, Milton. Review of "Man for Himself." *Ethics* 57 (1947/48): 220–222.

Silver, Abba Hillel. *A History of Messianic Speculation in Israel: From the First through the Seventeenth Centuries. With a New Preface by the Author.* Boston: 1927/1959.

Silver, Daniel Jeremy. *Maimonidean Criticism and the Maimonidean Controversy 1180–1240.* Leiden: 1965.

Simmel, Georg: *Hauptprobleme der Philosophie.* 6th ed. Berlin: 1927.

R Singer, Milton. Review of "Man for Himself." *Ethics: An International Journal of Social, Political, and Legal Philosophy* 57 (1947/48): 220–222.

M Smith, William Aloysius. *The Writings of Erich Fromm: A Detailed Critique and In-Depth Evaluation.* New York: 1970.

Social Sciences Citation Index. Philadelphia: 1970ff.

R Sonntag, Werner. Review of "Anatomie der menschlichen Destruktivität." *Stuttgarter Zeitung* 235 (Oct. 10, 1974): 35.

A Sowa, Julia. "Sur certaines définitions de la santé psychique, une analyse critique des idées de E. Fromm et de K. Horney." In *Moralność i spoleczenstwo, Ksiega jubienszowa dla Marii Ossowskiej* (*Moral und Gesellschaft. Festschrift für Marie Ossowska*). Warsaw: 1969.

Staehelin, Balthasar. *Haben und Sein.* Zurich: 1969.

Steinbüchel, Theodor. "Karl Marx. Gestalt—Werk—Ethos." In *Sozialismus,* edited by Alfons Auer, pp. 1–35. Tübingen: 1950.

———. "Zur philosophischen Grundlegung des marxistischen Sozialismus." In *Sozialismus,* edited by Alfons Auer, pp. 36–68. Tübingen: 1950.

———. "Zur Ethik des marxistischen Sozialismus." In *Sozialismus,* edited by Alfons Auer, pp. 69–98. Tübingen: 1950.

Steiner, Hans Friedrich. *Marxisten-Leninisten über den Sinn des Lebens. Eine Studie zum kommunistischen Menschenbild.* Essen: 1970.

Stoeckle, Bernhard. *Grenzen der autonomen Moral.* Munich: 1974.

———. *Handeln aus dem Glauben. Moraltheologie konkret.* Freiburg/Basel/Vienna: 1977.

———. "Christlicher Glaube und Ethos der Zukunft." In *Normen im Konflikt. Grundfragen einer erneuerten Ethik,* edited by Joseph Sauer, pp. 125–144. Freiburg/Basel/Vienna: 1977.

M Stoev, Stoiu. *Chovek, neofroidizum, marksizum. Kritika na konschtschepziite na Osb'ri, From i Markuse sa choveka i integriraneto an neofreudisma c marksizma.* Sofia: 1972.

R Stojić, Ljuba. "Fromọs Frojd." In *E. Fromm, Misija Sigmunda Frojda,* pp. 105–108. Belgrade: 1978.

Suzuki, Daisetz Teitaro. *Die grosse Befreiung. Einführung in den Zen-Buddhismus.* Introduction by Dr. C. G. Jung. Leipzig: 1939.

———. *Zen und die Kultur Japans.* Translated and introduced by Otto Fischer. Stuttgart/Berlin: 1941.

———. *Living by Zen.*

———. *Studies in Zen.* Vol. I. London: 1955.

———. *Mysticism: Christian and Buddhist.* London: 1957.

———. *Der Weg zur Erleuchtung. Die Übung des Koan als Mittel, Satori zu erlangen.* Baden-Baden: 1957.

——— *Die Zen-Lehre vom Nicht-Bewussten. Die Bedeutung des Sutra von Huineng* (*Wei-Lang*). Munich-Planegg: 1957.

———. "Preface" to Eugen Herrigel, *Zen in the Art of Archery.* New York: Pantheon, 1953.

———. "Lectures on Zen Buddhism." In *Zen Buddhism and Psychoanalysis,* edited by Erich Fromm, pp. 1–76. New York: 1960.

———. *The Essentials of Zen Buddhism. Selected from the Writings of Daisetz T. Suzuki.* Edited and with an introduction by Bernard Philips. Connecticut: 1973.

———. *Amida. Der Buddha der Liebe. Shin Buddhism.* Bern/Munich/Vienna: 1974.

M Suzuki, Yogo. "An Examination of Doctrine of Man of Erich Fromm and Reinhold Niebuhr." Ph.D. dissertation, University of Virginia, 1971.

R Swanson, Guy E. Review of "The Anatomy of Human Destructiveness." *American Journal of Sociology* 80 (1975): 1243–1245.

A Sykes, Gerald. *The Hidden Remnant.* New York: 1962. Pp. 87–94.

R Tarbert, Gary C., ed. *Book Review Index.* Detroit: 1968ff.

A Tauber, Edward S. "Some Biographical Notes." In *In the Name of Life: Essays in Honor of Erich Fromm,* edited by B. Landis and E. S. Tauber, pp. x–xiv. New York: 1971. Also in *Contemporary Psychoanalysis* 11 (1975): 390–395.

———. "The Role of Immediate Experience for Dynamic Psychiatry: The Sense of Immediacy in Fromm's Conceptions." In *American Handbook of Psychiatry,* pp. 1811–1815. New York: 1959.

A ———. "Erich Fromm: Clinical and Social Philosopher." *Contemporary Psychoanalysis* 15 (1979): 201–213.

Taubes, Jakob. *Abendländische Eschatologie.* Beiträge zur Soziologie und Sozialphilosophie 3. Bern: 1947.

R Teschitz, Karl. Review of Erich Fromm, "Autorität und Familie." *Zeitschrift für Politische Psychologie und Sexualökonomie* 3 (1936): 176–178. Also in *Marxis-*

mus, Psychoanalyse, Sexpol, edited by Hans-Peter Gente. Vol. 1., Bücher des Wissens, Fischer 6056, pp. 307–309. Frankfurt: 1970.

A Thompson, Clara M. *Psychoanalysis: Its Evolution and Development.* New York: 1950.

———. *Interpersonal Psychoanalysis: The Selected Papers of Clara M. Thompson,* edited by Maurice R. Green. Foreword by Erich Fromm. London: 1964.

M Tilley, William Clyde. "The Relationship of Self-Love for the Other with Special Reference to the Thought of R. Niebuhr and Erich Fromm." Ph.D. dissertation, 1966.

R Tillich, Paul. Review of "The Sane Society." *Pastoral Psychology* 6 (1955): 13–16.

———. "Ist eine Wissenschaft von Werten möglich?" In *Collected Works,* Vol. III, pp. 100–106. Stuttgart: 1965.

———. "Christentum und Marxismus." In *Collected Works,* Vol. III, pp. 170–177. Stuttgart: 1965.

———. "Der Mensch im Marxismus und Christentum." In *Collected Works,* Vol. III, pp. 194–209. Stuttgart: 1965.

———. "Entfremdung und Versöhnung im modernen Denken." In *Collected Works,* Vol. IV, pp. 183–199. Stuttgart: 1961.

———. "Autorität und Offenbarung." In *Collected Works,* Vol. VIII, pp. 304–315. Stuttgart: 1970.

———. "Der Mut zum Sein." In *Collected Works,* Vol. XI, pp. 13–139. Stuttgart: 1969.

———. "Wieviel Wahrheit findet sich bei Karl Marx?" In *Collected Works,* Vol. XII, pp. 265–272. Stuttgart: 1971.

R ———. "Psychoanalyse und Religion." In *Collected Works,* Vol. XII, pp. 333–336. Stuttgart: 1971.

R ———. Review of E. Fromm, "Sigmund Freud's Mission." *Time,* Feb. 9, 1959, p. 49.

Tomberg, Friedrich. "Der Begriff der Entfremdung in den 'Grundrissen' von Karl Marx." In *Basis und Überbau. Sozialphilosophische Studien,* pp. 147–207. Neuwied: 1974.

Topitsch, Ernst. *Sozialphilosophie zwischen Ideologie und Wissenschaft.* Soziologische Texte 10. Neuwied: 1961.

———. *Die Sozialphilosophie Hegels als Heilslehre und Herrschaftsideologie.* Neuwied: 1967.

———. *Vom Ursprung und Ende der Metaphysik. Eine Studie zur Weltanschauungskritik.* Vienna: 1958.

———. "Über Leerformeln. Zur Pragmatik des Sprachgebrauchs in Philosophie und politischer Theorie." In *Probleme der Wissenschaftstheorie. Festschrift für Viktor Kraft,* pp. 233–264. Vienna: 1960.

———. "Marxismus und Gnosis." In *Sozialphilosophie zwischen Ideologie und Wissenschaft,* Soziologische Texte 10, pp. 235–270. Neuwied: 1961.

———. "Seelenglaube und Selbstinterpretation." In *Sozialphilosophie zwischen Ideologie und Wissenschaft,* Soziologische Texte 10, pp. 155–199. Neuwied: 1961.

———. "Atheismus und Naturrecht." In *Mythos—Philosophie—Politik: Zur Naturgeschichte der Illusion,* pp. 121–141. Freiburg: 1969.

M Torres, Mauro. *El Irracionalismo en Erich Fromm.* Mexico, n.d.

M Tschepnenko, W. A. *Politischeskaja philosophija i ekonomitscheskije bsgljage Erika Fromma* (*Politische Philosophie und ökonomische Ansichten Erich Fromms*). Moscow: 1969.

Turel, Adrien. *Bachofen—Freud. Zur Emanzipation des Mannes vom Reich der Mütter.* Vol. II. Bücher des Werdenden, edited by Paul Federn and Heinrich Meng. Bern: 1939.

Underhill, Evelyn. *A Book of Contemplation the which Is Called "The Cloud of Unknowing."* Edited by Evelyn Underhill. 6th ed. London: 1956.

R Vayhinger, John M. Review of "The Heart of Man." *Contemporary Psychoanalysis* 11 (1966): 24–26.

Vorgrimler, Herbert. "Negative Theologie." In *Lexikon für Theologie und Kirche,* Vol. VII, p. 864f. Freiburg: 1963.

A Vranicki, Predrag. *Geschichte des Marxismus.* 2 vols. Esp. vol. 2, pp. 865–877. Frankfurt: 1974.

R Wagerer, M. Review of "Anatomie der menschlichen Destruktivität." *Zeitschrift für psychosomatische Medizin,* Göttingen (1976): 398f.

R Weigert, Edith. Review of "The Anatomy of Human Destructiveness." *Psychiatry* 38, Washington (1975): 101–103.

A Weiss, Andreas von. *Neomarxismus. Die Problemsdiskussion im Nachfolgemarxismus der Jahre 1945–1970.* Freiburg/Munich: 1970. Pp. 12–95.

M Wertschenow, L. H. *Kritika sozialnoi teorii Erika Fromma* (*Kritik der Gesellschaftstheorie Erich Fromms*). Moscow: 1969.

A Wickler, Wolfgang, et. al. "Antworten auf Fromm." *Bild der Wissenschaft* 11, Stuttgart (1974): 98–109.

A Wieczorek, Zbigniew. "Humanizm Ericha Fromma: potizeby ludzkie, mitość, rzeczywistość i wizje przyszlości. (Der Humanismus Erich Fromms: Menschliche Bedürfnisse, Liebe, Realität und Vision der Zukunft)." *Studia Filizoficzne* (*Suppl.*), Warsaw (1969): 259–278.

A Wiegand, Ronald. "Psychoanalyse und Gesellschaft bei Erich Fromm." *Psychologische Menschenkenntnis* 6, Zurich (1970): 257–273.

A ———. *Gesellschaft und Charakter. Soziologische Implikationen der Neopsychoanalyse. Von Erich Fromm über Karen Horney zu Harry Stack Sullivan.* Kindler Taschenbuch "Geist und Psyche" 2098. Munich: 1973.

A Wiesenhütter, Eckart. *Freud und seine Kritiker.* Erträge der Forschung 24. Darmstadt: 1974.

Wilhelm, Kurt. "Religiöse Weltanschauungen im neuzeitlichen Judentum." In *Juden, Christen, Deutsche,* edited by Hans Jürgen Schultz, pp. 66–75. Stuttgart/Olten/Freiburg: 1961.

R Winthrop, Henry. Review of "The Sane Society." *The Journal of Social Psychology* 45 (1957): 125–134.

R Wirth, Louis. Review of "Escape from Freedom." *Psychiatry* 5, Washington (1942): 129–131.

A Witenberg, Earl G. "On Erich Fromm's 75th Year." *Contemporary Psychoanalysis* 11 (1975): 389.

———. "The Interpersonal and Cultural Approaches." In *American Handbook of Psychiatry,* edited by S. Arieti, pp. 1426–1433 (2nd ed. pp. 854–861). New York: 1959.

A Wyss, Dieter. *Die tiefenpsychologischen Schulen von den Anfängen bis zur Gegenwart. Entwicklung, Probleme, Krisen.* 4th expanded ed., esp. pp. 188–195. Göttingen: 1972.

A Xirau, Ramon. "Erich Fromm: What Is Man's Struggle?" In *In the Name of Life: Essays in Honor of Erich Fromm,* edited by B. Landis and E. S. Tauber, pp. 150–160. New York: 1971.

M Yonker, Nicholas, Jr. *Ambiguities of Love. An Inquiry into the Psychology of Erich Fromm.* New York: 1961.

Zima, Pierre Vaćlav. *L'École de Francfort.* Paris: 1974.

Zimmer, Heinrich. *Philosophie und Religion Indiens.* suhrkamps taschenbuch wissenschaft 26. Frankfurt: 1973.

R Zuger, Bernard. Review of "Man for Himself." *American Journal of Psychoanalysis* 8 (1948): 63–65.

INDEX